William Stebbing

Some Verdicts of History Reviewed

William Stebbing

Some Verdicts of History Reviewed

ISBN/EAN: 9783337203283

Printed in Europe, USA, Canada, Australia, Japan

Cover: Foto ©ninafisch / pixelio.de

More available books at **www.hansebooks.com**

SOME
VERDICTS OF HISTORY
REVIEWED.

By WILLIAM STEBBING,
LATE FELLOW OF WORCESTER COLLEGE, OXFORD.

LONDON:
JOHN MURRAY, ALBEMARLE STREET.
1887.

CONTENTS.

	PAGE
I.—THE EIGHTEENTH CENTURY	3
II.—PATRIOT, OR ADVENTURER?	
ANTHONY ASHLEY COOPER	25
III.—TWO POET-POLITICIANS.	
ABRAHAM COWLEY	47
MATTHEW PRIOR	82
IV.—TWO LEADERS OF SOCIETY AND OF OPPOSITION.	
HENRY ST. JOHN	125
WILLIAM PULTENEY	200
V.—AN AMERICAN REVOLUTIONIST AND AN ENGLISH RADICAL.	
BENJAMIN FRANKLIN	257
WILLIAM COBBETT	300
VI.—PURITAN AND CAVALIER ENGLAND TRANSPLANTED.	
NEW ENGLAND	351
VIRGINIA	380

INTRODUCTION.

I.

THE EIGHTEENTH CENTURY.

THE EIGHTEENTH CENTURY.

THE substance of this volume, though subjected to revision and re-arrangement, consists of a selection from biographical and historical contributions to monthly and quarterly reviews. Latest in order of composition are the studies of Franklin and Cobbett, and some notes, incorporated in the present introductory chapter, on Mr. Lecky's 'History of England in the Eighteenth Century,' which I am permitted to reprint, the first two from the Edinburgh Review, and the third from the Nineteenth Century. The essays on New England and Virginia, which were written before the War of Secession, together with others as early in date, for instance, those on St. John and Pulteney, appeared in the Christian Remembrancer and the North British Review, quarterly publications long since discontinued. The antiquity of much of the contents of the book will explain and must excuse the absence of reference to the labours in the same fields of others whom I have had the misfortune to precede by many years.

My sketches can pretend to no historical continuity; they will, I hope, be found to possess unity of sentiment and point of view. They whose fortunes and characters I have traced agree in their enjoyment of extraordinary distinction once, and in their condemnation, with the exception of Franklin, to odium or obscurity now. Franklin himself has lost his power of literary fascination; if the statesman and man of science survives, the moralist and controversialist musters no more readers than Samuel Johnson. Upon the rest, if they be not exposed in the pillory of historical obloquy, as Shaftesbury, or as Bolingbroke, the silence of indifference has descended. It has engulfed Cowley and Prior the poets, Pulteney and Cobbett the popular leaders, the magnates of New England, and of Virginia, all but Washington. To me the interest of the group of careers has been as much in this present neglect as in the former glare of concentrated regard. Diversities in the personal and moral judgments passed by contemporaries and by posterity should excite small surprise. Contemporaries are apt to be excessively grateful to the doers of acts by which they believe they have benefited. Often they are extravagantly resentful against the prominent figures in calamities by which they have suffered. Posterity can afford to be more judicial both in praise and in censure. It has the right as a court of appeal from the past to judge the men. It has no right to leave either them or their acts untried. It can exalt or abase; it ought not to forget. An age may be deceived in the virtues of its heroes; its aversions may have been as baseless; it rarely miscalculates the weight of persons as motive forces on their own times, and thereby on those which follow. A halo of notoriety encircling historical names is seldom a will-o'-the-wisp conducting nowhere.

We of the Victorian era may be right in classing as a convicted political gambler the popular idol, the author of the Habeas Corpus Act. Because she lavished affection on female friends, of whom one was adored by the greatest captain of the age, and the other captivated its greatest satirist, it may be our duty to despise as a weak gossip the Queen who quelled Louis XIV., and, from the hour of her accession to that of her death, held two mighty contending parties in the hollow of her hand. We may weary of the art of Cowley, and be sceptical of the social charm of the wit who signed the Peace of Utrecht. We may morally detest the inventor of Constitutional Toryism, and disapprove the personal spite of the Parliamentary wrestler who threw Walpole. We may be conscious of no attraction in the journalistic scourge, the blister that would not let the nation sleep under representative corruption. Our generation is free to set aside old valuations of human motives and integrity, as its predecessors were free to form them. It may be right, and they may have been wrong; or both may be wrong together. If popular contemporary judgments often were those of accomplices or of prosecutors, posterity as often popularly has cancelled them for mere failure to conform to canons which, when they were delivered, had not been established. The exact medium will always be a fair subject of dispute. But beyond question an age abandons an inestimable clue, as well to the present as to the past, when it turns its face from the builders of the institutions under which itself lives, in defiance of the certain truth that every structure retains, and will reveal, an impression of its makers.

Posterity is guilty of the same kind of error when it consigns the eighteenth century to the lumber-room of history. There are dull ages and brilliant ages. Posterity is not bound to discover graces in a past which laid no claim to them for itself. But a period is a trustworthy witness to its own gaiety or torpor. The eighteenth century could hardly have imposed upon its children as a focus of radiance, if it were the chaotic and tedious morass it has been pronounced by its grandchildren and great-grandchildren. These are themselves far from treating it in act as the dead level they choose to proclaim it in words. From its depths they have not disdained to draw most of the mental nourishment upon which they were reared. Almost every movement which enriches and elevates the soil of the nineteenth century started in the eighteenth. All who desire to hold personal converse with such bright spirits as Addison, Swift, Gay, Pope, Gray, Goldsmith, Gibbon, Johnson, Fielding, Hume, Adam Smith, Handel, Garrick, Reynolds, Gainsborough, Chatham, and Wolfe, must travel thither. Only on the spot can we hope to solve the riddle why a period tenanted by inhabitants so delightful, and the parent of ideas so fruitful, should, as cannot be denied, exercise as a whole a repulsion which warns off its confines all but resolute students; why it should induce even them to look at it through the eyes of Smollett and Hogarth rather than those of Goldsmith and Reynolds.

The political contests of the first fifty years of the eighteenth century are repellent when surveyed from a distance. They become interesting when St. John, Harley, Walpole, Pulteney, and Wyndham are discerned struggling hand to hand, when the flash of the swords is perceived, and the roar of the cannonade is heard. The century throughout appears dull and incoherent when discussed by distant and cursory glimpses. Successive application to its several sections and aspects of the method of treatment by personal types and representatives interprets and illuminates the political chaos; it enables the entire age not merely to reveal, but to justify itself. Regarded as a whole, as a single chapter of national life and history, in its proper perspective, and with its due allowance of light and shade, it ceases to be tiresome and monotonous. The eighteenth century surveyed in its unity will be seen to be as harmonious, distinct, and instructive, as the confusion of its politics grows exciting when lifted from the swamp of annals, and embodied in living men.

Proximity, and the consequent absence of the assistance of time to marshal and sift the crude mass of materials, must in any case have rendered it hard for the nineteenth century to catch a bird's-eye view of the eighteenth. A literary accident has superfluously added to the prejudice of the one age against attempting to discern the resources for entertainment in its predecessor. Mr. Lecky censures the reigns of the first two Georges for the withdrawal of Government patronage from literature. Among other instances he gives of the cold shade under which men of letters were allowed to languish, is the fate of Tobias Smollett. "Smollett," laments Mr. Lecky, "was compelled to degrade his noble genius to unworthy political libels, and, at last, after a life which was one long struggle for bread, died in utter poverty in a foreign land." Our age has to blame Sir Robert Walpole and the Duke of Newcastle for the works their neglect compelled Smollett to undertake even more than for the possible 'Peregrine Pickles' and 'Roderick Randoms' it has lost us. The versatility of genius was never more fully proved than when Smollett turned historian. Put to the trade of book-making he became the ideal bookmaker. The language cannot show a more complete example of the dismal art than the history compiled by a prince of the domain of fiction, a master of fancy as fertile, and of a pen as vivid as English literature has ever produced. To Smollett's 'Continuation of Hume,' and the book trade which tyrannically forced it upon several much-enduring generations of readers, must be imputed not a little of the extraordinary superstition that the eighteenth century is the most tedious portion of English history.

Students of morals, of theology, of politics, and of the belles-lettres know what a delusion this is; but men generally, even when they are readers, are very far from students. It would seem to many persons a paradox, but it would be simple truth, to say that the eighteenth century is the best period from which to begin the study of contemporary English history. The real obstacle is that the century is too rich in distinct phases. No sooner is attention concentrated on one problem of which the age promises a solution than another and yet another present themselves. This is the century which a multitude of people would pronounce barren. Reigns are supposed to be without human interest which saw to their close the careers of Bolingbroke and Swift, which had moralists like Addison and Johnson, preachers like Butler and Whitefield, an economist like Adam Smith, metaphysicians like Hume and Berkeley, jurists like Hardwicke and Mansfield, a musician like Handel, an actor like Garrick, poets in verse or prose, or both, like Pope, Gray, and Cowper, Sterne, and Goldsmith, novelists like Richardson, Fielding, and Smollett, a historian like Gibbon, an orator like Chatham, a leader of society like Chesterfield, and an administrator like Walpole. Never was there an age fuller of variety and contrasts. Jacobitism and sneers at Divine

Right, Deism and the theology of the October Club, constantly face each other, and not only in the character of St. John. The Establishment rears at once a Warburton and a Wesley. Parliament acknowledges the sovereignty, now of a Walpole, now of a Pitt. Country gentlemen believe that the Church ritual is essential to salvation, and the communication of vital truth dependent on the imposition of a bishop's hands, yet expect their chaplains to rise with the entrance of the pastry, and to marry their wives' waiting-maids, or worse. Passive obedience is an article of faith among squires, but the heir of the King *de jure* marches through England and gathers scarcely a recruit to his standard. Women are whipped at the cart tail, or publicly burnt to death by the executioner, and Pope is the poet of society. While we recognise the near general relationship of the age to our own, we may be well satisfied that our lives are set in smoother places than a generation which shot Byng for an error of judgment, and connived at the wholesale purchase by a Minister of Parliamentary votes; which sat by turns at the feet of Hume and of Wesley, believing now in evil spirits, and now in no spirit at all; in which young gentlemen thought it a merry jest to bore out the eyes of quiet wayfarers with their fingers, and wrecking was a vocation. But the period, at all events, cannot be set down as tame, except by those who survey it at such a distance that it becomes a catalogue of names.

The interest of the eighteenth century has suffered in comparison with other periods of English history, partly because it presents none of those epochs which belong to constitutional history in the making. Not merely does the array of Catholicism against Protestantism lend unity to the reign of Elizabeth, but even its literature has a mutually illustrative consistency of its own. Marlowe throws light on Shakespeare, and the prose of Bacon enables us to measure the stately roll of Ben Jonson's verse. The battle of privilege against prerogative is the keynote to the reign of the first Charles. The degradation of England under his son has its special interest too. We hear through its hollowness the arming of the nation for the crowning vindication of its liberties. England had no such mortal combats to wage in the eighteenth century. Anne respected the Constitution, and the Georges had as little power as will to assail it. Abroad hopes were cherished of restoring the Stuarts, but the Foreign Powers which adopted their cause used them as a mere wheel in a complicated machinery which was put in motion with a view much more to Continental than to English politics. Readers look even upon the trophies of Marlborough with something of the same disgust at their supposed futility from an English point of view as that which Harley and St. John felt. The alliances in the next two reigns with or against France, and with or against Austria, seem to most Englishmen now, as to most Englishmen at the times they were contracted, simple devices for wasting English money for the benefit of Hanover or Hanoverians. The Septennial Act appears no more than a temporary device for preventing the election of a Tory House of Commons; and Excise Bills, Toleration Acts, and Marriage Acts, show like measures of parochial legislation by the side of the Test and Habeas Corpus Acts of the previous century.

But it is not only that in the eighteenth century the English Constitution has reached the harbour, and the grandeur as well as the terror of the tempest is matter of the past; the century as a century has suffered neglect still more from the presence of so many different points of interest that every one can pick out what he chooses and leave the rest for lumber. The student of the art of war has in the campaigns of Marlborough and Frederick the Great a vein he can work without concerning himself with the tortuous intrigues of Harley, or the place-mongering of Newcastle and Bute. The metaphysician can pit the theologians in whom Queen Caroline delighted against each other, without bestowing a thought on the miracle of political management by which a nation with a majority of its population still loyal to the cause of the Pretender, Old or Young, was being converted to as absolute faith in the House of Hanover as if it had reigned from before the Conquest. The Methodist, as he traces the crusade the authors of his creed led against latitudinarian and moral theology, is hardly conscious that the elder Pitt was rivalling Demosthenes in the House of Commons, and adding Canada and the Indies to the British Empire. The novel reader, as he dwells on the sorrows of Clarissa Harlowe, or the adventures of Joseph Andrews, or even the barbed experiences of Gulliver, need not be dazzled by the flood of light on contemporary society shed by the first two, and on contemporary politics by the last. Only the student who views the century as a whole, in its letters, its philosophy, its divinity, its manners, and its politics, knows how completely they illustrate each other, and that all, considered together, make a mirror of national life in which may be discerned not only what England was in the days of Bolingbroke and Walpole, but what it had been in the days of Laud, and was to be in those of Canning and Peel.

Certain periods of history are watersheds. It is possible to see in them currents flowing down into the plains on either side. The eighteenth century is one of those periods. Therein lies its special value to students of history, and also perhaps the secret of the repulsion it exercises on those who are not. The mass of the people still revered shibboleths which had been living realities in the seventeenth century; their rulers repeated them; but protests had already begun to be raised; and means had been found to nullify their despotism. The Test Act remained in force, though Swift mocked and Speaker Onslow deplored, a law which, as, Cowper complained,—

> . . . made the symbols of atoning grace
> An office key, a picklock to a place.

The Act continued on the Statute-Book; its severity was neutralised. Whig Parliaments and Ministers rejected by overwhelming majorities proposals for its repeal; but they passed annual Indemnity Acts which rendered it nugatory. The Act which punished witchcraft with death was repealed in 1736; but it was in active operation a little earlier in the century; five persons, according to Dr. Parr, had been executed for this imaginary crime at Northampton so late as 1722. After the formal abrogation the lower classes clung to their belief in witches; and the early Methodist preachers vaunted their rescues of the victims of demoniacal possession. Henry Pelham passed in 1755 an Act for legalising the naturalisation of Jews; it had been introduced first in the House of Lords, and had there received the assent of the bishops; but Conservative members complained that Ministers were welcoming a people who, as soon as they had obtained power through the elevation of Queen Esther, used it to "put to death in two days 76,000 of those whom they were pleased to call their enemies without either judge or jury." The fear of another Feast of Purim was so great that Mr. Pelham had, in 1756, to repeal the law. An Act of the reign of George the First forbade Popish recusants to come within ten miles of London, and gave them the alternative, on their refusal to recant Catholicism, of exile or death; but such laws were enacted more to keep up the tradition of English irreconcilableness with Rome than from any serious desire for a new religious persecution. While Parliament menaced the believers in Transubstantiation with death, a majority of the clergy preached a Gospel of which it might have been much more truly said than was alleged by Whitefield of Tillotson, that it had "as little of true Christianity as the religion of Mahomet." Bishop Wilson was evangelising the Isle of Man, and Bishop Butler reconciling faith and reason; at the same time the Minister who controlled the ecclesiastical patronage of England for nearly a generation laid it down as his principle of selection, that he "would no more employ a man to govern and influence the clergy who did not flatter the parsons, than he would make a man Chancellor who was constantly complaining of the grievances of the bar, and threatening to rectify the abuses of Westminster Hall." The same Minister had a fine taste for art, and understood obscenity to be equivalent to wit. The kingdom was yearly growing in wealth; but the poor-rates and the amount of able-bodied pauperism kept steadily increasing. It was growing in general intelligence, yet Whitefield found close to Bristol, the second city in the Empire, a population of many thousands "sunk in the most brutal ignorance and vice, and entirely excluded from the ordinances of religion." Highwaymen were so audacious that, wrote Horace Walpole, " one is forced to travel even at noon as if one were going to battle." Drunkenness was so little a shame that retailers of gin were in the habit of painting announcements outside their houses that men could be made " drunk for a penny, dead drunk for twopence, and should have straw for nothing." Past the middle of the century a panic was aroused by the reform of the calendar, and people thought they had been robbed of eleven days of life. In the meantime Clarke was popularising the philosophy of Newton, and Berkeley sounding the depths of metaphysics.

The nation had not awoke to the calls of philanthropy; it could give £100,000 to the relief of the sufferers by the earthquake of Lisbon; but a few men like Oglethorpe had not yet succeeded in making charity fashionable. Not only was sympathy with other types of humanity wholly wanting among Englishmen, but there was little appearance of any with their own. The kingdom continued to insist on its monopoly of the supply of African slaves to the Spanish West Indies, and its own laws against domestic crimes were as savage as its measures to repress crimes were inefficient. A hundred and sixty offences were punishable with death. No pity was shown for the criminal, or horror at his guilt, but there was plenty of curiosity. Famous felons, like Jack Sheppard and Dr. Dodd, were exhibited by the turnkeys in the press-room for two hours before execution at a shilling a head. Criminals had the chance of a speedy release from prison by the hangman; insolvent debtors at the Fleet and the Marshalsea might linger amid horrors unspeakable till smallpox or jail-fever freed them. Yet Englishmen who viewed these atrocities of their law as matters of course, cherished an excessive suspicion of designs against their liberty. They scented despotism in Walpole's wisely conceived Excise Bill, and plots against their commerce in Bolingbroke's project for a treaty of free-trade with France; but they outlawed three-quarters of the population of Ireland, and did all that in them lay to destroy the whole of its trade. The House of Commons was made up half of placemen. For a member to be inaccessible to a bribe was virtue so extraordinary that the repute of the singularity weighed down the odium of a life passed in concerting schemes for subverting the dynasty. Yet a most corrupt Parliament reflected the national will, and registered finally each national decision that this Minister should resign and that Minister return.

The first George remained a petty German Prince to his death, and the second, though he could speak a kind of English, cared more for the Electorate than all the British Empire. They never violated the British Constitution, or pillaged the public domain, and their wars, whether or not undertaken in the interests of Hanover, were more fruitful to England than the great victories of Marlborough. Their Court was stolid and coarse, and their private lives did not bear inspection; but their German environment set them apart from ordinary English society; thus, their vices did not lower the tone of public life a hundredth part as much as the profligacy of Charles the Second. Their subjects did not affect to love or admire them; they sympathised heartily with Pitt's invectives against George the Second's "absurd, ungrateful, and perfidious partiality for Hanover;" but they had accepted them for their sovereigns once for all. The warm devotion to the House of Stuart professed by millions when George the First ascended the throne, and not repudiated during the reign of his son, was a mere sentiment deluding foreign Powers into a belief that they could retort attacks from England by lighting the flames of civil war. The nation burst into periodical paroxysms of passion for war; but it hired Hessians to fight its battles. Englishmen who thought it natural that the kingdom should mix itself up with European politics, and with the quarrels of thrones based on innumerable legions, continued to declaim against standing armies in England. Pulteney, become Lord Bath, lamented in 1760, when the nation was exulting in the triumphs of the Seven Years' War, that "our nobility, born to be the guardians of the Constitution against prerogative, solicit the badge of military subjection, not merely to serve their country in times of danger, which would be commendable, but in expectation of being continued soldiers when tranquillity shall be restored." The erection of barracks was resisted even by so calm and temperate a jurist as Blackstone; and a soldier like General Wade acknowledged that "the people of this kingdom have been taught to associate the ideas of barracks and slavery, like darkness and the devil." They saw nothing atrocious in the manning of the navy by the pressgang; nor did they extend their tenderness for their own liberties to any regard for the condition of the soldiers. So scandalously was this neglected, that in 1707–8, sickness, want of firing, unwholesome quarters, and desertion reduced the garrison of Portsmouth by half in less than a year and a half.

This picture of the eighteenth century has abundance of harsh shadows. The charge, however, popularly brought against the age is not that it was immoral and cruel, but that it was dull. On the contrary, the century, if only it be looked at near enough, is seen to be full of movement and colour. A writer whose bold pen sketched, so that they actually live before us, the varied, though, by preference, the less healthy, features of English existence, from the country squire's household and the miseries of a British man-of-war, to the humours of a Prime Minister's levee in Lincoln's Inn Fields, must have found it hard to fetter his imagination, and to libel his own times in a history which is about as broadly philosophical as the Annual Register, and as absolutely without the air of reality of the Annual Register as one of Pinnock's Catechisms. He did exactly what he was paid to do. But it does not follow that every historian as determined to do his duty by the century as was Smollett to give his customers no more than their mean money's worth, will be equally successful in his more magnanimous design. The task in which the novelist did not attempt to shine is not one to be lightly undertaken. The only mode in which as yet it could be really accomplished would be by treating the century as matter for a series of dramas. Lord Macaulay might have accomplished it, if he had lived to a hundred instead of sixty. Mr. Lecky has produced two charming volumes, generous and liberal in sentiment, picturesque in style, and running over with information, laboriously collected and skilfully filtered. He has selected St. John and Walpole, Pitt and Wesley, as exemplars of the movements and counter-movements of the century, or rather its first three-quarters. He has lucidly delineated their characters and careers, and he has connected them with groups of essays, full of the variety, point, and thought we should have anticipated from his previous works on the social and political phenomena of the time, and on the prejudiced mistakes of another eloquent writer. But when we have read them we find ourselves still asking, "What, then, is the secret of the eighteenth century? What has it which other centuries of English history have not? What has it not which they have?"

A history of society would be the truest history of the eighteenth century. Its work was the fusion of classes. The English Constitution was defined by a succession of struggles from the reign of John to that of William the Third. The reigns of Anne and the Georges could contribute nothing to the history of the Constitution in its broad outlines. Those had already been drawn before the century opened; but its full operation was as yet far from ascertained. Its principles were understood, but they had not been thoroughly applied. The present century has shown, by its Reform Acts, and its repeal of an infinity of legal disabilities and some legal immunities, that the Constitution had not been followed out to its logical conclusions. It has shown by its financial and commercial measures that the State often interfered formerly when its interference was useless or injurious. It has shown by its factory and educational legislation that it omitted formerly to interfere when it was its duty to interfere. But it is only in tracing the history of the eighteenth century that we begin to be conscious of shortcomings in the State and the Legislature needing a remedy. We are ready to complain of the age for its poverty in social reforms in which the nineteenth century has been rich. We do not censure the seventeenth century for such deficiencies, for in those times we do not expect to find them supplied. The intermingling of classes which set in with the Revolution, and was encouraged by Whig and Tory rule, gave Parliament, in spite of all its rotten boroughs, a sense that it represented the whole of the nation, and inspired courage to interfere with class interests. In the seventeenth, as in earlier centuries, different classes had allied to secure the nation's constitutional rights against the Crown and Court; there was no fusion. Occasionally a member of one class passed into another, but he ceased to belong to the class he had sprung from. Trade, manufactures, and finance were the social solvent which last century applied to England. The great landowners bought out the small; contractors of loans and merchants, and later in the century, the "nabobs" bought out both. Borough-mongering, with all its mischievous and immoral scandals, promoted the general tendency by tempering the dominant country-gentleman element in Parliament with the capitalist element. Government by a Whig aristocracy or oligarchy gave vogue to the economical aspects of politics which Whiggism had always encouraged. When the House of Lords displayed as much interest in the Bank Charter as in the balance of power in Europe, the House of Commons, though landowners monopolised the seats, was not likely to resist very successfully the tendency of the age to attach special importance to trade and commerce. Mr. Lecky says: "A competition of economy reigned in all parties. The questions which excited most interest in Parliament were chiefly financial and commercial ones." A century in which a Parliament, with a majority made up of country gentlemen, attends more closely to finance and trade than to questions of constitutional safeguards and foreign politics, is at the threshold of current history. Mr. Lecky is surprised that St. John could not win favour for his proposed treaty of commerce with France. The wonder is less that merchants were so short-sighted as not to perceive the advantages of free-trade with France, than that they could rouse the passionate interest of the whole country in the defeat of a measure which they feared might diminish the profits of their class. The rottenness of a multitude of constituencies was flagrant. Nothing was done to cure the evil in the eighteenth century; but in the eighteenth century the scandal began to be noticed and condemned. In the reign of Elizabeth, and even under Charles the First, there were as many rotten boroughs; they caused no odium. The country took them for granted, and candidates for them could scarcely be found.

The eighteenth century is so much more like the century which followed than those which preceded, that a temptation arises to measure it with later times rather than the earlier. Thus Mr. Lecky truly remarks, that "in no respect does the legislation of this period present a more striking contrast to that of the nineteenth century than in the almost complete absence of attempts to alleviate the social condition of the poorer classes, or to soften the more repulsive features of English life." But no one would reflect on the Parliaments of James the First, or Charles the Second, for not reforming social abuses, or not providing wholesome dwellings for the working classes. Parliament in those days did not try to smooth asperities in English life, because it had no sense of an obligation to interfere with such matters. It was unconscious of an obligation, because classes were not sufficiently blended for the representatives of the nation, who belonged to one class, to feel it their duty to set right the private wrongs of other classes. By the reign of George the Second Parliament was beginning to understand that it was answerable for the whole country. When Mr. Lecky expresses surprise at the inertness it showed in accepting its liability, he is applying to the age a standard then still in process of creation.

Englishmen were studying each other in the eighteenth century; they had not arrived at the conception that they might or ought to legislate for the conduct of each other's homes. An Englishman's house was still his castle; but a castle is no longer a fastness when the minutest details of its internal arrangements become the concern of all its neighbours. The eighteenth century was an age when the favourite classic was Horace, and the favourite poet was Pope who never wrote a line which was not an epigram, and did not inclose a portrait. The facets of his verse, so exquisitely cut that we pardon some want of purity in the water, occupy a place in English literature from which they will not easily be dislodged. But we can form but a faint surmise of the impression they must have made on his contemporaries. We admire the archer and listen with literary sympathy to the sharp whirr of the arrow; his own age followed it to its mark, and shuddered or mocked at the spasm on the countenance of its victim. Every line of Pope is a witness how, in the eighteenth century, courtiers and citizens, statesmen and men of letters, watched one another in towns; every page of Boswell tells how they dissected each other's thoughts. Cowper sings, and, later on, Crabbe, in tales which our generation has not the wit to appreciate, narrates, how the same spirit of personal criticism moved the village. Classes were breaking up and melting together. The town was experimenting in rural life, though satisfied as yet with the Arcadia of Bath and Tunbridge Wells, and with a taste of the pleasures, hitherto unknown, of the sea-shore. The country was migrating to cities. A wave of mutual curiosity was rolling over and through English society. Dettingen and Minden were toughly contested fields, and Frederick's campaigns had a certain political importance to England; to the England of the Georges they were most of all important as furnishing illimitable themes for talk. Chesterfield lamented after the Convention of Closterseven, that "we were no longer a nation." Are we to suppose that he ceased his polished trifling for an afternoon, or savoured a scandalous anecdote a whit the less? Methodism scourged, in sober earnest, the frivolities of life; but it had the same effect as the other social movements of its day, of rendering one class inquisitive as to the sayings and doings of every other class. It was no age for those who "do not much delight in personal talk;" the English Lakes had not yet been discovered. Such recluses in vain, like Cowper, sought a rustic refuge from the life of busy idleness Horace Walpole depicts. On the banks of the Ouse they could not escape being touched themselves with the humour of their time.

The century has bequeathed to us letters like Lady Mary's, and Walpole's, addressed to a sister or friend, but written for a circle, diaries which are a gallery of miniatures, occasional verses still witty though blurred to us by time, comedies which keep the stage and kill their modern rivals, and novels which inspired Waverley and Pickwick, which Waverley and Pickwick have not superannuated. In the belles-lettres of the eighteenth century is embodied its history, and a sparkling history it is. So studied, its attractiveness and variety are precisely proportionate to its dreariness when read in Parliamentary history and Gazettes. But to study it as it deserves to be studied leisure is needed such as not all can command. The secret of a period furrowed by a religious or civil war may be communicated to those who would never have discovered it by themselves; it is hard to teach the true character of a period when it depends on the perpetual shifting of its lights and shadows, and the transitions from one scene to another. It is the drama of the nineteenth century which is being rehearsed in the eighteenth. The players do not know their parts thoroughly; the prompter's voice breaks the thread of the action; there is no audience but the company of the theatre; and the author seems to have not yet decided upon the catastrophe. On the other hand, an absence of formality and stiffness atones for much confusion; we see how the points are made which give the piece its final success, and we hear the stage directions. We must study the two centuries of English history together to understand either. In the earlier we can watch the preparations making for the work the later has done or has to do. In the one the legislative history is the more instructive, in the other the history of society. England has won more signal political triumphs in other centuries than the eighteenth, and has produced a nobler literature; but on those who love to speak face to face with another age than their own there is none in English history which will fasten a tighter grasp.

The period has its charm, and it has its enigmas. Among the enigmas which are not without the charm are divers careers corresponding so intimately with the age that fully to decipher them would be to decipher it. Those which furnish the subjects of this volume, though all are not comprised within the chronological limits of the eighteenth century, as a whole raise the same problems, and severally might all contribute towards their solution. Shaftesbury and Cowley, whom I have been tempted to introduce principally that I might examine the remarkable phenomenon of the decadence of their fame, died long before the eighteenth century opened; but their influence, extinct for themselves, survived in it. The liberties for which Shaftesbury fought, with whatever sincerity or insincerity, made a basis for the political emancipation of the coming generations. In his want of enthusiasm and of moral earnestness, in his readiness to accept a popular mandate, and become the instrument for the promotion of national rights and tendencies, he is much nearer to the professional politicians of the next age than to the struggling zealots of his own. If Cowley had already ceased to be read, his mental tone is more audible in the literature of the next century than that of the Elizabethan dramatists, or of Milton. The other chapters of biography and history which I have endeavoured to analyze manifestly touch the borderland of two centuries, the eighteenth, and either its predecessor or its successor. St. John's riotous youth was spent, and his character was shaped, in the seventeenth century. In that century Prior passed his apprenticeship to diplomacy. Pulteney was born in the reign of Charles II. Franklin, who lived and died in the eighteenth century, belongs in spirit, and in his work, as much to the nineteenth. Cobbett is altogether of the nineteenth, though he happened to be born in the eighteenth. The most absolute nineteenth-century entity, the United States, dates back by its double keystone, Virginia and New England, as essentially to the seventeenth century, when the former in fact, as well as the latter, was planted, as to the eighteenth, when their provincial life which I have tried to depict suddenly transformed itself into a great nationality.

II.
PATRIOT, OR ADVENTURER?

ANTHONY ASHLEY COOPER,

1621–1683.

ANTHONY ASHLEY COOPER.

The period of the Restoration is at once the most degraded in English annals, and the age in which, socially and politically, modern England can be seen preparing to take its definite shape. The unpicturesque space in history covered by the reign of Charles II. was formed of debris from the preceding era. The constitution and the standards of life were, in the apparent decay of patriotism and decorum, really being nursed then under influences inherited from earlier generations. To us the better qualities of the time are so absolutely the air we breathe that we fail to see in their original development either novelty or cause for gratitude. The affinity between that stage of the past and our present makes us more keenly and indignantly note the attendant elements of rottenness and corruption.

No one of the politicians who are accused of having used, abused, and perverted, to serve their selfish ends, the nobler party impulses of the previous epoch, has been so universally stigmatised since he died as Anthony Ashley Cooper, first Earl of Shaftesbury, and Lord Chancellor. Posterity has been content to accept as a judicial conviction the Court poet's magnificent onslaught on the popular champion. It has not sought for evidence, and knows little more than that which is told it in 'Absalom and Achitophel.' Manuals of history inform it in addition that Lord Ashley owns a letter in the word "Cabal," and that Lord Shaftesbury was author of the Habeas Corpus Act. Some persons are aware of a connection between him and the ethical philosopher of 'The Characteristics.' They have not thought enough about it to be amused at the opinion of a celebrated American authoress that the statesman and the writer are one. In general the name is passed by without inquiry on the gibbet to which contemporary malevolence assigned it, with its superscription of low cunning, vice, hypocrisy, and recklessness. The charter of personal liberty Shaftesbury won for the nation is accounted proof that he was so utterly shameless as to fight in the colours of a soldier of freedom for the mere gratification of his personal vindictiveness against his royal boon companion. The party itself which he organised has, in the person of Lord Campbell, contemptuously repudiated his advocacy of its cause, as the general disowns a deserter through whom he has gained a victory.

Happily materials exist for the redemption of Shaftesbury's memory from some, not the whole, of the unrelieved blackness which has been permitted to darken it. Mr. W. D. Christie, formerly British Envoy in Brazil, employed such leisure as diplomacy allowed him in collecting and collating the original evidences in a work, which appeared in 1859, entitled, 'Memoirs, Letters, and Speeches of Anthony Ashley Cooper, First Earl of Shaftesbury, Lord Chancellor.' Nobody can read the volume and not be convinced that the vulgar condemnation of its subject as a selfish and unscrupulous political weather-cock requires some modification. As certainly none will rise from a perusal of the morsels of autobiography without regret for their incompleteness, and no little personal interest in their author as a man, though more for his candour than for his magnanimity.

The first autobiographical fragment refers to the years from 1621 to 1639. It begins with the excuse that " the villainous slanders dispersed about its author under the authority of both Church and State have forced him to follow the French fashion," and write his own memoirs. He proceeds to give an account of his youth and position in the country. His name of Ashley, or Astley, and the manor of Wimborne St. Giles he obtained from his mother's father, a comrade of the first Devereux Earl of Essex, and original planter of cabbages in England. With Hampshire he was connected through his father, Sir John Cooper, who gave him for stepmother "a co-heir of Viscount Camden, a discreet woman of a large soul, who gave some jealousy to both her husbands." A German doctor, Olivian, took his horoscope at his birth, and the boy's tutor was a Mr. Guerden, chosen for his severe principles, which were not very sincere, by Sir Anthony Ashley, the grandfather. Old Sir Anthony thought "a youth could not have too deep a dye of religion, for business and conversation in the world wear it to a just moderation." On the death of Sir John Cooper, a reckless gambler, he became ward to Sir Daniel Norton. His estate had to fight for life against a host of his father's creditors, who strove to pay themselves from it. Against him were arrayed men powerful enough to have themselves appointed by the Court of Wards commissioners for the sale of lands which they were intending to purchase. His only ally was the famous blackletter lawyer, Noy, the inventor or discoverer of ship-money. At the head of the freebooters were his great uncle, Sir Francis Ashley, and "old Mr. Tregonwell, who never knew generosity or kindness but for himself, his horse, or his dog." They succeeded partially in cutting up the property for their own benefit, though his acuteness in detecting flaws in their title subsequently enabled him to retaliate. Meanwhile he made the legal persecution a plea to his own affections for eluding the proffer by his guardian's wife of the hand of her youngest, and probably portionless, daughter, with whom he seems to have been in danger, but for his precocious prudence, of falling in love. A young gentleman of fortune, so sage as, though possessed of a large estate, to decline an alliance which would not have increased it, was marked out for worldly success.

At Oxford, to which he now went, he displayed as determined a character. He soon, we are told by himself, became popular among the seniors by his learning and affability. He earned the admiration of undergraduates both by "letting his name in the buttery book own twice the expense of any in the University," and by leading the "coursing," originally, he says, a competition in logic and metaphysics, but latterly in strength of hissing and jostling between Christ Church and the tall raw-boned Cornish and Devonshire men of Exeter. His authority, puny and weak as physically he was, he upheld by generously ransoming his companions when caught in the act of stealing a neighbouring farmer's poultry. Another of his heroic deeds was a rescue of the Exeter beer from a threatened diminution of its malt. He terrorised the authorities by threatening them with a secession of all the elder sons. Those who could afford to be expelled he persuaded to send the defiance, while the rest who had to live by their studies he warned to be passive. Finally, to him is due the abolition of "that ill custom of tucking freshmen," which, for the benefit of all thorough Conservatives and opponents of academical reform, had better be described in the revolutionist's own words:—"The abolition of tucking was a harder work, it having been a foolish custom of great antiquity, that one of the seniors in the evening called the freshmen to the fire, and made them hold out their chin; and they, with the nail of their right thumb, kept long for that purpose, grate off all the skin from the lip to the chin, and then cause them to drink a beer-glass of water and salt. The time approaching when I should be thus served, I considered that it had happened in that year more and lustier young gentlemen had come to the college than had done in several years before, and that the freshmen were a very strong body. Upon this, I consulted my two cousins—german, both freshmen, both stout and very strong, and several others; and, at last, the whole party were cheerfully engaged to stand stoutly to defence of their chins. We all appeared in the hall, and my Lord of Pembroke's son calling me first, I, according to agreement, gave the signal, striking him a box on the ear, and immediately the freshmen fell on, and we easily cleared the buttery and the hall; but bachelors and young masters coming in to assist the seniors, we were compelled to retreat to a ground chamber in the quadrangle. They pressing at the door, some of the stoutest and strongest of our freshmen, giantlike boys, opened the doors, let in as many as they pleased, and shut the door by main strength against the rest. Those let in they fell upon, and had beaten very severely, but that my authority with them stopped them, some of them being considerable enough to make terms for us, which they did, for Dr. Prideaux, the Rector, being called out to suppress the mutiny, the old doctor, always favourable to youth offending, our courage uniting with the fears of those we had within, gave us articles of pardon for what had passed, and an utter abolition in that college of that foolish custom."

His University exploits showed a mixture of boldness and of skill both in calculating means and in using a victory. He continued to exhibit this combination of gifts when he quitted Oxford. Not even the counsels of his friend Olivian, the astronomer, could induce him to woo a certain Miss Banister on the faith of predictions, which he regretfully saw subsequently fulfilled, that she was to succeed to a fine fortune. He preferred to contingencies dependent on the stars a solid alliance with Lord Keeper Coventry. He was accepted as suitor for the hand of one of the great man's daughters. The "unswerving prudence of the lady" caused her to overlook the invidious phenomenon that her lover, in the nervousness, doubtless, of his passion, had talked much more agreeably to her sister than to herself. The marriage, at any rate, accomplished his purpose of increasing his local consideration. When released from attendance at his father-in-law's mansion in the Strand, and the villa at Canonbury, famous for the residence as well of Oliver Goldsmith as of Queen Elizabeth, he could now vie, not unsuccessfully, with the pomp of a rival squire, Rogers, Miss Banister's half-brother, who had lorded it without a peer, in his coach and six, about the Dorsetshire villages and bowling-greens. At present, all his anxieties pointed to an utter overthrow of that unhistorical magnate's county supremacy. His allies were Sir Walter Earl, an old campaigner, who, like Uncle Toby, cut his garden into copies of the redoubts he had stormed or defended in the Low

Countries; John Tregonwell, who, so that he had his "nightcaps," probably not remotely related to punch, "and his poached eggs, thought no farther of the world;" Lord Digby, "justly admired by all, but disadvantaged by a pedantic stiffness and affectation;" niggardly Sir John Strangways, and cunning Mr. Gray, Colonel Brigham, and Sir John Trenchard. Sagacious politicians like Holles, and old-fashioned country gentlemen, seem to have been studied by the young squire of Wimborne St. Giles with simple reference to the aid they might contribute towards the baffling of his neighbour's "malicious rivalry." His proficiency in the art of management at this juvenile stage is demonstrated by his influence equally with courtiers and with rustic grandees of the stamp of Mr. Hastings of Woodland. His delightful sketch of Mr. Henry Hastings was extracted from the Memoirs, and printed originally in 1754. But Mr. Christie's transcript reproduced it for the first time with perfect accuracy:—

"He was low, very strong, and very active, of a reddish flaxen hair, his clothes always green cloth, and were all worth when new five pounds. His house was perfectly of the old fashion, in the midst of a large park well stocked with deer, and, near the house, rabbits to serve his kitchen, many fish ponds, and great store of wood and timber; a bowling-green in it, long but narrow, full of high ridges, it being never levelled since it was ploughed; they used round sand bowls; and it had a banqueting house like a stand, a large one built in a tree. He kept all manner of sport hounds that ran buck, fox, hare, otter, and badger, and hawks long and short winged; he had all sorts of nets for fishing; he had a walk in the New Forest and the manor of Christ Church. This last supplied him with red deer, sea and river fish; and, indeed, all his neighbours' grounds and royalties were free to him, who bestowed all his time in such sports, but what he borrowed to caress his neighbours' wives and daughters. . . . The husband, brother, or father was very welcome to his house whenever he came; there he found beef, pudding, and small beer in great plenty ; a house not so neatly kept as to shame him or his dirty shoes, the great hall strewed with marrow-bones, full of hawks' perches, hounds, spaniels, and terriers, the upper sides of the hall hung with the fox-skins of this and the last year's skinning, here and there a pole-cat intermixed, guns and keepers' and huntmen's poles in abundance. The parlour was a large long room as properly furnished ; on a great hearth, paved with brick, lay some terriers and the choicest hounds and spaniels; seldom but two of the great chairs had litters of young cats in them, which were not to be disturbed, he having always three or four attending him at dinner, and a little white round stick of fourteen inches long lying by his trencher, that he might defend such meat as he had no mind to part with to them. The windows, which were very large, served for places to lay his arrows, crossbows, stone-bows, and other such like accoutrements ; the corners of the room full of the best chose hunting, and hawking poles ; an oyster table at the lower end, which was of constant use twice a day all the year round, for he never failed to eat oysters before dinner and supper through all seasons. The neighbouring town of Poole supplied him with them. The upper part of this room had two small tables and a desk, on the one side of which was a church Bible, on the other the Book of Martyrs ; on the tables were hawks' hoods, bells, and such like ; two or three old green hats with their crowns thrust in so as to hold ten or a dozen eggs, which were of a pheasant kind of poultry he took much care of, and fed himself; tables, dice, cards, and boxes were not wanting. In the hole of the desk were store of tobacco pipes that had been used. On one side of this end of the room was the door of a closet, wherein stood the strong beer and the wine, which never came thence but in single glasses, that being the rule of the house exactly observed, for he never exceeded in drink or permitted it. On the other side was a door into an old chapel, not used for devotion ; the pulpit, as the safest place, was never wanting of a cold chine of beef, pasty of venison, gammon of bacon, or great apple-pie with thick crust extremely baked. His table cost him not much, though it was very good to eat at, his sport supplying all but beef and mutton, except Friday, when he had the best sea-fish, as well as other fish he could get, and was the day that his neighbours of best quality most visited him. He never wanted a London pudding, and always sung it in with 'My part lies therein—a.' He drank a glass of wine or two at meals, very often syrup of gillyflower in his sack, and had always a tun glass without feet stood by him holding a pint of small beer, which he often stirred with a great sprig of rosemary. He was well-natured, but soon angry. . . . He lived to a hundred, never lost his eyesight, but always writ and read without spectacles, and got to horse without help. Until past fourscore he rode to the death of a stag as well as any." Such was a son, brother, and uncle to Earls of Huntingdon, "a copy of our nobility in ancient days, in hunting and not warlike times."

Young Sir Anthony's acquaintances were not confined to Hants and Dorset. He had many intimates in Somerset, among them that "cunning old fox, Lord Pawlett." Everywhere, as in all stages of his career, he made friends and enemies too. The "pleasant lazy humour," which made him, in the midst of dreadful pains in the side, "hate pitying, and laugh and joke when the drops fell from his face for agony," was not readier for a jest than for a rivalry. Not so much a love of grandeur incited him, as a determination to be first in his company, and a passion for notoriety. For some time he was satisfied to shine for the astonishment of his own orbit. His own country's side was the mark at which he aimed his various fascinations, his skill in palmistry and fortune-telling, and the knowledge of family secrets which he derived from the cleverness of a favourite servant. But chancing to visit Tewkesbury, he won the hearts of the bailiffs of the town by an encounter of wits, in which, on their behalf, he thoroughly worsted bitter-tempered and tongued old Sir Harry Spiller. Sir Harry had availed himself of a civic feast to abuse the Corporation, and Sir Anthony triumphantly defended their common hosts. In gratitude they returned him to the Short

Parliament "without a penny charge." Here, in the middle of an account not particularly accurate of the Reformation and its political consequences, the first autobiographical sketch leaves him just launched on public life. The reader's consolation for the abrupt close of this part of the diary is that the whirl of affairs must in any event have speedily deprived the ambitious writer of leisure or care for the further collection of agreeable scandal about his rural neighbours.

Sir Anthony's next contribution towards his biography overlaps the first. The narrative glances at his career from 1621 to 1650. In the Long Parliament he claimed the seat for Downton, but was excluded by a party manœuvre. A majority in the House refused to call for the report of the Committee, which was known to be in favour of his election. In disgust, if it were not a suspicion of his Royalist proclivities which had caused his ill-treatment, he accepted a Royal Commission, after the war had commenced, for the capture of Weymouth and Dorchester. They had, he says, long been under the absolute sway of "their parson, Mr. White, one of the wisest and subtlest of that sort of man." He succeeded, nevertheless, and was rewarded by Lord Hertford, the King's Lieutenant in the South West, with the Governorship of Weymouth and other places. He kept his post for a time, though Prince Maurice desired it for a friend of his own. But whether in consequence of a Court intrigue, or patriotic scruples of conscience, he after a time resigned both it and his loyalism. His enemies attributed his defection to disappointed ambition. He professes indignation at the charge, and argues that selfish motives would have weighed in the contrary direction. The King had promised him a barony, and he left his estate at the mercy of Cavalier spoliation. His single reason, he asseverates, was his discovery that Charles's aims were "destructive to religion and the State." Certainly they were; yet it would have been satisfactory had he alluded to any new signs of the truth which had been revealed to him in the very brief interval since he took up arms for his sovereign.

After his secession, according to his own account, he displayed remarkable generalship for the Parliament, in his own and neighbouring counties. Though his story, with the emphasis it lays upon minutiæ, does not observe the rules of proportion, there is no reason to doubt the details. He raised sieges, helping, for example, to relieve beleaguered Blake at Taunton; he stormed castles; and he performed, he intimates, all kinds of glorious martial exploits. They did not hinder him from enjoying the usual amenities of a country gentleman's life; and that is very characteristic of the crisis. Sometimes a black spot shows that war must be war, whether in Wessex or in Westphalia. He mentions that, when the besieged townspeople at Amesbury cried for quarter, he, "considering how many garrisons of the same nature we were to deal with, gave command there should be none given; but they should be kept into the house, that they and their garrison might fall together." His object was to starve them into terms. But generally, Englishmen seem to have thought and acted, when not actually engaged in hostilities, much as at any other time. Thus, Sir Anthony, in the midst of his victorious campaign, could find leisure to visit Tunbridge Wells with his wife, and drink the waters there for six weeks. He could stay with connections, and spend long summer days in bowling-greens. He could pass weeks at lodgings in Holborn, seeing after the letting of his property in the neighbouring Ely Rents, and the raising of loans for the liquidation of small debts, or for the improvement of his estate in Barbadoes. He loved speculations in finance as well as in politics, and his campaigning could at discretion be interrupted for the purpose. If he were at home, other country affairs beside arms shared the versatile notice of this hero, statesman, man of pleasure, man of business. He describes himself at Dorchester certifying, with satisfaction at the incidental testimony to the guilt of a convicted murderer, how the body bled at the prisoner's touch, or sentencing to death "pressed soldiers that ran away of the 15th of January, 1646," or permitting the lives of criminals, "who had been faithful soldiers to the State, to be begged." One year he is High Sheriff. The King had nominated him while he was still a Royalist. It was the Parliament which, when his turn arrived in 1647, he served. His journal dwells with some pride on his "sixty men in liveries to receive the judges," and on the ordinary kept for all gentlemen at Lawes's, at 4s. a head; "I paid for all."

He did not subside after his shrievalty into obscurity, as the various local dignities he filled prove. But in 1649 his wife died, and a new chapter in his career began. They had lived affectionately together; and he eulogises her, as well for many noble qualities, as for "preserving, works with the needle, cookery, so that her wit and judgment were expressed in all things." She had made his home so happy and sufficing that, had her life lasted, he might have gone on content to be a Dorsetshire squire. The closing of his house happened, however, to be contemporaneous with the opening of new avenues in statecraft for a character and faculties like his. The diary is silent on the circumstances of the King's trial and execution; the diarist was already engaged in fishing in the troubled waters. General Ludlow's 'Memoirs' testify to his activity, if not to his good faith. The references are not to be found in the Memoirs as they were published in 1698. Shaftesbury's reputation was still at that period important to the Whigs. They induced Ludlow's representatives to cancel the posthumous insinuations of the stern Republican who confesses that he never trusted him, and thought him inclined to play fast and loose. Mr. Christie discovered the suppressed passages among the Locke Papers. In them, Sir Anthony is sneered at as "of a healing and a reconciling spirit of all interests that agree in the greatening of himself." Cromwell had nominated him a member of his Council. According to Ludlow, he used his appointment to "labour to convince the people that it was desirable to choose as representatives men of healing spirits." Shortly afterwards he went into opposition, and was removed from the Council. Ludlow assigns as the cause of his conduct disappointment at the rejection of his suit for the hand of the Protector's daughter, Mary, and his discovery that "Cromwell was resolved to act in the Council as the chief juggler himself." He and the military party in the Commonwealth, to which Ludlow belonged, were declared foes. Much weight apart from independent evidence is not to be allowed, therefore, to Ludlow's imputation of motives. His assertion of the political prominence Sir Anthony had gained may be accepted as indisputable.

There can be no question of his importance, especially in the disturbed interregnum which followed the Protector's death. He was summoned to the Council, and defeated an intrigue to expel him as "assured to Charles Stuart's interest." Finally, he succeeded in establishing his title to a seat in the restored fragment of the Long Parliament, on his bygone election for Downton. Both there and in the Council of State the "smooth tongue and insinuating carriage," which Ludlow decries, ensured his ascendancy. Notes of a few of his speeches survive. They contain pithy apophthegms, unusual in modern Parliamentary oratory, such as "words are the keys of the cabinet of things; let us first take out the people's jewels before you part with that cabinet." Occasionally the point of view is hard for posterity to appreciate. It seems far-fetched to us, though it would not be to a generation near the era of Gustavus Adolphus, for Englishmen to be warned against Sweden as a Power which "may overrun Spain, Denmark, Pomerania, Italy, and make itself master of this part of the world." But for the most part his policy is sensible and well argued. His influence was consistently exerted against harsh measures towards manifest or presumed opponents of the Commonwealth, such as Nevil, Sir Henry Wroth, and his future accomplice of the Cabal, Villiers of Buckingham. Whatever the topic, the diction is invariably bold and eloquent. Its chief themes are the absoluteness of the Protector's despotism, and the absurdities of his House of Lords. Though the attacks on the Protectorate were principally made after the death of its wonderful founder, the House of Cromwell still, it must be remembered, reigned. He execrates, he cannot despise, Oliver's autocracy, "a government so absolute as the Florentine, Machiavelli, and he that sat in the great throne of the world, if they had met together, could not have made." Cromwell's Lords he simply mocks at as a ludicrous burlesque of the order to which he was very close by county rank, and had been promised elevation by Charles I.

On this subject there is a constant ebullition of sarcasms. In one discourse, in support of a motion that the Upper House should last only for the Parliament held after Oliver's death, and then sitting, his contemptuous fury boils over. Some extracts will indicate its tone: "I dare freely declare it to be my opinion that we are this day making good all the reproaches of our enemies— owning ourselves oppressors, murderers, regicides, supporters of that which we do not only acknowledge to have been a lawful government, but, by recalling it, confess it now to be the best; which, Sir, if it be true, and that we now begin to see aright, I heartily wish our eyes had been sooner open: and for three nations' sakes, that we had purchased our convictions at a cheaper rate. We might in '42 have been what we contend to be in '59; and our consciences would have had less to answer for to God—and our reputations to the world. This House of Lords is a house that inverts the order of slavery, and subjects us to our servants. In a word, Sir, it is a house, of so incongruous and odious a composition and mixture, that certainly the grand architect would never have framed it, had it not been his design, as well to show the world the contempt he had of us, as to demonstrate the power he had over us. . . . The foundation of this noble structure was laid in perjury, and was begun with the violation and contempt, as well of the laws of God, as of the nation. He who called monarchy Anti-Christian in another, and made it so himself; he who voted a House of Lords dangerous and unnecessary, and too truly made it so in his partisans; he who with fraud and force deprived you of your liberty when living, and entailed slavery on you at his death; it is he, Sir, who has left you these worthy overseers of that his last will and testament, who, however they have behaved themselves in other trusts, will, it may be confident, faithfully endeavour to discharge themselves in this.... And all this according to the 'Humble Petition and Advice' which he was pleased to give order the Parliament should present to him—for, as the Romans had kings, his Highness had Parliaments among his instruments of slavery; and I hope it will be no offence for me to pray that his son may not have so too. His Highness, of deplorable memory to this nation, to countenance as well the want of quality as of honesty in the rest, has nominated some Lords against whom there lies no other reproach, but only that nomination.... But, Mr. Speaker, can we, without indignation, think of the rest? He who is first in this roll, a condemned coward, one that out of fear and baseness did once what he could to betray our liberties, and now does the same for gain. The second, a person of as little sense as honesty, preferred for no other reason, but his no-worth, his no-conscience, except cheating his father of all he had, was thought a virtue by him, who, by sad experience we find, hath done the same for his mother—his country. The third, a Cavalier, a Presbyterian, an Independent, for a Republic, for a Protector, for anything, for nothing; but only that one thing—money. It were endless to run through them all; to tell you of the lordships of seventeen pounds a-year land of inheritance; of the farmer lordships, draymen lordships, cobbler lordships, without one foot of land but what the blood of Englishmen has been the price of. These, Sir, are to be our rulers—these the judges of our lives and fortunes; to them we are to stand bare, whilst these pageant lordships deign to give us a conference on their breeches.... I say not this to revile any man with his meanness.... I remind you of their quality, because they themselves forget it; it is not the men I am angry with, but their lordships. Sir, for great men to govern is ordinary, for able men it is natural; knaves many times come to it by force and necessity; and fools sometimes by chance; but universal choice and election of fools and knaves for Government, was never made by any who were not themselves like those they chose. I might tell you, Mr. Speaker, that the same honour is not purchased by the blood of an enemy and of a citizen; for victories in civil wars, till our armies marched through the city, I have not read that the conquerors have been so void of shame as to triumph. Even Cæsar had no days of thanksgiving to his gods and anniversary feasts for having been a prosperous rebel! To speak nothing of one of my Lords Commissioners' valour at Bristol, and of another noble lord's brave adventure at the Bear-garden, I must tell you, Sir, that most of them have had the courage to do things which, I may boldly say, few other Christians durst so have adventured their souls to have attempted. They have not only subdued their enemies, but their masters that raised and maintained them; they have not only conquered Scotland and Ireland, but rebellious England too, and there suppressed a malignant party of magistrates and laws; and that nothing should be wanting to make them indeed complete conquerors, without the help of philosophy they have even conquered themselves. All shame they have subdued as perfectly as all justice; the oaths they have taken they have as easily digested as their old General himself could; public covenants and engagements they have trampled under foot. In conclusion, so entire a victory have they gained over themselves that their consciences are as much their servants, Mr. Speaker, as we are."

This speech is said to have been made against time, and in a half empty House. Its consistency, argumentative and political, is not unimpeachable; and some of the valiant defiance of the new Protector's Government may conceivably have been introduced in a revised edition. At all events, it is an answer to the assumption of Hume and his school that the oratory of the Commonwealth was made up of nothing but lengthy dissertations divided into a multitude of heads as tedious.

Shaftesbury's oratory speaks for itself. His political opinions and combinations passed through so many phases that as definitely favourable a judgment can scarcely be expected for them. His memory has had the misfortune to be bound up with a great satire remarkable more for genius than justice, and to have been revived by having to contribute to the vast repository of entertaining but unsifted historical gossip, entitled 'Lives of the Lord Chancellors.' As Mr. Christie proves, Lord Campbell has poured out many random assertions. When two explanations, one favourable, the other the reverse, were given by contemporaries of Shaftesbury's acts, he invariably takes the latter. When there is no contemporary condemnation, he discovers one in his internal consciousness. For instance, Shaftesbury was not a practising barrister, and therefore Lord Campbell declares his legal training to have been acquired at theatres and fencing schools. He opposed Cromwell, and so must have been actuated by envy. He had sworn fidelity to Richard Cromwell; consequently, he was perjured for aiding in the restoration of Charles when Richard had been deposed by a military oligarchy.

Shaftesbury was not the strange monster of cunning, selfishness, hypocrisy, greed of power, and tergiversation painted by Dryden and caricatured by Lord Campbell. On the other hand, he is not to be furbished up as a hero and a patriot. He took sides too easily not to change them without any acute internal struggle. Had more notice been paid him by King Charles's courtiers, he might have remained a Cavalier. Had the Cromwell family, from Henry, whom he addresses in letters as "My Lord and Father," up to the majestic father, favoured his suit to "musical glib-tongued Lady Mary," he might never have joined in overtures, justifiable as in the circumstances they were, to the exiled Prince. A more scrupulous legal amateur, though it is a calumny to assert him to have been ignorant of law, would not have aspired to be at its head. While it is unfair to accept partisan sneers, and his own jest at himself, as evidence of unmitigated profligacy, it is useless to contest the unchallenged testimony of the public opinion of his time to the looseness of his morality. He had the misfortune to be no zealot, yet to have to act with zealots, to be possessed of brilliant talents and a fiery ambition for their display, without any special impulse towards one or another party object. He could see the use of other men's aspirations and beliefs as a motive force better than he could sympathise with them. He could persuade men to follow him as their leader. They could not pardon him when they found he regarded and treated them as tools. His lot was to work among, with, and by means of politicians suffering from colour-blindness, who viewed all acts and characters through a distorting medium. Because he was not equally blind, or animated by the same ardour, posterity as well as his contemporaries have proclaimed him a traitor all round. He was not an Ormond or a Goring, a Hampden or a Fifth-Monarchy man; therefore to the Cavaliers, and now to eulogists of Sidney too, he must be nothing better than an impostor. The reproaches heaped upon him from various quarters are not altogether groundless. It is a dangerous game to league with an Algernon Sidney and a Major Wildman, yet not be a Republican either of the Cato or of the Harry Vane class, to subscribe to Titus Oates's figments without a Puritan's apology of spiritual panic, to abet plots of a son against his father, and of riotous courtiers against their royal ringleader, without a Buckingham's boastfulness of incapacity for principle, or the passion of a determined regicide. So unnatural a coalition is sure to taint a cold-tempered statesman with the grossness of the extremes with which he has allied himself, while he misses their redeeming frankness or fire.

Shaftesbury's party shiftings and desertions might be explained or pardoned. Not many leaders in that lamentable period were attended by their original principles for all the stages in their career. A few alone, like Holles, and they not of the rank of chiefs, remained throughout faithful to the political type and theory they had adopted in youth. More resembled Clarendon, a Constitutional Liberal, whose end was to be impeached for bribery, and to expiate by expatriation his real crime of having been the dupe of a traitorous King. Shaftesbury's frequent secessions from parties, led as parties commonly were, would not by themselves prove him guilty. A brief personal experience of a Court in which the Palatine princes ruled, his native keenness being sharpened by his private wrongs, might convince him that the fruit of victories gathered under their auspices would be baneful. Clarendon, we know, and Falkland, and Newcastle, privately thought as much. Cromwell, again, he might follow gladly at first, when an interval of dictatorship seemed necessary for the prevention of anarchy. With equal honour and sincerity he might desert the usurper of a prerogative exceeding that of royalty. There was no self-evident fickleness in efforts for the restoration of the second Charles as an alternative to a military oligarchy or a tyrannic ghost of a Parliament. On the same principles might be defended his early co-operation with the companions of the sovereign's exile. When the old counsellors were found incompetent to rise to a comprehension of the growth of the Constitution during their absence, when Clarendon, for example, modelled on Lord Burleigh his estimate of a Prime Minister's prerogatives, a man of the highest integrity and moderation might have withdrawn from the returned Cavalier coterie as impossible. Some apology could be attempted for the Minister, who, perplexed between a master determined to treat the national resources as his private patrimony, and an Opposition conspiring with the enemies of all kingship, and enlisting every class of malcontent and revolutionist, had for a moment connived at unconstitutional acts to carry on the King's Government. More excuse might be made for his defection from his master when required to conduct a provisional crisis as a permanent system, and for a remorseful employment of his information, influence, and energy to cancel the evil precedent he had furnished. There might have been an indemnity even for a statesman hurried onward, by the growing consciousness that the King would have either absolute power or none, into the extreme position in which the line between rebellion and constitutional resistance becomes indefinable. History has pardoned it in Lord Russell. But then Shaftesbury was not a Russell. He was not even an Algernon Sidney.

Each of his changes might singly be explained, and the character of the seceder for good faith have been left unimpaired. In the mass they form an irrefutable indictment. It is useless to urge in extenuation that his transfers of allegiance were often against his interest. He might have been Oliver Cromwell's right hand, and have guided Richard. No game could have been more dangerous than the restoration of an outcast royalty. Later, from the inmost confidence of Charles he stepped spontaneously into hopeless opposition, with the Tower and exile as its goal. Instability has always proved ruinous in statesmanship. That the deserter suffers as well as his abandoned party can never be admitted as evidence of honesty. Unless Shaftesbury's apologists be able to show that, at the instant of each new movement, he could not have hoped to win the captaincy of one party in exchange for the lieutenancy of another, his actual losses are no proof of disinterestedness. It is unfortunate for him that his diaries, letters, and speeches afford no evidence which can clear his fame. They exhibit his subtlety, and his power of acting on men's minds, and on their perception of their private advantage. They indicate a master genius for creating a new party out of old materials. They are not without tokens of courage in attacking the dominant party when the storm which was to shatter it was as yet a speck in the distance. They contain not a word to imply that he believed in any principle, religious or political. His modern advocate appeals to them against the recorded judgment upon him. They are searched, and their answer is wholly negative. Not a spark scintillates from them of generous self-denial in himself, or admiration of it in others.

He was no thorough-paced villain, and he was no patriot. He was simply a dexterous party leader in circumstances demanding rather the character of a demagogue, or that of a tyrant, neither of which was he inclined to play. He could not endure a superior, and scarcely an equal. His misfortune was that, like his most illustrious predecessor in the guardianship of the Great Seal, he was endowed with a burning ambition and no enthusiasm of heart, with a quick brain-power and a slow moral pulse. His crime was that he chose his allies and his causes with a view to their power to promote his pre-eminence rather than their national merits. His failure was due as much to the limitations of his unscrupulousness as to that itself. We cannot but think he must have surveyed his career at its close with wonder how a course of political manœuvres had landed him in exile, a suppliant to a state of which, though it had never harmed him, he had, in the bewildering tangle of party tactics, vowed the extirpation. Refugee as he was at his death, and proclaimed traitor, it is still hard to pronounce whether he ever designed a revolution, or even an insurrection.

III.
TWO POET-POLITICIANS.

ABRAHAM COWLEY,
1618–1667.

MATTHEW PRIOR,
1664–1721.

ABRAHAM COWLEY.

COWLEY'S career started from a much lower social level than that of Anthony Ashley Cooper. It never approached the same pinnacles of political and official splendour. It encountered no dangers so virulently deadly; and it may be supposed never to have suffered so tremendous a fall. In reality, though the man and his character were safe from the storms in which the fortunes and personal reputation of the potent Cabal Minister, the brilliant Lord Chancellor, and the popular idol sank, Cowley's noblest distinction has undergone a more irreparably ruinous shipwreck. The author of the Habeas Corpus Act is secure against historical oblivion. The blaze of fame of the incomparable poet has dwindled till it is saved from absolute extinction only by the favour of compilers of Elegant Extracts.

Before me is an advertisement sheet of Tonson's, affixed to the tenth edition of Cowley's poems, issued in 1707, which, post-dated by a few years, well represents the literature and literary society in which that poet was supreme. It is an obituary of departed reputations. The wits of Button's and Will's, the courtiers of Whitehall, and scribblers from Grub Street, satirists, playwrights, pseudo-travellers, divines, and the great blind bard himself, make this single leaf a page of history. There are Dryden, Milton, Waller, Denham, Suckling, Rochester, Etherege, Garth's Dispensary, Addison's Campaign, works by the Tory L'Estrange, a 'Voyage to the Island of Love,' by Afra Behn, "our envy, her own sex's pride," as the moral Cowley calls her. The list is completed by congratulatory poems by Rowe, heavy booksellers' histories by Lawrence Echard, scandalous 'Memoires' by St. Evremond, a life of Pythagoras, by Madame Dacier, and, finally, various versions from the classics, the favourite reading of that lazy, spuriously scholarly era, and probably fully bearing out in letter, though not in spirit, Cowley's recommendation that translators should not servilely copy the original. It is curious to look on a muster-roll of dreary battalions from the Dunciad mingled with giant names, and mournful to think how many of these antitheses are now in annihilation not divided. Some volumes are seen just trembling into fame, some already illustrious, though with the seeds of quick decay in them, others destined to shine forth unexpectedly, far beyond and above the rest, when these, their coevals, should have become mere names of history, notable as representatives of a very peculiar social epoch, but with no distinct literary lustre. There Waller shows his seventh edition, put forth in an age when the court and the bar were an author's public, and Denham his fourth; and there, where Milton has apparently not yet passed beyond his first impression, Cowley overtops them all with the glories of a tenth. Where now are those "celebrated hands," nay, those "most eminent hands," great in society and the coffee-houses, who joined in Dryden's translations? Where are the much belauded patrons of literature, those courtly men of letters and plagiarists of Horace, the Dorsets, Godolphins, and Rochesters?

Abraham Cowley has been, perhaps, the most unfortunate of all, as he was as their chieftain far the most renowned. The rest deserved their fate. It is hard for us to put ourselves into the proper position for comprehending the admiration of our ancestors for them; in him are seen glimpses of glorious poetry, and a poetical, though not, it may be, a philosophical depth and truthfulness, which should have preserved him, as politico-poetical vigour has saved Dryden. His works could not, perhaps, be now a text-book; they deserve to be a classic. Cowley is a kind of proverb for the instability of popularity. Each successive age has stolen away one of the ornaments of his chaplet, till the present scarcely comprehends how the infallible Doctor should have thought it worth his while to accumulate reasons why men do not study a bard whose very name they but seldom hear. We know well the contour and bulk of the volumes of the eminent, the most incomparable, or, as Wood loves to call him, that prince of poets, Mr. Abraham Cowley. They lie stranded in every old library, like the beams and keels of wrecks, or the piles of drift-wood, described as obstructing navigation on the Mississippi. The larger sympathies and the central position in literary history of Dryden, give him the power to put forth green branches from a decaying trunk amid the turbid flood of time which has drowned much even of his celebrity. But many noble logs of timber lurk beneath the waters, unseen and almost unsuspected, until students, piloting their way through the bygone history and literature, suddenly strike upon them, and are startled at the mass which blocks their course. The current of literature flows over many such submerged heaps. Some patience and resolution are necessary before these relics of other systems can be properly appreciated, so thick a barrier of temporary prejudices has first to be surmounted. Of all of them, Cowley most deserves forbearance; as also perhaps most determination is needed to discover something precious in him as compensation for wading through the deliberate eccentricity of his style and versification. When readers have bound themselves apprentices to his handicraft, it is not difficult to discover how much harmony is consonant with art and stiffness, and what grace may be shown in dancing in shackles.

Possibly not a little of what we think forced, unnatural, and artificial in Cowley's poems, may be traced back to his precocious facility of versifying, which by out-running his power of conception, tempted him to look to novelty in manner for originality, and for the satisfaction of his absorbing thirst for literary glory. Next to Chatterton, he is the most remarkable instance of success in the ambitious imitativeness of childhood, which sometimes developes into poetry, sometimes proves to be nothing but the effervescence of youth and passion. His 'Pyramus and Thisbe' was produced at the age of ten, 'Constantia and Philetus' at twelve, and 'Love's Riddle' shortly after. Though it would be too much to say that we can read these poems with pleasure, at least in rhythm and sentiment they seldom offend the ear or judgment.

Cowley's poetical power was hardly hereditary, unless the narrow circumstances of his parents may be supposed to indicate that, being unsuccessful traders, they were literary geniuses. His father is supposed by Dr. Johnson, from the absence of any note of the poet's baptism in the register of his parish church, St. Dunstan's, to have been a dissenter. According to Aubrey he was a grocer. A reference in the Calendar of State Papers of the reign of James the First to a bond owing by a certain Cowley, a grocer, to two other citizens, would seem to corroborate that statement. The posthumous son of a little shopkeeper, born within the democratic city of London, beneath the shadow of Temple Bar, just where Chancery Lane strikes the end of Fleet Street, he did not start under very favourable auspices for winning the smiles and patronage of a Jermyn and a Buckingham. Mrs. Cowley, to whom was left the task of bringing up three sons, was a tender mother, and gifted with the power of exciting an affection in her children which no years or fame could diminish. But his friends confess she knew no more about poetry than her neighbours, and possessed no larger stock of books. It so happened, however, that in her window, along with the whole of the family library, lay a volume, the most gracefully artificial of English classics, Spenser's 'Faerie Queene.' Amid its bright pictures, Cowley tells us, he basked and grew up into poetry, till the solicitations of Mrs. Cowley, and the interest of some powerful patron with the head-master, removed him to the great school at Westminster and the hard business of life in the shape of Latin grammar.

It was the most aristocratic school of the day, and, from particular circumstances, the especial home of a political party; yet it does not seem that the boy was looked upon as an intruder, or exposed to unkindness from masters or scholars, on the score of his humble birth. His name was long and proudly treasured up among them, and his boyish poems heralded in stately rhymes by admiring school-fellows. Very quickly he vindicated his claims to consideration, though fits of poetic rhapsody did not at first exactly harmonise with the quaint hexameters of the præ-Busbeian grammar. Sprat has recorded Cowley's natural and boyish aversion for hard technical rules, as a portentous token of his friend's genius. He has been rebuked by the greatest master of the art of putting down, and the paragraph treated as a bombastic intimation that Cowley was no better than other boys. There was doubtless no lack in the days of Charles the First, any more than in our own more prosaic ones, of idle schoolboys or of rods, the maiden Queen's perennial benefaction from the royal forests to Westminster School; and the poetical aspirant's prophecy of his own future glories, in a juvenile dedication to Sir Kenelm Digby,—

"The birch that whipt him then would prove a bay;"

intimates that he had scarcely as yet experienced the results of so agreeable a botanical metamorphosis. But the disgust of the lad at those jingling prosodiacal barbarisms might well proceed less from want of application than from the desire, fostered by his previous process of self-education, to grasp at the results without going through the stage of mastering details. At all events, he speedily exhibited very remarkable classical taste. An ear for Latin verse, inferior to Milton's in sweetness and delicacy, but stronger, and showing on the whole more freedom and power of thinking in the language, is sufficient testimony to his early industry. Hand in hand advanced his power over both English and classical diction. In 1628, when the Parliament gained its first triumph over the King, and in the more advanced days of 1630, when the sovereign's violence was swelling by repression the growing passion for liberty, Cowley's muse tried its first flights. His 'Pyramus and Thisbe,' and 'Constantia and Philetus,' poems composed in those years in an English dress, were, envious contemporaries often whispered, superior to his mature works. His masters grew proud of him, and cherished the genius from which they expected yet riper fruits. One, Mr. Jordan, Cowley's gratitude for kindness, and not the necessities of a school exercise, led him to commemorate in an elegy.

Had he remained exposed to the feelings and influences most powerful both in his own home and his school, the future professed Royalist might have developed into an associate of Milton and Andrew Marvell. Westminster was a hotbed of Parliamentarism. In a school supervised by Williams, once Lord Keeper, and successor of Bacon, now Bishop of Lincoln, Dean of Westminster, and Laud's rival, and taught by Osbaldeston, alias Osbolston, alias, and as Cowley writes it, Osbalston, the poet was in the direct way of becoming imbued with the popular spirit. The earliest extant poem by the satirist of Cromwell was dedicated to the schoolmaster, who, even then suspected, was no long time after sentenced, for an unpublished libel upon Archbishop Laud, to stand in the pillory at his own school-gate. It is placed near a general dedication and congratulatory verses to the Bishop of Lincoln himself, on his release from the Tower, to which he had been sent for his part in this very transaction. But a time was coming when all were to be compelled to take a side, when it was no longer possible to praise the private virtues of a statesman without denouncing his political adversaries. It was not merely the general feeling among undergraduates in favour of Charles, as opposed at Cambridge, to a powerful party in the neighbourhood on the side of the Commons, but something also in Cowley's disposition, which developed his politics in a very different direction to that which might have been anticipated from the pupil of Osbaldeston and extravagant eulogist of the ex-Lord Keeper. He belonged to the section which will always comprise many men of letters in a time of popular commotions. Like Waller, like Selden, like Falkland, Cowley hated despotism, though scarcely with the fervour of judgment of the last two. But he was slow to seize on the salient points in the proposed changes and he dreaded the consequences. He could praise "*excellent Brutus*" and flatter and co-operate with a mean-spirited Jermyn, without any consciousness of inconsistency.

At Trinity, whither he proceeded in 1636, he had to fight his way without any regular patron. As, however, Mrs. Cowley could not well have equipped a son for college out of her unaided means, he may have been subsidised by the Lord Dorchester, whom he commemorates, or the son of the Sir Everard of Guy Fawkes and Gunpowder-plot notoriety, the celebrated Sir Kenelm Digby, of whom the gossip-mongering Aubrey speaks as "ever very kind" to our poet. For some reason unknown Cowley had failed to be elected to a Trinity scholarship on the Westminster foundation, but the renown of his school successes procured for him almost immediately an open one. He was soon distinguished favourably by the notice of the fellows of his college, especially the learned Mr. Fotherby, the uncle of his future friend, Matthew Clifford, and by the Master, Dr. Comber. Among his fellow-students his chief associates seem to have been William Hervey and the famous Crashaw, one of the sweetest of religious poets; though, like the rest, artificial. We have pleasant glimpses into the academical life of the poet and his friend, and their long walks along the meadows and dykes of that green region.

> "Ye fields of Cambridge, our dear Cambridge, say,
> Have ye not seen us walking every day?
> Was there a tree about which did not know
> The love between us two?"

In the same poem, written in honour of his friend's memory, he appeals to the reminiscences of long winter nights,—

> "Spent not in toys, in lust or wine,
> But search of deep Philosophy,
> Wit, Eloquence, and Poetry;
> Arts which I loved, for they, my friend, were thine."

His own assertion of assiduity as a student can have been no vain boast. His devotion to Latin scholarship was evinced by the production in 1638 of a dramatic medley, 'Naufragium Joculare,' though the title expressed its literary fate. Beside this, he found time for the composition of most of that ponderous poem, the 'Davideis,' which has hardly floated down the stream of time to us on the fame of its author. It was commenced in the boyish belief that the doom of all great poets is to compose epics; but the venial self-delusion was not regretted properly in after years by its author. Though not devoid of grand lines and noble sentiments, or of bright, happy conceits, it is, on the whole, as heavy as Prior's 'Solomon,' which was partly designed, in emulation of its repute, as at once a continuation and rival. More cannot be said against it. It is crowded with unblushing plagiarisms, such as "So a strong oak," and so on, *ad nauseam*. They are not, like Milton's imitations of the ancients, so beautified with new hues and shades playing over them, that we begin to compare Virgil with him, rather than him with Virgil. Sir John Denham could scarcely have perused the 'Davideis,' when he wrote of his friend,—

> "Horace's wit and Virgil's state
> He did not steal but emulate."

Sense there is; no fire is there to vivify the dead bones of rhymes. We miss all power of imagining a scene. How faded is Cowley's description of Hell, in comparison with that in 'Paradise Lost'! Milton is intentionally vague and misty; we feel as men groping in the dark, that ghastly forms are lurking behind the veil, modelled with as scrupulous fidelity as the carved goblins behind the stalls in Gothic cathedrals, though, like them, meant to remain hidden. In the 'Davideis,' there is a veil with nothing to hide, or thrown on merely to cover the barrenness and baldness of the author's conception. Sometimes, but rarely, the guardian angel of English poesy, the spring-tide spirit of Chaucer, breathes through and animates the struggling verse. "Uprose the Sun and Saul," perhaps betrays even more than sympathy with the patriarch of our literature. Now and then there are lines like these:—

> " Queen of the flowers who made that orchard gay,
> The morning blushes of the Spring's new day ; "

or we may chance to stumble on the racy vigour and earnestness which are never entirely wanting to political poetry; as, for instance, in the passage beginning,

> "'Tis jest to tell a people they are free."

But instances of natural feeling and power are few and far between. If the Bishop, his biographer, were not misled by friendship, or the wish to turn a sentence, the statement that, " with all the faults of the 'Davideis,' it is a better instance and beginning of a Divine Poem than he ever yet saw in any language," is to be accounted for only on grounds injurious either to Sprat's width of reading, or to religious bards. We may be excused, too, a slight wonder how far the poet can have believed the result to harmonise with his own lofty and terse prelude of invective against "the cold meats of the ancients" dragged into sacred verse; or against the " turning of a story into rhyme, which so far from elevating Poesie is only abasing the Divinity." At all events, he has cruelly abased the divinity of Milton's war-demon, kingly Moloch, by describing him as a nursery-tale giant, who—

> "Still did eat
> New-roasted babes, his dear delicious meat."

Public opinion respecting the volume when subsequently published, as that of the Bard's friends at an earlier period, by no means accorded with ours. He was hailed as the coming poet by the University and his College, of which he proceeded major fellow in 1642. His Royalism and his literary fame together pointed him out as the proper person to be selected for planning a dramatic piece for the entertainment of the young Prince of Wales, when passing, in 1640, through the University on his way to join the King at York. The result was 'The Guardian,' a rough-drawn farce, he himself tells us, not written out, but learned by the *dramatis personæ* from his extempore dictation. But the progress of the troubles brought evil days upon him. In 1643 he was, with his friend Crashaw, expelled from his fellowship and the University by the Parliamentary Commissioners, for delinquency in refusing the oath then tendered to all members of Cambridge. St. John's College, Oxford, the college successively of Archbishops Abbot and Laud, afforded him shelter, while the friendship of Lord Falkland gave him distinction with the courtiers assembled at Magdalen and Christ Church. He appears to have thus drifted into confirmed partisanship, with no very active zeal for party politics. Possibly, though some of the links for proving this are wanting, the influence of Sir Kenelm Digby, who had long been his friend, or some other powerful patron, may have acted upon him in this direction. Poets and scholars in those days occupied a more dependent, though at the same time less laborious, condition than now. In the later general revolution of political and social ideas they held a commanding position. The result was not fully attained till the reign of Queen Anne, when the golden age of literature became the golden age of men of letters. They were still part of the great man's household, and still looked to his purse and countenance for support as of right; but he began to use them for the political ends which were monopolising his own energies. Men such as Cowley did not hire themselves out as party tools; but when, as scholars, they had been attracted within the sphere of some patron's orbit, and exposed to all the influences which surrounded him, it was natural that, on his conversion into a statesman, their neutrality should be modified in accordance with the only theory on the subject with which they had had an opportunity of becoming imbued.

Thus Cowley, shortly after his migration to Oxford, appears to have betaken himself to the protection of Jermyn and the Queen's faction. In that focus of partisanship his own speedily became confirmed; though, apparently, it was always more the partisanship of habit and the accident of association, than of passion. 'The Puritan and the Papist,' a savage satire, delighted his companions, though it subsequently terrified both himself and others. Only at Dr. Johnson's earnest instance with the publishers was it at length inserted in a complete edition of his works. But he chiefly devoted his time to the composition of a heroic poem on the civil wars. Much of it was compiled from his own note-book; for he seems to have attended the King on several of his expeditions, and to have been employed in others as a confidential agent. When his locality and circumstances were different, the violence of the sentiments of the composition appalled him, and the poem was carefully suppressed. It was continued down to the time of the second battle of Newbury, when the catastrophe of Royalist hopes was too evident to admit even of a poet's favourable interpretation. Soon after this calamity, the Royalist cause became so desperate, that, along with a throng of compromised courtiers, divines, and authors, he fled to Paris.

Materially it was fortunate for him that he had gained the countenance of Jermyn, Lord St. Albans; for it was a matter of notoriety and scandal, that this nobleman alone of the refugees in France kept open house, living in comparative splendour, while the Prince of Wales was half destitute. Into his household, and consequently the Queen's, whose chamberlain Jermyn had long been, Cowley was admitted as a favoured confidant. His fame, which, though no remarkable work had proceeded from him, had long resounded throughout both the Republican and Royalist camps, as that of the coming poet, while 'L'Allegro,' 'Il Penseroso,' and 'Comus' were comparatively neglected as Elizabethan archaisms, made him a welcome inmate. Jermyn, with all his bad qualities, had sufficient taste to judge of literary power. The guest on his part appears to have used his advantages so kindly and benevolently as to escape the envy liberally dealt out to his host. By his help Crashaw, who had lost his fellowship at Cambridge at the same time and for the same reason, was kept from starving. Eventually, having turned Roman Catholic, he was despatched into Italy with such warm recommendations from Henrietta, procured by his friend's intervention, that Pope Innocent X. gave him one of the richest benefices in Italy, a canonry at Loretto. Cowley himself found active employment as Jermyn's secretary, in the routine but confidential employment of ciphering and deciphering the correspondence between the King, now a captive, and the Queen, and other Royalists. The drudgery took up all his days and two nights every week. When so distinguished a copying clerk was no longer needed, his services were put in requisition in various other ways. The intervals between political journeys were filled up with poetry and visions of some such happy sinecure as the mastership of the Savoy, of which the reversion had been promised him both by Charles I. and his son. He still retained the post of private secretary to Lord St. Albans, and managed the correspondence between the little Courts of Henrietta and Prince Charles, in his various removals to Bruges, Spa, and Cologne. Letters which have been preserved from Mr. Secretary Bennett, afterwards Lord Arlington, one of Charles II.'s favourite Ministers, from April 1650, show that the poet readily became a serious man of business; disappointing as this may be to those who would have a bard's eye always in a fine frenzy rolling. The consideration which he, a man of no pretensions to nobility or audacity in camp or council, enjoyed in the Queen Mother's Court, is of itself a sufficient indication, not only of his poetical renown, but also of a somewhat dignified character always keeping its place. We are told, both by himself and Sprat, that he had peculiar opportunities for becoming conversant with Courts and the splendour of palaces: that he was no mere pensioner and dependent, but an active member of the royal establishment.

When not writing letters to Charles's councillors or spies in England, he was principally engaged in political missions to the Prince from his mother. Whenever some plan required fuller exposition than was safe or possible through the medium of an ordinary council letter, the poet seems to have been despatched to communicate the opinion of the

Queen and her chamberlain. With this object he visited successively, Jersey, Scotland, Flanders, and Holland. No records, however, of the purpose of his journeys or the incidents to himself have been preserved, with one exception, consisting of an answer sent by him from the Channel Islands, to a copy of verses addressed to him when there. In his epistle he endeavours to emulate "the Sweet Melody of Native Insular Rhymes, written by ———— Esq. the year of our Lord, sixteen hundred, thirty-three." Perhaps on this expedition finding himself, as he tells us, without any books but Pindar, he was induced to study that poet's dithyrambic poems. The result was the introduction into the waters of the English Helicon of a rivulet of harshest verse, in which it tasks the benevolence of the most kindly reader to detect any melody. While settled in France in the year 1647, he thought it his duty to show his conformity with the principles, not the practice, of the Cavaliers, by composing his 'Mistress.' The subject quickly made it popular, rather than the special merits of the poem. It is not without occasional beauties :—

> "Love in her sunny eyes does basking play,
> Love walks the pleasant mazes of her hair,
> Love does on both her lips for ever stray,
> And sows and reaps a thousand kisses there."

At times a turn or a tone is caught which appears an anticipation of Tennyson. But the general impression on the modern reader is laborious monotony. Cowley's own explanation of its origin is enough to reveal the causes of its barrenness. He declares it was written because no poet can be esteemed a freeman of his company till he has sacrificed to Venus. A habit of concerting systematic, cold-blooded conspiracies for winning literary renown was the taint in Cowley's poetical character. His line—

> "What can I do to be for ever known?"

is an index to all his poetical cravings. He wrote the 'Davideis' as Haydon painted his oppressive pictures, because an Epic has the primacy among poems, and Abraham

Cowley must, therefore, put himself in a position to emulate Virgil, and Homer, and Tasso. He wrote the 'Mistress,' not because the subject, or the thoughts rising out of it, suited his tastes, nor only because the poet of the Jermyns and Wilmots must pretend to have analysed love; but mainly because each master poet had shown himself a votary of Cupid. Starting from such a confessed theory, he exhausts the whole subject as to its topics, though nowhere does he penetrate below the surface. He was unwilling to leave room for the detection of a single defect in his treatment of it. He was resolved there should not be a rock he had not visited and planted his flag upon. The laxity in moral sentiment which he was at great pains to display was itself a literary parade like the rest. There can be no worse reproach to the age or to the Cavalier party than that grossness of manners was so ingrained in it as to colour deeply the language of one practically well conducted as was Cowley.

A tradition preserved among Pope's sneering remarks upon his predecessors, says, that the lady meant to be fascinated by panegyrics, many of them of a kind now to be esteemed insults, was the Leonora celebrated by Cowley as his last and enduring love in that sparkling, but scandalous 'Chronicle' of his flames, which took Johnson's admiration by storm. Though he never actually asked her hand himself, her acceptance of a brother of his future biographer, the Bishop of Rochester, is said, on the same authority, to have soured his temper, and contributed mainly to his disgust at a Court. It seems unlikely that this respectable lady can have suggested some of the feelings of either poem; at all events, he had soon an opportunity of returning to her society. In 1656, the stagnation of the Royalist schemes in France, and the strength of the Protector at home, inclined many of the exiles to make compositions with the revolutionary government. Cowley had no estate to compound for; so it was supposed he would have the less difficulty in returning to England, and that while there, he might still be able, as opportunity served, to co-operate with his friends. It was not then thought dishonourable for a partisan to take to the profession of a spy. For Cowley, who hoped for nothing from Cromwell but to be overlooked, it appeared a most innocent thing to do what Evelyn, who was protected in his estate, thought perfectly becoming. It had been thought advisable that he should remain incognito; and this is the chief circumstance revealing that his duties were to consist in espionage. His character would have led us to suppose he had intended now to throw off all political obligations whatsoever, and live for literature and science; but, as it happened, almost immediately upon his landing he was seized as a returned refugee, by mistake for another against whom the warrant lay. His real name quickly became known; and the famous Court poet and confidant of the Queen and the detested Jermyn was looked upon as a prize. Several times was he examined and menaced by the Protector and his Council, but to no purpose. It nowhere appears, except from an obscure report of a saying of Clarendon's, that the enemies of Cowley hinted he had betrayed any secrets to Cromwell, to whom they accused him of unworthily truckling in other ways. Perhaps he had no secrets to reveal. The exiled prince's applications to every sovereign in Europe for a little ready money could scarcely have interested the mighty parvenu much. At length he was dismissed, though only on bail to the amount of £1,000, a sum which vastly raises our notion of the poet's political value. His surety was the celebrated Dr. Scarborough, of whose loyalty to the Protector there was no doubt. Scarborough's resolute Protestantism was alleged to have been the reason many years later for concealing from him, though royal physician, the accouchement of James the Second's queen.

Now the poet was free to make trial, if he chose, of some positive realisation of the hope breathed in the drawing-rooms of Paris:—

> "Ah! yet, ere I descend to th' grave,
> May I a small house and large garden have!
> And a few friends, and many books, both true,
> Both wise, and both delightful too!"

He actually betook himself from town into Kent, to study botany and rival Virgil's Georgics. From the earnestness and width of curiosity which distinguished his character, medical and natural science soon absorbed his attention. He sought for and, probably by the influence of Scarborough, obtained from the Government a command to the University of Oxford to grant him the diploma of M.D. By his application for a degree in medicine he may have wished to manifest his determination to leave politics. Its grant by favour of the Protector was thrown in his teeth by detractors as a species of apostasy. Whatever the motive, he really devoted himself to science, after his manner; and the result was the first four books of his Latin poem on Plants. In the year 1656, he brought out a collection of his poems. The measure was rendered necessary, as well by the unscrupulous abuse of his name by English publishers to screen paltry rhymes, such as a work called the 'Iron Age,' as by the numerous and defective editions both of his juvenile and his later poems. But the volume scandalised his friends; it had a copy of verses to the Protector inserted in it by way of dedication. Compliments to a political adversary who had treated him courteously by a poet, a prisoner upon parole, are no atrocious crime. But it is to be regretted that the Bishop extenuates the obnoxious preface on the ground of the necessity under which the author was of allaying the fears of Government, in order more fully to discover and betray its counsels to his employers. Cowley had, we may hope, a better apology, even if such were the excuse for the biographer's own 'Pindaric Ode, dedicated to the happy memory of the most renowned Prince Oliver, Lord Protector,' wherein it was declared, rather equivocally, that

"His fame, like men, the elder it doth grow,
  Will of itself turn whiter too."

At any rate, Cowley's dedication brought him no profit; his bond still remained uncancelled; and the indignation of the Royalists against verses, only, after all, expressive of admiration of that energy in the Protector's rule which had elevated the national character, was so violent that the writer was weak enough to suppress them after the Restoration. Altogether the visit was a failure; if he came to collect information, his detection and the suretyship of Scarborough effectually baffled the mission. He had become an able botanist among the Kentish orchards, and was recognised through the introduction of the friendly physician, as a man of science, and a master poet: but penury and the cold looks of friends and foes embittered his life at this period. Such was his despondency that he even used to consult his friends on a migration to the American plantations, to study botany and medicine, and write poetry at leisure. His genius had a practical side to it, and he was wise enough, while sighing for solitude and a wilderness, to include a good library in the list of necessaries for Virginia and Maryland. Still it was fortunate for him, wearied though he was with the world, that he could never put his vision to the test.

As this fancy floated off his mind the times rendered the distant prospect of the Savoy less dream-like, and he accepted an invitation to resume his duties in Jermyn's household at Paris. They do not seem to have been obtrusive, for there is no appearance of the poet's surety having been mulcted for this new delinquency. At last came the joyful day of the Restoration, and, of all men, the poet and author of 'The Mistress' expected that in the "cheerful fit of folly," which was to do away with the remembrance of "the twenty years of melancholy," he should not be passed over. But his petition for the long-promised boon was rejected. Wood declares this arose from some "enemy of the Muses." The mysterious assertion may refer to the dull George Monk, dubbed "honest," or even to the ultra Royalist Cavaliers of the Queen Mother's household. The story of Charles's response to the petitioner, "Mr. Cowley, your pardon is your reward," if it rested on any foundation, might favour the latter supposition. He would have been hardly a poet not to exclaim at such treatment. His 'Complaint' was temperate and loyal, but it and its author, "Savoy-missing Cowley," were ridiculed in Suckling's witty poem of the day on the choice of a Laureate, as exhibiting a pitiful incapacity for outspoken resentment. As it was, he remained a dependent of Lord St. Albans, a poet by trade, and man of general science by taste. His professional character of M.D. had been thrown off after the publication of the poem on plants. Soon came out, in prose, with verses interspersed, his 'Discourse by way of Vision concerning the Government of Oliver Cromwell,' a grand composition. The reader's indignation at the renegade-like vehemence of the revilings is tempered by the feeling that the praises which pretend to be ironical may have been an outburst of admiration. Hume has, with the change of a few words, openly borrowed them for a panegyric; they were probably in substance identical with 'The Lament of the Death of that Great Sovereign,' a poem, though Wood records its existence, now no longer extant, except as inserted in a setting of abuse. The 'Discourse' is a noble eulogy, full of the fervour of a man exulting that England had produced such a son, however much loyal subjects might disapprove his usurpation. In few compositions is the prose more perfectly akin to poetry. Cavaliers could not have been at all satisfied with a work in which every epithet and censure revealed a sense of the gigantic in the deceased. The favourite phrases of scurrilous songsters and pamphleteers, 'Red Nosed Noll,' 'Brewer's Son,' and such like, seemed to have evaporated amid the strong stream of the poet's execrations. By the side of the enumeration of the national glories, won by the dead Protector, the flattery of the young King's locks—

"If gold might be compared with angels' hair,"

is tame and bald.

This work elevated the poet to an undisputed supremacy in contemporary literature, if it gained him no rich sinecure. He remained a follower of Lord St. Albans, though passing his time chiefly with men of letters and science.

His companions were Evelyn, from Deptford; Boyle, the most modest and abstracted of philosophers; Sir Kenelm Digby, who frequented the society of the sages at Gresham College in a long mourning cloak, peaked hat, and Oriental beard; Hobbes, in his selfish green old age; Shakespeare's godson, Sir William Davenant; Lord Broghill; Denham, his associate in politics and poetry; and Sprat, somewhat pompous, but a fervent and affectionate admirer. A little further off in this circle of his intimates might be seen men of fashion like Buckingham, constant to nothing but patronage of literature; Waller, from whose recollection the shame of confederates betrayed to the hangman, had easily glided off, and not from his memory alone, but from that of friends and foes, whom his gentle wit then and long after captivated; politicians, who excused no variableness, except in themselves, like Clarendon; accomplished debauchees, like Wilmot Earl of Rochester; Dryden, soon about to take up, as it were, Cowley's sceptre, and rule literature after him; and Matthew Clifford, reputed co-author with the Duke of Buckingham and Sprat of the 'Rehearsal,' and deemed worthy of the dedication of the life of Cowley, one of those anomalous men of letters who are admitted as honorary members into the guild, without performing its exercises, and sometimes, as this connoisseur himself, with his coarse comments on Dryden's Fables, miserably disappoint their friends when at length they have been flattered into authorship. All these, and, tradition says, Milton himself, were among his professed admirers. As recognised sovereign of letters he received the homage of the men of science, the fashionable votaries of taste, the philosophers and divines. Beside all this, there were domestic duties which the poet never neglected. His mother, probably still alive at the Restoration, and brothers, one at all events prosperous, and living in King Street, Westminster, shared in the advantages, such as they were, of his fame.

Though not, as he has been termed, one of the six or seven founders of the Royal Society, Cowley was on the list of the men who were to be first asked to join. His general fame and his acuteness in experimental science, especially botany, made him a valuable recruit. Doubtless even experiments for the restoration of youth by the transfusion of the blood of the young into the old, and other ambitious speculations, found from his ready imagination perfect sympathy. It was not only his co-operation in that way which was desired; the philosophers hoped from his social rank and pen to obtain vogue, and to be screened from the popular ridicule which irritated even the serene philosophy of Evelyn. He acceded to the invitation of the latter to give them "a divine song," to vindicate them from the satire and scoffs of the drunkards. Accordingly, he wrote, in the year 1667, a poem which it is a shame on our age to have forgotten. Nothing in didactic poetry can be finer than the lines on Bacon, beginning,—

"Bacon, like Moses, led us forth at last,"

and the apology for the theorist's failure in practice; or than the bitter retort on the men who were trying to laugh down science—

"The things which these proud men despise, and call
Impertinent, and vain, and small,
Those smallest things of nature let me know,
Rather than all their greatest actions do!"

The praises of the Royal Society were undertaken by him cordially, for the whole scheme of that institution approached a design which he, in common with Milton, Evelyn, Boyle, Sir William Davenant, and Sir William Petty, was always debating. This was the erection of a philosophical college in accordance with the suggestions of Bacon, in the "Advancement of Learning," for the promotion of general, but especially experimental, knowledge. As might have been expected, Cowley's designs were not altogether practical; scarcely so much so as Evelyn's. The latter would have been content with £400 a year as a foundation; but then, apparently, each member was personally to contribute all the little ornaments and elegancies required by philosophers, whose wives were to join them in college, and hold musical soirees. Cowley's scheme required an annual expenditure of £4,000. He proposed to erect two quadrangles, the second opening upon gardens and green lawns, and to procure no contemptible endowment in the shape of appointments of £120 a year for each of the professors, and £20 for each scholar, exclusive of incomes for travelling fellows to collect rarities. The plan branched out into details respecting the division of the profits of new discoveries between the college and the inventors, and the establishment of a grammar school and boarding-house for rich pupils. From the profits of these gradually a fund was to be accumulated for the maintenance of poor men's sons, "as plentiful as for the rich, there being nothing to be expected from a low, sordid, and hospital-like education." In one point especially, the poet, as compared with a man of the world like Evelyn, betrays himself when he gravely lays down the rule for his seminary, that the professors should "all keep inviolable and exemplary friendship with each other." Cowley agreed with Milton as to the proper instruments of education. Greek and Latin, especially the latter, were to be taught, but Varro and Cato, Columella, Celsus, the Georgics, and Manilius were prescribed as text-books, to carry out the design that the students should learn things as well as words.

Amid the convulsions of politics and society, many Utopias of the same sort were being projected, all with the same negative results. While republican theorists were constructing their impossibly perfect polities, the men of science were planning how to turn the political changes to the advantage of physics. They had all looked with unselfish covetousness to the sequestrated bishoprics and royal domains, and Cromwell's proposed University of Durham was viewed as an instalment of large donations to learning. Even on the Restoration, undaunted by the crowd of eager individual claimants, the philosophers put forth their collective requisitions. So late as Queen Anne's reign, and in the sardonic mind of Swift, a hope was harboured of persuading Ministers to endow colleges for the improvement of the language. Cowley and his friends had already entertained a similar design. If it came to nothing, at least it gave the projectors an interesting subject of discussion. They used to walk through what were then pleasant fields to talk literature at Gray's-Inn. They thus anticipated the Kit-Cat Club, which had itself existed for purely literary purposes, under the auspices of a famous bookseller, long before it was taken up as a party organ. Though there were but few meetings, they seem to have been continued at intervals during two or three years. They were interrupted by the Plague, and above all, writes Evelyn, " by the death of the incomparable Mr. Cowley." He was the centre of the whole, the most fashionable of poets, and esteemed the greatest. To this age such a rank is incomprehensible, though Milton's 'Paradise Lost' had not yet appeared.

Cowley had a reputation independent almost of the merit of his published works. This must have been mainly based on his character, for his friend and biographer tells us that "he did not surprise at first in his conversation," and further, that none but his intimates would have discovered he was a poet. There was nothing brilliant or showy to make up for this in his general demeanour. When his eulogist declares that he was possessed of perfect natural goodness, great integrity, and plainness of manners, though he had lived in France; that there was "nothing affected in habit, person, or gesture;" that "he understood the forms of good breeding enough to practise them without burdening himself;" finally, "that he was modest and humble excessively even to the appearance of dissimulation, unless for other equal virtues," we have no great difficulty in representing to ourselves a person destitute, like Addison, of external graces, but without Addison's capability of warming into eloquence and wit. It is not necessary to go so far as to believe in the truthfulness of his friend Denham's epigram—

"Had Cowley ne'er spoke, nor Killigrew write,
They'd both have made a very good wit."

But perhaps it was the conjunction of his brilliant fame with apparent unconsciousness of it, which chiefly charmed by its contrast with the affectation and pretentiousness of other literary men of the day.

Such as it was, his popularity, like Dryden's, though it survived them, had met with one or two checks. While association with courtiers gave literature fashion, and taught literary men the profitable art of making their compositions popular with society, not only did they sometimes find in the noble a competitor who forgot the patron in the rival, but any deviation from the tone which the great man believed himself fully competent to prescribe, or any appearance of isolation in life and severer morals, exposed to the chance of a persecution. Courtiers leagued with his brother authors to degrade Dryden by treating Settle as a rival, from jealousy of his literary dictatorship. The attack on Cowley had more of a political or party character. In 1663, he had remodelled and produced upon the stage, 'Cutter, of Coleman Street,' the play originally represented before Charles, when Prince of Wales, at Cambridge, under the title of 'the Guardian.' In itself a witty and well-managed comedy, with abundance of brisk action, it seemed adapted to please the Cavaliers by much illiberal caricaturing of the Puritans. To the horror and surprise of the poet it was hissed off the stage. That seemed to him the catastrophe, not only of his social, but his literary aspirations. He feelingly laments, in a preface to a library edition of the drama that, "from all he had written he had never received the least benefit or the least advantage, but on the contrary, had felt sometimes the effects of malice and misfortune." He himself ascribed the disaster to an incongruous and predetermined union of parties against him. He was condemned, he writes, by a faction before being heard; of profanity, for attacking hypocrisy; of disloyalty, for exposing a few disorderly and sham Royalists, who had joined the party only to disgrace it. This was the reward of his sacrifices for twenty years.

Apart from reasons grounded on some unexplained envy, to which his character would not seem to lay him open, the doom of the play may have been owing to the fact that its tone was out of date. It laid stress on the roistering qualities on which the Cavaliers had, as a party, once prided themselves; and it held up Puritan sobriety and love of constitutional liberty as the sentiments of canting rogues. Personal loyalty was put in the place of all the virtues, when already all sensible Royalists were beginning to be disgusted with the qualities of their old comrades which favoured despotism and licentiousness. The poet, though personally always moderate, and averse from the extreme practice and doctrine of the Cavaliers, had not been prepared, more than Clarendon, to discover that the radicalism of the beginning of the troubles was become the liberal conservatism of their conclusion. He had written in accordance with the sentiments to which he had been of old habituated. He did not comprehend the ramifications of the Court and Country parties. If he had been free to study the matter for himself, and then to take sides, he would probably have been against extreme principles. He had assumed, without investigation, the folly of all but simple Royalism. As it was, he was thoroughly disheartened by his reception, though the play subsequently, when a new Cavalier party was reviving, was acted with applause. Perhaps he may have been conscious of sinning against his conscience, by stretching his dislike for fanaticism and austerity to the semblance of a boon-companion's love for debauchery and riotousness, in order to please the courtiers. In any case he discovered that a spirit which suited the atmosphere of Bruges or of Prince Rupert's camp was out of place in the vicinity of St. Stephen's and the City of London. Sneering Dennis reports an expression of surprise by Dryden that Cowley did not bear the news of the fate of his drama, when conveyed to him by himself and Sprat straight from the theatre, with anything like the philosophy to be expected from so great a man; as though, bitterly comments Johnson, who himself had experienced the same sensation once, they had a right to anticipate haughty tranquillity at the damning of a piece produced in the sanguine hope of popular applause.

More eagerly then than ever the poet resumed his intermittent longings for leisure to rear trees and flowers, and search out the secrets of nature. Previously he had been unwilling to quit all hopes of advancement from the Court, while reluctant to reside in town. As an intermediate course he had, very soon after the Restoration, when his hopes of the Savoy were not yet blighted, taken up his abode successively for a short time at Deptford, in the neighbourhood of the sympathetic Evelyn at Sayes Court, at Battersea, and at Barn-Elms. But at these places he only hired temporary residences. They afforded no scope for putting in execution regular schemes of rural retirement, till at last a gleam of prosperity made his permanent plan of life feasible. Even now he was not indebted to the direct bounty of the King, whom and whose cause he had served long and faithfully, however calmly and without enthusiasm. His preferment was due to the solicitations and influence of Buckingham and the Earl of St. Albans, his constant friends. Through them he was pensioned in the year signalised by the catastrophe of his comedy with a lease for life of the Queen Mother's dower lands in the manor of Chertsey, on terms so favourable as, with prudent management, to promise him £300 a year net income. In Aubrey's account of the preliminary negotiation the chief merit of the gift is attributed to Villiers, whose memory stands in woeful need of a few such kindly traditions: "The Duke of Buckingham, hearing that at Chertsey was a good farm of about fifty pounds a year, belonging to the Queen Mother, goes to the Earl of St. Albans to take a lease of it. They answered that it was beneath his Grace to take a lease of them. That was all one, he would have it, paid for it, and had it, and freely and generously gave it to his dear and ingenious friend Mr. Abraham Cowley, for whom purposely he bought it."

The gift permitted Cowley to try his ideal life of a poet and searcher after scientific truth, without too violent a wrench from his established habits; for in all his Utopian schemes he was sufficiently wise not to expect happiness from pursuits perfectly alien from those in which he had spent his youth and manhood. From Deptford, Battersea, and Barn-Elms he had been in the habit of resorting to London occasionally, and there indeed the failure of his 'Cutter, of Coleman Street,' had found him. Now he resolved to dwell altogether in the country, though glad to admit the visits of old friends. It is not strictly true, as Sprat relates, that "he gave over thoughts of honour and riches when he might have gratified them;" nor, lastly, is it very probable that "he refused many invitations to return to business." Neither his character nor his talents were fitted for doing the work, or pleasing the humours of that capricious Court. But we are ready to give all credence to the Bishop's assertion of his friend's disgust at a Court like that at Whitehall, " a sort of life which, though his virtue had made it innocuous to him, yet nothing could make quiet."

Before his visits to London wholly ceased, in his lodgings at Barn-Elms, as later on his Crown farm, he had entirely thrown aside the politician. That " unaffected modesty and natural freedom, easy vigour, cheerful passions, and innocent mirth," which had found themselves under constraint in the miserable squabbles of the exiled Stuarts, expanded in a rural life which admitted the cultivation of all such qualities. Gardening was one of his staple employments; he writes to Evelyn from Barn-Elms, acknowledging himself his reverent disciple, and full of gratitude for a gift of plants and seeds, and of curiosity respecting the success of some which he had already set. At Barn-Elms the last two books of his didactic Latin poem on plants were composed. They testify to his study of the botanical characteristics of the neighbourhood. A modest letter to Dr. Busby, chief of all schoolmasters that ever were, accompanying a presentation copy of his poem, has been preserved by Nichols, the antiquarian. Poetry, which he had never intended, in all his schemes for the future, to abandon, he now made " together with himself," says his friend, " an anchorite dedicated to drive evil spirits from the human heart." His solitude continued to be crowded with silent aspirations after literary renown. Then were produced the delightful essays, which we can well believe to have been real expressions of "his thoughts on the point of his retirement," though they appear to be fully as much designed to persuade himself as others of the charms of isolation. He had meant, though they were never sufficiently completed to admit of such a form, to dedicate them to his early patron Lord St. Albans, who appears, from what Sprat says, to have felt displeasure at the poet's retirement. Doubtless the "eminent and celebrated Mr. Cowley" was an ornament in those days of Mæcenases even to Jermyn's household, and the lease of the Crown farm may have been intended as a pledge and retainer rather than a reward for the past. The beauties of prose and verse are happily united in these compositions. They contain none of the sketches of society which pervade the Spectator and Tatler; none of their wit and humour. But gardens with green pastures, and solitude, are described with an exquisite grace, and over all meanders a transparent current of pure sentiment.

Another large design, which at intervals occupied his attention, was a history of style, which Sprat and Clifford and others of his admirers had persuaded him to undertake. He meditated also a general analysis and review of the original principles of the primitive Church, as they might be gathered from its records of the first four or five centuries. His wish was as well to satisfy his own mind, and that of his old companions in exile, of the truthfulness of Anglican doctrines, as to vindicate their sincerity in professing them, which their connection with Queen Henrietta had caused to be suspected. The plan was too vast for his learning or leisure, and was never prosecuted. In preparation for the history of style, some rough characters of ancient and modern authors were drawn up, but never fitted together. Literary ambition was as capacious in him as in Gray and Coleridge. All three had the academical development of literary curiosity, uncorrected by the feeling of what is practicable. All exhibit the same largeness of literary aspiration. The entries of their schemes read like the catalogue of the labours of a literary society. Programmes of huge out-of-the-way histories are scattered up and down their correspondence and memoranda. Chains of philosophy were to be constructed to link together sequestered settlements lately reclaimed from the backwoods of metaphysics. Whenever it seemed to them that the student has to search for himself a dozen works, or infer a principle from a hundred scattered instances, an obligation appeared to lie upon them to compose a book. Cowley was not satisfied that a scholar should be left to learn from Demosthenes and Cicero themselves the secret of their eloquence. In like manner Coleridge designed an epic on Titus's capture of Jerusalem, because it ought to be done; a score of dramas merely to fill up the void in Shakespeare's national scenes illustrative of English history; and for the same reason a gigantic corpus of philosophy or register of every possible dogma or shade of a dogma which could find birth in a German mind.

Cowley's literary cravings were not likely to diminish on his removal to the deeper solitude of Chertsey, though they were counterbalanced by the cares of his farm, and his taste for natural philosophy. The latter was an abiding love, as compatible with his poetry as was the pursuit of medicine with Akenside's very inferior but not very dissimilar muse. He did not find all the leisure for it which he had expected, though now in the position relative to London, which he had designed for his philosophical College. But farming was a more anxious pursuit than gardening, and making a living out of a leasehold estate, let at however low a rental, was not the same as having a foundation of £4,000 a year to fall back upon. Sickness also interfered with his plans, though it did not efface them, or make him miserable. Probably in disgust at his reception at Court and on the stage, he had been in too great haste to quit London, and consequently did not select his place of residence with sufficient caution. The three Thames villages in which he took up his abode successively were all more or less unhealthy from damp. He lived at Barn-Elms, whither he removed from Battersea, near the old manor-house. A neighbouring villa became famous later as the residence of Jacob Tonson, and the resort of the Kit-Cat Club. The manor belonged, by the gift of King Athelstan, to the canons of St. Paul's; but by compulsion, as was her custom, Queen Elizabeth had extorted a lease from the chapter. By her it was assigned to her sagacious councillor, Francis Walsingham; and there he had the expensive honour of entertaining her and the Court. From him it devolved upon the Earl of Essex, in right of his wife, Walsingham's daughter, the widow of Sir Philip Sidney. Mulberry-trees, which love old country seats, still bear witness to the times of Walsingham; the more modern traces of Cowley long since disappeared. Rich meadows spread about it, and the river glistens near at hand, overshadowed by the tall elms which gave the name. Beneath them was a fashionable promenade, where Pepys loved, on a summer evening, as he often recounts, to display his newest and gayest plumage to the admiring and admired company. Cowley must have often thus caught, not so unwillingly, an echo from the town he professed to have abandoned for ever. "Barn-Elms no longer has," wrote Lysons, "the reputation of being damp and marshy." In Cowley's time the place had it with reason. He was prostrated by a bad fever, from the effects of which his constitution never entirely recovered, though he soon resumed his old pursuits after it, and put the last touches to his poem. His position at Chertsey, still by the Thames, was not immaculate, though healthier. The Porch House attached to his farm is shown, with a verse from Pope's 'Windsor Forest,' slightly modified, inscribed over the door:—

"Here the last accents flowed from Cowley's tongue."

It was just within the town, but surrounded with ample gardens, and skirted by a brook, with St. Anne's steep declivities rising at a little distance. There, not yet far advanced into middle age, he determined to settle himself for good. He had abjured the town; but he was always glad to receive his old friends, and speedily made new among his neighbours.

Many interesting facts might have been learnt from letters passing between him and his friends, had not Sprat's and Clifford's scruples about the propriety of publishing compositions designed for those only to whom they were addressed, led them to suppress the entire correspondence. Whether the letters were destroyed or only secreted, is still a curious question. The reverence for documents containing precious information, though, in the opinion of the depositary, unsuitable for publication, allows a hope that they may be lying concealed among old family archives either of Sprat or Clifford. An antiquary might be rewarded who endeavoured to clear up the problem. The fashion has been to bewail or ridicule Cowley's resolution to retire from London, as though it had resulted from disappointment. He has so long occupied the poet's reserved niche among the unrequited great, along with princes reduced to merchants, schoolmasters, or market-gardeners, premiers made into graziers, and court beauties into lady abbesses, that it would be rather perplexing to have to find another bard of fame for the vacant post, or a proper station for the late occupant, high enough, yet properly sequestered from the vulgar necessity of being read. As "the melancholy Cowley," he is always sufficiently before the eye of the literary public to satisfy the requisitions of his celebrity in his own age. He is dismissed with a well-turned phrase, and people suppose they know all about him, without having to gauge his actual merit, in order to rank him suitably. It might be otherwise, if the conscience of the student were burdened with a "celebrated," a "most incomparable" Mr. Cowley, and obliged to give reasons for adoption of the epithets handed down from a former generation. Yet no authority exists for asserting that he was a disappointed man. The three authentic bodies of evidence as to him are Sprat's Life, and Evelyn's and Pepys's invaluable Diaries. The Bishop says, "his retirement suited his mind better than his body;" that is, he was happy and sickly. Evelyn and Pepys speak of his fame as pre-eminent; and the former refers to his life with invariable respect, but nothing like pity. In Spence's amusing but untrustworthy colloquies of Pope and his friends, his disappointment in love is mentioned, and consequent inclination to be, in each remove, "farther and farther from town." A blighted lover, if he ever were that, is not identical with a soured courtier. His own poems and essays show no feeling that his dreams of rustic retirement had been premature. All the indications, even when he had quitted the Court, are of a contrary sentiment. The one basis of the epithet, is his application of it twice to himself in the 'Complaint,' a poem written simply to reproach the failure of the Court to reward his long fidelity, and comprising no reference to a country life, on which, at least since the Restoration, he had not yet entered. On this slender evidence he has been converted into a proverb, and a warning to all who happen to think the charms of a villa in the country exceed those of a house in town. One of his few extant letters, on personal matters, that to Sprat in May 1665, has been thought to confirm the popular report of his dejection in his suburban retreat. Surely, the catalogue of ills in this epistle was compiled in sport, and by a very cheerful mind. The sorrows of the amateur farmer over trespassing cattle, and the rest, cannot have been very deeply seated to disperse in a moment at the prospect of a ramble over the slopes of St. Anne's Hill.

Agricultural perplexities at all events are known not to have clouded his apparent serenity, or to have hindered his enjoyment of local society. His ailments in his retreat were, as his friend lamented, physical and not mental. His constitution had been impaired by his sickness at Barn-Elms. This was succeeded, on his removal to Chertsey, by another illness of some months' duration. All warnings he appears to have neglected, and to have continued his usual way of life. Perhaps he was tempted by his new situation and prospects to imprudent exertions. Staying out late with his reapers he brought on a stoppage in the breast and throat. In spite of his medical training he treated the malady as no more than a cold. It was thus suffered to increase, till it resisted all remedies, and resulted in his death, at the age of forty-nine, after a fortnight's illness. Pope's peevish memory retained a story of the occasion of the death of a different complexion, and probably untrue. He declares that Cowley, with Sprat, then on a visit to him, went to visit a neighbour, who would not let them go till evening. The two friends set out, bewildered by the country lanes and the claret, till they irrecoverably lost their way, and were compelled to pass the night in a ditch; whence the poet's cold and mortal disorder. We are told that the parish still talks of the "drunken Dean Sprat." At any rate, Sprat's fair fame may be exonerated. Cowley, in the letter to Sprat, to which I have alluded already, speaks of a convivial country neighbour as "the Dean." Pope, or his informant, would be unaware of the nickname; and having heard some local gossip that the poet died from a complaint contracted by accidental exposure to the night air, might suppose Sprat to have been the "drunken Dean," though not appointed to his deanery till 1683.

Whatever the precise circumstances in which the fatal cold was caught, its issue was bewailed as a national calamity. It cut short a bright career. At a selfish, frivolous Court it excited something like sorrow. The Court indeed owed him funeral honours; it had spoilt an immortal poet. The Duke of Buckingham reared his monument in Poets' Corner; Sprat composed his epitaph, and Denham his elegy. Nobles attended his bier on its passage down the river to the Abbey,—

"Tears the river shed,
When the sad pomp along its banks was led."

King Charles passed on him the eulogium that "Mr. Cowley had not left a better man behind him in England." His fame and authority had bloomed and ripened early. He had been passed over in the distribution of honours, and abused in the theatre; yet it was assumed by all that he had been and

was at the head of contemporary literature. Part of this
exalted praise may be ascribed to his gentle disposition,
which, as it prevented him generally from arrogating precedence, saved him from exposure to the worst violence of
envy. He was rather a centre for literary men to group
themselves round than their captain. Neither the man nor
his works provoked attack. Though he invented new metres
and experimented in rhythm, men, while their ear was
caught by novelty of sound, heard no thoughts of a kind
to offend their conservatism. Sprat declares that "his
rough verse was his choice, not his fault," that he affected
variety to divert men's minds. It is no great merit in a
poet to hunt after variety in this way. But it helps and
explains both the subsequent neglect, and also his favour with
his contemporaries. He allowed no affectation, the Bishop
tells us, in his language; that is to say, "he neither went
before nor came after the use of the age." He forsook the
conversation, but never the diction, of the city and Court.
Though Sidney's it might be, this was not Shakespeare's and
Milton's way of avoiding affectation. They discovered how
to speak in the language of the nation, not of any section of
it. Good society was not to them the nation as to language
any more than as to life and manners. For Cowley, not
more from the aristocratic tone then prevalent, than from
the Puritan assumption of indifference to such things, the
whole national taste for literature was absorbed within the
narrow boundary of the Court and aristocracy. They might
have understood a poet speaking to the whole nation, of
which they were a part; they appreciated him with far
greater zest, and he lost few readers or admirers, because he
addressed himself to their class habits and sentiments in
their own everyday language. Cowley has become for us
not equally antiquated with Waller, because mental greatness
and want of exclusive sympathy with his party and the
Court prevented him from reflecting their tone alone. But
his general reflection of the fashion of his day explains his
burning popularity then as compared with present neglect.

The qualities which caused Cowley to be worshipped have proved a bar to his posthumous fame. He had attributes which must otherwise have secured him permanent favour. He whom Milton, notwithstanding party hostilities, ranked with Spenser and Shakespeare, in the first rank of English poets, whom Rochester, chief of wits and courtiers, made the pure gold standard to try base poetry by, whom the jealousy of Pope allowed to be a poet with all his faults, a seventeenth-century writer, lastly, whose works ran through ten editions in twenty years, must have had solid claims to admiration. He has no pathos, and little of the largeness of conception fitted for the wide canvas of an epic; his rhythm is wanting in subtlety and glow; but in his verse we find ingenuity of fancy, depth of thought, and an astonishing earnestness of intellectual fervour, coloured with passion. His variety is inexhaustible. As an epic poet his contemporaries admired him, though we cannot; now as then his lofty rank in the neighbouring class of solemn didactic bards is not to be disputed. Thence he suddenly passes on almost to the splendour of Pindar in poetic narrative. His master could scarcely have improved on the tale of the infancy of Hercules. Now he soars upwards, high as ever poet mounted, in his noble elegies on Crashaw, Hervey, Lord Balcarres, and Vandyck; then off he flutters into the brisk vivacity of the 'Chronicle.' Nothing is more Anacreontic in Anacreon than the song, still a favourite, 'To a Grasshopper,' and that to drinking, 'Come Man of Morals.' Waller has no prettier strained conceit than the verses 'On a Lady tiring herself.' It would be hard to instance a freer or more splendid outburst of fancy than the poem 'In the chair made out of Relicks of Sir Francis Drake's Ship.' His translations of congenial passages are elegant and spirited; those from Pindar are often something more. When he met with suitable material, as an epistle of Horace, he could all but outdo his original. His dainty rendering of the ode to Pyrrha is superior to Milton's. But perhaps the neutral territory between poetry and philosophy, tinted with cross lights from fancy and from reason, is more peculiarly his own. Bacon shines on the one side of the boundary line, Cowley on the other. Each catches the reflection of a ray from the opposite star. The Novum Organum appears to suggest the ode 'To the Royal Society.' That in its turn interprets in poetry thoughts which were verse disembodied in the mind of the reformer of physical science. Inferior as is Cowley to Wordsworth as an original thinker, he had an extraordinary and almost an unique faculty for inspiring his imagination with grand philosophical ideas not his own. He is not so much a metaphysical or philosophical poet, as the poet of science and philosophers. I have more than once referred to that famous ode 'To the Royal Society.' Men when they hear it seem to recognise it, though they never read it before; it rings through our literature. In those to Hobbes and Scarborough and Harvey, and in the Hymn to Light, are lines equally grand, though fewer. They cry shame upon our neglect. Any reader who is sceptical has but to study Cowley as a whole and not in fragments, and his conversion is certain. He may commence by despising Cowley's contemporaries for worshipping his genius; he will end by blushing for the modern desertion of the shrine.

It is good now and then to take the muster of extinct literary luminaries, and require an account of their former brightness and present obscurity. At first we see all as through a haze of prejudices from time and circumstances. Gradually the quivering lines and bars, through which the mind dazzled by the novelty surveyed the scene, dissolve away; we begin to discover that the beauties which our forefathers saw were happily not all imaginary. If a past age had been so grossly deceived, we might well doubt the stability of our own estimate of modern genius. It is reassuring, while we feel in accord with our own leaders of thought, to be able to understand why previous generations felt in sympathy with theirs; to perceive that genius is not mere fashion; that the great in their various degrees are always great, though not always famous.

MATTHEW PRIOR.

VERY few years separate Cowley and Prior; they are an age apart in the characters they played, and the temper in which they played them. Both were of humble extraction and rose to high renown. They were scholars of the same Royal school. Both were poets, and eminent poets, though of different degrees of distinction. Both were employed in serious public business, though their comparative importance was there reversed. Literature was for both the ladder by which they climbed; and neither ever disdained its services. Yet, amidst a multitude of points of resemblance in circumstances, the general impression the two careers produce is of utter dissimilarity. It was not only that the men were different; their periods were more different still, and emphasised their varying tendencies. Cowley in literary history stands, though on the verge, within the period when the literary profession was a profession of dependence on the doles of patrons, when men of letters solicited, and did not make a maintenance. Prior's lot was cast in times when literature was beginning to be acknowledged as essential a constituent of social organisation as law, physic, and divinity. . The writer could not be dispensed with; and he exacted his wages in what coin he would. His commercial value had risen with his new utility. Literature, not in one form alone or another, but as a whole, was growing into a necessary vehicle of public opinion, to be measured by general standards, and to be employed, with its professors, for general public purposes. That is to say, Matthew Prior happened to be born one of the moderns and not one of the ancients.

Two periods may be contiguous, yet one appear within the verge of ancient, the other of modern history. Even in those times which must be called by a common name modern, one epoch impresses us with a feeling of the closest affinity and analogy; we can understand the passions and point of view of its chief characters, and instinctively penetrate to the springs of their conduct; when we survey the list of events occurring, it may be, but a single reign before, we grope about in a kind of darkness. We hear party names and party cries, and we know that the objects for which these factions were striving, are the same as those which roused the desires and regrets of our own fathers. The people which assumed the appellations, and strove so angrily for the privileges and rights, is to us altogether foreign. Thus, as we ascend in English history from the reign of Henry VIII. to that of his father, a sense of isolation in a strange land and people comes over us. Bosworth field, and princes smothered in the Tower, appear legends of the Dark Ages beside the Reformers, and Hugh Latimer preaching at Paul's Cross.

We pass forward, through the reigns of Edward, Mary, and Elizabeth, into the epoch of the Stuarts, and start to find the scene again changed, though many of the actors, the Bacons, Cokes, Cecils, and Raleighs may be the same. It is a new departure. When we compare men and things, the one era seems ancient, the other modern history. The same periods will appear modern or ancient according to the presence or absence throughout them of particular characteristics which happen for the time to be commanding the inquirer's attention. In one sense, all on that side of Constantine is ancient, and all on this is modern history. In another the ecclesiastical revolution of the sixteenth century draws the boundary line. In a third, for England, the constitutional conclusions of the first half of the seventeenth, make the age of the Pyms and Hampdens ours also, and all before it antiquity. Yet the division even then has not been carried far enough. The age of the Star

Chamber, and "ex officio" oaths, of monopolies of soap, and compulsory knighthoods, scandalum magnatum, and sales of peerages, cropped ears, and Harrington's Oceana, is to us unnatural and alien. We know that the men of that age fought for the liberty which we now enjoy, and we recognise at a general election some of the arguments which Pym and Hampden first made watchwords. The private life and manners of the heroes of our political reformation are black-letter to us. They seem as unreal as the descriptions of men and women in historical novels. We cannot imagine a Falkland or a Strafford walking the streets of London, or an Aston and a Wilmot at Aldershot Camp. Between West-end dinner parties, and the rioting of Royalists in the Strand or Whitehall, or the debates of the Long Parliament, and the harangues of our modern House of Commons, yawns the same impassable gulf as between the dark countenances frowning from the canvases of Vandyck, or Lely's beauties, and a miniature by Ross, or the portraits of Lawrence.

It was reserved for another reign and generation to roll back these heavy folds of the curtain still stretched between us and our ancestors. The Revolution of 1689 did not reform the working of our Constitution alone, it changed manners. It was not achieved by the energy of one class exerted against another class, as had been that accomplished by the men of 1642. Its operations were not confined to the atmosphere of high politics which the majority of a nation scarcely breathe. They were attained, equally, by the dexterity of statesmen, and by the passive resistance to oppression of the ranks which had cowered beneath the horrors of the Bloody Assizes. Freedom of opinion was the reward of Nonconformists for having detected behind the mask of an occasional lenity the persecutions of the High Commission Court, and the Corporation and Conventicle Acts. The great nobles had been at the head of the movement; the masses, which followed and approved, or murmured, gave the moral weight and momentum indispensable for success. Feudal lords were no more; influence, rather than privileges, belonged to the order. Never had public opinion, in the wide sense of the term, been appealed to more consistently or fully. When the object had been attained, and the succession to the throne changed, as a guarantee that the policy most antagonistic to the old would be carried out, the battle still raged. Every inch of ground had to be defended by the strength of half the confirmed partisans in the kingdom against the attacks of the other half.

No period is so favourable to the approximation of classes, as one in which known and recognised chiefs have led a movement, but by the choice and election of the people. Every feature, mental or even physical, every little peculiarity in manner or conduct belonging to the leaders, Whig or Tory, was marked. The eccentricities of caste, which prevail when an order, is so separated and bound up in itself, that each member is sure of his position, and can, in the wantonness of impunity, transgress all established rules, that audacious trampling upon decency which the annals of Charles II.'s reign lavishly display, subsided beneath the inquisitorial censorship of public opinion under William and Anne, and the biting sarcasms of the pen. Wharton was, at last, decent, though as finished a profligate as ever. The notorious Buckhurst, of the crew of Sedley and Rochester, became, in the latter scenes of his life, a legitimate subject for gratitude and odes, under the name of the Earl of Dorset, the protector of literature. The aristocracy, as candidates for the popular leadership, were forced by dread of antagonists ever in the field, and ready to seize on some occasion for decrying them, to submit themselves to the decorous rules of society. They were able to remain representatives of the nation, on condition that they adopted the fashions and ways of thinking with which their constituents could sympathise. Villiers might have still, in this generation, been the hope and chosen leader of the Puritans, but he must have assumed their demeanour to qualify himself. A reign earlier, Harley would not have deemed himself obliged as head of the Tories, to wear the guise of a High Churchman, nor St. John to pretend to be a Christian.

Much of this result had been effected by the efforts and vigour of the writers whom the Revolution brought forth armed in all the panoply of satire and invective. From the Court of the Restoration they had imbibed social ease and polish. The Revolution changed the aim and the form of their efforts, while it was the means of elevating their profession. They ceased to amuse society by ridiculing it in comedy or burlesquing it in the rant of tragedies with plots laid in Asia. Their arms were keen satire, whether in prose or verse, levelled against the blemishes of prominent champions. They did not attack vaguely and uncertainly whole classes; for the dart would often have flown wide, and hit a friend. The Revolution had initiated no class-war. Its reproach, on the contrary, is, that its contests were mere battles of factions, each under leaders of the same condition and rank. Individual defects in the opposite chieftains were the stock-in-trade of authors; to know the vulnerable points they were obliged to live in the same circles, and affect the same usages. No longer were they mere hirelings, scribbling savage libels in taverns for the eleemosynary guinea of a noble. They wrote as partisans, as themselves personally interested in the event of the struggle. They did not simply draw the outline, and leave their employers to embellish it with point and personality. A fee was not that for which they looked as their pay and reward. Every student of Swift remembers the bitterness with which he repudiated a gift of money from Harley. They claimed a share in the division of the booty when embassies and departments were to be filled up.

If such were the duties and rank of writers in this age, it might naturally be anticipated that, the more furious and doubtful the contention, the more magnificent would be the recompense to the chief agents and instruments in the strife. More peculiar claims would they have, who rose to gratify the ever ready demand, when the issue of the struggle of parties was as yet uncertain. That palmy condition of authors is the prominent feature in this exceptional epoch. Under Charles II. literature flourished. A legion of poets lived on the taste for dramatic exhibitions and the nauseous flattery of dedications, with which the eminent personages of the day were fed. There was a "wits' coffeehouse" then, as later; and courtiers, and men of fashion, loved to throng the winter table, or summer balcony, where sat enthroned the king, John Dryden. They dined at the tavern with authors: they gossiped with them at the coffeehouse; on occasion, they adjourned in their company, from the long-protracted debauch to break windows and worry watchmen. But this familiarity had been all on one side. Writers, who in public were bosom companions, had found often the great man's doors rigidly closed against the suitor for the customary acknowledgment of an adulatory inscription on the frontispiece of the last new poem. Suddenly, and to the manifest surprise of some among them, they found themselves elevated, by the novel relations of the Revolution, and the personal tone of parties in that period, into custodians of the most tremendous political engine. Cadets of noble families, who would, under the old state of things, have begun by being courtiers and companions of royal follies, now inaugurated their career with a dash at literary fame. Charles Montague, grandson of Lord Manchester, had no mean title to promotion at the Court of a liberal and revolutionary monarch. He challenged and proved his claim to favour there, and in Parliament, by winning first the glory of a successful satirist. Prior, the son of a joiner and nephew of a butcher, would have been, in different circumstances, as much, if not, perhaps, something more of a wit; his name had, most undoubtedly, unless for exigencies flowing from the events of 1689, never been connected with a peace, which is one of the landmarks of politics, and with the fate of the two illustrious statesmen, whose real character is yet a problem.

Prior is as consummate a representative of this phase and order of things as it is possible to find. Apparently he was not designed by nature or tastes for a professional states-

man, as was Montague. As a writer, he had not genius, like
Addison's, to compel the world to accept as truths of human
nature the humours of a special period. Yet, by tempering
literature with politics, and politics with literature, he made
a high reputation among his contemporaries, and won lofty
official rank. By the mere weight of the frequent repetition
of his name, in one relation or another, in the records of the
period when he flourished, his fame, as a diplomatist and
poet, has descended to an age which recollects little of the
circumstances of his negotiations, and not much more, in
reality, of his muse. The creation of a considerable reputation is never without an interest of its own. No effect can
be without a cause. Men may praise something which
contains not a germ or spark of what is really praiseworthy;
they never praise by accident. Either in the object of their
laudations, or in themselves and their circumstances, is to be
found the explanation of the halo which surrounds some
names. It is often necessary to recollect this in contemplating the life of Prior. At first, the humble attendant of wits,
and the patrons of wits; then the college contemporary of a
man destined to be the most powerful agent in carrying out
the spirit of the Revolution; renowned for a piece of humour
which carried the coffee-houses triumphantly over to the
Liberal side; an active and favoured cooperator in every
great scene of William's foreign policy, while not less influential in furthering it as a co-founder and luminary of the
Whig committee of wit, the Kit-Cat Club; then, a seceder from
the standard he had long followed, but not altogether, even
now, alienated from his old companions, nor ever visited by
them with revilings and hatred as an apostate; naturally,
among his new friends, assuming the same position as among
his former connections; always associated with, never
leading, any prime movement of policy; though assisting
enemies of its spirit, still negotiating on the principles of the
Revolution, and not of the previous period; a chosen companion and equal intimate of the master minds of his new
side; in the crisis of his disgrace, and the fall of his chiefs,

not condemned to a subordinate's ignoble punishment, neglect and obscurity, but conspicuous by examinations before secret committees, and imprisonment by the Commons; lastly, when at length released, though excluded from the profession of politics, the idol, as a poet, of society—he affords, in his history, a complete epitome of his times. For his tastes and conduct he would have been a good representative of the old; he is, in his fortunes, a better illustration of the new temper of the age, with its suspension of caste distinctions, and its appeals to the nation at large by arguments drawn from the scandal of the drawing-room, than either Montague, with his historic name and high talents for finance, in an age when finance was government; or Addison, with his exquisite taste, which must have, in any age, elevated its possessor above the masses; or Swift, with his keen political perceptions, and constitutional exuberance of controversial venom, in an epoch of personal and party rivalry.

Prior had no family claims, nor sufficiently manifest ambitious propensities to excite the envy and jealousy of the great houses which had effected the expulsion of the Stuarts, and claimed the benefit of that exploit. But, beside negative qualifications, the business-like tastes he possessed contributed materially to his advancement. They were just enough to hinder him from being a clog on serious hours; they proved a most important accession to the utility of a companion in days when affairs of State were discussed over tokay, and the capacity to entertain a Queen or her waiting-women at the tea-table was an essential gift in a politician. Business and the pleasures of life were in that brilliantly artificial portion of our history curiously intermingled. The combination in Prior's disposition of an inclination for pleasure with bureaucracy made him an efficient agent throughout it. The aristocracy which had expelled the old dynasty asserted its title to be the instrument in developing the new system. The sovereign no longer was the head and source of all political action. William and Anne had been parties to the conspiracy. On its success they shared in its fruits.

But they had been accessaries only, not the designers, confederates rather than patrons. As the relative power of the two main factions in the State rose and fell, the monarch gave in his or her adhesion to the conqueror. William naturally had been a member of the great Whig junto; his sister-in-law, through life, manifested a timid but persistent bias to the side of the Tory and Church of England confederacy; yet, with all the feelings and tastes of their several natures interested and bound up with one party or the other, we find each, in turn, compelled to have recourse to that which had demonstrated its superiority for the time in the dubious struggle. The nation in the name of which the battle was being fought, which was the ultimate arbiter, did not claim to appoint demagogues from the masses as defenders of the popular standard; it selected from the limited aristocratic caste. The administration of affairs continued to be a monopoly vested in a Court, though not dependent on the sovereign, and all government to be an incongruous medley of politics and pleasure.

Prior's period is enveloped in a bright confusion of personal love and hatred, intrigues at home and abroad, national alliances cemented by presents of strong liquors and champagne, liable to be dissolved and interrupted by a fire in an ambassador's house, or the abduction by a Popish Countess of her Protestant son. In reading the records of the time, we might imagine ourselves engaged with the Court of Charles II. or the Orleans Regency, till the casual mention of the "Crisis," or some appeal to the people against the efforts of an Opposition hourly gaining ground, drives home to our recollection the fact that we are still in the purlieus of that prodigy, the popular Revolution of 1689. The powers of Prior were drawn out, and turned to account by the predisposing influences of the reigns of William and Anne. His wit and poetry were political weapons, when *vers de société* were an important part of the machinery of statesmanship, when Ministers of State roamed about to find a bard to celebrate a battle, and a Lord Treasurer could win popularity by parading his white staff through a crowd of admiring courtiers to compliment no greater a versifier than the amiable and ingenious Parnell. As a diplomatist Prior was criticised by Sir Robert Walpole, perhaps rather harshly; for Walpole disliked men of letters who took upon themselves the style of politicians. It was fortunate for him that circumstances required not so much a master-mind, as an obedient and industrious secretary and mouthpiece, the popular name and manners of a poet, rather than an inventive politician. English diplomacy was almost the creation of his age, and in diplomacy he found the freest scope for his abilities. The deeper and more subtle mysteries of negotiation were beyond him, but he was never without chiefs to whom the conduct of these fell, who would hardly have suffered him to take the initiative, had he felt the desire. William notoriously was his own foreign minister. The mind alone which had designed it could hold the threads and clues of a complicated net-work of plans embracing the whole of Europe. The peace of Utrecht again was too delicate a matter to be entrusted to the casual intuitions of some ingenious envoy; nor would the pride or the vanity of Bolingbroke have brooked intermeddling with the mazes of his comprehensive scheme. The indifference of intellectual capacity in Prior's character, rather than its many-sidedness, explains, not the continuity of his employments only, but also his peculiar fortune in being the point of contact for competing coteries. All projects of ambition and pleasure were then much more concentrated than at present, and drawn into a smaller and more contracted space; but he had a peculiar facility and coolness of temperament, which connected him at different times with combinations the most dissimilar or even mutually repulsive.

For one so prominent and active, remarkably little is to be learnt of what is personal to himself. The details of his life are but his relations to the history of his time and its most illustrious characters. The demand for anecdotes of a celebrated man's boyhood often produces the supply. But the school reminiscences of Prior are meagre. Though he was a contemporary at Westminster of Montague, with whom his name was hereafter to be closely associated, whose powers, though with the same component elements of a taste for poetry and for politics, were weak and strong exactly in the converse proportion, the grandson of a peer and the nephew of the butcher and vintner were not school friends. Their acquaintance was strengthened at Cambridge, through the medium of another Old Westminster, Stepney, called by courtesy a poet, and made into one of those classics who are never read, by his somewhat contemptuous admittance among Johnson's famous biographies. At school Prior had been fortunate in his master, Dr. Busby, whose pupils have procured for him an honorary place in any history of English poetry. We are told that he distinguished himself highly. But he was prematurely withdrawn to be apprenticed to his uncle at Charing Cross. To have passed through College at Westminster was in those days an important advantage to an ambitious youth; for the " Challenges," a competition, now, the Minor as well as the Major, become a bygone memory, in which each lower candidate turned examiner of his rivals in his turn, were then a fashionable spectacle. According to the politics of the headmaster for the time being, or the accident of political or family relationships to the competitors, party leaders, influential peers, and prelates, thronged the antique schoolroom. We read in Bolingbroke's correspondence of his attendance in the plenitude of power and place, to encourage a friend's cousin, and watch spitefully, with the old rancour of the Christ Church and Bentley feud, the manœuvres of the tyrannic Master of Trinity inflexibly resolved, " pro solitâ humanitate suâ," that is, writes the indignant minister, " with all the good-breeding of a pedant," on choosing the best scholars for his own college. At a later period, we have Pulteney writing to his nephew Colman with fervour and enthusiasm on the same subject, and expressing his desire to be present at the contest. Many boys had an entrance into public life secured to them by the acuteness and quickness they manifested on these occasions. Prior, who had scrambled into the school with difficulty, had not the opportunity of signalising himself thus. Traditions vary as to his plans and hopes on leaving. There is a tale that he even served the office of tapster at his uncle's house. But his talents were too useful to be lost at this epoch of our history; and his ingenuity and wit appear to have been exactly suited for pushing his powers into notice in the only way then possible.

The Earl of Dorset, and Horace, the standard of poetry and of well-bred morals for the age, furnished very appropriately Prior's introduction to society and fame. Lord Dorset represents the Court of which he was the brightest ornament in its light and its shades. We may at once reject his protégé's judgment of him as a writer. The song

> " To all you ladies now at land,"

though not of the highest merit, or entitling its author to rank with Alexander or William III., because he could touch it up the night before a bloody sea-fight, is to be commended for neatness and gaiety. According to Prior, "the manner in which he wrote will hardly ever be equalled;" "every one of his pieces is an ingot of gold, such as wrought or beaten thinner would shine through a whole book of any other author." The adulation is excusable only from the extravagant courtesy of the age, the laudable grief of a friend writing to a son of his dead patron, or, lastly, a prejudice in favour of profligate wits. The panegyric of one member of the class is balanced by allusion to the forgotten lucubrations of another, Wilmot Earl of Rochester, as "the other prodigies of the age." As a friend, a gentleman, and a courtier, Dorset probably deserved the praises lavished upon his generosity and universal affability, though frequent gusts of passion, however short and speedily atoned for, and an uncontrollable taste for satirising, not vice, but social faults, must have made his temper trying, to say the least, to his associates. But a casual allusion to the gross debaucheries and mad follies of many years, scenes which have done most to taint the memories of Charles II.'s reign, as "the little violences and mistakes of a night too gaily spent," is terrible evidence of the radical corruptness of society, which could pardon everything, and forget everything, when the perpetrator was a Lord Buckhurst. His merits as a patron are less equivocal. He seems to have possessed that instinctive apprehension of the neighbourhood of genius, which often beguiles friends into the belief that he who can so skilfully estimate power in others must be himself endowed with the same species of capacity. Intimate relations to Waller, and Wycherley, Dryden, Butler, and Prior, which, with the last three, were the relations of a patron, point to no common appreciation of intellect or ordinary keenness of discernment. To the gratitude of Prior he is principally indebted for the preservation of his fame and the memory of his munificence.

They met at an annual dinner of the noblemen and gentry of St. Martin's parish, held, according to custom, at the Rummer Tavern, kept by Samuel Prior. From wine and talk of love there had been a transition, usual in those days, to the poet of both. A discussion arose on the exact interpretation of some inspired platitude in the Odes about the twin pleasures. One of the company happened to recollect that a schoolboy was in the house, the nephew of their host, whose memory might be fresher on these points than their own. Courtiers and authors were astonished at discovering the delicacy and quickness of perception of the destined vintner in their own peculiar subject. Lord Dorset at once recognised the lad's genius, and charged himself with his maintenance at Cambridge and future advancement. The determination did honour to his sagacity. The life of Prior is henceforth, at home, the history of coteries, which have made themselves niches in history; abroad, of famous treaties, appealed to even now as articles of faith in the creed of the balance of power, and, in many of their provisions, fresh and lasting. At St. John's College, he soon grew into fame as a wit of the very first rank in the then sense of wit. Mathematics had scarcely as yet, notwithstanding the world-wide reputation of Sir Isaac Newton, begun to engross the lion's share of the interests of Cambridge. Latin verse composition was its primary occupation; and each tenant of the throne of letters in London counted it among the burdens of greatness to have to peruse, or pretend it, the prolix Latinity of ambitious gownsmen. Prior's good scholarship secured his election as fellow of his college shortly after taking his degree. He became a centre of that society of which, at an earlier date, we discover many picturesque traces in the quaint biography of Matthew Robinson. In the vacations he and other University men might have been found pressing round the upper table in the "Wits' Coffee-house," or the famous summer balcony. There they listened reverentially to their chief, "proud to dip a finger and thumb into Mr. Dryden's snuff-box, thinking it enough to inspire them with a true genius for poetry, and make 'em write verse as fast as a tailor takes his stitches," as a carping contemporary asserts. · He appears to have been at least on repartee terms with the great man at the date of the publication of the 'City Mouse and Country Mouse,' apocryphal as is the anecdote, that the veteran shed tears of annoyance and indignation at the fact of "two young men, whom he had always treated well, treating him so ill."

Never, indeed, had anything been welcomed with more riotous exultation and a heartier burst of applause than this parody of 'the Hind and the Panther.' The smartness of the insinuations and innuendoes so pleased and gratified the party-feeling, which had now drowned every other sentiment, as to insure it against cool and temperate criticism. Dryden had already, by a proud self-assertion, and, at the same time, by his competition, due to the narrowness of his circumstances, with the crowd of hack-writers, roused envy and jealousy. Now there had arisen an additional motive for rage against him in his change of religion, and, in the partisan fear of the admirable powers of satire and criticism, which had worked havoc in his 'Absolom and Achitophel,' among Shaftesbury's Whigs. He has been avenged upon his over-praised juvenile assailants by the neglect with which posterity has chosen to visit their work. Such has always been the case with themes of ephemeral interest, and almost in proportion to their temporary popularity. The 'Two Mice' is never republished, for it could have no readers, unless for its historical interest. The authors were at once enrolled in the select company of wits who were in the habit of meeting at The Judge's Head, in Chancery Lane, the sign of the celebrated Jacob Tonson, publisher of the maltreated 'Hind and Panther.' This society was the germ of the prince of dining clubs, the Kit-Cat, more regularly established in 1700. Originally it was a publisher's dinner and conversazione, at which literary projects were discussed, and the first stone of a clever epigram laid. Gradually, as the fame of its wit and conviviality grew, peers and politicians of the Liberal party petitioned to be admitted, till at last, though preserving the idea of a party of guests, with Jacob Tonson for host, it grew into a focus of the literary and statesmanlike brilliancy of the Whig houses. Along with its summer expeditions to the Upper Flask, amid the distant wilds of Hampstead, it kept its conclaves at Jacob Tonson's country house at Barn-Elms. There it amused itself with the proud condescension of their host, who thought himself the greatest man among them, in taking the post of their secretary, and with his pompous horror at the sacrilegious insolence of wild Lord Mohun, in breaking off the gilded emblem of office from the publisher's own sacred chair. But all this was at a later period, when Prior was lamented as a deserter to the Tory camp. At present it was more exclusively an association of young authors, or genuine literary lords.

The poet's puns and bon-mots secured him a high place in this fraternity. But there was an undercurrent of prudence in his disposition, which made him crave some more stable position than that, in itself no sinecure, of a man of wit and fashion. The times were favourable to his ambition. By the political excitement the importance of authors had been disproportionately increased. The professional services of poets and satirists were required to rivet national assent to the results which a comparatively minute body of prominent individuals had achieved. All those most versed in the routine of public business had been servants of the defeated Government, and were bound over to promote reactionary principles. Their place had to be supplied; and the owners of a fluent pen were the natural reversioners. To his confessed surprise Prior nevertheless was at first passed over. He complained with a mixture of humour and querulousness—

> " My friend Charles Montague's preferr'd;
> Nor would I have it long observ'd,
> That one mouse eats while t'other's starv'd."

His murmurs were hardly justifiable. Not only had Montague exceptional capacity for business and eloquence, but his name and connections would give him a sure title to notice from the ruling oligarchy. Prior, however, might be pardoned for overlooking the fact that the immediate event, the publication of the satire, which led to his friend's elevation, was not the sole reason. He could not help remembering that the co-author, who seemed in danger of ending his days as a senior fellow, had contributed all the vivacity of the burlesque, except what merit the preface might possess. "Did not Hallifax write 'The Country Mouse' with Mr. Pryor?" asked Spence once of Lord Peterborough. "Yes," said Lord Peterborough, "just as if I were in a chaise with Mr. Cheselden here, drawn by his fine horse, and should say, Lord! how finely we draw this chaise." He fretted that his right to promotion was vested, but not made payable. His grievance was redressed through his friend Fleetwood Shephard, an old courtier of Charles II., to whom two amusing " Conversation " poems are addressed. Shephard revived the interest of the poet's old patron, the Earl of Dorset, in his fortunes, and Dorset procured him an introduction to the King. In 1690, just three years after the publication of the 'City Mouse and Country Mouse,' he was gazetted to the Secretaryship of Legation at the Hague.

Here begins his political career. It was altogether diplomatic, though he held other offices, with nominal duties; and it was almost the same in its demands upon his talents and political principles in the days of his Toryism and his Whiggism. Fortunately for his fame the times immediately succeeding the Revolution were as remarkable for their negotiations as for their wars. Then first began to be understood the doctrine of a balance of power. Formerly it had only existed, as a principle, in the speculations of profound international lawyers. The mutual fears and jealousies of neighbouring great states had been the substitute for it in the period following the condensation of the myriad of independencies, which, under the feudal system, had rendered such a doctrine unnecessary. Practical statesmen had been forced to recognise it through the insolent ambition of Louis XIV., which made the terrors and suspicions, formerly intermittent, continuous. The comprehensive policy of William of Orange gave the banded nations of Europe a chieftain and centre, and facilitated the adoption of measures in conformity with it. The negotiator recognised in the terms he was instructed to ask, and the conditions the ministers of hostile cabinets were constrained to accept, the vast and energetic mind of his King. A sentiment of veneration for the champion of the Whigs appears to have survived in the Secretary's mind his defection to the Tories. He himself was no mere makeweight in these transactions. A spiteful saying of Walpole's, and his reputation as a poet, have prejudiced posterity against receiving him as a statesman. For no real cause men have been led to conclude that he was an incapable diplomatist. William, and Bolingbroke, his subsequent patron, were not in the habit of choosing incompetent instruments. If there were any merit in the local labours of the embassies in which he was engaged, undoubtedly to the Secretary we must assign the praise, and not to the great Revolution Lord who might happen to be the chief figure in the pageant.

His possession of abilities for the work there can be no reason to question; if his name only had been wanted to give an air of literary distinction to the Government, plenty of glittering sinecures could have been found for him. What the work really was, and the sort therefore of talent needed, is not so apparent. As William was his own foreign minister, so he was, and especially in Holland, all but his own diplomatist. Bolingbroke imitated him in this respect. It would have been strange had it been otherwise. The rights of nations were much more perplexed then than now; the complications which had been growing more tortuous since the feudal system, were then first being mapped out. The statesman who had conceived the plan, and who held the chart of the track in his own mind, could alone embody the result in a treaty. No certain rules had as yet been established to determine the relations of states; the application of them was not the only difficulty, but the principles themselves. For envoy a man was required shrewd enough to comprehend the bearing of things, and not too egotistical to communicate all to his principal, and to obey orders implicitly. He had to be pliant and able to adapt himself quickly to foreign customs in an age not yet abounding in travelled experience. A reputation for *esprit* was wanted to render him acceptable in foreign society, and the art finally, to avail himself of all secret influences in an age of female stratagems and finesse. The correspondence of Prior at a later period shows how well he fulfilled these multifarious conditions.

We have not full particulars of his conduct as a negotiator during William's reign. We know that he answered the expectations of his patron, and satisfied the King. Without any impeachment of his business gifts, he appears to have been looked upon as ornamental too, not from personal attractions, since we are told by a friend, that he possessed "un visage de bois," but for his sparkling wit. He figured, accordingly, on all occasions of show and pageantry. He did not dislike being forced to become part of a spectacle, though he anticipated with some shame the humble condition to which he would have subsequently to return. His movements were watched by all the quidnuncs at home with a curiosity which must have been gratifying to the nephew of the butcher and vintner of the Rummer, and perhaps yet more to the fellow of St. John's. Narcissus Luttrell, in the diary published in 1857 by the Oxford University Press, records carefully every rumour of his elevation and doings. From him we learn that, after having been four years at the Hague, attending the congress of the Anti-Gallic powers of the West of Europe, he was appointed secretary to the King himself. Being now regularly retained for diplomacy by Government, he assisted at the peace of Ryswick in 1697, and was selected for the honourable duty of bringing home the news to the Lords of the Regency. Bonfires and bell-ringing welcomed him as though he had been a conqueror. The same year, as a reward for his exertions, he was gazetted Irish Chief Secretary, but was speedily called upon to attend Bentinck Earl of Portland, William's prime favourite, on his mission to Paris to exchange ratifications of the treaty. With the exception of the Duke of Bedford's mission to France, in the last century, and that of Lord Castlemaine to the Pope, in James the Second's reign, this was perhaps the most sumptuous ever dispatched by our country. The occasion was important. Not one, but a series of wars had ended. There was a desire also to show that England, in changing its dynasty, had not abdicated national splendour; to publish to all Europe a manifesto of insular pride and spirit. The whole was conducted on a scale of rude and boastful magnificence. The starving peasants, who thronged the highways to welcome the bearers of peace, were astonished at the droves of fat oxen imported from home, and the French capital flowed with English ale. The Secretary was allowed £300 for his equipage on the occasion of the solemn entry into Paris; and the exact number of shillings thought by the Administration sufficient for such an official's daily expenditure is specified by the minute philosophers of London taverns and coffee-houses.

His tact and wit recommended him to the same office under Portland's successors, Villiers Earl of Jersey, and Lord Manchester. With his reputation for fashion and dexterity of repartee, combined with real application, he was a most valuable representative of England at a Court of politico-amatory intrigues. He seems to have been gifted with a coolness, or coldness of temper, which made him, though no Machiavelli, a capital Secretary of Legation. The dignity of his position, as envoy of England at that special time, and a genuine admiration of the obstinate heroism of William's character, of which the object of his mission was so material a proof, gave an air of sincerity to his famous saying, when paraded before Lebrun's pictures of Louis's Flemish campaign at Versailles, that "the monuments of *his* master's actions were to be seen everywhere but in his own house."

He continued to reside in France, with but two short intervals. One was devoted to a visit to King William at Loo, on matters connected with diplomacy. The other was occupied by his temporary charge, in default of work for him at Paris, of the Under-Secretary's portfolio in Lord Jersey's office. The curious in England were very inquisitive as to the business which could have gained for Prior admittance to the monarch's favourite retirement, and the conference has been considered evidence of his statesmanlike qualifications. His second absence from Paris was rumoured to be connected with a negotiation of marriage between himself and the dowager Lady Falkland. Whether there were grounds for the report does not appear. Prior, at all events, never succeeded in contracting any advantageous alliance. He was unhappy in his attachments. Previously he had paid his addresses, during the leisure of a Gentleman of the Bedchamber, to Mrs. Singer, subsequently the celebrated Mrs. Rowe. From a Mrs. Bessie Cox, who responded more favourably, his friends thought him fortunate in escaping, even by the last resource of dying. He was soon summoned back to Paris from the caresses and caprices of society in London. To be employed at all is no disagreeable lot in life; to be employed as was Prior is rare good fortune. Any one should remember what sort of mind and tastes his were, and ought to read a page of his poetry, who feels inclined to regret that a poet's life was frittered away in the circumlocutions of diplomacy.

Yet we must not underrate Prior's Court poetry. A poet in office was considered indebted to the King or his ministers in so many bundles of panegyrics or condolences, just as if he had been a salaried Laureate. But Prior laid his tribute before the throne with a frankness and elevation of tone, which showed it not to be wrung unwillingly from him. The character of the King, as a general and sovereign, notwithstanding forbidding traits in his ordinary demeanour, might have inspired a less ready muse. Johnson is forced to allow, when speaking of the Carmen Seculare of 1699, that William was, in his public character, heroic, and that Prior may have told the truth, when he declared that, while he praised others out of compliance with fashion, he lauded his king from inclination. The poem itself is too laborious, after the manner of odes generally, and especially those of his age, to be read with pleasure now, let alone its wearisome mimicries of Horace. Still it has some fine lines, contrasting with William's more complete character, as he thought it, the mixture of iron and clay in Roman heroes. He proceeds in the vein of Dryden:—

> " With justest honour be their merits drest;
> But be their failings too confest :
> Their virtue, like their Tyber's flood,
> Rolling its course, designed their country's good.
> But oft the torrent's too impetuous speed
> From the low earth tore some polluting weed;
> And with the blood of Jove there always ran
> Some viler part, some tincture of the man."

The humorist and inditer of clever epigrams could rise on occasion; yet readers may be pardoned for not searching a poem, and that an ode, of some five or six hundred lines, for a few dignified passages. Why the 'English Ballad on the Taking of Namur' has not kept its popularity, it is much harder to explain. Perhaps, as in the 'City and Country Mouse,' the labour of hunting out the parallels in the parody of an obsolete French poem may be the reason. At all events, Prior's verses have an admirable freshness and animation. In lieu of thought, there is, what is no bad substitute sometimes, true zeal for his subject. There is plenty of animation if there is scarcely genuine poetic fire. The poem is full of open daylight and plain sound English.

Prior's change of party is a fact of history. There is no mystery in it which calls for explanation. He was no devotee of political purity, no constructor of theories of the Constitution and Government. The interest of his career is its representative character. He simply pursued with more than ordinary success the object of a multitude of clever men of his age. He was not sufficiently energetic for the bar; nor could the son and nephew of tradesmen have gained direct admission to the Court. From Parliament, as a profession, he was excluded by the deficiencies which unfitted him for Lincoln's Inn or the Temple. But he chanced to combine a taste for the splendour of a courtier's life, and abilities for the desultory industry of bureau statesmanship. His powers, such as they were, were well attempered, and in perfect unison. Poetry and patronage in his youth were the regular and legitimate resource for men of education, narrow means, and social aspirations superior to their rank. Prior, therefore, became a poet, having an ear, and an especial taste for Horace, the hierophant of the mysteries of Court versification. Dorset had the honour of lighting upon him for a protégé. The characteristics of Charles's reign passed away. The Court, as a Court, no longer absorbed all the talents of the nation. Sedley, and Buckhurst, and Wilmot could no longer affect, with repute, to blaspheme. But the people, though not content to go on being beaten and insulted by a gang of young nobles, who esteemed it fashionable to play the ruffian, retained too much of the impulse of the Restoration to refuse to let them subside into secretaries of state and ambassadors. Their followers became politicians with their patrons; and Prior, without abandoning his profession of a wit, grew in time into a minister plenipotentiary.

He took up politics as the natural bread-winning resource, in those times, of a wit and a poet. He had no sympathy with the fervour of either of the two religious parties. His political tenets were not much more clearly defined than his religious, though he had a practical liking for the oligarchical system which succeeded the expulsion of James. The attraction exercised upon him by some of the chief agents in that event, had set him on his first literary performance, and carried him forward along the same track. His strongest sentiment on the side of 1689, admiration for the great qualities of William, was of the same personal sort. But political partisanship, grounded merely on personal dependence, not cemented by reminiscences of personal risks and trophies in the strife and struggles of principles, is unsteady. So it proved in Prior's case. Suddenly, and without notice, we find him on the opposite side. His migration occurred the year after his election for East Grinstead, and his appointment to the seat vacated in 1700 by Locke at the Board of Trade. The occasion seems to have been the motion for a Bill of Impeachment against the Privy Councillors, who had irregularly connived at William's conclusion of the Partition Treaty. At the same time a future friend, destined, by the baleful lustre of his genius and ambition, to blast the dawning hopes of the Tories, Henry St. John, made himself remarked. It has been supposed that Prior records his own original dislike of that convention, in spite of the part he had taken in it, in 'The Conversation.'

> "Matthew, who knew the whole intrigue,
> Ne'er much approv'd that mystic league."

But as this is said in the character of a false pretender to intimacy with the negotiator, and the next couplet—

> "In the vile Utrecht treaty too,
> Poor man! he found enough to do,"

is an attack upon the triumph of his diplomatic career, the contrary inference might more plausibly be drawn. Uncharitable critics who choose to construe his conduct as St. John interpreted his subsequent intercourse with the Whig Ministry on the fall of the Tory cabinet, will suppose him to have been influenced now by a fear that the mechanical share he himself had in the transaction as secretary to the King, might involve him in the criminality. But explanations, when we once allow the possibility of perfidy, are endless. Jealousy of his old comrade, Charles Montague, would be as probable as any; only it has not the least basis of proof to rest upon. It is best to impute his secession to a mixture of motives, a little dread of the odium waiting upon a sinking party, long accumulating discontent at the slowness of promotion, a faint conviction of the impropriety of unconstitutional measures in politicians who had expelled a sovereign on this plea, and, finally and chiefly, the formation of new connections.

A vote against Somers and Montague clearly indicated his intention, but he had never sufficiently pledged himself as a partisan to be open now to execrations as an apostate. His present change was rather of masters than of principles. Scarcely, in the heat, if the term can be used of a diplomatist, of envenomed controversy, during the later years of Queen Anne, did Prior engage himself to præ-Revolution doctrines. For a long time he seems, notwithstanding Pope's assertion to the contrary, to have maintained his acquaintance and cooperation with many of the subordinates in the party he had left. He kept the regard of men, who had, like himself, taken to politics as the proper profession for men of intellect. Stepney, for instance, on his death in 1707, associated his two opposed schoolfellows in his will, bequeathing to Halifax books and a gold cup, to the other fifty guineas. We find, a year after, in the height of the party war, when the friends of Prior had recently been ejected from office by a coalition of Whigs and Liberal Tories, the 'Phædra,' a play by the Whig Edmund Smith, brought out with an epilogue by him and a prologue by Addison.

If he had changed from motives of interest, he was rightly punished with a long interval of enforced leisure. He was repulsed in 1701, when his new allies were in place, in an application for the Keepership of the Records at Whitehall, vacant by the death of Sir Joseph Williamson. The circumstance is alluded to in Addison's answer in the Whig Examiner to his criticism on Garth's verses. It is insinuated that his bitterness against the quondam Tory, Godolphin, was not truly patriotic. Literature, and plots, and all the trivialities of a man of fashion occupied him, voluntarily or otherwise, for nine or ten years. Some of his time was given up to the foolish dissipation of the period. Yet he was not a notorious tavern-haunter, or a man to spend, like Addison, whole days and nights in a coffee-house. He preferred privacy in his pleasures, and the character of his wit was better suited for the meetings of a select club, or a lady's drawing-room, than for the publicity of the favourite resorts of that age. His lodgings in Duke Street, Westminster, were often glorified by the presence of Addison himself, and Swift and Steele, who all, at times, could merge the accidents of political hostility in the common brotherhood of literary genius. At some of these meetings the conspiracy of Isaac Bickerstaff's predictions against the astrologer Partridge's peace of mind, and belief in his own existence, conceived by the same fiery fancy from which flashed the idea of Lilliput and Brobdingnag, was elaborated and embellished by the others, assisted by Rowe, not yet a Whig, and Yalden, a consistent Tory.

Much of his leisure was passed at the houses of Lord Dorset, Fleetwood Shephard, near Stamford, and Sir Thomas Hanmer, at Euston. Part he spent in his rooms at St. John's, where, no doubt, he was duly admired as a great politician and London wit. Still, with all these varied sources of interest, the late diplomatist repined at being without employment. He kept his Commissionership of Trade, having been confirmed in it on the accession of Anne; but he made it all but a sinecure. Besides, he was subject to chronic apprehensions of poverty, though, according to friendly testimony, totally devoid of the prudent habits by which it might have been avoided. Rather later, responding to an invitation to Euston, he complains, that " he does not perceive that his fortune does any way intend to lessen his liberty," and commissions Hanmer to get him, not only "a pretty nag," but also any available "Welch widow, with a good jointure." The narrowness of his circumstances, at the same period, appears to have made him hesitate about declining an offer of the secretaryship to the Bishop of Winchester, with a kind of general agency to the estates of the see. He had weighed the matter in his own mind, and was decided against acceptance as much by a discovery that the income was less than what report made it, as by a fear of compromising his prospects with a Liberal Tory ministry. He expresses himself vexed at the rumour that he was to " set up High Church, and cut down all the bishop's woods into fagots to burn dissenters."

The first cabinet of Queen Anne's reign had been formed on Tory principles. Though many subjects had been turned into open questions to let in the new partisans of the Duke of Marlborough discontented with the regular Tories, it had preserved enough of its original character to allow the ex-envoy to hope for a fresh mission. The successes of Marlborough left no scope for abilities so peculiarly adapted as were Prior's for the atmosphere of the Paris and Versailles of Louis XIV.'s reign. On the rupture among the Tories, he attached himself more and more to the section of Harley and St. John, less from any especial devotion to their principles, than from the courtesies of which these leaders were prudently profuse to all men of letters. The death of Dorset in 1706, and of Stepney in 1707, left their friend more at liberty to follow his own bent. He was not ordinarily inclined to exult passionately in the triumph of his friends or the fall of his opponents; so we must not expect songs of victory on the virtual defeat of the prosecutors of Dr. Sacheverell. But for a moment, he! let himself be borne away by the violence of his associates, and was one of those Tories who sympathised with the wrath of the October Club at the lenity displayed to their foes by Harley. When the Examiner was set up by St. John, who at first conducted it, Prior was enrolled among the contributors, and signalised his accession by a contemptuous critique of Dr. Garth's verses to Godolphin on the loss of his white staff.

The genius of Prior was brought to bear upon the most vulnerable points in the enemy's ranks by his editor, a very complete master of all the artillery of political literature. Notwithstanding the poet's zealous cooperation in the earlier numbers of the Examiner, the kind of warfare does not appear to have altogether suited his capacity. We miss in Addison's answer the grace and neatness of the Spectator. Addison was not better adapted for a hand-to-hand combat in letters than in Parliament. His satire is obscure, and the virulence clumsy. Prior himself had equal deficiencies of a different description. He was open to attack himself, and was too self-conscious to take up those positions from which alone, in such conflicts, at some risk of personal exposure, any mortal injury can be done to the adverse side. He could point and wing a javelin, not "the sort of sledgehammer retort" which Swift, with scarce an effort, would heave at ancient friend and present foe. But he had his aptitudes too, and they fitted the period. In the intervals of the "dreams of cockets, and dockets, and drawbacks, and jargon," by which, as a Commissioner, he declared himself to be haunted, he dressed smart sarcasms, organised clubs, and did much of the work of a Whip among the polite and fashionable adherents of his two chiefs. It was an age of epigrams. Society was a more important element in the life especially of politicians and authors than now. Newspapers had not yet begun to report faithfully the heaviest and the longest speeches for future reference, so that oratory, to be remembered, had to be terse and pointed, rather than elaborate and argumentative. The author had no large reading public at his beck and call. Even in the upper classes, books were not a necessary. A bon-mot, on the other hand, travelled with the swiftness of every sedan chair, and made its inventor famous where he most desired to shine. The example of France, even the prevalence of the French language, encouraged this taste. The sharpness of political contests, and the fusion of a man's political and social life, rendered the class of literary ability which can embalm a party cry or invective in a stanza invaluable.

Prior's powers as a wit were employed by his party, till the policy of its leaders created fresh scope for his services in diplomacy. Peace with France had been, since the Revolution, a rooted sentiment of the Tory party; and the recent Whiggism of Marlborough, the only born general England possessed, rendered negotiations, in the judgment of a hostile cabinet, inevitable. The nation, however, could not bear the thought of resigning the fruits of an incomparable series of victories, even while it murmured at the expenditure of which they were the result. The equipment of a formal embassy on a contingency was too perilous an enterprise for an unstable cabinet. Prior received in 1711 a secret commission to prepare the way. Unluckily the whole transaction was bruited abroad through his detention on his return from Paris in company with Mesnager and Gaultier by the officious patriotism of some provincial politicians. We can imagine how the city of Canterbury, or Deal, which other accounts represent as the scene of the incident, would triumph at the capture at last of the celebrated Mr. Matthew Prior, so long a suspected character, in the company of a notorious French Abbé. Occasion for invectives as noisy against a Tory and Popish Government would be furnished by the order in Council for their release. The 'New Journey to Paris,' by the Sieur de Baudrier, was composed by Swift in ridicule of the monstrous reports to which the clandestine expedition gave rise. The quiet demureness of the satire is excellent, as is the picture of the airs of the pretended narrator, whom we discover from internal evidence to have been the English envoy's prying valet. The incident had, at all events, the effect of habituating the country to the idea of peace, and it precipitated the preliminaries.

Next to St. John, Prior was the most active and conspicuous personage throughout these negotiations. At his house in Duke Street the managers of the preliminaries met; and he signed the articles along with the Privy Councillors. Often, after the business of the day was over, did the aspiring Secretary of State resort to these same lodgings in quest of "cold bladebone of mutton at the hour of midnight, despatched after the drudgery of office, with much talk," and that, often, we may suspect, not of the gravest or most statesmanlike character. The poet was named Ambassador Extraordinary, to act at Utrecht with the Resident, Lord Strafford; but the indignation of the latter justified Swift's apprehensions, and hindered the ratification of the nomination. He was consoled by being selected to attend his chief and comrade, the "all-accomplished" Secretary of State, to Paris, where he participated in the glory of a deliverer of a harassed nation from an internecine war. On his own account he was acceptable to Louis, who doubtless had never heard of his advice how without peril to earn the laurels of a martial king:—

> "Are not Boileau and Corneille paid
> For panegyric writing?
> They know how heroes may be made
> Without the help of fighting."

Voltaire, indeed, remarks in his 'Lettres sur les Anglais' that down to the time of the poet's last visit to France, Paris was not aware that he had ever written verses of any kind. It is, however, hard to reconcile this statement with facts.

The correspondence with Bolingbroke, on the return of the latter to England, throws light upon Prior's character in this the most exalted scene of his career. He was not a great master of the art of letter-writing, but neither were his immediate coevals. Queen Anne's reign was that also of epigrams; the next two reigns lost this secret; we find a bluntness even in Pulteney's bon-mots; they excelled in epistles. Nowhere can be discovered more exquisite models of this branch of literature than in the correspondence of Pope, and of Lady Mary Wortley Montagu, both, though contemporaries of Prior in a literal sense, belonging more properly to the era of the Georges, of Gray, and Horace Walpole. The letters of the famous men of Anne's reign, of Swift himself often, of

Bolingbroke, and Prior usually, are stiff and spoilt by classical quotations, and stilted attempts now and then at smartness. Their epigrams and sayings are pointed and as happy as can be. The distinction is due to the varying influence of the social element in the two epochs, and to the different objects which called out and developed it. A good epigram is, in its own way, as certain evidence of the prominence of the social features in an age as a picturesque style in letter-writing. Its neatness and pungency require a highly educated audience. That is not enough by itself. The audience must be composed of persons living so familiarly together as at once and simultaneously to catch the intention of an insinuation. A perfect epigramatic style implies, as precedent to its formation, large enough an audience and eager enough an interest in its neighbours' concerns, to reward the pains of the wit. Such was the age of Marlborough, Addison, Wharton, and Bolingbroke. Politics had become sport and excitement for a number of leaders of society, plotters in drawing-rooms as well as in cabinets. The interests with which they coquetted were national; the heart of a whole people and the life of ministries were the strings on which they played. But too many instruments and agents were required by the demands of national and party enterprises, to be compatible with perfect social freedom. The entire reciprocity of sympathy and even prejudices, a sense that the relations of writer and reader are settled once for all, whether they be those of mutual equality, or the reverse, and that rank and position are recognised and fixed, all necessary conditions of epistolary ease, were wanting, for example, between the tradesman's son and the heir of the St. Johns. Hence, in the letters of Prior to Bolingbroke there is an appearance of effort in the familiarity. Only when he gossips of common acquaintances does this vanish.

Otherwise, they are curious records of the business of the representative of a powerful nation. They throw much light on the real functions of a plenipotentiary in that age, if not in others, during the negotiations for a great

European peace. The proofs of the dependence of the Minister at Paris on instructions from home on every single point, however trivial, diminish our wonder at the elevation of Prior to so important a station. With two short intervals, when Bolingbroke and the Duke of Shrewsbury were at Paris, he was in full charge. On the departure of the Duke he assumed the public character of ambassador; nevertheless, his correspondence with the Secretary of State is filled throughout the entire period with details of petty vexations, little triumphs, and little duties. The letters chiefly refer to events subsequent to his visit to England in October 1712. We hear incidentally about that visit, that stocks rose on his arrival. He went up to Cambridge to display the plenipotentiary to his wondering brother-fellows. The Master of St. John's, to show he at least was not dazzled, let the great man stand before his elbow-chair. Prior, in half-feigned indignation, indited an epigram to the effect that the dignitary should not have his interest for a bishopric.

He returned to France, to be harassed with a legion of petty perplexities. His complaints that his salary was always in arrear, and trouble at the ambiguity of his position, as envoy with full powers at one time, and at another, as during Shrewsbury's residence in Paris, without a definite name, though with a public commission, are distressing. Accompanying nearly every official despatch to the Secretary of State, is an epistle from "Matt to Harry," detailing his embarrassment from want of equipages. Now and then he affects to despise the parade of a public entry into Paris, except for the honour of England and the Queen's commission. In March his murmurs are answered by Lord Dartmouth, the Secretary of State for France, with a reproof of his craving to be part of the spectacle on the entry of the Duke of Shrewsbury. He had been allowed a sum of money for equipage when only secretary to the Earl of Portland, at the peace of Ryswick; he is now censured for supposing his commission gives him any representative character, and informed that he need only assist at the ceremonial as a private gentleman. "Did I ever desire to be a lion in Arabia," he cries to St. John, in a burst of hurt pride, "any more than to be an Ambassador at Paris?" His friend "Harry," who to every disappointed applicant for Government patronage always returned expressions of commiseration and readiness to aid, were it not for the senior partner in the' ministerial firm, had often reiterated, "My friendship, dear Matt, shall never fail thee; employ it all, and continue to love Bolingbroke." Now, he advised him not to ask for such things, but to get them on credit. Matthew did this to his cost, finding, on the fall of his chief, that he was held personally liable. In April 1713, however, the old querulousness again breaks out. "Those people, you know," he writes, "who are curious and impertinent enough upon such heads, begin to question me so closely that I sometimes wish I knew how to turn the discourse." In July, he feelingly complains, that "if he be left plenipotentiary, he must have a house and a parson." His troubles were considerably lessened in September, for his friend had now become Secretary of State for the half of Europe in which France was included. The envoy seems to have been told, in St. John's magnificent way, to order all he wanted; for he bemoans, with manifest vanity, the necessity of keeping "ten horses in his stables, and knaves in proportion." We know that no part of all this splendour was as yet paid for, even the salaries of the State messengers being in arrears.

His public business consisted mainly in learning and transmitting the propositions of the French Ministry, not in disputing or discussing them. His less mechanical duties, beyond the subjects of constant meditation with which his unsatisfied wants in the way of services of plate, Royal portraits, and coaches supplied him, concerned the maintenance of the national glory by hospitality to foreigners and Englishmen, the transaction of Bolingbroke's private business at the French Court, and the provision of truffles for the Queen's kitchen. The last care is prolific of Ministerial despatches. The history of the truffles was this: Mme. de Tencin had sent some to the Secretary of State through the agency of Prior. St. John, knowing the Queen's taste, loyally transferred them to the royal cook in the plenipotentiary's name, following up the event by the grave announcement: "the Queen liked them, wished them *marbré* within; I give you the hint." Hence more truffles, and fervent thanks from Paris for "the hint as to the *marbré* in truffles; non sunt contemnenda quasi parva sine quibus magna constare non possunt." Prior recompensed his friend's kind offices in the propitiation of the royal palate by undertaking the apportionment of St. John's gifts among his fair or political allies in France. There is much correspondence on the important subject. One consignment was composed of honey-water, sack, and "eau de Barbade," and several high dames had, it appears, equal claims in the "Nectareous liquor eau de Barbade," known to us under a less recondite name. "I protest," writes St. John, "I contributed to make the partition of Europe without being so much at a loss as I should be how to make that of this cargo!"

But a blight was about to fall upon all his political prospects. Harley and St. John had quarrelled; and the hopes of foes and fears of friends rose to a tremendous height. Prior had often vaunted his preference of "some small establishment at home" to all his ministerial grandeur, and indulged in affected regrets for the modest poverty of Duke Street. Still the Queen's illness, in January 1714, had struck him with a panic, and induced the trite but well-founded foreboding, "if the prospect be dreadful to the masters of Mortimer Castle, Hinton St. George, Stanton Harcourt, and Bucklebury, what must it be to friend Matt!" No sooner had the immediate danger disappeared, than in the very next month came the terrible rumour of a schism in the Tory party. "We have reports here," he says, on March 3, 1714, "that frighten me all day, and keep me awake all night." They compelled him "to put his mind into 10,000 postures, as the caprice of every man that comes from the enchanted island requires." Again, renouncing his old longings for a lowly refuge, he encourages himself and his chief to determine to make their retreat, respectively, to Bucklebury and St. John's, "as late as possible." Then he urges upon the Secretary, that, "though it may look like a bagatelle what is to become of a philosopher, when that philosopher is Queen's plenipotentiary and on such an occasion, and friend of one of the greatest men in England, one of the finest heads in Europe," it is unbecoming he should be left to the ostentatious patronage of a Frenchman, de Torcy, who had offered to remind "Robin and Harry" of his claims. He disdains the Baden legation, and even the Commissionership of Trade, "having been put above himself, and not liking to return to himself." In a little while he would gladly have compounded for the poorest official asylum. In vain had St. John assured him that there would be no Tory schism, and reiterated that, "though he laugh at the knave and the fool who is advanced, he will never go about to disturb the only Administration he ever liked, the only cause he can ever like." In vain did Prior urge the scandal of open quarrels between his masters at Whitehall, and bemoan his own ruin as involved in theirs; "Am I to go to Fontainebleau? Am I to come home? Am I to hang myself? From the present prospect of things, the latter begins to look most eligible." The rupture was to be; St. John was to snatch the crown of victory from his rival Harley's hands, and find it turn in his own into a mere bunch of withered weeds.

Within a month all the fears of the party were realised, its councils convulsed by an internal revolution, and the Queen dead. Prior lingered in Paris till March in the next year, in a sort of amphibious condition, between an ambassador and a political refugee, vexed by debts contracted to support the dignity of his station, and watched by his own countrymen as, perhaps, now already intriguing with the Pretender. It was a sad reverse, after he had gaily congratulated himself and the Ministry on St. John's "beautiful daughter, the peace," to be looked upon as a traitor for the very treaty which he had proposed should be depicted on medals, impersonated, and enthroned in a triumphal car, as "Pax missa per orbem."

At last he was relieved from his official pillory, by the arrival of Lord Stair as his successor, and the tardy payment of his debts, not the less tardy that Lord Halifax, his old schoolfellow, who still called himself his friend, was King George's First Commissioner of the Treasury.

No bells were rung or bonfires lighted, on this occasion, on his arrival at Whitehall; but men's eyes were not the less fixed upon him with eager expectation. Though never upbraided for treachery his political career had scarcely given evidence of any rigidity of principle. His partisanship had seemed the result rather of personal connections and friendships than of conviction. His disposition was unenthusiastic, and his intimates appear to have considered him, though careless, selfish. Enemies could not be blamed for hoping to intimidate or corrupt such a character. They adopted measures to suit both alternatives, committing him to the loose custody of a messenger in his own house, and inviting him to dinner at the mansion of Walpole. The most appalling evidence of the common opinion, even among his friends, as to his weakness of will, or bad faith, was that conveyed in the flight of Bolingbroke the night on which the news of this certainly most suspicious entertainment reached him. Happily there are strong reasons for believing that Bolingbroke's terror was groundless. Prior, if he had really led the Whigs to hope anything from his confessions, pretended readiness to turn king's evidence only to concentrate on himself exclusively their expectations of startling disclosures. He may have calculated that, if the confidant of the late cabinet in all the inmost mysteries of negotiation should, when divulging all he knew, be found to have revealed no plan bordering upon treason, the party would be cleared of criminality in the eyes of the nation. The details of the rage of the Whigs on discovering the trick played upon them, as furnished by the pen of the poet himself, are amusing and piquant. They vented their wrath on the author of the failure of the mighty secret committee, by voting him the honour of an impeachment. For a second-rate poet and diplomatist this ought to have appeared the acme of his career. He himself was not content with such glory. Though he never was in any fear for his life, notwithstanding his own account of the origin of his deafness, that "he had not thought of taking care of his ears, while not sure of his head," the wreck of his career as a politician, and the cloud under which he lay, seem to have weighed upon his spirits.

He remained under surveillance over two years, being discharged shortly after the passing of the Act of Grace in 1717, from which, however, he was excepted by name. At first he had attempted to make light of his misfortunes, and to give himself to poetry; the clever but unsystematic 'Alma' was the production of this period; but the permanence of his equivocal position, aggravated by a constitutional cough, produced great dejection. In October 1716, he writes to Sir Thomas Hanmer, his steady friend, and too moderate a Tory to have been dangerously implicated in the plots of his brother Ministers:—"I have been for the last two years a stranger to health and pleasure;" and, in November of the same year, "Melancholy I can't help indulging even to stupidity." He had never been a sufficiently bold or earnest politician to be properly impressed with the grandeur of acting the martyr to his maintenance of the tenets of the October Club, so long as the dignity interfered with his personal comfort. His circumstances, besides, were bad, most of his small savings from official salaries having been swept away in 1711 in the failure of Stratford's bank. He was forced to meditate a sale of his house and effects. His friends, on hearing of his necessities, exerted themselves nobly. They were a numerous body. The correspondence with Bolingbroke was never renewed. In that dark suspicious mind, an impression once planted unfavourable to a friend grew till it overshadowed all reminiscences of ancient kindness. His rage against the memory of Pope exemplified later his temperament. He always recollected, with resentment, that the fear of Prior's disclosures was the immediate cause of his own rash and ill-judged flight. The closeness of the relations between Prior and Lord Harley, his old rival's son, kept his anger fresh. Swift and Pope might remain on a friendly footing with the house of Oxford, yet be his friends; but the poet-diplomatist was now become its attached and regular retainer. With the bulk of the party, however, Whig persecution was accepted as convincing testimony to the constant good faith, as well of Prior as of the Harleys. The halo of an impeachment blinded it to all old shortcomings.

Instead of a testimonial, which would now be the course, an edition of his poems by subscription was proposed by Lewis and Arbuthnot, and strenuously furthered by Swift, Pope, and Gay. "No advertisements," writes the first mentioned, "are to be published, and the whole affair will be managed in a manner the least shocking to the dignity of a plenipotentiary." In addition to the 'Alma,' the collection contained another new work, the fruit also of his detention. 'Solomon' was his chief pride and boast, but, notwithstanding Cowper's approbation, and some few stately passages, is an attempt wholly outside his powers. The poem is an experiment at embodying Proverbs and Ecclesiastes in a romance, embellished with lively scenes and highly-wrought descriptions of banquets so complete, that

> "Not e'en the Phœnix scaped."

The design wants method; but more radical defects are that the bard had no heart in what he portrayed, and, perhaps, little comprehension of the grandeur of the sentiments he aspired to versify. The enterprise is said to have been undertaken in rivalry as much of the fresher laurels of Pope as of Cowley and his 'Davideis.' Consequently he petulantly rejected Pope's preference of the Hudibrastic 'Alma.' Pope judged rightly; he also praised discreetly:—

> "Our friend Dan Prior told, you know,
> A tale extremely à propos."

Even the jealous author could sometimes criticise impartially and in the same spirit, the child of his matured abilities—

> "Indeed, poor Solomon in rhyme
> Was much too grave to be sublime."

The edition produced £4,000, which, with the addition of the same sum lent by Lord Harley, in whom the estate, subject to the poet's life interest, was vested, purchased Downe Hall, a pretty and pleasant seat in the west of Essex, which had ancient associations with the de Veres. He did not spend much of his leisure there. He divided his time thenceforward till his death chiefly between "the little house close to the noise of the Court of Requests," the mansion of Lords Harley and Bathurst, and St. John's College. Though making over the emoluments generously to a deprived fellow, the learned Baker, he had steadily refused to resign his fellowship in the height of his fortunes. He was in the habit of replying to the railleries of friends on his collegiate pluraity that it would procure him "bread and cheese at the last." The event justified his prudence.

The Brothers still met occasionally, and he with them. But clouded with thoughts of the faded past, the society pined and at length died out. Prior did not keep up his friendship with the more professed political followers of St. John, such as Wyndham; but a close intimacy subsisted between him, and not only Hanmer, a type of the Hanoverian Tories, whose Conservatism included acquiescence in the Revolution, as un fait accompli, but even, though subsequently their affection waned, plotting Bishop Atterbury. If at his death St. John affected regretful surprise that he should have been abandoned by his wealthy patrons to comparative poverty, the remark was rather a sneer at the Harleys than the expression of a literal fact as to Prior. There can be no question that he enjoyed a very fair amount of comfort at this period of his life. It certainly approached what he had himself often represented to his friends as his ideal of happiness. Nevertheless, we can detect, in his correspondence, the shadow of a lingering hope that he might once more be floated into political consideration, not through any exertions of his own, or even the agency of the Tory party, but in the train of Lord Oxford. The South Sea Bubble so marred the credit of the Whig Ministers that a vague expectation arose of the late Lord Treasurer's restoration to his old authority. Prior reckoned upon a share in his patron's prosperity, though not entertaining the same opinion as the public of that statesman's character. He disbelieved the popular explanation of all Lord Oxford's conduct as ruled by the laws of a profound cunning. The apparent caution and astuteness he knew to be nothing but dilatoriness and indecision. At all events, the crisis passed by, and the supposed sagacity had no opportunity of being again found out.

Prior's regrets and longings, his querulousness at straitened means, and determination to enjoy to the full the pleasures within his reach, lasted till his death, which occurred shortly after this final disappointment. He left behind him the brief memory of a very everyday character, most remarkable for its contrast with the grandeur of the scenes in which he had figured as a principal agent. Both parties in turn trusted him as an active ally. He was the favourite, as a negotiator, of two sovereigns, one his own, the other an enemy. Notwithstanding this, he was no statesman. In the so-called golden age of our literature he ranked among eminent poets; he was confessedly the first to introduce that more polished rhythm, which Pope's 'Rape of the Lock' displays in its highest perfection; Pope, who disliked him for his quarrel with St. John, placed him along with Shakespeare, Spenser, and Dryden, among the eight "authorities for poetical language"; he was vindicated fiercely by the moral, devout, and natural Cowper, from Johnson's "rusty fusty" remarks on Henry and Emma; and he had the honour to furnish large stores of quotations to the tenacious memory of Scott; yet his claims to lofty poetic fame have been disallowed by the popular judgment of posterity, and his neatest love-odes are totally neglected. Without thought or passion, no writer can long keep his rank among poets; and Prior had neither. He was more regularly engaged in politics than Swift; some of his bon-mots, Hazlitt says, are the best that are recorded; but who would dream of comparing him with the author of the Drapier's Letters and Gulliver as a politician, or even as a wit? In the unique social epoch of Queen Anne's reign, he occupies no place apart, no individual position among the many luminaries with whom he familiarly consorted. Scarcely an idea has been handed down to us of his demeanour and general appearance. He did, said, and wrote many things which are remembered; he himself is not. A nation did not mourn for him as for Cowley; and the grief of his other old friends was as well under control as Atterbury's, who was content to be kept away from his funeral by a cold. He had to remind posterity by a bequest for a sumptuous monument in the Abbey who he was, and what he had been.

IV.

TWO LEADERS OF SOCIETY AND OF OPPOSITION.

HENRY ST. JOHN,
1678–1751.

WILLIAM PULTENEY,
1682–1764.

HENRY ST. JOHN.

FROM Prior to Bolingbroke is a transition from agent to principal, from an instrument to the hand which wielded it. The two were intimately connected with one another by association with the same events and persons. Both represent their period, and their careers unite in reflecting its peculiar characteristics. But the men played their parts with very different powers, and with very different effectiveness. The second is so identified with his age that he seems to sway it as much as it him. He does not merely exemplify it; to study it apart from him is virtually impossible. An exposition of the first half of the eighteenth century which was not also a biography of Henry St. John would be lost labour.

That it is so follows from the qualities of the age, and from the spirit which constitutes its charm. In it the trait which specially engages our fancy is the strong personal element manifested as clearly in literature as in the conduct of affairs. Queen Anne's era must be interpreted in a liberal chronological sense. The current of some great rivers can be traced far out to sea; and in the same way the impetus of the spirit Queen Anne's era set in motion outlasted a reign. The period in many ways extends over the following generation, which its influence governed. As a whole it has the relation to sober history which Lord Beaconsfield's novels bear to a serious political treatise. It is as though the spirit of the Parisian coteries of the time of Louis XIV., and the regency of Orleans, had blended with the violent humours and passions of an English electioneering season. In Anne's reign itself, not till the catastrophe, which astonishes us from its complete independence of the vicissitudes of the struggle itself, do we detect the national pertinacity of adherence to a deliberate decision. The interval is given up to a chaos of drawing-room schemes, back-stairs plots, and the intrigues of club-committees. We feel, with a certain fascination in the discovery, that the State is, after all, not an abstraction, but a concourse of living beings, moved by the same impulses, and susceptible of the same vexations and pleasures. Posterity is admitted further behind the scene than at other times; and more of specific character appears in the prominent agents than can usually be perceived in the instruments of a nation's will. Above all, these servants of a national policy did not pass away with the measures they shaped. Round one of them, the master-spirit of an Administration once, gathered subsequently all the strength of Opposition. His influence we trace in each more important act of the close of the Queen's reign. He, by fashioning the most shining of political and literary societies, when out of power, and half an outlaw, has brought both politics and society within the verge of the same sympathies.

Violent partisanship ran in Henry St. John's blood. His ancestors, when they came forward, chose no safe or moderate course, and delighted in extremes. The grandeur of the family dated back from the marriage of a scion of the powerful Saxon family of Port, settled at Basing, with the heiress of the Norman St. Johns. It had never been obscured since the days of the Conquest, though, till the seventeenth century, chiefly conspicuous in the details of county history. During all that century, and far into the following one, it was in the van of all political movements. Henry St. John could count in the male line among his near relatives the Earls of Bolingbroke of the Parliament, and the chivalrous Viscount Grandison of Clarendon's History, one of the first victims of Charles's cause. Through females, he was grandson of the gloomy Chief Justice of the Commonwealth and nephew of the High Church and Tory Earl of Nottingham. He himself was destined to run the gauntlet of principles seemingly contradictory, and to illustrate in his own life the extreme conclusions of the most adverse political factions of the preceding age. Tradition tells of the splendour of the old house at Battersea, the gift of Charles I. to Viscount Grandison, with its forty rooms on one floor, the cedar parlour, still existing, where Pope loved to compose, and the terrace overlooking the Thames, so often paced by the statesman and the poet, only in death estranged. There he was born. In his boyhood he witnessed an unfortunate contrast of strict theoretical principles with the example of a lax private morality. The sternest moral discipline was maintained by the old Puritan, his grandfather, throughout the household, even to his death in 1708. Abroad, a libertine father made a jest of all political and religious sincerity. It was the worst possible training for one whose versatility of character disposed him to mimic tenets, and to indulge every wayward gust of passion.

His school-days at Eton, where he had Walpole for a contemporary, foreshadowed that strenuous idleness, that petty ambition of supremacy in licentiousness and genius, which distorted into something at once grotesque and picturesque, repulsive and attractive, the whole course of his life. It is easy to see in the boy a historical Vivian Grey, leader of the school and terror of masters, already preparing the minds of his friends to expect the statesman. He continued his education at Christ Church. Under the rule of Dean Aldrich, famous for port and music, architecture and logic, "Priest of Bacchus," as Whigs styled him, "Champion of the Church," as Tories, a more than modern licence was allowed to students of noble families. St. John possessed the perilously happy constitution, both of mind and body, which enabled and tempted him, like Alcibiades, to enter into excesses, which must have else quickly degraded him to the condition of one of his future partisans of the October Club. His model was Wilmot, the fantastic friend and rival of Charles II., whose genius had a spontaneous bouquet, which has, in evaporation, left behind it nothing but a deposit of vapid immorality. In emulation of the Court wits, he became a poet, as poets were then. Various very wretched compositions are ascribed to his muse, too weak and poor, with a few exceptions, even for Dodsley's Collections. He had already propitiated the favour of Dryden with eulogistic verses on his Virgil, and been admitted to the vinous conclaves over which the poet presided. In him all this licence was not a mere result of youth, but an indication of incurable restlessness of organisation. The manners of his family had not implanted in him any fixed principles. The manners of the time were not likely to supply the defect of education. Of all men he was the most incapable of supplying it for himself. Higher capacity and abilities the world has rarely seen. There was nothing for which they were not prepared. They were tools of the finest temper, but wanting a soul to guide them. He had not enough conscientious patience to conceive and maintain a code of action for himself in an age when factiousness was the only consistency. He was without the moral sagacity and self-restraint needed for accepting the fundamental theory of a party, and identifying himself with it, heart and soul, after the manner of Nottingham among the Tories, and Cowper among the Whigs. All he cared for was to guess, with his marvellous shrewdness, the petty selfish motives which instigated the policy of parties. He possessed the instinct of leading men, or rather of constituting himself their spokesman, in perfection; but the spirit he poured into them was rarely higher than their own, only, heated and enkindled with his fiery energy, and consciousness of power. In the days of Henry VIII. he would probably have been another Cromwell; under the Commonwealth he might have copied his maternal grandfather, though with less of stern consistency; in the semi-literary, semi-political agitations of Queen Anne's reign, he became the representative of the Gallic sympathies and the Court intrigues of the second Charles, coloured later by the new philosophico-political spirit which came in with and mystified the Hanoverian dynasty.

The wit and debauchee of Oxford was not very widely separated from the hard-drinking zealot of the October Club.

The doom of his nature was that it was ever eager to constitute itself the centre of a faction rather than a party, of a knot of personal adherents, who would make him their lodestar, and look on his conduct, however irregular, as a law carrying its own theory. No period could have been better adapted for the encouragement of his special temperament than that commencing with the year 1700, when he first entered the House of Commons. At any time he must have proved himself a remarkable man, full of the statesman-like power of seizing opportunities, however wanting in the unerring sagacity which teaches the most prudent use of them. He could not but have led, whether an Opposition or an Administration. But portions only of his character and faculties might have been matured and illustrated. The attraction and repulsion of other luminaries in the political firmament might have restrained his aberrations, and kept him in one certain orbit. The revolutionary aspects of William's reign, and the unstable basis on which rested the boasted legitimacy of Anne's title, with its regular inconsistency of party-badges, and glaring contradictions in political creeds, formed a lurid and troublous atmosphere, in which blazed and strayed at will his disorderly genius.

He had made a marriage of convenience, if we may judge from the fact that the co-heiress of Sir Henry Winchescomb possessed a fortune of forty thousand pounds, and that the pair lived in a state of perpetual discord, though never legally separated. Contemporaneously he entered Parliament as member for Wotton Basset, in Wiltshire, the seat of his own and his wife's interest. The same year was signalised by the return of Robert Walpole for Castle Rising, in Norfolk. Both were as unscrupulous in the details of political morality as free in their maxims of private conduct. But something in the nature of Walpole at once attached him to the ranks of the great Revolution party; and something in that of St. John, notwithstanding, or perhaps partly in consequence of, early associations, drew him to the side where all was yet to be won, and a party constructed from the foundation.

The anarchy and humiliation of the Tories served only to attract him. Of the best blood in England, he felt the envy and jealousy of the close oligarchy of the Whartons and the Churchills which might have roused a young noble of Ancient Greece or of the Middle Age Republics of Italy to seek in a tyranny vengeance upon the ruling Houses. With the consciousness of originality and resolution sufficient for a whole Cabinet, he wanted no established system, no groove, along which the wheels of his policy might smoothly glide. Followers he needed, and not champions or counsellors, a strong cry, and not previously settled rules of action.

It was the epoch of the peace of Ryswick; and the title of the Revolution dynasty was recognised at home and abroad. Now at last, might the Tories argue, had arrived the time for testing the benefits to arise from the expulsion of the Stuarts. Yet the Protestant Government ruled by the military arm which had terrified Church and Cavaliers into revolt from the son of the "Blessed Martyr." William unhappily possessed no pliability of temper. If the nation proved resolved on a measure, he could not but acquiesce; but the manner was most ungracious. His enemies pretended they saw in his hesitation evidence rather of a tacit protest or reservation of a right to retract, than of conscientious reluctance to assent to a policy he thought dangerous. Though he felt himself bound by the will of the majority, he was ever too open in his denunciations, and too bold in his expressed forebodings of the evil consequences likely to ensue. The King threatened to abdicate if the army were disbanded. The Whig leaders supported him in vain. Their old arguments against a standing army had been too deeply imprinted on the minds of the mass of their followers, and afforded too convenient a handle for the Opposition. Rather hastily William construed this defeat by a coalition of Whigs and Tories as a sign of a sure preponderance on the side of the latter. He at once replaced Somers, Sunderland, Shrewsbury, Orford, and Montague, by Rochester, and the pliant Conservatism of Godolphin.

St. John soon flashed his maiden sword in the battle of

parties. He had cast in his lot with Harley, that pre-eminently clever upholder of principles at least not Tory by the help of Tory adherents. With him he had supported the Act of Settlement, and carried the insertion of clauses meant to coerce the prerogative of the new family. With him and all the chiefs of the " Young England " Tories, he carried up an impeachment of Portland, Somers, Orford, and Halifax, to the Peers, in April, 1701. Now the young statesman felt for the first time, what he was to experience in subsequent stages of his political career, that the Tory majority in the Commons, though elected by the nation from discontent at the conduct of affairs by a Whig Ministry, were watched with suspicion by their own constituents. They were sent up to Westminster to gratify a popular pique; their commission executed, the kingdom had no intention of letting them play their own game. St. John was among the foremost in inflaming the ready passions, and not so ready courage, of his fellow-members against the Kentish petitioners. The imprisonment of these persons for what was called a libel gave the Whigs a watchword, which they employed to ruin their adversaries. This blunder, and the ineffectual menace of impeachment thrown out against the late Government, provoked the incomparable efforts of Swift and De Foe, soon to become opponents. The House of Commons felt how powerless it was unless as the representative of the people, and bowed to the storm it dared no longer openly resist. William's last days were cheered by a more unanimous sentiment of national loyalty than had ever before been elicited even from his own political partisans. Anne, on her accession found a Tory majority in Parliament, eager to gratify all her blind instinct of animosity to the memory of her brother-in-law. She found the powerful Revolution families exposed to popular rancour; charged with unconstitutional subservience to the monarch's will; with a denial, finally, of the right of Parliament to discuss the preliminaries of grand and permanent measures. But she also found the principles of the Revolution recognised, and registered in the Act of Settlement, which she could not impugn, since her own title depended on it, and the nation as little inclined to concede unlimited discretion to Tory squires as to Whig peers.

In this state of things her first Ministry, though composed of Tories, was scarcely representative of that party. The Sovereign's personal predilection was rather the title to admission within it, than the fact that its members were the organs of a certain pronounced policy. Harley and St. John were still left without office. There were great Tory families as there were great Whig families. Finch Earl of Nottingham, Godolphin, sure of place, from his long experience, his wariness, and his connection with Marlborough, and Rochester, both as son to Clarendon, and as the Queen's uncle, had a sort of hereditary claim to be employed. When not courtiers of the King, they had been courtiers of the heiress; and to them the sovereign naturally looked as the legitimate chiefs of Opposition. It had been so throughout the life of William, but, during his reign, a strong and genuine Tory confederacy had been reviving, the potent country interest. Politicians, whom we may term social Tories, Tories not because there were Whigs, but as a consequence of the entire tenor of their lives and circumstances, had put Harley into the Speaker's chair, and maintained him there in Anne's first Parliament. They recognised him and his lieutenant, St. John, as their spokesmen; they did not adopt measures at their dictation. Harley had a decided bias, in many respects, to the Nonconformists, but he only committed himself to vague professions, and never compromised his position by a vote. St. John was a libertine in practice and doctrine; yet he protested against latitudinarianism in doctrine and discipline, along with the most vehement county members.

The new Parliament, which had met in the October of 1702, speedily evinced its tendencies. Its first act was to vote thanks to the General, while it showed that the intention of the vote was rather to reflect on the late King than to exalt so doubtful a Tory as Marlborough, by refusing him a pension on the Post-office revenue. But the most significant measure was that against occasional Conformity. The bill, though vehemently supported by St. John, was dropped for this time, in consequence of a quarrel between the two Houses artfully inflamed by the leading Whigs. There had existed, since the Revolution, two fruitful sources whence the thirst of the rival factions for reciprocal calumny might be readily quenched. The Whigs accused the Tories of advocating the cause of arbitrary power, and the Tories the Whigs of culpable laxity in religion. Never was a motion introduced reflecting on the one side, but forthwith, blast and counterblast, came retaliation in the shape of a bill reminding the nation of all it had to fear from the other. The Whigs saved themselves on this occasion by a manœuvre of an analogous kind to those often practised by Shaftesbury. Their turn had now arrived to attack. They moved that every attempt to disturb the Protestant succession as established by the Act of Settlement should subject the offender to the penalties of treason. Harley, with his Trimmers, could not reasonably oppose a resolution, superfluous perhaps and supererogatory, yet in affirmation of a measure they claimed as their peculiar work. St. John took an independent part. Already his ambition was to be identified with the country Tories, while he acted with Harley. None of these measures were strictly what we should call Ministerial. A Whig administration really represented the Whig party. It was not so with the Tories. Although in Godolphin's cabinet, as originally constituted, the majority was Tory, its members, not having been called to office by the voice of a party, did not conceive themselves individually pledged to any special course. Thus, when Rochester had resigned the Lieutenancy of Ireland in a fit of jealousy at Godolphin's ascendency, and Lord Nottingham, after finding his reiterated complaints of the sway in the Council of the Whig Dukes of Somerset and Devonshire disregarded, had retired, there was nothing self-contradictory in the appointment in 1704 of Harley, Hedges, and St. John, the first two to be Secretaries of State, and the last Secretary-at-War.

Though Tories, they represented a different body to that

which gathered round Rochester and Nottingham. The Hydes and Finches were themselves parties in the State; their successors were influential Parliamentary partisans. A Tory Lord Treasurer might, in those days, adopt means for the exclusion of Tories who were personal rivals. Such procedure exposed him to no imputation of treachery to his party. It evidenced no wish or intention to resist the royal determination to maintain the Tory element in the Government. The whole change was simply the result of an intrigue in the Cabinet, however the victory of Godolphin might foreshadow a future divergence from the pronounced opinions of his ejected colleagues.

The Ministry was, in truth the last for a long time openly formed on the old principle that the Sovereign, as responsible for the executive, had a right to choose the most capable subordinates he could discover. The accession of the House of Brunswick, which depended originally for its crowned existence upon the Whigs, caused this doctrine to be obscured for half a century. George III., whose title was more secure, revived it. For many years under him every Minister forced into office by the voice of the nation had to endure the presence in his Administration of certain men, who, as "King's friends," deemed themselves chartered to play the spy, in council and the public informer in Parliament. King's friends, however, but partially resembled the discordant element in the Godolphin Government. Godolphin, unlike the Pitts and Norths, represented no known party in the State, while Harley and St. John were admitted actually as leaders of a division of Tories. Their junction with Godolphin could be called neither a coalition nor a defection. It was no coalition, for they succeeded to the posts of notorious Tories; it was no defection, since their chief voted for Tory resolutions. If Walpole found in the reconstituted Ministry a seat at the Admiralty Board, the appointment of Simon Harcourt to be Attorney-General was a full Tory counterpoise.

But the two friends were far too acute not to comprehend

the tendencies of the Ministerial modification. The sagacity of the elder, especially, was seldom at fault, when his own interests were concerned. He saw in his own elevation a design of warding off Tory opposition by securing the co-operation of Tory placemen for half concealed Whig measures. When the chiefs should have been thus compromised, they might be cashiered with impunity. He calculated that, whatever the present views of Godolphin, the instinct of Marlborough, the dictator, must teach him to look to the party of the Revolution as the only permanent support for his war policy. Finally, he did not believe that any Premier, except perhaps himself, had the art to balance in those days two antagonistic interests in the same Cabinet, and to treat all critical topics as open questions. For the present, especially after the elections of October, 1705, dimmed the prospects of their party, the two new Ministers confined themselves to the work of their offices. The glittering abilities of the Secretary-at-War proved no bar to the display of capacity for business, which· won golden opinions from the great captain, whose commissariat he superintended. Repeatedly, in his correspondence, Marlborough entreats the Treasurer to confide in Mr. St. John. In Parliament they were less conspicuous than formerly. It was at once dangerous to provoke dismissal by too violent Tory partisanship, while their plans remained immature, and to offend the Queen by the appearance of an active alliance with the other side. At length, the now open Whiggism of the majority in the Cabinet, and the inveterate mistrust conceived by it of Harley, united in bringing about the Bed-chamber Plot of Harley, Mrs. Masham, and the Queen, against the tyranny of the Marlboroughs and the family compact of the Administration. The expulsion of the most active conspirator and the triumph of his Whig adversaries in the new Parliament of 1708 ensued. Godolphin yielded himself absolutely to the counsels of the "Junto," Somers, Orford, Halifax, Sunderland, and Wharton.

Harley had earned his dismissal. The red eyes of the Queen, remarked by the suspicious curiosity of the courtiers, bore witness to many a midnight conference, enlivened only by continual tea. St. John had scarcely found an opportunity for displaying his knowledge of character and his ability for intrigue. Yet his resignation accompanied that of Harley. Walpole, who always dogged his steps, succeeded to his office. He had the additional mortification of exclusion from Parliament. His seat, gained by a combination of family influence and his presumed adherence to the political creed of his Whig grandfather, had been retained by the authority of place. Now, suspected as a factious Tory, and a foe of the Government, he had to betake himself, with a poor attempt at self-congratulation, to literary pleasures, and others which were not so innocent. He had not yet attained to the stoicism or hypocrisy which could give vent to the lofty sentiment, "no life should admit the abuse of pleasures; the least are consistent with a constant discharge of our public duty, the greatest arise from it!"

General odium, however, both in country and in Parliament, was quietly preparing the downfall of the Ministry. All the complicated forces implied in the Greek Nemesis, the intrinsic self-destructive action of all self-confident prosperity, were at work to overthrow this too strong Cabinet. There was ingratitude, real or supposed, to a host of adherents, who were for the most part no genuine Whigs, but merely scented the carcase of patronage. There was a growing discontent at the burdens of taxation, which, as the condition of Marlborough's grandeur, Sunderland and Godolphin felt themselves pledged to keep up. Harley, who knew by instinct all the ins and outs of faction, nursed this increasing disaffection. He hoped to be enabled to turn it to account by means of the naturally anti-Whig prejudices of the Queen, now exasperated and roused by the capricious insolence of Lady Marlborough. St. John still had only a subsidiary part in this long and dexterous extra-parliamentary campaign. When the object was to seduce from a rival the affections of his partisans, there never existed, as Harley found to his cost, a more incomparable intriguer than he. He possessed, in perfection, the gift of displaying himself in the aspect most attractive to each man's peculiar temperament. But it is one thing to win over individuals, another to have grown by long study and practice so morbidly sensitive to every thrill and throb of national or party feeling, as to be able to predict infallibly the direction which a popular movement will take. Harley, in virtue of that facility, was sole "undertaker" for Opposition. But it was not till the impeachment of Sacheverell for impugning the doctrines of the Revolution, and calling the Lord Treasurer Volpone, that the secret interviews of Anne with him were renewed. He was at his country seat, and at table, when news came of the rash prosecution to which Ministers had committed themselves. He set off for London the same hour. The Whigs found that they had, in St. John's language, burnt their fingers in trying to roast a priest. Hardly could the managers, Boyle, Smith, Walpole, and Stanhope, prevail with the House of Peers, the natural stronghold of the Revolution, to impose a sentence of two years' suspension. The Doctor employed the beginning of his leisure in solemnly visiting all the London churches, to offer up thanks for his virtual deliverance. Bonfires, addresses, and civic banquets, shouts, and substantial presents, proclaimed the awakened strength of the party, which the semblance of a Tory element in the Government, in the person of Godolphin, had lulled to sleep. Jealousy of the Dutch, our rivals in commerce and in the Protestant confederacy, and suspicion of a subsidising foreign policy, were the common ground on which the nation and party met. The cry raised was loud enough to overbalance, for a time, the pleasure the people derived from the sweets of positive military glory after William's succession of drawn campaigns.

Harley's time was come. Not a High-Churchman at heart, he had found matter for sarcasm in Harcourt's interpretation of Sacheverell's sermon as an exposition of the doctrine of non-resistance to the two Houses of the Legislature, the true sovereign power in the State. His feeling towards the man was not more friendly than to his discourse. Swift says of Sacheverell, April, 1711: "He hates the new Ministry mortally, and they hate him and pretend to despise him too. They will not allow him to have been the occasion of the late change." Harley's words in public conveyed a different impression, as did also his suggestions to the Queen. The scheme of government which he laid before her was both in itself plausible, as was everything which originated with him, and most dexterously adapted to her temperament. She felt much jealousy of the appearance of subservience. The new fact in the English Constitution, the necessity of choosing a Ministry wholly from one party, conveyed no idea to her mind. It seemed to her, naturally enough, to reduce the Sovereign from a personally influential agent to the condition of a machine for registering the results of a party contest. Her secret adviser recommended an Administration selected on a different principle. It was to be composed of men influential in the Houses, yet not chosen in the mass for their party prominence, but taken one from this section, and from that section another, according to the character of the departments they were required to fill. Godolphin had tried the plan. Long after, St. John advocated it. But the Queen's extreme aversion to all connected with the then Ministry, Cowper and the Somersets excepted, condemned the scheme to failure, however well suited to her own theory of the royal prerogative. Otherwise, the first experiment must have demonstrated the impracticability, now that the superintending control of Parliament was acknowledged, of carrying on a Government without reciprocal confidence among its members. The dread of a colleague's Parliamentary manœuvres and intrigues was sure to have vitiated all unison of operation. Harley, it may be suspected, less with any patriotic design of mitigating party rancour, than from the love of coalitions, a radical feature in all his policy, and in the hope of warding off the violence of the Whigs, or the vehemence of the undisciplined Toryism, of which he seems to have conceived an instinctive dread, made the attempt. Lord Chancellor Cowper and Walpole emphatically repulsed his overtures. In vain he insinuated that "a Whig game was intended at bottom." The Chancellor declares in his diary that he saw how shuffling were all Harley's explanations, and that, "in a little time, when any Tory of interest would press for the place, he must have it." Probably prejudice against the new Minister's candour rendered Cowper unjust. Harley's constant policy was to temper the Tories with the Whigs, that he might not become an instrument of Jacobite intrigues. But the Whig policy was not to temper Whigs with Tories; and, after a flourish of trumpets, in the dismissal of some subordinates, Godolphin surrendered his beloved white staff. Though Marlborough retained his command, his fall was the slow but certain consequence of the overthrow of his connections. The Treasury was put in commission, Harley being head of the Board. Rochester, as President of the Council, in the absence of a Lord Treasurer, was in rank Premier; and St. John assumed, with a Secretaryship of State, his historical position of statesman.

The suddenness of St. John's elevation dazzles the student of history. He had spoken often, and with effect; he had discharged the duties committed to him with zeal and tact; but he was only the follower of Harley, rising and falling with him. The plot which brought him his promotion was not of his devising. To his chief the honour belonged, if honour there were; yet St. John reaped the lion's share of the profit. He had been lost in a party; all at once the nation resounded with his voice, and Europe, for half a century, felt the effects of his policy. Harley knew better than any man how to adapt himself to weaknesses. St. John compelled adhesion from admiration. The one could never lead a party boldly and decidedly; the other could never collect a party; he was made to be the spirit and soul of one already formed. The audacity of conception, which aroused fear in his adversaries, gave confidence to friends. Few joined his ranks because they had been convinced by his acts or arguments, but, once gathered round him, they obeyed implicitly. He did not entrench himself in the camp of Toryism. Toryism was not recognised as the national policy. Whig principles were alone constitutional, Whig statesmen the only authorised interpreters of the Constitution. The object of the Harley Cabinet was to impugn the deductions from the principles, and the integrity of their custodians, without attacking the premisses on which the inferences were based. St. John was an instrument in carrying out this policy, and he secured the aid of the press; but his aim was higher and it was independent. In that aim is to be found the link between his Toryism and his Radicalism. Shaftesbury was by turns a Republican and a Royalist, and we shall see that the Royalist St. John could recognise, at one time, an obligation upon the sovereign to consult the popular will on every occasion; at another, his right to govern his territories according to the absolute bias of his own will. Both theories flowed from the same mental character. The dislike to a Venetian oligarchy is an original sentiment in certain minds, and no invention of Mr. Disraeli's imagination. St. John appealed from the dogmas proclaimed by a league of great lords, among whom it enraged him that he was not himself counted, to the individual majesty of the Sovereign, and the collective majesty of the people. It was not the capriciousness of a disposition ever attempting innovation for the sake of showing craft, which inspired his peculiar political career. It was not disgust at the haughty disdain of the lords of pocket boroughs. It was hatred of a system which exacted blind submission to a creed of the past, and required a party to act in a particular way because it had acted so before. His feelings moved him to adopt a cause in which he would be most of a real agent; the organ, it might be, of a monarch; it might be, of a democracy; but, at all events, not a colleague of a set of mummies.

In mere numbers the Tories probably exceeded the Whigs; but the Whigs had achieved the Revolution; and their work had never been renounced by the nation. To win over the people, to secure, not its incorporation in the Ministerial, but its defection from the opposite party, was the object of the eager patronage now extended to literature. From this line of action the characteristic lustre of the last four years of Queen Anne's reign is derived, set in relief as they are by the neighbourhood of Walpole's unillumined administration. Now, not a few isolated exceptions, as Addison and Montague, among writers, were caressed by Cabinets; all were accepted as, of right, equals in society, by their employers and patrons. Literary men of the same political opinions were courted for the aid they brought, and, if adversaries, less for the harm they might do than out of compliment to the profession. Not only were Prior and Swift reckoned high among statesmen, but Steele retained his Commissionership, and Addison was always an honoured guest of St. John's. Authors responded by a spirit and manifest consciousness of power over affairs, unknown in the days of Charles II. Proud of being acknowledged partners of politicians equally sympathetic with literature, and prominent in that practical faculty of ruling men which unpractical men appreciate so intensely, professional writers became at once sworn advocates of the policy of the statesmen, and protectors of their fame. Robertson attributes the unjustifiable glory of Francis, as contrasted with the very indifferent reputation of his rival the Emperor Charles, to his zealous patronage of letters. No small part of the renown of St. John is due to the openness with which he confessed the power of literature, and the manner in which he conciliated the admiration of its professors by his own devotion to the art.

The high rank maintained by the reign of Anne, as the Augustan age of English literature, is intimately connected with the favour shown to authors by the Minister on whose subsequent reputation the celebrity of some of them has signally reacted. A condition necessary to the promotion of any especial epoch to this rank, is a high state, not of caste culture, but of national culture; that state in which a whole people is able to appreciate a production, in proportion to the distinctions of social grades. No author will write so as to move a nation, unless his countrymen be in a condition to be moved. Only thus will the spirit of a nation be so changed or modified by literature as to become a force reproducing like effects in the minds of after generations. Whenever in such circumstances great authors arise, as great authors surely will, they must exercise an enduring influence. But place them, with this condition of general intellectual culture fulfilled, in a crisis of political agitation, or social progress, and enforce among them the recognition of a standard, by forming them into a community for reciprocal criticism; then the influence of the era will have no bounds. Its best intelligence will be directed to the training of national and political feeling, and will exert an ever fresh and living power. The writings may be scarcely intelligible as to their immediate objects, when these have been obsolete for generations; they never lose the interest with which a thorough perception of popular tastes and temper originally invested them. Gulliver's Travels and Sir Roger de Coverley cannot become unmeaning. The title to be a golden age of letters is determined by the coincidence of a popular taste for literature with a call to advocate popular objects. The Elizabethan age demonstrates the extreme height to which the English mind can aspire. But Addison, Swift, Pope, Steele, De Foe, and Bolingbroke, are still practically our literary models. Their age continues to set the standard by which we test the works of our contemporaries.

All the literary strength had hitherto been on the side of the Whigs. De Foe, Steele, Addison, and Swift, at first in the train of Somers, were a host. St. John perfectly comprehended the importance of such an engine in the uncertain political state of the kingdom. Later, wearied with the various attacks on his measures, and without the hopefulnes of the youth of an Administration to sustain him, or in the confidence of power, he brought forward a sweeping enactment against the freedom of political tracts. Though he failed in carrying that, he persuaded Parliament to lay a heavy tax upon newspapers and pamphlets. At present as he could not, or would not, curb the Opposition press by force, he resolved to write it down. The Post-boy, a ferocious party paper, and the much more characteristic Examiner, commenced August 3, 1710, undertook the task. The benefit to be obtained by the Government from a clever literary organ could not be overrated. It was in a most exceptional position. While it enjoyed the decided confidence of the House of Commons, and, by inference, the squires, it was hated by the most energetic portion of the community, by the middle classes and the trading interest. They saw in it a faction exemplified by its leaders, some the personifications of selfish unscrupulousness, some careless of everything but the gratification of personal ambition, or personal vanity. It was no answer to this that its opponents were as mere a faction; that they cared nothing for the interests of their country, or for the liberties of the people; that they had always been ready to intrigue for party ends with foreign powers, and actually, in this reign, concerted with Marlborough and the Elector a scheme for introducing Hanoverian troops to fortify the Protestant succession. Their success in changing the dynasty had stamped all their measures with the authority of legitimacy. Both alike were factions, utterly regardless of the will of the majority. Both would have been inclined to sympathise with the temper of the Duchess of Marlborough, who loved to dabble in philosophy, when she denounced the patience of Socrates under a legal sentence awarded by "a villains' majority." The difference remained, that the one faction seemed to have none but private aims, the other to have identified private with public. To offer to its own party a plausible theory of the plans of their leaders and the calumnies of enemies, was the object of the Examiner.

It was supported by St. John's sparkling style, in which the English language seemed to have reached its ultimate pamphleteering force of expression, and by the fierce but cold humour of Swift. Its greatest strength was in the confident tone, which assurance against pillories and actions of libel, and acquaintance with secrets of State, naturally taught all its contributors. The Review, edited by De Foe, exhibited, together with a residuum of positive Whiggism, the conciliatory tendencies of Harley. The Examiner displayed against Steele's and Addison's Tattler the Secretary's uncompromising hostility, not to the principle of the Revolution, at least openly, but to the deductions drawn from it, and to the characters of its agents. The bitterness which flowed freely from his pen he would probably have justified by his tenet, that " to form a good and great character, the heart must be touched with esteem and contempt, with love and hatred." While Swift hurled the imputation of mean rapacity against the General, and of analogous conduct to that of David towards Uriah, and bigamy, against the Whig Chancellors, Somers and Cowper respectively, St. John vented, in a letter to the Examiner, his detestation of the ambitious Duchess, and his exultation that "the Fury, broke loose to execute the vengeance of heaven on a sinful people, is restrained, and the royal hand reached out to chain up the plague." State measures were freely discussed, and in a way to provoke, even invite, free discussion on the other side. Steele answered Swift, and Cowper St. John. This was St. John's own design. His instinct told him, truly, that the one thing to be dreaded by Ministers was the feeling of a mystery and concealment, which made the nation suspect more than met the ear in everything done or attempted.

When the start was fairly made, he had resigned the editorship to hands strong enough to uphold the most dubious cause, to the portentous mixture of fury at will and plain shrewd sense which composed the mind of Swift. Swift was, with more sincerity, St. John's literary counterpart. His diseased constitution, both of body and disposition, was not fitted for the fine balancing of party combinations which was Harley's peculiar delight. The writer who stigmatised the Chancellor, himself no half partisan, as " Trimming Harcourt," for disapproving the charge of cowardice against the most accomplished of English generals, could be no sincere adviser of coalitions, unless as temporary manœuvres. Whatever he undertook he lent his whole being to achieve; though he might change his politics, he had a capacity of believing always in his work, of never doubting the obligation which lay on him to do what he had undertaken, as a matter of conscience. Now, too, at last, disappointed ambition had driven him into the party which really suited his nature. He loved to fashion men's thoughts and institutions after a pattern furnished by his own fancy. There was in him an element of destructiveness, controlled and corrected by a passion for reconstruction. A Church establishment which should endure no occasional conformity, a monarchy which should not be at the bidding of an oligarchy of birth or riches, were the two fundamental conceptions in the soul of Swift. As with St. John, there was an assumption in his projects that the Church and the monarchy should be exactly fashioned after his own, and not other men's ideas; and that as abstractions cannot act, their organs should be himself and his friends. But, to effect all this, the present state of things must be changed; and the change could be accomplished only through an appeal, not to the great Revolution families, but to the people. In this, the Radical side of his politics, as of St. John's, is the point of contact between the two. Yet he does not appear to have altogether liked the Secretary. One party could scarcely afford free scope for two such men. Each had sufficient self-confidence and ambition to rebuild the entire edifice of society, and each believed himself to be an infallible touchstone for all measures. Besides, there was a grand seigneur air at times about St. John, as about Byron and Frederick the Great, in his intercourse with literary men. The demeanour of a man affecting to look on such employments as a graceful condescension, not perhaps in the statesman, but in the man of the world, could not but offend his companion's earnestness and energy. The one had not known what leisure meant, and still remembered, with loathing, the lofty graciousness of Sir William Temple. A man whose life had been never free from anxiety about petty wants, who threw himself with all his heart into the work before him, could not be satisfied to see another, who profited by his efforts, professing to look upon all this as not the real business of life, as not entitled to come into competition with a saunter in the Mall or an assignation. Harley's complaisance and spirit of concession were more to the Doctor's taste. That statesman had learnt, in his partly neutral position of Speaker, not to affront his clients with the ostentation of patronage. Even when he annoyed the proud spirit, which rated its services at a mitre, with the offer of £50 for his parallel between the late and present Cabinets in the 26th number of the Examiner, the blame was laid by the offended author rather on a want of delicacy of perception, than on the contemptuousness of a man who thought money could buy brains. Swift's letters and sayings betray a deeper sentiment of friendship for Harley, sincere admirer as he was of the genius of the Secretary, his own more immediate coadjutor.

The ascendency of character which at length obliged Swift to recognise in St. John the chief of the party, while he deprecated his patron's deposition, began, soon after the formation of the Cabinet, to be exerted. Not only was the foreign policy shaped by the Secretary as of course; the scope of the general policy of the Administration was also mainly marked out by him. The office of countenancing the Cabinet, and procuring for it the favour of the hereditary Tory families, was left to Rochester, otherwise a mere obstructive. Harley's genius was best adapted for conciliating opponents. He did not hope to convert professed partisans, but to blunt the edge of their hostility, and to gain the votes of dubious members. The respectable appearance made by the Whigs in the new Parliament pleased him. It gave room for the practice of the art of management of the House of Commons, which none understood more exactly. He saw in it a prospect of escape from the thraldom to party principles and violence which he abhorred. As Swift represented St. John, so De Foe expounded, though with truculent earnestness, the views of Harley, to whom he owed his liberty. He had been sentenced to Newgate for the authorship of 'A Short Way with the Dissenters,' a sarcastic burlesque on the Establishment, which was, it is said, for a long time applauded in the combination rooms of Cambridge as a grave and judicious suggestion to Government. Thenceforward at peace with the Ministry, he advocated, with his deliverer, a larger comprehensiveness and a widening of the basis of party.

But Harley was not a statesman of originality or farsightedness sufficient for such an undertaking. Any union of parties effected by him could be only a coalition of men. It could not reconcile principles, by tracing them up to and including them within something higher. Unhappily for him, a temper was at work in the country, and an unquiet spirit astir in his own Cabinet, which swept away the cobwebs of his intrigues, and undid all his clever Parliamentary patchwork. The Country party was at last thoroughly roused. In its red-hot vigour and strong with the unpopularity of the war policy of the late Administration, it complained of conciliatory schemes as treason against it, and a violation of the right of the conquerors. Now it had a leader far superior to Rochester or to Nottingham, and him it resolved to make head of the Government, as he was already of the party. The attempt on the life of the First Lord by Guiscard, a French Abbé, part profligate, part infidel, which, well managed, might have caused the evil day to be put off indefinitely, did not defer for long the transfer of the preeminence. At the moment Harley's wound excited a degree of national enthusiasm and generous sympathy only to be paralleled by the feeling of the country on the murder of Mr. Perceval. He was held up as a martyr to the vengeance of disguised Jesuits. A peerage was the least of his honours. The opportune death of the Lord President opened his way to the High Treasurer's staff, a badge of supremacy which could not be bestowed in Rochester's lifetime.

The incurable bitterness between the colleagues, which infuses so painful and personal an interest into the catastrophe of the Administration, dates from this event. St. John, who had at first manifested all becoming indignation at the crime of Guiscard, grew envious of the glory his friend had acquired, especially as the previous request of a private conference with himself seemed to indicate him as the original object of the assassin's fury. The fervour of Harley's popularity with the nation at large seemed to defer, perhaps for ever, the elevation which the Secretary's influence over the Tories had given him a right to expect. Not his ambition alone was attacked. His vanity was wounded by the subsequent conduct of the Premier. Vanity was an insatiable passion in him. A morbid craving for opportunities of action and the exercise of his abilities is the key to his career; he intended not only to be, but to seem, the prime mover of the Government policy. But even to be left undisputed leader in the House of Commons he thought a small thing beside a grant to Harley of the heraldic honours of the de Veres and Mortimers. Perhaps Harley's perception of his own comparative obscurity in Council made him feed the flames of jealousy in his colleague's breast by a proud sequestering of himself, while he resolutely claimed the exclusive distribution of all patronage. "We who are reputed to be in Mr. Harley's intimacy," writes St. John to Lord Orrery, May 1711, "have few opportunities of seeing him, and none of talking freely with him. As he is the only true channel through which the Queen's pleasure is conveyed to us, there is, and must be, a perfect stagnation till he is pleased to open himself, and set the waters flowing." This festering prejudice had been nursing itself in the hearts of the two, before their common friends discovered its existence. In February, Swift expressed his satisfaction to Lord Peterborough at their love for one another, in spite of the scandal of inconstancy under which Court friendships lie. In May, he was forced to write, "I am not now so secure." Well might he doubt. It was unlikely that St. John would long consent to sit as a subordinate in the Cabinet to which he dictated. It was even improbable that he would consider it prudent to rest quiet in a position, in which all his plans had to be submitted to the carping and timorous supervision of such a principal. The delay, in which he was forced to acquiesce, irritated his appetite. The time was not ripe in the moment of national enthusiasm for another bedchamber plot, which should rudely set aside the popular idol. But it was not in St. John's nature to forget a scheme of aggrandisement, though friends might, as Swift attempted, demonstrate it to be fraught with ruin to himself, as well as his adversary.

He had converted the press into a powerful machine for cementing his party, by concentrating round himself a vast amount of literary power to be pointed and directed by him. Now he devoted his abilities to the task of impressing his political associates with a sense of his own talents, in contrast with his rival's incapacity. His force of character, and mastery over the mysteries of social intercourse, enabled him to employ to this end the collective weight, and the electric sympathy of mind with mind, of which by his day political clubs were become reservoirs. London taverns had been from of old, before the tone of good society had shrunk into a tone of reserve, the favourite resort of men of pleasure and leisure. Every one will remember the brilliant picture drawn of them in the 'Fortunes of Nigel.' Coffee and chocolate houses were of later origin; they did not supersede the life of taverns, but extended it; they afforded, as any number of the Spectator, or the details of Addison's own day indicate, a more habitual resort for the purposes of conversation or business. "Button's" and "Will's" are become names of history. Yet all these were obviously ill adapted for centres of political movements, however well they served for the rendezvous of authors. Clubs filled up the void. The name is an anachronism, when applied before the age of the Revolution. The conception was not realised in the conclaves which listened to the Republican dreams of Harrington and Sidney. That was reserved for the comparatively free epoch of the reign of William, and the adventurous propagandism of the statesmen of the next.

The Kit-Cat Club, founded by Lord Somers, in conjunction with Prior, Congreve, and Jacob Tonson, the bookseller, met in summer at the Upper Flask, Clarissa Harlowe's

Upper Flask, on Hampstead Heath; the rest of the year in Shire Lane, at the house of that inauspiciously-named baker of mutton-pies, Christopher Cat. Whig it was, heart and soul. Whig sentiments alone were given; Whig witticisms alone were allowed; Whig beauties, as we learn from Lady Mary Wortley Montagu, who herself had, as a child, enjoyed the distinction, were the only toasts. Wit or rank was a necessary condition of admittance; and dinner was served at the ultra-fashionable hour of three. Hard drinking seems to have been, though not its monopoly, at once the principle and art of the Beef-steak Club, rather than politics. Presbyterian Liberals do not appear to have had any such society. The Calves'-head Club was a reunion for the remnant of the implacable Cromwellians, being designed to commemorate the execution of Charles I. The October Club, so called from the devotion of its members, mostly country gentlemen of the rank of squires, to mighty October ale, was instituted for party purposes, and comprehended almost a third of the Commons. Harley was no favourite within the walls of the Clock tavern, in Westminster, where the members met. They supported his measures; they did not disguise their dislike to his character, nor their suspicion of his ulterior intentions. St. John, on the contrary, they received with open arms; the licence of his private life was excused in their eyes by his persecution of everything unorthodox, in a generation which had no spare energies for the championship of morality, whether against him or a Wharton. They may have thought him too clever; his fierceness atoned. But even of St. John they would make no inspired prophet: he must first conquer their confidence. At a subsequent period, he wrote savagely to Wyndham of the House of Commons and the Tory members, that "they grew, like hounds, fond of the man who shows them game, and by whose halloo they are used to be encouraged." A blinder confidence was kept for men such as Nottingham, or, still more, Rochester.

The death of Rochester did not merely remove an

obstruction from the path of the Treasurer, but also, by depriving the Tories of their hereditary leader, abandoned them to the conduct of the younger statesman. St. John, however, required a more manageable and more obedient centre, from which his theories and principles might be propagated through the nation. The society of The Brothers —they would not call it a Club—was instituted in June, 1711, for twelve, and afterwards sixteen members. It included, beside St. John, the Dukes of Ormond and Shrewsbury, the latter a discontented Whig and a most fatal convert to Toryism, Swift, Prior, Arbuthnot, and Wyndham. Neither the Treasurer nor Harcourt was a member, though their sons were admitted. In it was contained the germ of the literary "Scriblerus Club," far better known to posterity. The members and their wives were supposed to be linked together by the closest friendship. It was but an extension or modification of the Saturday dinner at Harley's house, with St. John substituted as president. As Harley's guests, before the outbreak, in May, of the bitter mutual jealousies, the Secretary, Swift, Harcourt, Rivers, and that capricious faithless genius, Peterborough, the Tory hero, and the Don Quixote of his age, for valour, though not for truthfulness, had met weekly to dine and confer. Over their beloved champagne, or more beloved tokay, they had listened reverentially to the counsels of the despotic Dean, as Scipio and Lælius to the poet Ennius; only, the viands were rather superior to the pot-herbs which, on Cicero's authority, we must believe formed the staple of the Roman banquets. The "society" really served chiefly the purposes of St. John's rivalry. He pretended that its object was to correspond, in the higher ranks of the Tory party, to the influence among the Whigs of the Kit-Cat. "The first regulation," say St. John's proposals for the formation of it, "and that which must be inviolably kept, is decency. None of the extravagance of the Kit-Cat is to be endured." The founder required a standpoint from which to propel popular opinion. All his friends became apostles to spread his views: some of them are accepted as of finer intellect than their master; from him came the impetus which set their minds working. He might safely embellish his projects with their wit and thought, or borrow ideas from them; as Mirabeau pressed the masterpieces of ancient and modern eloquence into his service. All came forth bearing the genuine stamp of his genius. The preachers of the new gospel traced their inspiration to him.

The defect of his nature was, that there was not sufficient ballast for the weight of sail. He would be first always; and not borrow, but found a system. His talents made him lead; there was not enough of judgment, patience, sympathy, or, above all, consistency, to constitute a successful leader. His career, in all its several divisions, had ever the same features. It left a profound impression of force, which may be traced in contemporary literature, but he could never keep his levies long from disbanding. His immediate survivors were unable to explain the sudden decline of the influence of his ideas, when the man, with his contagious strength of will, was gone; posterity cannot understand whence arose his influence at the first. In his own day, the momentum and energy of his character, with its extraordinary subtlety and keen perceptions, were sufficiently visible impulses. His is one of the periods when an individual palpably moved Europe. The proper circumstances were given; the spot on which the machinery was to be set up had been prepared. He had reorganised and collected the scattered powers of the Tories, turning against the Whigs their own peculiar artillery of the press. The author and head of the Cabinet had been reduced by his lieutenant's superior capacity to a titular dignitary, his friends detached from him, and his programme forgotten. The victor now put forth his strength to achieve a measure which he regarded as the index of his own and his party's predominance, and a patent for it of perpetuity. The hatred felt for a league with the Dutch by the Tories was only equalled by their hatred of a war with France. Yet they had found it necessary to accede to both these measures, from the patriotic fear of royal treachery, in the reign of

Charles II., and of popular feeling, in their brief intervals of power under William. Godolphin's originally Tory Administration had yielded to this incubus. Harley, and the majority of his Tory colleagues, though encouraged by the Queen, did not venture to throw it off. St. John, however often wanting in moral fortitude, had abundance of political courage. The difficulties which deterred others were a spur to him; he preferred having the whole of the risk, and the whole of the glory. It would be a noble exploit, he thought, in itself; and would ensure his pre-eminence among his adherents, and with Anne. The negotiation of the peace of Utrecht was the glory of his term of office. It was not merely the conclusion of a sanguinary war; it was the inauguration of a change of European policy, which lasted till towards the retirement of Walpole, when that great Minister resigned his peaceful tactics in deference to clamour.

Even at this distance of time, opinions diametrically differ on the expediency of the peace, apart from any suspicions of treachery in its author. His own declared contrition for having compromised the balance of power by deserting the United Provinces, and not forcing a breach in the brazen wall of France, will not be taken at more than its proper value. The confederacy of Walpole and Fleury was wonderfully efficacious in opening his eyes to the want of patriotism which any alliance with France indicated. There could be no doubt of the danger to Europe from the not improbable union of two contiguous realms like France and Spain, had the Duc de Berri died and Philip disavowed his renunciation of the French succession. A forgetfulness of family ties, even should the two crowns remain separated, was no certainty, as the subsequent alliances of those powers against us proved. On the other hand, the nation had a right to consider whether there were any proximate hope of success in an undertaking, by deserting which no sacred obligations, except perhaps the engagement to the Catalans, would be compromised. It might well hesitate to pronounce authoritatively that a free nation should take a sovereign of another's choosing, and not the next heir. Again, the peril from the present union of the Empire of Germany and Spain, in the person of Charles, was to be set against a possible future conjunction of France and the Peninsula. Men then still believed in the tradition of Spain, as head and fountain of violent Catholic propagandism; they had not forgotten the collective might of Charles V. They were not able to discern, as we can, that the apathy of Spain respecting the Netherlands in William's reign was the result, not of corrupt government merely, but thorough national exhaustion. In addition to all this, we must remember the character of the Imperial House of Austria, always ready to demand subsidies, and to break its own engagements, which might frighten some statesmen from the delivery into its hands of the keys of West Indian commerce. All Ministers felt the impracticability of dealing with a policy essentially and hereditarily selfish. It was not only Harley's Cabinet. Stanhope and the rest who reprobated the desertion of Charles of Hapsburg, confessed that they were induced to form the Quadruple Alliance by the prospect of confining the grasping covetousness of the Emperor within specific limits.

St. John's motives in concluding the treaty which left Spain under the Duke of Anjou, are estimated generally by the light of his subsequent connection with the Pretender. When men had before them the facts, that St. John made peace with France, and afterwards joined the Stuarts, they found no difficulty in imagining an union of cause and effect between the two events. St. John's sincerity in his negotiations with James at the end of Queen Anne's reign is now a foregone conclusion. The Stuart papers, and his own confession to Lord Marchmont, prove it completely. If he acknowledges so much, posterity is to be excused for conjecturing an earlier, though not so complete a collusion with the Court of the exiles. His misfortune was, that this probably true inference, which the country had no right to draw from what is known of the negotiations at Utrecht, it took for granted on the weak evidence of party, or anti-French prejudices. Partly circumstances, and partly the bias of St.

John's disposition, are chargeable with the obloquy attaching to him on the score of the treaty. It was his own particular work, and transacted by him with that appearance of self-confidence and selfish exclusiveness, which rendered him a bad coadjutor in any political enterprise, unless it were an attack. Secrecy and mystery may be necessary in preparing an assault; they are not popular qualities when the captured fort is to be governed.

Hence the peace became the natural point of aggression both for former friends and for open enemies. Harley, as head of the Cabinet, was a party to the conclusion, but had been excluded from knowledge of many of the preliminary manœuvres, in which he might not have had the courage to engage. His personal friends, aware of this, bore no good will to a treaty which was a mark of their chief's humiliation. We may be sure that he himself, the clever Parliamentary Trimmer, the friend of the Nonconformists while leading the Tories, would hardly care to conceal the fact from the Opposition. On the contrary, he blazoned abroad his own insignificance. " While this was doing," writes St. John, " Oxford looked on, as though he had not been a party to all which had passed; broke now and then a jest . . . ; and, on those occasions, when his station obliged him to speak of business, was absolutely unintelligible." The whole Whig connection felt itself aggrieved by such an end to such a war. The memory of its great "Deliverer" was insulted by the commonplace termination to all his confederacies and toils. Whigs exclaimed, that the pledges of England to the Protestantism of Europe had been dishonoured, and its presidency of the league against the breaker of the Edict of Nantes deliberately disowned. Even many Tories had expected more from all the burdens they had borne, and from the splendour with which Marlborough, whom yet they affected to depreciate in comparison with Webb, had suffused the national name.

There were two divisions of the Tory party, which, though united generally against the Whigs, were always suspicious of each other, and not seldom at open war. There were the

Parliamentary Tories, and the great "Country party," the Abhorrers of Charles II.'s reign, the Cavaliers of his father's campaigns. Not so much fear for the Constitution had made the latter recognise the de facto government of William, as fear for the Church. They liked the old peaceful foreign policy of England, though they nourished a prejudice against France, not the less for the thought that there the Stuarts had learned the doctrines which made them unfit rulers of England. William's policy, as Shaftesbury's two reigns before, had caused this national dislike to be transferred to Holland and the allies generally. War with France had become the watchword almost of the Whigs, and the dreaded Hanoverian succession was bound up with the same idea. Thus, with this Tory section the peace was decidedly popular, although, as soon as it was signed, the old jealousy of our neighbours revived, and prevented any concerted resistance to the murmurs of Opposition. The other division, the Parliamentary Tories, had been for the most part implicated in the Revolution, and had too much to lose to approve of any measure which might pave the way for the restoration of the Stuarts. They had conceived, besides, a rooted distrust of the leaders of the larger portion of their own party. The country gentlemen of that section had chosen chiefs of their own, not those hereditary chiefs who become at last fixtures in a party, but active instruments for carrying out and representing their views. Of these the Parliamentary Tories suspected Harley, but they absolutely feared St. John. They saw in him an unscrupulousness, whether rightly or wrongly, which would lead him into any situation best fitted for a display of ingenuity. His evident determination to gratify an inordinate vanity, as his enemies would term it, his talent for affairs, according to his friends, dismayed them, unchecked as he was by the least self-restraint in the choice of means or occasions. Stanhope and Nottingham alike saw in him a resoluteness, which would, to accomplish a party measure, lead him to conspire, though in office, against the established order.

Domestic suspiciousness grievously increased his difficulties as a negotiator. He had, at once, to convince the French Court of the large concessions it must make before peace could be guaranteed by his Administration; to outbid the Dutch and Austrians in popularity at home; and to conceal his procedure, till he should have so far compromised the nation, as to make it virtually impossible for Parliament to draw back. With the array of friends and foes against him, Whigs and Tories, he could not have escaped from a similar storm to that which broke upon Somers and Portland towards the end of the last reign. His morbid love of working in darkness deprived him of the kindness and charity of all sections of opinion in the hour of that fall which public men might in those times count upon with certainty. No nation, no party, suffers itself with impunity to be circumvented, to be duped, even into being done good to against its consent. This was what, according to his own interpretation of his conduct, he did. He deceived the kingdom into deliverance from a war, which was become a nightmare, but henceforth was invested in the popular fancy with ideal lustre. England was tricked into a peace which, however necessary, was an inadequate compensation for so much glory and exhaustion. In vain was the captious rejection of more advantageous conditions, offered at Gertrudenberg, retorted upon the Whigs. They rejoined, that nothing had occurred to justify the acceptance of terms so inferior, or, yet more, to extenuate the infamy of abandoning the Catalans. Secretaries of State might wonder at what they deemed " the stupid obstinacy " of patriots, fighting for their hereditary liberties, as St. John called it in a letter to the Queen; but nations often have a conscience, which party leaders, as Walpole, who have it not themselves, know how to rouse, for selfish purposes, against official violators of justice.

The whole affair was involved in mystery. Secret agents, the Abbé Gautier and Prior, traversed in disguise England and France. Mesnager, and Dubois, the future statesman, appeared in London. Informal powers, countersigned by no Minister, not sealed with the great seal, were forwarded from Windsor; Harley and Shrewsbury were hurried on by the audacious Secretary; and, suddenly, the nation woke up to find the campaigns of Marlborough matters of history, and itself committed to articles of which no party, no statesman approved, but one with the reputation of a political adventurer.

His work was still by no means over. The allies might rouse the nation to disavow its diplomatists. Marlborough and Eugene might open a campaign so brilliant as to necessitate a rise in our demands. Parliament might refuse to ratify what had been so informally done as to be the act of an individual, and not of a cabinet. Swift's journal to Stella depicts the confusion of parties, and excitement of St. John, whose spirit rose to the level of the occasion. An amendment to the Address was actually carried in the Lords, since the Revolution a Whig assembly, to the effect, that no peace could be safe and honourable which left the Spanish Indies and the Peninsula in the hands of the Bourbons. Harley, who did not dare to cast off his dangerous colleague, yet would not openly subscribe to his measures, was not present. The friends of the Secretary and himself affected surprise at the apathy of the head of the Government, as if in all the transaction he did not feel his degradation from that position, though without the boldness to break with the man, now the only intermediary between him and advanced Tories. In the Lower House the fascination exerted by St. John kept the party together. The same amendment was rejected there by 232 to 106. All the resources of intrigue and faction were called out by his inventive mind. De Foe, ever grateful for his freedom, though calling himself a true Whig still, wrote, unconscious of the estrangement of the Treasurer from his colleagues, to vindicate the peace from the charge of being a desertion of William's constant policy. Swift, with a less scrupulous partisanship, poured forth a whole hail-storm of Grub Street parodies and invectives on the leader of the " Hanoverian " or " whimsical " Tories, to use St. John's phrases—

"The orator dismal of Nottinghamshire,
Who has forty years let out his conscience for hire."—

whose junction with the Opposition on the peace silenced resistance to the long-mooted "Occasional Conformity Bill." The same scourge fell, in the "Windsor Prophecy," on the Whig Duchess of Somerset, against whom Swift enigmatically warned the too partial Queen, "Beware of carrots;" and on the great General, who had long been used, though he never grew reconciled, to the names of "Harpy" and "Crassus."

At last, the partisans of peace felt strong enough to strike openly at their adversaries. It was not Swift's insulting pen, nor the unpopularity of a tedious war, nor the Ministerial majority in the House of Commons, which left them at liberty to commence the assault. It was the Queen's detestation of the whole family connection of the Churchills, comprising the Godolphins, Sunderlands, and the Duke and Duchess themselves, which freed St. John's hands. He had leave to propose in the Commons a Committee of Inquiry into the public expenditure of the late Lord Treasurer. In vain did Walpole declaim and argue. The October Club had its eye on him also, though for the moment there were older foes to be singled out. The integrity of Godolphin himself was unimpeachable; but Marlborough did not escape. Custom, and the Queen's direct permission, were pleaded, in excuse of his malversations, to no purpose. The plea, though perhaps true in form, was, when we consider the Duchess's despotism over her mistress, too little equitable, in fact, to justify Lord Stanhope's indignation, in his able History of England, at the "baseness of bringing a charge of peculation." Anne gladly took advantage of the doctrine which screens the Sovereign from the reproach of inconsistency. She deprived the Duke, at a blow, of employments from which, and his wife's places, he derived the enormous revenue of £64,000 a year. Notwithstanding Harley's caution, the Cabinet had at length succumbed to the dictates of the October Club. The news of so radical a measure, which could be attempted with safety only by the creation of twelve peers in the equally divided House of Lords, where the General's interest was strongest, struck dismay into the Protestant and Germanic confederacy. Prince Eugene came over, in the futile hope of dissuading the Queen, or the not unreasonable expectation of creating such a storm of personal enthusiasm as to compel the resumption of the old policy. The former danger was dispelled by the insensibility of Anne, and the vigilance of St. John, who, in a royal audience accorded to the famous Captain, bore the brunt of the conversation. The latter, and more formidable one, was obviated by the momentary popularity of the peace, and some ridiculous reports of an intention on the Prince's part to seize the reins of government.

All the heads of the Whig party were marked down for destruction by the October Club. Harley shuddered at the large majorities which affirmed Ministerial motions. St. John did not participate in these fears. He must in far different times have looked back with regretful exultation upon the day when a charge of peculation, a terrible engine for those corrupt days, was brought to bear on his enemy Walpole. All this time only his name appears in State affairs. The Treasurer still had the disposal of patronage; his influence over Anne had already passed into the hands of the friend and flatterer of Lady Masham. We see traces of this in the secret cooperation of the Sovereign. While England believed the negotiations were being conducted at Utrecht, St. John was quietly transacting the whole matter with Torcy. Ormond, whose presence in arms in the Netherlands still kept the Opposition quiet, was secretly instructed, by order of the Queen in Council, to refrain from any deed of active hostility. But the veil was soon to be lifted. Pulteney, a name inseparable from opposition, though sometimes with, and sometimes, as we shall see, against St. John, detected the difference between the public and private instructions to the General. The leader of the Commons boldly avowed his plan, and took credit for his management. On the 6th of June, 1712, the Queen came in state to communicate to the Houses the propositions for peace.

On the prorogation, which shortly followed, St. John was

elevated to the peerage as Baron St. John of Lidiard-Tregoze, and Viscount Bolingbroke, ancient titles of two branches of his family. It might be thought the culmination of his prosperity. The grant of a peerage, unless to a lawyer, is considered an equivocal compliment to a politician, as, in fact, an intimation of past rather than present vigour. This was not the opinion, even so late as Anne's reign. The power of the Commons had been acknowledged since the Great Rebellion; but the House was scarcely the place where a Minister preferred to publish his larger schemes of policy. In the Commons the leader was too much the slave of a violent and prejudiced mob like the October Club. We may fairly question whether the desire of a serener political atmosphere were the influential motive with St. John. As a Tory, even as a Minister, he was a radical; but his radicalism was that of a nobly-born demagogue, who advocates the popular privileges to cast down some superior of his own order. The chagrin he evinced at the inferiority of his title to that of Harley, a man " bred up in the Inns of Court," bears out this view. His consent to be ennobled was due not so much to the wish for leisure from the daily contests of a popular assembly, nor again, to the need of a counterpoise to the tremendous weight of Whig eloquence and sagacity in the Upper House, as to the vanity of shining with a title, and the ambition of arguing in the Painted Chamber with his hat on. The party does not seem to have lost much from his transplantation. The Tories hardly wanted a champion in the Commons. There it was esteemed a weakness, if not a sign of corruption, in a member to change sides on account of an eloquent speech. The Minister could, though sitting among the Peers, yet grasp the reins, and know how and when to loosen them. The thorn in his coronet was his colleague's earldom. He had coveted a revival for himself of the just extinct earldom of Bolingbroke. In after-life he wrote, that he " was dragged into the House of Lords, in such a manner as to make his promotion a punishment, not a reward; and was there left to defend the treaties almost alone." With no gratitude to his Queen and country he set off for Paris, where the open conferences were to be held.

The brilliant statesman of thirty-two was sure of favourable judges at the Court of Louis XIV. He was fitted to shine in that rendezvous of politics and pleasure. He laid the foundation of some friendships which served him well when a fugitive; and he may, perhaps, have had, as his enemies reported, confidential communications with the Stuarts. His journey did not conduce to the popularity of his Administration. The tone of sympathy with France was disliked, and the Jacobite relations of the Tories furnished a fruitful topic for whispers of treason. On the whole, however, in spite of the natural murmurs of Opposition, he was well satisfied with the definite conclusion of the negotiations. In the midst of his triumph he attempted to conciliate the Whigs. Willingly, at Swift's request, he invited to dinner their common literary adversary, Addison. The party was rather constrained, till drinking, protracted from two or three o'clock till midnight, at last warmed the distinguished guest to a friendly political fervour. In his enthusiasm he made his host toast Lord Somers, and began sociably to discuss the peace with the negotiator of it. It was always St. John's policy, and perhaps inclination, to stand well with literature. Especially, on the eve of the first appearance of "Cato," was there reason for seeming to be on good terms with Joseph Addison. He might hope to ward off an application of the moral of the play to his own conduct, by the conscious innocence indicated by intimacy with the poet. His dexterous reference of the tirades against Cæsar to the patent for life which the Whig Commander-in-Chief had once demanded is well known. A harder conflict awaited Bolingbroke in Parliament than at a drinking-bout. All Arthur Moore's and De Foe's sagacious arguments for free trade with France, with all the zeal of the Minister's private following in the same cause, were ineffectual to save the eighth and ninth articles in the Treaty of Commerce. The House of Commons feared that the free importation of Bordeaux and Burgundy would destroy the gainful woollen trade with Portugal, and refused to resign a certain advantage for an uncertain. Calculations were made, showing that the annual balance against England, had the articles been approved, would have probably been not much under a million and a half.

The national jealousy of France gained for Opposition this unexpected victory. The feeling extended even to the moderate members of the Tory party, as represented by Sir Thomas Hanmer. They had been eager to check William's continental policy, but could not be won over to confer anything resembling a favour on the ancient enemy. A more statesmanlike and nearer anxiety respecting the succession was added to this hereditary prejudice. The apprehensions were, in some measure, justified by the characters of the present holders of office. Of them, Harley had accumulated so confirmed a character for insincerity, that he was trusted neither by his own nor by the opposite party. Not opponents alone would cordially hate a man, who "loved tricks, when not necessary, from an inward satisfaction in applauding his own cunning." "If any man was born under the necessity of being a knave, he was," writes Lord Cowper in January, 1706, when his colleague and guest. Even partisans suspected a chief, " who," says Lockhart in his Commentaries, " was indeed very civil to all who addressed him, but, generally, either spoke so low in their ear, or so mysteriously, that few knew what to make of his replies; it would appear that he took a secret pleasure in making people hang on, and disappointing them." His friend Swift charges him with thinking, "that there is something profound in politics, which men of plain honest sense cannot arrive to." Much of the earlier portion of his political life was passed in hopeless opposition to a party which had placed upon the throne the actual Sovereign. He had become imbued with the spirit of intrigue and distrust of all men. A man can hardly escape imbibing such sentiments who sees his firmest adherents perpetually seceding from him under the temptations of office, and his ranks recruited only by insurgents, or by politicians who intend to pass there their political apprenticeship, and to approve themselves fit for place, by showing themselves to be dangerous; who, lastly, is forced to cut down and pare all his schemes, from dread of detaching one element of the incongruous faction by measures suited to the tastes or passions of another.

In such a school Harley had learned with consummate dexterity to maintain different opinions, at the antipodes in all but their advocates' exclusion from office. He had not learned how to conduct a Cabinet, when the position had at length been attained. He was perplexed by the conflicting claims of friends, Nonconformists and Churchmen, whose sole common topic was love or hatred of the "Occasional Conformity Bill." His habitual "Poh! poh! all will be well;" "Let us go gently," and "Leave it all to me," were rather inadequate watchwords for a faction whose trust was in action, and, it might be, revolution. In his perplexity he remained neutral, a spectator of the proceedings of his own Cabinet, allowing his colleagues to carry through, uncurtailed, measures certain to disgust half his supporters. He cherished the vain hope, as well that he could not be held responsible for acts he had never advised, as that he might gain a sublime and evident ascendency over his subordinates by sequestering himself from their petty quarrels, and by being known among them only as the dispenser of all patronage, and the Sovereign's friend. With such a character opponents could expect from his treachery or weakness no guarantee for the Protestant succession. If he found the Jacobite cause clearly the stronger, they could not hope that he would refuse his adhesion to any Jacobite plot of his fellow-Ministers. The mere fact that he remained nominal head of the Cabinet, though scarcely one of its proposals had his hearty assent, though against his express advice] it pardoned apologists for the Stuarts, though it instigated the Queen to rebuke addresses of the Lords against the exiles, and to compel Marlborough's favourite officers to sell their commissions, proved how little reliance could be placed either on his paternal love for the Act of Settlement, or his antagonism to his Jacobitish

Secretary of State. The selection of Bromley, the suspected member for the University of Oxford, as Secretary, in Lord Dartmouth's place, and the appointment to the Exchequer of Sir William Wyndham, close friends, as both were, of the banished family and of St. John, gave additional reason for fearing the preponderance in the Ministry of a spirit much more daring than that of Harley. The promotion of Dean Atterbury, a zealous writer in the Examiner, to the See of Rochester was as significant.

The elections of August, 1713, only partially showed how the nation construed all these signs. Popular discontent was chiefly manifested in the strength of the so-called Hanoverian or Protestant Tories returned by the old decaying market-towns under the influence of the clergy. The Opposition had at length a good cry of its own, and Government found no retort to the reproach of the desertion of the gallant Catalans, and the odium of its defeated Reciprocity Compact. There was no persecution now of a Sacheverell; there was no military dictatorship, with which to alarm the nation's suspicions. Ministers could only call upon their partisans to stand by the throne, the security of which their principles, it was contended, alone endangered, and rehearse equivocal sentiments upon the beauty of hereditary right, which a foe on the opposite coast was eager to illustrate. With this for their only standard, and not even a Cabinet ready to risk an open assertion of the belief, there were fatal dangers ahead for the Administration. We cannot think Bolingbroke judged wrongly, on his own principles, in intimating quickly the course he meant to pursue. It may have been an instinct before, which made this favourite of the October Club intrigue to wrest the first place from Harley; it may have been vanity. Now, it was the last desperate resource of a tottering party. His cause was certain to lose much numerical strength could he succeed. A much more furious hostility would proceed from opponents with whom Harley had kept up relations, and been a sort of bail for the loyalty of his companions to the Constitution. But the confederates would at length have concord in their own body, and liberty to deliberate unreservedly about their concealed projects. Concealed they were only from Cabinet Councils. The whole of England took them for granted, so that the Ministry which had espoused such opinions had at once the disadvantage of their unpopularity, and a prohibition imposed upon them, both of repelling insinuated charges which they refused to consider relevant to themselves, and of taking measures for accomplishing that revolution to which these charges pointed.

Perils were on every side. A majority in the Commons, in spite of Whig denunciations of the unfortunate Treaty of Commerce, and the general show of Whig woollen "favours" at the late elections, still mechanically endorsed Ministerial resolutions. Expulsion from the House by a majority of a hundred votes, for the authorship of the "Crisis," taught Steele that it was a libel on the October Club to maintain that the Protestant succession was in danger. The Whigs were not disheartened. In the House of Lords they had always been in a majority, as far as intellectual power went, and, previously to 1712, numerically. They avenged Steele's cause by committing the publisher and printer of Swift's anonymous answer, 'The Public Spirit of the Whigs.' Only by the shrewd device of instituting a prosecution against the same two victims did Harley save his friend from the consequences of their evidence. In vain Government endeavoured to check popular suspicions by motions that the Protestant succession was in no danger under her Majesty's Administration. In the Lords, the resolution was the signal for an ominous secession. Lord Anglesea, an old friend of St. John, exclaimed, glancing at the unlucky Treasurer, "that he durst pursue an evil Minister from the Queen's closet to the Tower, and thence to the scaffold!" Even in the Tory Commons, the effrontery of the thing reduced the majority to 48. The Treasurer grew frightened and more Constitutional. The manœuvre of the Whig Junto, in making the Hanoverian envoy demand a writ of summons for the Electoral Prince, as Duke of Cambridge furnished him with an occasion for manifesting his disagreement with his colleagues, and attachment to the House of Brunswick, as well as his pique at the Queen's estrangement. Yet he could not be forced to declare himself sufficiently anti-Tory to furnish a pretext for his ejectment from the Cabinet. He escaped the ambush of Wyndham's Schism Bill by the plea of not having considered the matter. He listened in silence to St. John, an almost avowed deist, arguing for it as a bulwark of the Church; nor could be drawn to defend a friend, even by the vengeful attack of Nottingham, who had the self-restraint to reject the bait of the Bill in his desire to conciliate the Nonconformists, on "a certain divine who, hardly suspected of being a Christian, is in a fair way of being a bishop."

It has been sometimes assumed, that Harley had at heart the Restoration of the Stuarts, and was only converted to the opposite opinion by his rivalry with the favourite of the October Club. The hypothesis is hardly even plausible. He had never been a Jacobite. Chosen leader of the country gentlemen, he soon gladly exchanged his prominence among them for the headship of a coalition characterised by one broad feature, opposition to the great Whig houses of the Revolution. We cannot suppose that his cautious nature and liberal tenets coexisted with a craving for arbitrary rule. His genius was altogether Parliamentary, and not made, as that of his rival, for the office of vizier to an almost absolute Sovereign. His passions were not strong enough to move him to purchase the right of persecuting at the risk of enduring the same treatment in turn. His negotiations with Marshal Berwick, and the equivocal admonitions to the Pretender to quit France for Venice, prove no more than the mission of his brother to Hanover, if so much. Now, at all events, Anne's alienation, and his desertion by all the high Tories of the Government, ensured his Constitutionalism. Traces are discernible of a convulsive attempt by the falling statesman to effect a coalition with the Whigs and the Hanoverian Tories, by the instrumentality of his former colleague, Cowper. The taint of insincerity throughout his career must finally have vitiated any such negotiation; but St. John's vigour disconcerted the preliminary advances. The Queen had a parting interview with her old servant. She accused him of indolence in the conduct of public business, of a complete want of truthfulness, of unintelligible mysteriousness in all his statements, and of often coming drunk to confer on matters of State. It was a strange collection of her wrongs as a lady and as a Sovereign, and evinces how intermingled as yet were the two ideas. Either she had never liked him, and, with her prudent egotism, merely accepted his aid against yet more detested personages, the Marlboroughs; or, a term of office had exaggerated his natural slovenliness and carelessness; or, more probably still, the sway of St. John over the great party which Anne, by a monarchical instinct really loved, even while sometimes fearing it, had communicated a sentiment of aversion for the man who hindered the consummation of its projects. She had, to enforce this propensity, the perpetual company of a woman, once the friend of Harley, now his bitterest foe, on account of shameful ingratitude on his part, as she would have said; for having refused to bribe her with public money, according to the report of his adherents; both explanations being, the Treasurer's character allows us to believe, at one and the same time correct.

The defection of his old followers seems to have been partly the result of dread of his extreme wariness in a crisis requiring boldness; principally, of the extraordinary capacity of St. John for infusing into his immediate intimates confidence in his energy and genius. At any rate, no man could have resisted the combination of his own colleagues and the majority in the Commons. The final scene appears to have blended historical solemnity with the petulance of a catastrophe in genteel comedy. The personal connection of Sovereign and Minister, of which the Government of Lord North is our latest perfect example, conjoined with a sense of Ministerial responsibility to the country, fully recognised, though not always acted upon, gave to the interview at once the air of a private quarrel between friends, each accusing the

other of faithlessness, and the lofty tone of a patriot's warning
to rulers ready to put in jeopardy their country's happiness out
of private spite. St. John and Lady Masham were there, to
keep the Queen to her resolution, and to triumph over their
old friend. Almost to the moment they had maintained
their ancient appearance of intimacy. In the midst of all
this history of mines and countermines, we hear of friendly
little suppers at the Mashams, of strolls together in the Mall,
and familiar conversations. Now the parting was indeed come.
Harley, with all the wrath of a betrayed friend, and the pro-
phetic forebodings of a retiring Minister, predicted the anger
of an incensed nation against the miserable ambition and
traitorous schemes of the Cabinet he had formed. The prophecy in part brought its own accomplishment. Anne had
been deeply agitated by the scene. She had long been per-
turbed both by remorse, at having, on her own view of the
indefeasible right of kingship, usurped and kept her brother's
inheritance, and by resentment, that her most loyal subjects
were calculating on her death as the removal of an obstruction
to the reversion of the crown to the rightful owner. Under
this conflict of emotions her vital powers gave indications
of decay. Her mortal disorder manifested itself on the
29th of July, 1714. A Council was summoned, at which the
Duke of Shrewsbury presided. He had been, as a youth, a hero
of the Revolution. Once again his old liberalism revived;
and he openly rejoined that party which had till then looked
on him as a deserter. The appearance of his name in the
Elector's secret instrument of Regency, which had been for
some time past in the hands of the Hanoverian envoy, proves
he must have so acted as to be counted upon by the chiefs on
both sides. Few statesmen of this age can, we fear, be placed
for honesty far above the systematically false Sunderland
and Marlborough. At Shrewsbury's invitation, the Whig
Dukes of Argyle and Somerset took their seats in the Privy
Council, though not members of the Ministry. Probably on
their proposal, though St. John's friends declared it was on
his, Shrewsbury was nominated to the Queen High Treasurer.

Alas for Bolingbroke! "The Earl of Oxford was removed on Tuesday—the Queen died on Sunday! What a world is this, and how does Fortune banter us!" It is St. John's groan to Swift in a letter of August 3. The prize had been wrested from the grasp of his rival; he had gained nothing by it, except a schism in his party. All the work of so much intriguing, eloquent pamphleteering, and subservience to the littleness of factious spleen, was nullified in a moment. His plan, as future head of the Government, had been elaborated. It shows much judgment and self-restraint in him that he had decided on retaining the Seals of the Foreign Office, in preference to the glittering bauble of the Lord Treasurership; while the names of Wyndham, Ormond, Harcourt, Buckinghamshire, Bromley, Mar, and Atterbury, point, at least, to a more decidedly Tory policy than had prevailed in the old Cabinet. At the same time, envoys had their instructions for coquetting with the Electoral Court. Now, when he acted on his own sole responsibility, he began to comprehend the caution of his predecessor. He even sought to establish friendly relations with the principal Whigs. Would that we had the details of a banquet at which he entertained Walpole, Stanhope, and Pulteney, a few days before the Queen's death, at his mansion in Golden Square! What speeches full of flowing courtesy were there delivered! What disclaimers of private enmity, notwithstanding the strifes of political interests! Little could a stranger have augured the fierceness of the cry for blood, which those amiable guests would soon raise with one accord against their host, or the yet more rooted rancour of disappointed friendship, which should avenge him in the future enmity of all the three.

Had the Queen but sanctioned the Minister's nominations one half hour before her death, he might have selected his policy in safety, and either restored the exiles, or made terms for himself with Hanover. As it was, with a Cabinet all his own, with Anne willing to accept his counsels, the deadweight of three Whig Dukes, backed by and backing the Constitution, could not be resisted. The Ministry had a great majority in Parliament, but chiefly of country gentlemen, independent members, each acting for himself, and joining in the same votes from choice, and not in obedience to the dictation of their leaders. The Whigs were a compact body. They had faith in their champions, and these could advocate any measure with the certainty that it would be supported. They had overturned an ancient dynasty. Their names far outweighed those of men like Bromley, and Mar, and the unstable Peterborough.

Added to the mortification at the loss of all the advantages of his machinations, were many petty vexations inseparable from so peculiar a conjuncture. The Regency, appointed already by secret instructions of the Elector, did not attempt to soften them. He was superseded in all the real duties of his office, and compelled to attend with his bag outside the Council Chamber, where he had so long ruled, till it should please his enemies to admit him. Very few men would have the philosophy to bear patiently these trivial affronts. Bolingbroke was not of the few. His troubles were not to end here. He took up an attitude neither of defiance nor of submission. With Harley he assisted at the coronation of the new King, and, we are told by Lady Cowper, "bowed three times down to the very ground" in doing homage. He intimated his willingness to take office, should it be the policy of the new dynasty to rule independently of party. "On the same principle," he writes to Lord Strafford, as he had served Anne, " will I serve the King, if he employs me." But it was not the policy of the Whigs to encourage coalitions. When offered place by Harley they had refused. It was unlikely that they would now, in the day of their triumph, consent to share their power and forego revenge. Lord Cowper, in a memorial presented to the King, argued that it was not for the safety of his House to attempt any such partition of favours, and intimated that the Whigs would not consent to have the experiment tried.

They were not of a temper to spare an enemy who refused

to solicit their mercy. His whole demeanour was that of a man who may have been mistaken, but, having acted conscientiously, keeps his own opinion, though not condemning the opposite. He proposed in the Lords, in a fine oration which lived in men's memories, the substitution of the word "maintain," for "recover," with respect to the reputation of the kingdom in its foreign relations. The Duke of Shrewsbury, the immediate cause of his present downfall, in vain supported the amendment. Everywhere he saw nothing but hostility. The country had returned a Whig majority to the Commons, of 244 to 138 who still dared to call themselves Tories. The names of the new Ministry, notwithstanding the admittance of the Hanoverian Tory Nottingham, indicated what reliance could be placed on the King's assurances that he would not be a partisan. Harley trusted to his late ignominious expulsion from the Cabinet, and to his carefully preserved relations with the Nonconformists and the Electoral Court. St. John's hope was, not so much in the justice or mercy of Parliament, as in the impossibility of his condemnation even by Whigs, without proof of collusion between him and Versailles or St. Germains. His compromising papers were in security; and only one confidant existed who had anything dangerous to tell. This was Matthew Prior. Never was a friend more trusted than he by St. John, never a dependent treated more as an equal. We may well pity the fallen Minister, when he heard that Prior had landed at Dover under an engagement to reveal all. He could not tell, what we have reason for believing, that the whole was a device to concentrate expectation on the envoy's disclosures, and then, by their triviality, to convince the nation of the injustice of its suspicions of the late Government. He only knew that Prior had been granted an audience by the King, that he was now at dinner with Townshend and Stanhope. The news, communicated according to an uncertain rumour by Marlborough, followed him to Drury Lane Theatre on March 26, 1715. He sat through the spectacle, bespoke the performance for the following night, and then, in the disguise of a French

Messenger, set off for Dover. In another day and a half he was on the French shores, and a ruined exile.

His flight was a blunder. It betrayed a want of moral courage, and was esteemed proof presumptive of criminality. Yet not many would have acted differently in the circumstances. The Whigs raged against him; a doggrel ballad expressed the thirst of the populace for his blood. His imagination pictured the late victorious leader of Parliament reduced to supplicate its compassion, and dwelt on the humiliation of kneeling at the bar before his Peers in a partnership of odium and guilt with the detested Harley. His personal friends were dispersed; Swift gone to Ireland, in wrath against the disunited Cabinet, "to die like a poisoned rat in a hole;" Prior presumed a traitor to friendship; his Jacobite followers furious with their chief for his procrastination; he furious with himself for the same. His fears were not altogether groundless. The two-years' imprisonment of his rival proves, that, though he had escaped the scaffold, a dreary doom for his impatient temperament would have awaited him. On release from prison he could not hope to be allowed to return to public life; and his nature was too fiery to have rested satisfied with the literary leisure which contented Lord Oxford. Harley in his gardens and magnificent library, in the chief treasures of which his name still survives, enjoyed the repose, never lost sight of by him in the most tempestuous season of his intriguing life. The plots of St. Germains, and the feverish extravagances of the Regent's Court, alone might deaden the younger statesman's regrets for the sweets of power so briefly tasted, and his lust of revenge upon old friends and old foes. His departure from England scandalised his few remaining partisans, and seemed to sanction the vituperations of his enemies. His coeval, Robert Walpole, his evil genius, born to affairs with him, and destined to die to political activity almost at the same time, was the fitting chairman of the secret committee for investigating the conduct of the Ministry in the negotiations of Utrecht. Robert Walpole presented the report and moved the impeachment, not, in the first place, of Lord Oxford, but of Henry Lord Viscount Bolingbroke.

It was a foregone conclusion. Only two voices were raised in his defence, those of General Ross and Mr. Hungerford. The news of the resolution, which passed on the 10th of June, and of the readier process by bill of attainder, founded upon it, soon reached its object. He had already established a secret connection with the Pretender, in anticipation. Sometimes it has been questioned whether his intercourse with that Court had been of long continuance. The Stuart Papers and de Torcy's Memoirs show that scarcely a single statesman of any account, of any party, whether in or out of office, in the reign of William and Anne, refrained from corresponding with the exiles. It is paradoxical to seek to clear the chosen companion of the chiefs of semi-Jacobite clubs from the general reproach. The declared Jacobitism of many of his especial instruments in the Cabinet, as Mar and Ormond, with his hostility to all supporters of the Protestant succession, is circumstantial evidence. The conclusion is corroborated by his bias against the Dutch, however weak an argument if standing alone. We are, at all events, justified in agreeing with Count Rémusat's summing up in 'L'Angleterre au Dix-Huitième Siècle,' a work to which all students of the period are deeply indebted: "La trahison envers la succession hanovrienne entra au besoin dans ses calculs, et fut au nombre des expédiens qu'il se réservait.".

St. Clair, on the left bank of the Rhone, near Vienne, had been the retreat of the fallen statesman. When the tidings came of the vindictiveness of the Whig Parliament, neither its charms, nor the greater of Madame de Tencin, the fascinating and dissolute mother of D'Alembert, could restrain him, though ill in bed with a low fever, from responding at once to an invitation from the Chevalier. With the royal courtesy and tact, which contrasted favourably with the German brusqueness of the first Georges, the titular earldom of the Bolingbrokes, their descendant's never forgotten object, was revived for him. "I cannot, you know," wrote the

Prince, "as yet, give you very essential proofs of my kindness; but the best I can do for so good and faithful a servant" —perhaps a poor compliment to one who always described himself as now for the first time a Jacobite—" is in sending you the enclosed warrant, which raises you a degree higher than my sister had done before, and which will fix your rank with me beyond dispute." The Jacobites, with the active cooperation of Ormond, still braving Whig violence in London, had resolved upon two movements, one in the south of England, the other in the Highlands. St. John persuaded them that the two, to have a chance of success, must be simultaneous. The secret of his influence at St. Germains and Commercy consisted in his perfect acquaintance with the spirit and sentiments of the present French Ministers, through whom advantage might have been taken of the capricious change in popular opinion now exalting Ormond and Harley into martyrs as representatives of the Church party. His ill-luck dogged the Pretender's new Secretary of State. At the beginning of July he had arrived at the little Court. On the first of September, 1715, died Louis XIV., and with him all the zeal of France for the restoration of the Stuarts, and all the authority at the French Court of the negotiator of the peace of Utrecht. The Regent Duke of Orleans was anxious for a good understanding with England, the Power most interested in supporting his title as heir presumptive against Philip of Spain. He had no kindness for the policy of a Cabinet from which he had been sedulously excluded. The small knot of exiles soon understood that their Secretary was not more powerful at the Regent's Court than themselves. They made him feel what a counterfeit his office was, as compared with the reality he had left behind in England. His positive experience, and perhaps a feeling of contempt, not entirely concealed, for minute unproductive intrigues, led him to display a conscious superiority which offended men, each of whom thought himself more of a victim to principle. He soon found reason to be disgusted with himself for his flight, and, as he declares to Wyndham in a famous letter, for his precipitancy in casting in his lot with a set of desperate outcasts. His sagacity saw the folly of the dreams of his associates, " some, who could read and write, having letters to show, and those who had not arrived to this pitch of erudition having their secrets to whisper." The crowd of "busy Irish faces," with their rumours of bulls and benedictions and subsidies from Rome, especially annoyed him, conscious as he was of the exclusive dependence of the cause on English Churchmen.

However, he counselled his new master to the best of his ability; and he intrigued in the Jacobite interest with the ladies of the French Court and the Regent's favourites with indefatigable diligence. Indeed, the entire history of the earlier portion of his residence in Paris is chiefly an unintelligible maze of negotiations with 'Mrs. Olivia Trant.' He rejected offers made by the French Ministers to use their influence with the English Government to procure the pardon of a man who might, on his return home, have greatly furthered their objects. All this was not for long. On the 13th of November the surrender of Preston sealed the fate of English Jacobitism; and on the same day the battle of Sheriffmuir proved of equally decisive importance in Scotland. By the last week in the next February the Pretender was back in Paris. The day following his return, St. John, whom he had received with the greatest demonstrations of affection, was discharged almost contumeliously from his service. This mysterious step was justified in the busy gossip of the Court by reports that the Secretary had joined the party in order, by betraying its secrets, to requite it for the losses his old attachment to the cause had inflicted upon him. An improbable tale can hardly be preferred to the unison of the testimony of Lord Stair, the King of England's ambassador, of Marshal Berwick, and of the published papers of the Pretender's Secretary's office, to his honesty and zeal. Here is the Marshal's opinion of his capacity and fidelity :—" It is admitted by all England that there have been few greater Ministers than Bolingbroke. He was born with splendid talents, which had raised him at a very early age to the highest employments; he exerted great influence over the Tory party, and was, in fact, its soul. . . . I was in part a witness how he acted for King James, while he managed his affairs, and I owe him the justice to say that he left nothing undone of what he could do; he moved heaven and earth to obtain supplies, but was always put off by the Court of France." There is a little more intrinsic plausibility in another story that the punctilious Prince's disgust was excited by the demeanour of his Secretary in one of his not infrequent drunken fits. The probability is that he had prepared the way for his abrupt dismissal by taking no pains to hide his discontent at the misery into which his rash adhesion had brought him. He afterwards asserted that his resolution had been already formed to quit his post, as soon as the affairs of the Stuarts should have been in some sort arranged.

Never was there a man of a spirit less inclined to sit down under an affront, or to neglect the opportunity, afforded by the severance of old ties, of following that in which his soul delighted, a new combination. He was once more the English agitator and pamphleteer, and in much the same attitude as of old. In office he had been the leader of a party opposed, both practically and in principle, to what was, since the Revolution, the actual Constitution of England. It was equally, when in power and in disgrace, a faction, however gallant. During his brief term of service under James, his capacity for organising a plot had been almost dormant; now it blazed up anew, and, from the circumstances which called it forth, demanded all the resources of ingenuity and irony which the friend and partner of Swift possessed. Malcontent Whigs were to be personally courted, and persuaded of the harmlessness of the writer; while sufficient animosity was shown to their doctrines to satisfy his Tory friends. Finally, all the wretched jealousies and disputes of the Court he had just quitted were to be withered up by the scornful pen of this political free lance. The home Government had, from the first, expected his secession from the Jacobite Court. Some, judging him so faithless that he could never refrain from betraying his employers, had authorised Lord Stair to purchase his confessions. Others, more truly, discerned in his character an intellectual restlessness which could never let things be, and must, sooner or later, snap the connection. He was not unwilling to prove them right in their conclusions. His letter to Sir William Wyndham, in its present state, is an attempt at once to justify himself to the English Tories, and to win favour with the Government. The character of the man is, as M. de Rémusat aptly remarks, well illustrated by the fact, that at the very moment when the relenting of the King and Whigs promised his restoration, he drew up, in the manner of Seneca, various reflections on the consolations of exile. If he thought he should no longer need them for personal use, and therefore could spare them to the world, he found himself for some time disappointed. His celebrated Letter was written in the September of 1716; not till 1723 were the incidents of the attainder so far mitigated as to restore him, when a resident in England, to the protection of the laws. The tedious delay was owing partly to the rooted suspicions of the Whig leaders, and partly to Walpole's jealousy of the opponent who had at the first far outstripped him. The discovery of various plots for the reestablishment of the Stuarts, of one especially in which Bishop Atterbury, St. John's ancient ally, was alleged to be implicated, excused their reluctance.

All parties were against him. He was at variance at once with the Jacobite section of the English Tories, though still the friend of Wyndham, and with the adherents of the late Treasurer. He never ceased to cherish a strange implacability against Harley, only to be explained by his belief that to Harley's pertinacity in retaining office had been owing the postponement, till too late, of those plans which might else have secured to their author a dictatorship under a new dynasty. The resurrection of Harley in 1717, through Walpole's coalition with the Tories against the Cabinet from which he had been ejected, must have spoiled many a dream of rural contentment at St. Clair. The popular cry of "High-Church and Harley" would sound in his rival's ears like the war-trumpet to a captive knight. The discord in the victorious Whig party, the cabals of Sunderland and Stanhope against Townshend, and of Townshend and Walpole against Stanhope, cannot but have vibrated even through the non-conducting atmosphere of divine philosophy. Yet in the meantime he did not let life slip by untasted. A main characteristic of his disposition was that, while there could be no one with a more pertinacious constancy in the pursuit of any objects, however various, or however minute, whether of pleasure or of ambition, his nature seems to have had so indomitable an energy and capability of enjoyment, as to employ itself with equal vehemence on a scheme for destroying a system of faith, and on an intrigue in Paris. Vainly did neglected Lady Bolingbroke use all her Hanoverian interest in her husband's service: her lord repaid her exertions with a sneer that his cession of his goods for her benefit to save them from confiscation eventually proved a serious loss to him. In the interval he was falling in love with the Marquise de Villette, niece of Madame de Maintenon, whom he married on the death of his wife, in 1720. For his sake she professed Protestantism. In that same year, under the safeguard of the Regent, whose companion in pleasure, though not in politics, he had always been, he was engaged in eking out, through the enterprises of Law, a subsistence which the £11,000 he brought from England could but ill have supplied. His usual residence was the Chateau of La Source, where, amid fair gardens, rises the Loiret. There, by the aid of Madame de Villette, who was wealthy as well as witty, he learned to despise the world, and studied the addition of new perfections to the marvellous political pamphlet style, destined in future days to gall the callous Walpole. But the gaieties of Paris not unfrequently drew him from philosophical and other speculations. He was peculiarly fitted, with the reputation of his name, the versatility and eccentricity of his genius, to delight alike the courtiers of Versailles and the new school of polite philosophers. Voltaire writes of Milord Bolingbroke in a strain of rapture, which may have been, he half confesses, somewhat heated by the compliments his idol paid to the "Henriade." He describes his universal learning, and the cosmopolitan tastes which French encyclopædists adored. That all these gifts met in a man who had been the greatest *roué* of his time, seems to have kindled in the Frenchman the same glow of enthusiasm as in Swift. He only spoke the general opinion. With the French philosophers of the Entresol Club, as Alary, Count Argenson and the Abbé Charles St. Pierre, with Swift in Dublin, his chivalrous champion against Jacobite maligners, with Pope, Gay, and Arbuthnot in London, down to the miscellaneous crowd of the French Court, the impetus of his mind, and his power of setting the stamp of genius on all pursuits alike, had gained him an universal sway.

At length, his residence in France drew to its close. In May, 1723, the pardon promised in 1715 passed the great seal; but he had no hope, at present, of a Parliamentary restoration in fortune and peerage. Walpole distrusted his professions of friendship, and replied to hints of his power to bring over Lords Gower and Bathurst, and Sir William Wyndham, to the Whigs, by warning him against Tory connections. The Minister had in mere deference to Melesina, Duchess of Kendal, waived the hostility, which in 1719 had drawn from him, in allusion to the acquittal, mainly due to himself, of Harley, the indignant words : "His rival in guilt and power even now presumes to expect an act of the legislature to indemnify him, and to qualify his villainy." On the whole, St. John's reception in England was so chilling as quickly to despatch him back to La Source. Not till the 25th of May, 1725, durst his advocates move his restoration in fortune. Then the bribed Court, the Duchess of Kendal receiving for her share £11,000, only extorted a sullen assent from the Premier by the menace of dismissal. St. John's Parisian friends contributed not a little to the result. They had lamented his departure in 1723; but they used all their influence to effect his complete restitution. Two visits were paid to England by Madame de Villette, whose own considerable English investments were imperilled by her husband's legal disabilities. During the second, she succeeded in buying the good offices of George's ugly mistress. Besides, his foreign acquaintances procured him information of highly serviceable Court secrets. The envoy, Horace Walpole, the Minister's brother, applauded himself for having learnt them "without having given to St. John any handle to become the negotiator of his Majesty's affairs." Lord Townshend, whom they enabled to triumph over Carteret, was more grateful. The Abbé Alary, founder of the Entresol, which, like all French societies of the period, was a social, philosophical, political, and literary reunion, exerted his influence on a visit to England in the same cause. What so many sought was at last granted to the active mediation of Harcourt, become a Whig in 1721, but still mindful of the merry dinners at which the early policy of the Harley Cabinet used to be moulded. The Whigs, on the one side, roused themselves to oppose the motion, under the leadership of Onslow, Methuen, and Poulett, though Walpole, without any affectation of magnanimity, intimated to his adherents that they might be content with the exclusion of their enemy for ever from office and Parliament. On the other, the memory of long severed associations, against the inclination of their Jacobite chiefs, Musgrave and Sebright, appealed for him to the mass of those country gentlemen whom his voice had once woke to victory. The motion passed by a majority of 231 to 113.

He was free to begin the world again; after being tired out, he writes to Swift, "with suspense, the only insupportable misfortune of life, and with nine years of autumnal promises and vernal excuses." Shut out from Parliament, the natural sphere of his talents, he made it his profession to be a Mæcenas to men of letters, and the pattern country gentleman to his neighbours at Dawley, as in the old days when he presided at the October Club. For his political friends he was the secret counsellor, who held in his hands the strings of many a Parliamentary struggle. We find his sway equally acknowledged by literary chiefs, and by Wyndham's political associates. Swift came to England, for the first time since his friend's banishment, to do him homage. He brought over a manuscript destined to overshadow the reputation of the Drapier's letters themselves. Another writer of an influence as yet almost of the future, but of more power to change a nation's spirit than that wielded by the author of Gulliver himself, soon joined the circle. Voltaire had been dazzled by St. John in Paris. Observation of the ardour of English admiration did not diminish his respect. To the contagion of St. John's intellect is owing the infusion of an English tone into Voltaire's works. It is to be hoped that to no indorsement by him of a lying tale current about Lord Cowper's family, and further distorted by the malice of Swift, may be due the account to be found in the 'Dictionnaire Philosophique' of doctrines held by a political adversary on the subject of marriage: "Il est public en Angleterre, et on voudroit le nier en vain, que le Chancellier Cowper épousa deux femmes, qui vécurent ensemble dans sa maison avec une concorde singulière qui fit honneur à tous trois. Plusieurs curieux ont encore le petit livre que ce Chancellier composa en faveur de la polygamie."

Without deserting literary society, the devotee of rural leisure immersed himself in politics as well. Walpole, he conceived, by withholding his readmission into Parliament, had forfeited all title to his gratitude. Tories mistrusted him as a party leader. A way was opened by the jealous and despotic temperament of the Premier for St. John's return to public life without open coalition either with Whigs, or with Tories. The Opposition, led by Wyndham, a Tory, and once a Jacobite, and by Pulteney, an old Whig, and ancient enemy of St. John, rested on a foundation both narrow and broad enough for any principles. Its basis was hostility, savage and uncompromising, to the "sole Minister," the "grand corruptor." Wyndham headed the remnant of the old Cavaliers, who had ruled at the beginning of Charles II.'s Long Parliament, the Tories of sentiment, not Conservative Tories, not the men of reflection and statecraft, who had been represented by the Nottinghams, father and son. Pulteney's classic wit and eagerness of temper shone in the van of the Whig revolters. Pulteney had long been the chief friend of Walpole. Now he agreed with St. John in regarding him as a man, who "had usurped on his fellows, by wriggling, intriguing, whimpering, and bargaining himself into the post to which he was not called by the general suffrage, nor perhaps by the deliberate choice of his master himself." The tie among these disaffected politicians throughout was unity of wrongs. Their new colleague explained to themselves and the public the theory of Government which their conduct in opposition illustrated. That the ruling faction should not look upon all things from its own single point of view; that the party which had carried the nation with it in one enterprise, should not assume all its objects were national ones; that, finally, though the will of the majority must prevail, the majority at any particular time is not to deem itself possessed of a right divine to oppress its adversaries, are the doctrines which he devoted his later political life to preach. By retrospective reference to them he now excused the earlier stages of his wild career as a statesman. For the present, he attacked Ministers, and not the Sovereign, in compliance with the modern constitutional text. He described them, not as instruments of the Sovereign's will, but as usurping tyrants over both him and the nation. The dynasty he accepted as an accomplished fact, though the deductions from the fact of its establishment he rejected. As a writer, as the author of a series of slashing leading articles, he did his main part in the active struggle, though Opposition was indebted also for many a clever Parliamentary movement to the inventiveness of the same energetic spirit. To him figuring as "Humphrey Oldcastle," Pulteney's organ, the Craftsman, commenced in 1726, owed its most stimulating passages. He scourged the Ministry as "the Occasional Writer." As specimens of measured invective, emanating from measureless intellectual contemptuousness and envy of success, it would not be easy to match the letters by "the Occasional Writer," in the February of 1727, on the subject of the Spanish quarrel.

All this time he had not declared open war with Walpole, whose neutrality had been essential to his return. But, beside fierce attacks through the press, he was incessantly intriguing against him with the Duchess of Kendal, who was jealous of the sway of any one over her royal lover. Fortunately for the Minister, the days when a Court favourite could make or unmake a statesman had passed away with the Sarahs and Abigails of Anne's reign. The defect of St. John, as a politician, was that he loved crooked schemes. All his experience had conduced to increase his constitutional belief in the efficacy of back-stairs plots. He had observed Cabinets changed and rechanged, from neglect of these minutiæ, when a ruler at home. The Court of Louis XIV., and the Regency, had confirmed him in the same faith. When the solicited interview, long sought in vain, at length granted with the consent of Walpole to the interested prayers of the Duchess, turned out a complete failure; when St. John found the King unable to comprehend the benefits of emancipation from a Minister, the mainstay of the Act of Settlement, who relieved him of the entire care of government, respected his solicitude for Hanover, and paid him his revenue regularly, baffled, not despairing, he patiently set himself to weave another net, and this time for the heir apparent. He began to concert measures for forming a "patriotic" Ministry with Lord Chesterfield, the guide and adviser of the Prince of Wales. Once more his plans were disappointed, though formed with the most plausible prospects of success. He had thought that the main object was to conciliate the mistress. Lady Suffolk was installed lady-patroness of the entire politico-literary coterie. She became Pope's muse, and Swift's correspondent. The King died. Walpole gave way to Sir Spencer Compton, the Speaker. All Opposition was triumphing, when it began to be whispered that actually to the wife, not the mistress, to the metaphysical Caroline of Anspach, belonged the keepership of the King's conscience. Walpole in a few days resumed his places and influence, and St. John in despair withdrew to his farming and hunting.

Never did there exist a more resolute and persevering mind, along with equal vivacity and ardour. The disappointment of his conspiracy with Lady Suffolk, as formerly with the Duchess of Kendal, did not make him relax his efforts in the Craftsman. His style is always animated. It is oratorical, slightly rhetorical, and flavoured with satirical wit. Its defects are the frequent use of an insinuation or a metaphor in the place of argument, and a want of speciality, a vagueness in the topics of declamation. Sometimes he enunciates an universally received maxim, in lieu of convicting his mighty adversary of the violation of it, and sometimes he rings the changes on an administrative triviality, without demonstrating the impolicy of the end which it served. The peace with Spain, in 1729, was in accordance with the general views, as he acknowledged, of the negotiators of the peace of Utrecht; yet he marshals a most elaborate series of attacks upon details in the preliminaries. His genius was better fitted for tracing and distorting a general idea throughout the ramifications of a Cabinet's whole policy. This talent shines out conspicuously in the series of letters published in the Craftsman, under the signature of Humphrey Oldcastle, entitled, "Remarks on the History of England." There he endeavours to prove that, in the annals of our country, the spirit of liberty and the spirit of faction have never coexisted; that the Administration, in complaining of the seditious and sulky tone of public feeling, as expressed by the Opposition press, was condemning the tyranny of its own rule. M. de Rémusat is surprised at such sentiments from the late leader of the Tories. He seems to suppose the Tory party, subsequently to the Revolution, to have been Conservative, interested, that is, in maintaining the existing state of things which secured the predominance of their opponents. In the 'Dissertation on Parties,' republished in 1735, with a sarcastic dedication to Walpole, St. John pleads with all parties that they should unite in a common opposition.

He argues that the party boundary stones are, in effect, only of antiquarian interest, though revived, and treated as realities, by an Administration which found its safety in dividing its adversaries; bribing some, persecuting others. A powerful Young England party, the Patriots, comprehending a multitude of men, condemned, as they professed, by the dictator to serve their country, and not the King, rallied under him and Pulteney, and accepted his essays as the exposition of their principles. They learned, catching his watchword, to declaim against the man and the system whence sprang "the tyranny of faction, by Whigs, factiously for the Government, and by Tories factiously and rebelliously against it." Perfect independence of political theory is compatible with a combination for the destruction of a Cabinet which disdains equally all theories. Not till that object has been attained is the impracticability of holding the reins of power, with an infinity of open questions, discovered by the confederates.

Walpole did not submit quietly to these savage attacks. Pulteney's personalities had almost provoked a duel; St. John's invectives against individuals, as impersonating vicious principles, irritated him no less, from the recollections of a lifetime of rivalry. He had little literary taste, and he could not conceive the existence of a passion for letters in other men. Swift he once invited to dinner; but he dozed while the Dean argued. So all the beaux esprits of the period were treated by him. Writers, he thought, could be bought like votes, when the occasion came. The consequence was, that the strongest Ministry ever known in England, the only one to be compared with the French Governments of Richelieu, Mazarin, and Fleury, or the Spanish of Ximenes and Alberoni, has been traduced to posterity, though with a cause by no means indefensible, and, most of all, by the miserable apologies of its own hireling panegyrists. The finest geniuses of the period sought the patronage of Chesterfield, St. John, and Pulteney to them always generous. The Premier's press retaliated by vague charges of sedition, and true charges of selfishness and disappointed ambition.

In Parliament, Walpole could defend his own cause manfully against Craftsmen in the Commons, and, by deputy, against the Rumpsteak and Liberty Club in the Lords. Wyndham might bring forward motions of censure, and Pulteney, his Whig coadjutor, thunder against " the monster, the many-headed monster, Excise." He parried attacks with more or less open menaces against the hidden worker of the machinery. Twice did Wyndham lead the onslaught. Twice, in the Excise Bill debates, did the Minister pass by the weaker foe, and strike at the traitorous anti-Minister, whose Parliamentary agent he asserted Wyndham to be. It was a desperate conflict. The majority of 125 on the earlier occasion diminished, by gradual desertions, all through the long struggle, till finally it had dwindled to sixty-one on the first reading of the Bill, and, on the second reading, to sixteen. Another such victory would have destroyed him. But Walpole was obstinate in nothing but in clinging to office. He did not care to injure himself, because Englishmen would not let themselves be benefited: the third reading was postponed, and the Bill was dropped. His majority rose again on the debate for repealing the Septennial Act to sixty-five. This was a change too democratic for the old Whiggism of Pulteney, one of the chief agents in passing the original Bill. It was forced on the Opposition by St. John; and his friends among the Tories, Bromley, St. Aubyn, and Wyndham bore the brunt of the battle. In this famous discussion, in rejoinder to Wyndham's noble picture of a nation with an automaton king, a king Log, and a tyrant Minister, Walpole drew the companion portrait of " the mock patriot." " Suppose," he exclaimed, " this fine gentleman lucky enough to have gained over to his party some persons really of fine parts, of ancient families, or of great fortunes; and others of desperate views, arising from disappointed and malicious hearts; all these gentlemen, with respect to their political behaviour, moved by him, and by him solely; all they say, either in private or public, being only a repetition of the words he has put into their mouths, and a spitting out that venom which he has infused into them; and yet we may suppose this leader really not liked by any even of those who so blindly follow him, and hated by all the rest of mankind. We will suppose this anti-Minister to be in a country where he really ought not to be, and where he could not have been but by the effect of too much goodness and mercy, yet endeavouring, with all his might and all his art, to destroy the foundation, whence that mercy flowed. In that country suppose him continually contracting friendships and familiarities with the ambassadors of those countries which at the time happened to be most at enmity with his own; and if, at any time it should happen to be for the interest of any of those foreign Ministers to have a secret revealed to them, which might be highly prejudicial to his native country, suppose this foreign Minister applying to him, and him answering, 'I will get it you; tell me but what you want, and I will endeavour to procure it for you;' upon this he puts a speech or two in the mouth of some of his creatures or new converts, and what he wants is moved for in Parliament. . . . Let us, further, suppose this anti-Minister to have travelled, at every Court where he was, thinking himself the greatest Minister, and making it his trade to reveal the secrets of the Court where he had before been, void of all faith or honour, and betraying every master he ever served." It was a crushing indictment. But it could not defer the Dissolution. The Opposition was mentally arranging its new Cabinet, and St. John planning the resumption of his long-interrupted Parliamentary career.

The Dissolution came. The new House met; and, to the consternation of their foes, the divisions showed that Ministers retained an assured preponderance. Bolingbroke perhaps feared to provoke the realisation of the threats thrown out darkly against him; perhaps he and his promiscuous allies were mutually dissatisfied; perhaps his fortune could no longer support the position at once of a patron of literature and a party-leader. At all events, he resolved upon withdrawing himself for a space from England. At fifty-seven he found himself still half an outlaw, with his means impoverished, the gay witty mistress he had married in France old, sickly, and dejected, and the mighty coalition, into which he had infused a meaning, ready to fall to pieces from hopelessness. The Tory section recognised his aid, and with gratitude; Pulteney's Whigs were willing to forget their obligation. Pulteney himself found his ascendency diminished by his contrast with a bolder spirit, with a man never contented with an inferior, or even an equal rank. The Whigs were frightened by the scandal of their alliance with one whose old treason had left its stigma in the shape of civil disabilities; against whom a Minister could launch, without any internal evidence of improbability, charges of correspondence with the enemies of our country. He was equally alien from them, whether he were more really an absolute Radical, a species of politician never much loved by the old Whigs, or a partisan still of Tory and Jacobite principles, though no Jacobite or positive Tory himself. He himself assigned as the cause of his retirement a craving for literary leisure and rural pleasures, without attempting to disguise his vexation at the seeming impregnability of his opponent's position. But he also complains three years later, in 1739, to Lord Polwarth, that "certain persons, who had supported themselves on his exertions, thought his name and, much more, presence in Britain, did them mischief."

Chanteloup, or, as he writes it, Chantelou, a famous chateau in Touraine, was his favourite place of residence; but he also possessed a hunting lodge, Argeville, on the borders of the forest of Fontainebleau, of which a near relative of his wife was ranger. There he read, and wrote, or followed the chase with the royal hounds. Pope speaks of his life there with enthusiasm. He of whom cynics like Swift, and Pope, and Voltaire, wrote, not only with admiration, but with respect and affection, must have had some peculiar radiance, not only of wit, but of nature, to counterbalance the allowed fitfulness of his temper. The earnestness with which he could throw himself into every different pursuit recommended to him by circumstances shows vivacity and spontaneity of intelligence. He possessed, above all, the gift of undoubting self-reliance, which impresses us also in Swift. He had always been a student of philosophy after the manner of men of literary tastes. Now, he began to apply his thoughts more exclusively, he writes, in March, 1741, "to those abstract meditations whose objects are generals and not particulars." He wished to wean his mind from sombre reveries on schemes of ambition frustrated, and years spent in vain. The pursuit of philosophy was, we may well believe, not a mere veil to hide, but a means of dispelling or healing, his chagrin. This result, it is to be hoped, was more perfectly accomplished than his design of teaching the world. In the intervals of the chase, he undertook the composition of a work, which should set at rest all the more dubious questions of metaphysics, and cut away debatable ground, through the simple method of demonstrating the nullity of the subject as a science. Most readers will be satisfied to measure the extent of his success in this wide but common enterprise of amateur philosophers by a perusal of Pope's 'Essay on Man.' It was deliberately written to embody the essence of those infallible processes of reasoning, which were to be fully, with all their steps, drawn out in prose by the teacher. Little that is new occurs, either in the noble verse of the disciple, or in the equally fine prose of the master. The third Lord Shaftesbury had already anticipated the praises of universal order, which so often indicate a tendency towards deism. Master and poet-pupil rather prematurely congratulate one another on having surveyed the entire circle of truth. They very unwarrantably assume that the assent of the Dean of St. Patrick's had been given to their conclusions.

While, however, his literary admirers were stimulating his researches in the bewildering circle of metaphysics, his political friends had continued to call for the aid of his pen against Walpole. His league with the Opposition had at no time been altogether interrupted. Correspondence with the chiefs went on vigorously; and the secession from Parliament, carried out, not to the advantage of the party, as secessions never are, in 1739, had been planned from of old by him. The occasion which the Opposition selected, the insignificance of the Ministerial majority for the address of congratulation on the convention with Spain, demanded rather, he thought, an appeal to the country at large; but he was decidedly opposed to Pulteney's opinion that the declaration of war with the same nation furnished a decent pretext for returning to the House. Once a professional politician always one, is a truth illustrated in every age and people. With an affectation of regret, the veteran statesman openly resumed his political machinations. The 'Letters on the Study and Use of History' was a work which had apparently been suggested by Lord Chesterfield, the chief counsellor of Leicester House, when George II. was Prince of Wales, and was addressed to Lord Cornbury, whose influence was great over the present occupant. The previous inhabitants of Leicester House, once firm "patriots," had adopted the sentiments of their new residence, when they migrated to St. James's. Now, the old house was tenanted by a new Court, which followed the time-honoured policy of the heir apparent of the dynasty, and, as reformers untaught by experience hoped, with more sincerity. In the 'Spirit of Patriotism,' Bolingbroke depicts to the Prince, in glowing colours, a coalition, in which parties should be merged, and men allowed to think for themselves while prosecuting, with all their energies, the few great common objects of all lovers of their country. In the second of the two privately circulated letters to Lord Lyttelton, a confidant of the same Court, is drawn the celebrated portrait of the Patriot King, whose prerogative is limited simply by the willing obedience of a grateful nation, and not by the rights of a dominant faction over the creature of their policy.

About the same period he had visited England, though with an appearance of secrecy. His presence was barely known outside the circle of his immediate friends; nor did the spectacle of the state of things incline him as yet to change his residence. In the seventh year of his scarcely voluntary exile, after a tumultuous session, Parliament was dissolved, and Walpole found himself in a minority, or what would have soon become one. He retired; and the contemporaneous death of Bolingbroke's aged father, Viscount St. John, in the spring of 1742, left him free in all ways, whether fear or poverty had induced his expatriation, to resume English citizenship. He could become at discretion again an English citizen; not an English peer; still less an English Minister. The coalition which he had nourished had in it no principle of union, when once the enemy was overpowered. Its sections and members had one common feeling, hatred to the holders of office; one common end, their dismissal. That end attained, community of sentiment and hopes disappeared. Each then had his list of positive desires to be gratified, no longer merely the negative passion of envy. All had accepted St. John's co-operation in their need; they were not ready to share their booty with an old enemy. Worst of all, the eloquence, acuteness, and friendship, which were blended together in the fiery soul of Wyndham, in whom even adversaries confessed that "everything seemed great," had been already, in 1740, quenched in death. He who had lost so many parties lost few living friends; and, of all his friends, Wyndham had been the most tried, and found most faithful. Though a vehement adherent of the Stuart cause, he had made that no plea for deserting his ancient political leader. He was mainly instrumental in effecting St. John's restoration, and as loyally followed his counsels, when himself a chief in Parliament, as when a subordinate in Harley's Cabinet. Well might St. John write, "multis fortunæ vulneribus percussus huic uni me imparem sensi." He had been the link between the politician of a bygone generation and the politician of the present; and this link was now severed. In vain St. John returned home. He found no compensation for his toils from his late companions. To this personal neglect has been confidently ascribed his discontent; probably in a great degree it was the cause. Can we blame the worn statesman excessively for murmuring at such forgetfulness? But, if he had been the purest and the least selfish of patriots, he must still have cried out on men who, after having denounced Ministers, rightly or wrongly, as a disgrace to English politics, then, when the outworks, to use his own metaphor, had been stormed, capitulated with the defenders; and, on this condition, that the miners and their under-workmen alone should enter in, and hold the fort jointly with the garrison; yet worse, on the old terms, which had been the sole pretext for the assault, acquiescence, that is, in the system of Walpole, and subservience to Hanover.

He found himself, whether from conviction or private disappointment, perhaps from both, forced again to betake himself to weaving those melancholy tissues of intrigues, which were always doomed, at the decisive moment to be swept away by some ordinary but unforeseen circumstance. It is wearying to contemplate this absolute master of the craft, like a squirrel in a revolving cage, seeing the goal ever just within his grasp, then suddenly put back. He might envy the fortunes of the old Duke of Leeds, Minister both to Charles II. and William, never without some dormant impeachment overshadowing his name, yet climbing, through all the gradations, to the head of the peerage. He might meditate over the prosperity of his more immediate contemporary, Sunderland, leader of the Tories and leader of the Whigs. He might even contrast himself, not unfavourably, with his late pamphleteering colleague, the former patriot, and "Great Commoner" once, Pulteney Earl of Bath. Of him Lord Marchmont writes to St. John, in 1744, that "he was mustering a set of *honest* men, who should be free from the fury of the Opposition, and consult the interests of their country without regarding the favour or offers of the Court;" and, with what great object of constitutional or social reform? "To intimidate the Court, so as to obtain the Garter." Amid the general depravity of statesmen, St. John, who almost alone had his deserts, chafed at his doom of perpetual disability, and thought it hard to have been singled out as scapegoat for acting a few months as servant of the Prince, openly, with whom Marlborough, and Walpole himself, did not refuse to maintain a secret correspondence. Some quality in his disposition prevented him from retrieving a fall. There was a restlessness, an incapability of stooping out of notice, till the gust of unpopularity had passed over, a taste for tacking in the tempest, without caring whether he made way or not, instead of putting in and waiting for calmer weather. This temperament made the one false move fatal; it kept him continually before the public in the light of an inveterate enemy determined on revenge, or a jobber snatching at power.

On the formation of the "Broad Bottom" Administration, in 1744, when he had taken up his regular abode at Battersea, he soon discovered that Chesterfield, though delighting in his wit and acuteness, did not care to act with him in politics. The Earl's exclamation on defects in his friend's morals, "Alas! poor human nature!" was a judgment also on the politician's instability. St. John need not have asserted so emphatically to him, his "joy in the privacy, to which circumstances and his own desire had reduced him ; and that all he had to request of those who had come into power, was that he might enjoy the private life he was in," without being exposed to what he calls *avanies*, that is, affronts from authority. Pitt, though an ardent admirer of the "inimitable beauty of style" in the Oldcastle essays, would have been more brusque than Chesterfield in rejecting him as an official colleague. It may be credited that he described the schemer who ventured to lecture him as "a pedantic old man who quarrelled with his wife." Pitt was of a higher spirit than all his contemporaries. He did not understand the "*astutia Italiana*," which the other had studied so exactly, and urged so cunningly. St. John comprehended as little that majesty of conception and singleness of policy, which were soon to astonish Europe. All the energy he set down to passion and anger against individuals, not to the confidence of original genius, and a detestation of minute intrigues. He saw only that his junior "of fair parts, but narrow, did not know much of the world, was a little too dogmatical and extremely supercilious." He writes bitterly, that, when he was a young man, Sir Edward Seymour and Musgrave heard him with more deference than had Pitt; and that "the coalition, which neither Lord Chesterfield nor Mr. Pitt had formed, but himself alone, younger men wished to manage and control."

We cannot look upon the relations of statesmen, especially at times of such political vicissitudes, from the same point of view as contemporaries. The succession of persevering exertions, though with ever the eventual disappointment, which forces many now, when contemplating the political history of the period, to end by pitying a statesman whom they can very seldom approve, would produce the contrary effect upon adversaries whose own power was in instant danger from those obstinately fierce assaults. It is too easy a thing for posterity to be generous. If it seems unwise in his enemies not to have relented at last towards the ruling spirit of Queen Anne's reign, it was far more unwise in him to battle against a destiny he ought by this time to have considered irreversible. His position was high in Europe. He was a patriarch among politicians; and was recognised as a Destroyer of Cabinets, though himself ostracised. Possessed of a competent estate by the death of his father, and of exceeding fame, he might have ended his days in a state of literary Epicurism. Round him at Battersea, as on the banks of the Loiret, at Chanteloup, the purlieus of Fontainebleau, and at Dawley, gathered all the most eminent in the ranks of the old Opposition. Marchmont was there, always formidable, though shut out from Parliament by the barren honours of a Scotch peerage; Chesterfield; occasionally Pitt; and, often, Murray, afterwards greatest of Chief Justices. There he dictated to his intimates their political and philosophical creeds, sometimes hearkened to, and sometimes not, but always with an eloquence which never lost its force or colour. Thence he beheld the growth of Wesley's and Whitefield's influence, without the clue which might have enabled him to comprehend the cause.

Though conscious of the little direct effect he produced on the national councils, he could never entirely forget politics, nor resign the excitement of State intrigues. With eager interest he watched every change in the Administration; contented with none; bewailing the impending ruin of England from the increase of the national debt; and criticising the policy of our wars, in "Reflections on the State of the Nation," composed in 1749. His fondness for management, after all his protestations five years before of a determination to retire for good and all from the world, bore him into all the agitations and mazes of Leicester House stratagems. He sought to guide the youthful Prince as he had the reigning King, in the vain hope of recovering, with the accession of his pupil, his old predominance, and exchanging the title, conferred by the Pretender, for the coveted actual earldom, for the denial of which he owed an undying grudge to Harley. Not till the death of Frederick in March, 1751, ended his manœuvres for a complete restoration. His own days were now numbered. Himself gradually pining away under a cancer in the face, and other acute maladies, he had the additional anguish of seeing his wife, the Marquise de Villette, " the comfort of his life in all its melancholy scenes," of whom, whatever Pitt may have thought, he never speaks without love and affection, go before him. In December, 1751, with the ardent feelings of youth still alive, with the consciousness of glorious gifts, which had only accomplished one positive work, the Peace of Utrecht, the statesman, who seems to link together the twilight age of the Stuarts and the grey dawn of visibly modern times, dropped into his grave. He left a void in the literature and politics of his day, which, at the moment, attracted more notice and more emotion than had attended upon his later living efforts. Soon it was closed up with new men and new interests. "It is strange," has been said, "that, of all the events which constitute a person's biography, there is scarcely one, none certainly of anything like a similar importance, to which the world so easily reconciles itself as to his death."

St. John knew long before he died that he had failed as a politician. He cherished a hope that he would survive and rule as a philosopher. Here too in life he had experienced disappointments. Thus he supposed that he had always been able to govern the mind of Pope; and had often, for his use, meditated arguments against the dogmas of Warburton. One of his chief employments, on his resumption of residence in England in the winter of 1743, was the confirmation of his sovereignty over the poet's convictions. Pope, in return, most suspicious and most timid of men though he was, ardently adored the genius of St. John. Probably, he had a real love for St. John's philosophy, with a yet more vehement fear of popular disapprobation. The history of the conflict in his mind between trust in the orthodoxy of Warburton, and reverent admiration of the brilliant deist, has been often recounted. His astonishment at discovering the practical significance of the opinions, of which he had in the 'Essay on Man' become the mouthpiece, was doubtless assumed. The "guide, philosopher, and friend," perceived, and indulged the weaknesses in his votary's character. With his approval Pope infused that ambiguity and vagueness into the doctrine of his poems, which made it possible for Warburton to defend them. But it was a cruel disenchantment to discover that finally his disciple had been so half-hearted in confidence in him as to choose his chief theological antagonist for literary executor. His wrath against Pope's memory may be attributed much more to this evidence of wavering allegiance in the pupil in philosophy than to the discovery of Pope's mean breach of faith in having had 1500 copies printed secretly of the 'Idea of a Patriot King,' entrusted to his care, instead of a score or so, according to agreement, and in having, moreover, altered parts, both of this pamphlet and the 'Letters on the Spirit of Patriotism,' and shown them to Warburton.

Still, though his success in the conversion of a poet had been so very partial, he expected better things from the great public which should be illuminated by the collected mass of his inquiries. He bequeathed his philosophical MSS.

to Mallet for posthumous publication. His vanity was apparent in his want of heart to suppress such splendid evidences, as he certainly esteemed them, of his powers of reasoning and breadth of thought; his cowardice, in that he was not ashamed, according to Dr. Johnson's indignant expression, "to leave half-a-crown to a beggarly Scotchman to draw the trigger," for which he had not nerve himself. Could he have replied to this accusation, he would have argued, as on a similar occasion, that his writings were "a vindication of reason against philosophy, religion against divinity, and God against man;" that he "not only disowned, but detested the character of *esprit fort*, a character usually applied to them whom he looked upon as the pests of society." But his defence of religion was an assertion of the government of the world by general laws alone, without the intervention of any particular providence; he advocated the encouragement of religion as a matter of police, "as a curb in the mouth of that wild beast, man, whom it would be well if we could check by half a score others." With the same plea, no doubt, to his own conscience, he attended his parish church at Battersea, and held forth, to the admiration of the parishioners, that "quarto Common Prayer-Book, fit for a decorous lord of the manor," which we find him commissioning a correspondent to purchase for his use. There is consolation in knowing that the bequest turned out most unprofitable to the literary executor, though not so much, we fear, public conscientiousness and disgust caused the writings to accumulate dust, as the want of that adventitious incentive to curiosity, which partisanship lends to performances out of a living statesman's track. Horace Walpole need not have complained that the cause of Moses and St. Paul was taken up fiercely by men who had applauded the author's patriotism, philosophy, and heroism, when he broke the ties of friendship, and plotted against his benefactors. The publisher's balance sheet is the true and mortifying measure of the efficacy of his attack upon revealed religion. The refutation by Warburton, the presentment by the grand jury of

Middlesex of the works, with a view to a bill of libel, the prosecution commenced by the Archbishop of Canterbury against the printer and editor, and the address of the London clergy to the King against the publication of dangerous and irreligious books, could not attract popular attention to the contents. The dissertations themselves, apart from the author's name, are too destitute of merit, except the grave dignity of style and correctness of emphasis, which never fail.

Their composition and publication are chiefly worthy of remark as closing in England an episode of fashionable deism. Bolingbroke had been the centre of a strong literary and political party, which, with Hobbes, pretended to reverence Christianity as an institution well adapted for maintaining order. They sought to construct in the place of dogmas, which they were too proud to take upon authority, a shadowy scheme of natural piety. Voltaire recognises Bolingbroke from this point of view as the philosopher of the eighteenth century; and his name lives on the Continent as that of a master in the school of unbelief. But the love of virtue for virtue's own sake, which he inculcated, was, in his teaching, as he showed in his practice, too vague a principle to coerce men's passions, or satisfy their affections. The positive part of his system has been long forgotten, the negative and destructive alone is remembered. He was a sceptic in philosophy as he was a sceptic in politics. For a man of powerful administrative genius, few spheres could have been more discouraging than an atmosphere of perpetual conspiracy; for intellectual vanity like his, no retribution more humiliating than the utter neglect which, the fear of retaliation and the motives of curiosity once removed, attended the cherished offspring of his meditative leisure. Yet many will part reluctantly from the spoilt child of the eighteenth century, from the plotter against the Constitution, the sophist in statesmanship, morals, and theology; they cannot help sympathising with his own generation, which, while it never fully granted him his own way, never took his manifold delinquencies so seriously as to punish them condignly.

WILLIAM PULTENEY.

To Lord Bolingbroke, with all his intelligence, his persistent exclusion from national confidence, and from a practical share in the party triumphs which had, mainly by his intervention, been won over Walpole, was an inscrutable problem. He never believed in the genuineness of public opinion, and fancied that he could hoodwink it at his pleasure. He perceived its force, and tried to make it his tool. He did not understand its sincerity, and that it had its positive objects, and was resolved to choose its instruments and representatives for their accomplishment. Far from desiring to repudiate and rescind the Revolutionary settlement, it was fighting against the contradictions in the practice to the theory which 1689 had established. For the overthrow of the despotism of the great Whig houses, it used the feuds and jealousies of the same order. For these reasons, it selected Pulteney, a Whig of the first rank, to overturn a system of Whig oligarchy; and the leader of Piccadilly was the favourite alike of the City and of the petty farmer. When the long conflict ceased, and the cause was victorious, it was not his silence about social reforms which brought down from his lofty pedestal the popular idol in a tempest of popular indignation and contumely. A few weeks could not have been expected to bear legislative fruits. It was that in his day of power, and when his decree was absolute, Pulteney sanctioned the system he had been commissioned to overturn. Men disbelieved the original sincerity of the antagonist of Walpole, who could leave his nominees and accomplices in office.

National aversion to the divine right of the Whig oligarchy was the keystone of the success of this famous Opposition. The people did not desire to elevate men of the people; but they would not allow a small, close body to claim a right of co-optation without respect to fitness for office. They were ever ready to catch at any symptom of mismanagement to utter, in a burst of rage, their protest against the whole system, their suspicions that their representatives were no representatives. They had a sense of want; they had formed no positive conception of wants; and their chiefs did not and could not interpret for them. The absence of social popular cries from the Opposition vocabulary is a curious and disagreeable feature in the history of the contest. It imparts an air of barrenness and unreality to the whole. Perhaps it was to be expected. The instrument must be first created: the work is subsequent. But it accounts for the evanescence of the fame of politicians, none of whom ever broke out into a proposal of electoral enfranchisement, some great scheme of education, a modification of oppressive poor laws, or a large project of trade. All that they did was to veto, unless the subject were war. War was always welcome, because the Minister loved peace, from his dread of financial embarrassments.

Pulteney was not more a statesman than the other champions of Opposition. A true orator he was, and he could run over the scales, from the sublimest tones of patriotism to the hottest blasts of indignation and the stormiest gusts of ridicule. Well might the harassed Minister exclaim, that he feared Pulteney's tongue more than another man's sword. From Pulteney the rest took their key. He surprised his followers and adversaries with a scope of eloquence which enlarged and rose with the occasion. All his contemporaries, whether friends or foes, agree as to the astonishing compass of his oratory. "He could state and explain the most intricate matters, even in figures, with the greatest perspicuity," writes Chesterfield, who had envied, and affected to scorn him after his death. "He was a most complete orator and debater in the House of Commons; he had arguments, wit, and tears at his command." Onslow, Walpole's Speaker, whose position was constantly being menaced by the assaults of Opposition, who watched a debate only to detect some breach of order in the harangues of his adversaries, was amazed at this man's eloquence. "He had the most popular parts for public speaking that I ever knew; animating every subject of popularity with the spirit and fire that the orators of the ancient commonwealths governed the people by; was as classical and eloquent in the speeches he did not prepare, as they were in the most studied compositions; mingling wit and pleasantry, and the application even of little stories, so properly to affect his hearers, that he would overset the best argumentation in the world, and win people over to his side, often against their own convictions, by making ridiculous that truth they were influenced by before, and making some men to be afraid and ashamed of being thought within the meaning of some bitter expression of his, or within the laugh that generally went through the town at any memorable stroke of his wit." He had trained himself carefully, long confining his part in Parliament to short business speeches. That he had not commenced orator at once was no bar later on to strains of continuous and impassioned invective. The habit of being always ready and able to speak to the point remained of essential service in the perpetual guerilla warfare which, as leader of His Majesty's Opposition, he had to direct. The quality of his style, which his enemies called "miscellaneous incoherence," was reckoned by his friends, and by the judicious among his opponents, as the perfection of debating.

In his private character defects there certainly were, and many of them. Not only filial resentment made Horace Walpole ascribe all the inspiration of his writings to "ambition and acrimony." Not only jealousy of superior power, talents, and honesty, or the passion for epigrams and point, led Chesterfield to declare, in his exaggerated style, that "resentment made him engage in business; that he could equally detect and practise sophistry; that his breast was the seat of all those passions which degrade our nature, and disturb our reason; that there they raged in perpetual conflict; but avarice, the meanest of them all, generally triumphed, ruled absolutely and most scandalously; that nothing exceeded his ambition but his avarice." Party feeling exclusively did not prompt Speaker Onslow's criticism on "the mixture in him of such natural defects and weaknesses, that no time, I believe, can produce an instance of a man of so variable and uncertain a mind, who knew not that he was so, and never designed to be so." Not a little in all this was true. He was ambitious and acrimonious; he was sophistical. He could be capricious in conduct, and was ever so in temperament. He was in petty matters ludicrously economical. It is told how his coach and six, outriders and all, were suddenly checked, to allow the opulent and compassionate Lord Bath time to grope in his pocket for a halfpenny to bestow on a decrepit old beggar. He haggled with his ward Colman about a few pounds for tutor's fees, and bestowed on him most earnest advice to look about for second-hand law books. Yet he could be nobly generous to a friend, while he esteemed it a reflection on his understanding to yield a "point in the way of bargain." Chesterfield's sarcasms on his ruling vice, it seems, arose from his refusal to sell some frontage land in Hyde Park for less than its market price, and are somewhat out of place from the great noble who bequeathed to his mistress, the mother of his son, £500, as some "small" (small indeed!) "compensation for the injury he had done her." That Pulteney had not been heroic or eccentric enough to disclaim a devise of the Bradford estates, was converted into another grave charge against him. But never was a demand made upon his liberality for public objects, or upon his sense of equity, in vain. Bishop Newton, who knew him perfectly, tells us that he was a constant and generous patron of literature; that many youths were brought up and advanced at his expense; that "the charge of gaining intelligence and of printing and publishing, and the like, for the party, was almost all his own; and there were very few who assisted now and then with so much as a subscription of five guineas." A man who, we learn on the evidence of Bishop Pearce, yearly bestowed more than a tenth part of his whole income in charity, and undertook the payment of the enormous debts of his deceased son, Lord Pulteney, voluntarily and without liability, could hardly have been the mean, ungenerous, even dishonest miser that family enemies and envious companions delighted to prove him. The country rated these calumnies at their proper worth. The West End might echo with whispers of a clever bargain, or a piece of minute economy; the nation at large knew him as the millionaire who rejected the lures of sinecures and pensions, who, from the time when first he entered public life, had always subscribed to every patriotic loan, however hazardous, whose accumulated wealth was available for all popular objects. It was ready to sympathise with his indignant outburst at being contrasted for a "sparing, scraping nature," with the magnificence and prodigality of the statesmen of the age: " Dost thou call the profusion of the public treasure on a worthless crew of pimps, spies, projectors, and abandoned scribblers, for thy own secret service, instances of personal generosity ? At this rate Catiline was a man of a frank, liberal heart."

His enemies reproached him with "outrageous bursts of sudden passion, with an affectation of good nature and compassion;" they did not deny that his fierceness of tone "was supported by great personal courage," and that, "perhaps, his heart might feel the misfortunes and distresses of his fellow-creatures." His friends could add, that he was religious in an age when scepticism was fashionable, and moral in a period of habitual sensuality; that in private life he was "so familiar and engaging, that you could not be with him half an hour, but you felt yourself entirely at ease;" that he never forgot the ties of school friendship, or, in his triumph, gave the rein to his thirst for vengeance; that he condescended to no low intrigues to embarrass his adversary; rejecting for instance, the proffered services of a man skilled in opening and re-sealing letters with the utmost scorn and loathing, though the Treasury did not; that, while leaguing with men of all denominations in politics, he had never deserted his ancient pledges, or in his anger with the Sovereign plotted with the Pretender.

William Pulteney entered public life with favourable prospects. His father had done little to increase the distinction of the family, which took its name from its original seat of Poultney, at Misterton, Leicestershire, and was of Norman descent. But his grandfather, Sir William, had long been member for Westminster, and his memory introduced his descendant at once to the heart of the Whig party. From Westminster he went to Oxford. At Christ Church, his Latin verses, spirited, but with no ideas above a schoolboy's, recommended him to the favour of Dean Aldrich and for the post of speaker of a very smooth and very tame address to Queen Anne, on her visit to Tory Oxford, notwithstanding his Whiggish connections. On leaving college he made the grand tour. He entered public life at the stormiest period of our political history, full of hereditary prejudices, and with a disposition to view all things through a medium of suspicion of men's motives. Wealth, which flowed in till his fortune swelled to the then gigantic bulk of £1,200,000, perhaps aggravated the natural blemishes of his temper. Love of money, confirmed by the growth of his possessions, rendered him envious of the illicit gains of his old friends and colleagues, while the consciousness of perfect independence in point of fortune encouraged him in an eccentric and impracticable opposition.

On his first entrance into Parliament, where he obtained a seat through the influence of Guy, the Secretary to the Treasury, for the Borough of Hedon, such defects were singular merits. All England was become one turbid scene of intrigue and disaffection. Party spirit had all the narrowness and sordidness of private selfishness. The Sovereign herself was looked upon as a conspirator against the principles which had set her on the throne by the vast party by which those principles had been defended. The defeated adherents of her brother were divided between sympathy with the Queen as secretly their supporter and fellow-thinker, and dislike to the usurpation which they were obliged to deem her sovereignty. Pulteney's wealth and name soon gave him weight in the deliberations of the Whig confederacy. His first speeches did not, nor was it intended that they should, produce much impression on the House. The Place Bill called him to his feet; but the country was first warned to expect a leader by his earnestness and vehemence in the prosecution of Sacheverell.

Through all the period of dejection, and, sometimes, despair for his party, Pulteney shrank from no part of the burden. The Tories testified their opinion of his resoluteness by dismissing his uncle, no violent partisan himself, from the Board of Trade. When Walpole was imprisoned for a transaction by him as Secretary-at-War, on abstract principles unjustifiable, though, according to the morality of those days, to the credit of his heart, Pulteney, who had been more particularly welcomed into the arena of politics by him, stood by his old patron. He was proud to be admitted as a partner in the games of nine-pins with which the silence of the Tower was often broken. When the 'History of the Last Parliament' came forth from Walpole's pen, Pulteney was selected, and gladly consented, to take the office of editor. With Walpole and Stanhope he was St. John's guest in Golden Square, when that Minister, having deposed Harley, had discovered, in his turn, in the plenitude of his absolute sway, the inconvenience of being a single party's nominee and slave. He never lost courage, though he could hardly have foreseen that the very crisis, when it appeared to most that all hope for the old Whig houses was gone, that nothing remained but to negotiate the best terms possible with the conquerors, was the beginning of the ruin of the Tories, and of their subjection to their adversaries for half a century.

On the final triumph of his friends, Pulteney's claims to office were recognised. He was appointed Lord-lieutenant

and Custos rotulorum of Yorkshire, and admitted to the Privy
Council. In defiance of the opposition of the Commander-
in-Chief, the Duke of Marlborough, to any adherent of
Walpole's, he was elevated to the post of Secretary at War,
which in his case, as in those of St. John and Walpole, was
regarded as a stepping-stone. Still, though high in the
ranks of his party, he was but the follower of Walpole.
He was not formed for a leader. He had no taste for responsibility, nor the steadiness required for such a character,
and the necessary patience. Circumstances alone forced him
into the post; and then his trophies were gained in the
desultory warfare of an Opposition which can pick its own
time for an assault. Never of his own choice was his
eloquence employed in promoting a positive course of policy.
He had acuteness at will to detect a flaw in the policy of
an enemy, not the subtlety which elaborates a plan of
action. Under the guidance of Walpole, he was a conspicuous advocate of a triple alliance between England,
Holland, and France, which, under the Orleans Regency, had
laid aside the ambitious schemes of the former reign, and
promised to be the guardian of peace in Europe. However,
soon again he reverted to the negative character, and burst
forth with a display of that fierceness which he had, in words,
ever at command. To him it fell to impeach Lord Widdring-
ton for the rebellion of 1715; and we find him, about the
same time, haranguing against a motion to address the Crown
for a proclamation of amnesty to all rebels laying down their
arms. Soon, too, he was hurried into opposition, a state from
which he never again completely emerged, even during the
ascendency of his friends. He had felt obliged to send in
his resignation in 1717 when Walpole's influence proved
inferior to Stanhope's in the Cabinet; though it seems from
the correspondence of Stair with Stanhope in January, 1718,
that Pulteney, then at Paris, was averse from that open
union between the Tories, as Tories, and Walpole's followers,
which had led, the year before, to the acquittal of the Earl
of Oxford. Unlike Walpole, who affected, to excess, the

character of an old-fashioned English country gentleman, Pulteney had not even a country seat. He loved London and the Continent. His present residence abroad may have been connected with his perplexity at his position as a seceder from the Government while he felt bound in conscience not to oppose its measures. He was discontented with Walpole for having implicated him in a factious policy. He had more enduring cause for dissatisfaction when Walpole's schemes for a return to power were crowned with success, through the reconciliation of the King and Prince, and the troubles consequent upon the South Sea Bubble. The zeal and eloquence of Pulteney had been among his chief resources, yet no worthy place was reserved in the edifice of his grandeur for the devoted friend, even when he became First Lord of the Treasury, in April, 1721.

It has been the fashion to blame the Minister for folly in having, by his suspicions and jealousy, himself collected the force which destroyed him. "He could forgive great faults, not great talents." With a different policy, he could not have grasped or retained that autocracy, which he enjoyed, so long as Hanover was safe, and enriched by English gold, without a murmur from the King, and, while he held the keys of the Treasury, with no need of yielding to troublesome demands of confidence from his subordinates. Though he had kept the nominal chieftainship which already the partnership of Stanhope had once wrested from his grasp, and that of Townshend threatened, he could not have played the dictator with Chesterfield and Pulteney asserting equal rank, and ready to snub every gesture of supremacy. Walpole was not a man to care for an empty name. He loved the reality of power, to feel other wills bowing beneath his own. Though cold-hearted and prosaic, he resembled the elder Pitt in the self-reliance which prefers the feeble Pelhams as coadjutors to the sharing of authority and responsibility with minds of larger proportions. Warned by his friend's reluctance to change principles with position, he embraced the opportunity of Pulteney's sacrifice of high office in sympathy with himself, to leave him permanently outside. It was mean conduct, and its moral is the day when, deserted by all, with the whole nation apparently thirsting for his blood, he gave way to his former liegeman.

For the present, Pulteney's enmity smouldered. Walpole did him the honour to be sufficiently jealous of his possible rivalry to offer a peerage, in the hope that his well-known wish to found a noble house might seduce him to a desertion of the natural sphere of his eloquence and popular manners, the House of Commons. The offer was declined civilly; the motive was indignantly detected. Pulteney was the more bitter internally that it was impossible to commence opposition on purely personal grounds. He continued to support the side which Ministers advocated; perhaps with the greater vehemence, to avert the suspicion that his now known dislike was inspired by private grievances. He moved the confiscation of the ill-gotten wealth of the South Sea directors. When Bishop Atterbury was accused of complicity in the Stuart plots, he moved the bill of attainder and the address of congratulation to the King. He condescended to ask for the post of Cofferer of the royal household, to prove himself, he argued, no renegade from his party, and not disaffected to the dynasty he had ever supported. Then, finding that Walpole looked upon his acceptance of the place as a pledge of peace, he determined to show that he was not compromised. In accordance with the tradition rather than practice, that office bound the official to the Sovereign, not to the Minister, he concerted a plan of opposition the most irritating, a system of perfect independence. He interpreted his place as letters of marque granted by the monarch against Whig and against Tory. He had plenty of allies in the mass of malcontents the Ministerial policy towards persons had made. As the year 1725 drew on, a very serious storm was seen blackening the political horizon. Walpole was determined not to part with a jot of his absolutism; he thought that the proffer of a Secretaryship of State to Pulteney was not really a departure from that resolution. Pulteney was wise enough to see that he was too far compromised to go back, or resentment stood him in the place of sagacity. To a hint that Townshend might soon cease to hold the seals, he replied with a bow and smile. To a second and recent offer of a peerage he had already bitterly responded: "Sir, if ever I should be mean enough to be sold, I promise you that you shall never have the selling of me. A peerage is what, some time or other, I may be glad of accepting, for the sake of my family; but I will never obtain it by any base method, or submit to have it got for me on such terms by you."

A cry was still wanting; and a cry the Opposition at last prevailed upon itself to think it had found. When the nation rose against Walpole, it did not mean to impugn the Revolution of 1689. The people were incensed against the Ministry, inclined to sneer at the Sovereign, and had no sympathy with the aristocracy. Yet they could not understand the point of view of those politicians who wished to lodge the little Court of Compiegne at St. James's. "Whig" and "Tory," though become somewhat obsolete, men recognised as old party names, and were ready to believe English principles were represented by them; the indefeasible title of the Stuarts was beyond the reach of their imagination. To the Revolution, and to the Whig principles on which it was founded, Pulteney and his allies appealed against the Whigs in office.

The Revolution had, once for all, marked out the boundaries between Prerogative and Privilege. There was no danger from Prerogative. Parliament had perfect liberty to act, if it would, for the kingdom's general welfare. To the nation, then, Pulteney preached, that it was betrayed by its own guardians, that the power it had extorted from the crown for them, they used for themselves; that the theory of the Constitution was infallible; that the Whiggism of the Revolution was the true political faith, but that the practice of the priests was corrupt. He bade them look to the Bill of Rights and the Act of Settlement, and see whether the

Revolution had not pledged their rulers against threatening their liberties with standing armies, or with armies of placemen, the Janizaries of a government; against robbing England for the gain of a foreign principality. He denounced the Treaty of Hanover, the Secret Service funds, Hessian and Hanoverian mercenaries. "The time might yet come," he exclaimed, "when we should see a tyrant Minister driving about with six members of Parliament behind his coach!" To the Parliament he employed a different tone. To the Whig rivals of Walpole, angry at want of place, he addressed one common argument. All were victims of the Minister's jealousy. In each the Minister saw a possible rival, and each who had no sufficient post conferred upon him, might deem himself not despised, but feared. Walpole was too needy and prodigal, he warned them, to let them share the public treasure. Houghton needed all that was left from the buying of votes and of boroughs. He pointed to a crowd of Whigs, known statesmen, ejected by the usurper; he terrified aspirants with the prospect that every year of the despot's rule was rendering him more absolute. To the independent he spoke of the worthlessness of their votes and wisdom, when one man had the command of wealth to purchase a majority at any time; to the corrupt, of the growing strength of their "grand corrupter," which would soon make votes a drug, and of the growing rage of their constituencies. The Jacobites he terrified with the friendship between Fleury and the Walpoles. Constitutional Tories were roused with the hope of emancipation from their political disfranchisement, by glorious prophecies of a future, when party should be no more, and by declamations against the present perversion of party badges into standards of faction and the watchwords of licensed robbers.

The charge of general corruption of Parliament sapped the foundations of the strength of a Ministry which existed by the will of a Parliamentary majority. The people could not tell what statesman on the Ministerialist side was guilty or not, what measure was the product or not of bribery. All alike, both men and measures, they were inclined to condemn, in order to crush the guilty thing at all events. Every vote for Walpole was looked upon as the possible fruit of corruption ; consistency in voting always on the Minister's side would be thought consistency in corruption, variableness would lose a man the confidence of friends and foes. One way was open to no doubt. Co-operation with the tactics of Opposition was a safe policy. No suspicion of bribery could attach to the adherents of the struggling cause. A member could not suspect his own candour, when he decided against his manifest interest. To the dishonest themselves that manifest interest was become dubious. With the country rising against the Government, with all the talents ranged against it, victory and the spoils of the vanquished were the sure reward of Opposition, sooner or later.

Pulteney was from the first not alone. He could reckon on the enthusiastic declamation of Wyndham. Many a fierce sarcasm pointed by Bolingbroke, and many a luminous idea hammered out in the fiery forge of that statesman's mind, shone forth amid the full flow of Wyndham's oratory. For an elaborate and sustained attack, Wyndham produced a greater effect than Pulteney ; he had not the same variety and animation, not the readiness and spontaneity. Commonly, though not always, Shippen ranged himself on the same side with his fifty followers, that systematic partisan, who could forget the old services of St. John and refuse to vote for his restoration, who could even in the final struggle support Walpole, consistent in the resolve alone to make all parties and doctrines his tools. More trustworthy was Samuel Sandys, a master of statement, provided the topics were supplied to him. Pulteney had Sir John Barnard, the representative of the section of the moneyed interest opposed to the bank directors, Walpole's staunch supporters, for his preceptor on all financial questions. Later, he could look for the aid, in the Upper House, of Chesterfield, the most finished, but not, therefore, the most effective orator of his time, with his studied passion and quaint thoughtfulness.

Among his enemy Walpole's enemies, rather than among his own followers, were arrayed in the Commons also the polished taste of George Lyttelton, and the majesty and truthfulness of Pitt. Pitt almost alone in the epoch had an actual object, a positive policy, to be elaborated in some future Utopia after the fall of the reigning Cabinet. About Pitt alone there is, in those artificial times of "Roman virtue and patriotism," an air of reality. It is strange that he was doomed throughout the whole of his political career to association with the least magnanimous and deserving statesmen of the period. Driven into opposition for a single vote given against Walpole, he became an intimate of Leicester House, without losing his uprightness in that hotbed of intrigues. His misfortune was to lack riches and influence enough to stand by himself in a tainted age. He was not a professed member of Pulteney's party, though he voted on Pulteney's side, and aided it by his eloquence. The Opposition could never thoroughly understand or control his flights, while it often profited by them.

Of George II. when Prince of Wales Pulteney had been a consistent courtier. He had been excluded from official knowledge of the negotiation, which led in 1720 to a reconciliation between the Prince and the King; and he never forgave Walpole for a reserve which, he believed, originated in jealousy. He was the more irritated that the communication to him of each step of the treaty by Mr. Edgcumbe, proved that others were thought worthy of initiation into the mystery. He went so far as to warn the Prince against letting himself "be sold to his father's Minister by persons who considered nothing but themselves and their own interest, and were in haste to make their fortunes." "What," he declared he had said to Walpole, when told that, as the reward for the pacification, the Prince was "to go to Court again, and have his guards, and such fine things," but not to be left Regent in the King's absence from England—"What! have you stipulated for a share of royalty for yourself, and is the Prince to live as a private subject of no consequence in the kingdom?" When the Prince had discovered that his adviser was right, and that his interests were totally disregarded in the new arrangements, he reverted to opposition. At Leicester House the campaign was concerted, and the vivacity of Mrs. Howard and the judgment of the Princess Caroline furnished useful suggestions. There met all the wit and learning which had survived the establishment of the new dynasty. Pope and Gay were welcome guests; and an occasional letter from Ireland would remind the town of the mighty intellect ever expressing hatred for mankind, but lashing its oppressors, and projecting measures of enlarged philanthropy. Mrs. Howard gathered her habitual train of admirers, her Peterborough, and her poets, while now and then a Butler, or a Clarke, fresh from some discussion before the Princess, on the depths and heights of metaphysics, mingled in the mistress's more brilliant levee. The Heir Apparent's Court was a pleasant contrast to the dull formalities of St. James's, where Walpole discoursed in bad Latin with his Sovereign, and Baroness Kilmanseck and the Duchess of Kendal held heavy sway.

Leicester House was the natural centre of the belligerents. The spirit which had animated the clubs of Queen Anne's reign had evaporated; the end and object of political combinations were not measures but men; no recognised social fellowship could now be formed on a basis sufficiently broad to comprehend all the members of an Opposition resting on motives of personal connection, rather than principles. The tendency of society was against such institutions; there could be no sympathy between Grub Street and Piccadilly, now that the denizens of Piccadilly actually made their mansions, instead of the coffee-house and the tavern, their homes. The charm of the Kit-Cat Club, of which Pulteney was a member, arose from the meeting of wit on terms of social equality with wealth and rank. It sat as a critical tribunal, adjudicating not only upon politics but upon literature. When wit was forced to show a pecuniary qualification, the ease of such associations disappeared altogether.

They were exchanged for the clumsy humour and unadulterated politics of aristocratic gatherings, such as the exclusive Beef-steak and Liberty Club. From the coffee-houses and taverns of Charles II.'s reign the passage had been smooth to the more select commonwealth of a club. Thence, under the Georges, the transit was abrupt to political conferences in drawing-rooms, and especially at Leicester House. Tories who were not Jacobites, rejoiced to predict the growth from Leicester House of a true Conservative policy which should be consistent in not challenging the Revolution and, at the same time, in discouraging fresh changes. Discontented Whigs beheld in it the seat of a prince who had no title but from the Act of Settlement, but was bound to the principle, and not to a special group of its official advocates. Radicals, lastly, men whose minds had contracted a bias to perpetual alterations, or whom the new order did not exactly suit, found there a delightful hurly-burly of murmurs and complaints, nothing positive to be opposed, but a fashion of resistance to all that existed.

Pulteney's place was high in the little Court, though he was no favourite personally with the Prince or Princess. After all, George II. and Caroline were as Hanoverian as George I. The measures which the Prince opposed as Heir Apparent he really loved. Walpole's cold temper and unimaginative method of government were, in spite of her *esprit*, much more in harmony with Caroline's German feelings than the cleverness and popular ways of his rival. The men of letters Pulteney introduced, who gave the Court an air of patronage of learning and wit, were men of Queen Anne's day, and more naturally betook themselves to flattering Mrs. Howard than her mistress. One lady his influence brought in, whose name was destined to become sufficiently notorious at a later period. The shameless Duchess of Kingston, the convicted of bigamy, and the mortal foe of Foote, was, as Miss Chudleigh, patronised by the statesman, who obtained for her the place of maid of honour. He condescended to watch over her studies, seeking to imbue her with a taste for good reading; but, with all his wit, the accomplished Pulteney, as a preceptor, seems to have proved a dull companion for the young lady. The men of letters, Gay and Swift, Pope and Arbuthnot, who met at Leicester House, as formerly at the table of Harley, or the dinners of the Brothers, had gained admission as his friends. They fell off from it when his interest there declined. Originally they had been no companions of his. A common antipathy was the bond among them; and Pulteney had the art to convert political fellow-feeling into personal friendship. Chesterfield, a competent judge, declares him to have been " formed by nature for social and convivial pleasures, to have had lively and shining parts, a surprising quickness of wit, and a happy turn to the most amusing and entertaining kinds of poetry, as epigrams, ballads, odes." " Good humour and the spirit of society dictated his poetry," writes the generally contemptuous Horace Walpole. " So familiar and engaging was he that you could not be with him half an hour but you felt yourself entirely at ease. He gained admiration by not seeking it; his wit was all natural and easy, arising from something then said or done," is the testimony of Bishop Newton. For social talents, Mrs. Grenville, who often saw all the chiefs of Opposition together at her husband's table, thought no one comparable to him. A bon mot of his echoed through the town, as his speeches roused the kingdom. In addition, it was not forgotten that he was wealthy, and not sparing of his riches, at all events, at the call of literature. Gay, his rival in glory and odium, as Swift styles him, he, as all, loved; he admired Pope, and Pope admired, or affected to admire, him:

" How can I Pult'ney, Chesterfield forget,
While Roman spirit charms or Attic wit."

With the great Dean over the water he maintained an intermittent but cordial correspondence. If there was not enough of earnestness or steadiness in Pulteney's character to satisfy Swift altogether, neither at present discovered the want. As an affectionate friend Pulteney invites Swift to England, engaging there shall be one and that an 'undisguised' dish; he shall have his cup of mixed small beer and wine, "no women at table if you don't like them, and no men but such as like you."

It is strange to find one of their most rancorous opponents received thus into the circle of the Brothers; it is stranger to see him and Bolingbroke, on Bolingbroke's restoration in fortune in 1725, become the firmest of allies. Of all men these two, having been once foes, seemed least likely to coalesce. There was the opposition, not of contradiction, between them, but of relation. Each united with wit and eloquence a political instability, which, in the one, originated from infirmity of will; in the other, from too absorbing and constant a contemplation of distinction as the sole end of life. Each was possessed by an overweening vanity. In the one it took the form of a determination to give the tone to every measure, and to society at large; in the other, to submit to no dictation. Resentment against Walpole, to whose character theirs were equally contrasts, was the bond of union. It silenced the antagonism of conflicting egotisms until his despotism had been shattered. The presence of Bolingbroke in the confederacy is its most interesting feature. His unscrupulous originality and individuality are set in relief by the nervelessness of his fellow-workers, even of their leader, men who made dislike of an individual the clue to guide them to a national policy. Sandys and Barnard, Bubb Dodington and Lyttelton, were indebted for their existence as politicians to the ungraciousness of a Minister. Pulteney himself might have been Secretary of State, or Premier, in other circumstances; he owed it to his rival that he became "the Great Commoner."

St. John must have been marked and famous at any period of history. He flits like a dark shade over the annals of the first two Georges, like a ghost behind the arras, with a tale to tell of the crimes of a bygone period descended as an inheritance to the present, which durst not confront the light of day. With an outward semblance of conformity to the established Constitution, he prompted measures inimical to it, yet not favourable to the restoration of the old order.

He assailed the Minister with strokes that fell with equal effect upon the throne and upon society. He argued as if all institutions were on probation, as if every polity stood on the same footing of propriety and plausibility, from an absolute monarchy down to a republic.

The junction of St. John, while it terrified Walpole, furnished him with a whole armoury of weapons against his Parliamentary adversary. Pulteney had been the most vehement member of the committee which condemned the Peace of Utrecht; he was asked why he had leagued with the author of that peace; why, a Whig, he called for the head of the champion of the Act of Settlement. The only answer, it was suggested, could be that he was "ambitious and aspiring, impatient and irresolute, unable to bear a superiority, conceiving unjust jealousies and discontents, full of himself and his own extraordinary merit, and determined to hold the highest offices in the State, and to censure and confound all the measures of the Government under any other Administration." Simply for these reasons he had "at length renounced at once all former friendships and principles, vowing the destruction of those who had distinguished him by peculiar regard, betraying private correspondences, and endeavouring to distress that Prince to whom he owed the highest obligation." That was the charge in the dedication of Sir William Yonge's 'Sedition and Defamation Displayed' to the patrons of the Craftsman. Pulteney rejoined in his 'Answer to One Part of an Infamous Libel' that "a certain closet is the only place in the kingdom where such assertions can gain belief, or where the gentleman traduced can be thought a Jacobite even for half an hour." "That he voted with Tories," he contended, "was no proof that he had gone over to them rather than they to him." He worked in harmony with Bolingbroke because enmity to the great traitor against the liberties of England was a more patriotic motive than the memories of old hostility, not that he repented of his past measures. One same principle underlay his condemnation of the treaties of Utrecht and Seville. At least, Bolingbroke had never been equal in depth of guilt to Walpole. "If the Ministers of that time did many things ill, have not you, sir, done things ten times worse?" The bygone Administration had been, at all events, free from the infamy of unlimited votes of credit, profusion of presents, and secret service money. And then, to compare the two chiefs in point of capacity; what "a pedler in politics" was the one by the side of the other! But charges of desertion of old pledges were out of date. The age of parties was past, or revived as mere matter of speculation by selfish placemen who gauged Whig and Tory principles by the standard of co-operation with, or opposition to Government. Now, "God be praised, the senseless distinction is almost sunk in general concern for the national interest." That was the text on which its original framer continually dilated in the Craftsman, with an eloquence never before known in the annals of English pamphleteering. Abandonment of party spirit was the only point of view from which the composition and tactics of Opposition could be cleared of the shame of personal pique, or covetousness of spoils. By it could be reconciled to the kingdom, and to the conscience of the Whig leader, private with national objects. The thought had long been brooding and smouldering in the breast of the people. Bolingbroke gave it a voice and a shape. To this mighty party organiser, to the man who was never aught but a partisan, whose measures, in power as well as in Opposition, were carried always by way of conspiracy, we owe the first steps towards an enlargement of the policy which made the Constitution favoured by the majority a tyranny for the minority, towards the development of the principles of the Revolution of 1689 into a national creed, and of the foreign dynasty imported by the Act of Settlement into the nation's choice.

The protracted campaign or campaigns, between 1725 and 1742, began in the former year with a fierce onset by Pulteney on the increase of pensions, which had exhausted the civil list and compelled an appeal to Parliament. "He was not surprised," he said, "that some persons were so eager to have the deficiencies of the civil list made good, since they and their friends had so great a share in it." Down to this time he had preserved the semblance of amity with Walpole and the Crown, and retained his place of Cofferer. He even, on the third reading of the bill for paying His Majesty's debts, voted with the Administration, on the ground that, while he believed it the duty of his office to resist the growth of so pernicious a system, he could not gainsay the King's argument, that the Opposition was hindering him from being an honest man. The plea was a strange one. An honesty might be left to shift for itself which can be saved only by a transfer of the burden of debt to others. In any case the Minister, who had been chiefly assailed, did not see much merit in his opponent's inconsistency. After a feeble overture towards reconciliation from the side of the Court, Pulteney was dismissed into hopeless opposition.

Yet it seemed not so at the time. The King was old and infirm. There could be little doubt that the Prince must shortly succeed, and as little that he would prefer the services of men who had for years been flattering him, to a Ministry which rather embittered than sweetened the relations of St. James's Palace and Leicester House. The King died; Walpole's proffered help in drawing up the proclamation of the accession of George II. had been coldly declined; and Pulteney was anticipating hourly a summons to Court. It never came. Caroline, who veiled an absolute predominance over her husband's mind under the appearance of unquestioning subservience, had only felt resentment at compliments and homage which she shared with the Prince's mistress. Bolingbroke and, through him, Pulteney, had been beguiled into a double game which might have suited the Court of Versailles, where it was learnt, but, to the credit of England, led to disappointment here. Moreover, the Princes of the House of Brunswick, with many faults both of head and heart, a narrow selfishness, and a Hanoverian patriotism looking like treachery to their greater kingdom, combined an almost preternatural instinct of self-preservation, which taught them that 1689 and the Act of Settlement had crowned them sovereigns of England. Mere envy and jealousy carried four heirs to the throne of England in succession into an undutiful and almost revolutionary opposition; yet this very conduct bore the fruits of profound sagacity. It introduced a tone of apparent loyalty into the spirit of faction, and reconciled a powerful minority in the nation to government by a party, through the natural expectation, that, with their royal chieftain, they must succeed to that despotism in the State which now crushed them. But, with the prerogatives, the Heir regularly assumed the hereditary prejudices of the throne. Liberal, almost republican tenets, which, never touching the other distinctions of rank, had employed all their strength in disproof of the absolute supremacy of the head over the scions of the reigning family, lost at once their charm. In their place he adopted mistrust of him who must, eventually, succeed to his new station as he quitted it. A young King's necessities enlisted him on the old side. The feelings of the ruling caste did not change with the demise of the Crown; the owners of pocket boroughs, the great Revolution houses, remained unaltered. With no majority in the Lords, the lustre of St. James's would be dimmed. With a minority in the Commons, how would the debts of the civil list be met? Where would be the civil list itself? Speedily news came that Spencer Compton, the King's confidant, had been allowed to seek the aid of the Minister's experience in drawing up the proclamation of the Accession; and that Caroline had accepted Walpole's pledge to secure her an income of £100,000. Swift's presents of Irish cambric were neglected, Gay insulted with the offer of a gentleman-ushership, and the witty courtesies of Pope and St. John forgotten.

Opposition and the Craftsman exclaimed at the perfidy of princes, and clamoured against the inconsistency of Ministers for condescending to serve one whom they had openly scorned and ridiculed, who had as openly reprobated them. Then, after a momentary pause, they recommenced at the point at which they had left off; only, with redoubled ferocity.

The war was war to the knife. On three occasions a series of pitched battles was fought. But the pamphlet conflict of the year 1731, the debates on the Excise Bill, and on the Right of Search, and the Convention with Spain, were preceded and connected by a continuity of savage sharp-shooting. In 1726, Pulteney had moved for a statement of the public debts, "with no other view than to give that great man an opportunity to show his integrity to the whole world, which would finish his sublime character." In 1727, the old charges are repeated. The sinking fund, he argued, was nothing but a convenient cloak for embezzlement of public money. It was a popular fund, which the nation was ever ready to keep supplied, and the Ministry had ever at hand as a reserve for its own necessities. If there were a deficiency, it had ways and means. It had nothing to do but borrow on the credit of some other fund. At present Walpole staked his credit that by this fund the national debt had been actually reduced. But what was it that he succeeded in proving? Why, that of the £6,648,000 by which the debt had been diminished, three millions had come from a late Parliamentary grant, and the rest been raised on the credit of the civil list. Like the secret service fund, it was a pretence which "made Parliament a mere form, and screened corrupt Ministers." After the appearance of the Craftsman the fury of the attacks deepened. The Craftsman began in 1726, with Caleb D'Anvers, of Gray's Inn, as editor, but really under the management of Pulteney and Bolingbroke. Though Bolingbroke gave it its leading theory, Pulteney's pen was as active as his. The language used there he at length used also in the House of Commons. In 1731, from the narrow boundaries of the Treasury Bench, where Pulteney and Walpole both sat as Privy Councillors, were bandied to and fro the cries of "traitor to his country," and "factious demagogue." Hitherto, notwithstanding Pulteney's ejectment from office, and bitterness against the King and Queen, whom he accused of treachery and ingratitude, the road had not been absolutely barred to a pacification. Negotiations were opened by Queen Caroline, some of whose especial favourites, as Bishop Pearce, were friends of the popular champion, on the terms of an independent coalition between Walpole and him. They were put an end to by his assertion that he would never join a Cabinet comprehending Walpole. Still, he had scarcely before set up the standard of Parliamentary rebellion, and thrown himself upon the country. The temptations of pamphleteering drew him into a position of pronounced and reckless antagonism both to the Cabinet and to the Sovereign.

The Minister became conscious of the need of stronger literary auxiliaries than his raw recruits from the 'Dunciad' battalions, and his "Turkish army of scribblers." He had authorised Sir William Yonge to compose his 'Sedition and Defamation Displayed.' Pulteney never attempted to restrain his temper. He seems to have been persuaded by the flatteries of the popular party, against whose enemies his irascibility was usually called into play, to deem it a virtue. He was the more wrathful now, that rumour ascribed the authorship of his caricatured portrait in the Dedication to the patrons of the Craftsman to a former friend and political pupil, Francis Lord Hervey, the Lord Fanny of Pope's scurrilous satire. He had replied with the biting personalities which terrified his adversaries in the Commons. Hervey was brave, though puny and sickly. The malignant insinuation of the author of the memoirs of 'Pulteney's Life and Conduct,' that Walpole stirred him up, by false misrepresentations of facts, to challenge his libeller, "in hopes that the point of the young gentleman's sword would despatch his rival," rests on no foundation. Freely and spontaneously he challenged Pulteney in a cause with which he had properly nothing to do. The result was a meeting in Kensington Gardens, a slight wound given and received, but no reconciliation.

The personal controversy did not end with an exchange of scratches. In the Craftsman of May, 1731, Bolingbroke, under his usual signature of Oldcastle, assumed the odd part of a witness to character, and vindicated his confederate from the reproach of treachery to the Whigs, imputed by Yonge. "They have left him, because they have left the principles they professed. He left neither. He inveighs against public profusion and private corruption. He combats both with a constant inflexibility, which might have done honour to a Roman citizen in the best days of that Commonwealth. They have left both him and virtue." Not spite had moved him to this course, but the dangerous ambition, insatiable avarice, and insolent behaviour of the Minister, exaggerated by the remembrance that to Pulteney he owed his elevation. "Which," the writer proceeds, "of the two was the more likely to have been actuated by private interest? Whose circumstances required most an increase of wealth? Which had given greater proofs of vindictiveness of temper, of avarice to gather, and profusion to squander? The one laid down a good place, and forced Ministers to take another way; and, if I am rightly informed, it will be hardly even in the power of the greatest man in England, to persuade him to accept of a third. There is the ambition of doing good, and of receiving the reward in fame. If any man in one age and country hath reason to be satisfied with his success in the pursuit of this ambition, it is the gentleman of whom we speak." Forthwith appeared in answer, 'Remarks on the Craftsman's Vindication of his two honourable Patrons,' full of personal abuse of the Opposition leader's conduct in all the relations of life. Pulteney thought he recognised in the topics of this paper, if not in its style, his prime rival's own hand. He writes to his brother-in-law, F. Colman, then Minister in Tuscany, that he must now "dip his pen in gall," to answer a pamphlet by Walpole himself.

It is not difficult, independently of external evidence, to distinguish the contributions of Pulteney and Bolingbroke, respectively, to their party-organ. The same animosity against the Premier marks both; but in the elder statesman's invectives is discoverable a solid substratum of constitutional and theoretical opposition; his companion supplies the place of this by personal allusions. Against Bolingbroke had been brandished in no equivocal language by the Minister and his scribes the menace of Westminster Hall or Tower Hill; he retorted by a glowing appeal to the nation against prejudgment by a faction. Pulteney's wrath and patriotism had been interpreted as the growth of malice, disappointed ambition, and all the littleness of spite. He was stigmatised as a brother conspirator with "the infamous retailers of lies, scandal, sedition, and treason, and as a copartner with hireling authors of Billingsgate, who applaud the Dutch precedent of De Witt for dealing with a political foe. But he must know that a man is not a patriot because he desires another revolution, nor fancy that the strutting and swelling Wat Tylers and Jack Straws of our days resemble the Northumberlands and Warwicks of old, or like them can make and unmake kings." In response the leader of the parliamentary Opposition, unlike the statesman of Queen Anne's reign, evolved no profound theory. He replied by a string of innuendoes, most of which cannot have been intelligible beyond Hyde Park. Mistaking the author, he levelled at the wrong man the most unmitigated abuse. "The little quaint antitheses," he writes, under the name of D'Anvers, "the great variety of rhetorical flourishes, affected metaphors, and puerile witticisms in this political nosegay," had at first made him ascribe it to some precocious Etonian, then to a boarding-school Miss, till at length he was, in great confidence, told that it was by "that circulator of tittle-tattle, and bearer of tales, and teller of fibs, that stationed spy, pretty Mr. Fairlove." While opining "that the toil of forty pages, even of such stuff, must have been almost too great for the dapper little author's delicate brain," and recommending in future a fan instead of a pen, he makes a fierce onslaught upon his patron. "A person," he burst forth, "of tolerable second-rate parts, below a genius, above the vulgar, of industry inferior to few, of impudence superior to most men, with a low education, mean habits, and a narrow fortune; an adventurer never caressed by the greatest general or the greatest statesman of their time; buoyed up by the stream of party, and a series of lucky accidents; this child of fortune rises to the first post of Government, with talents scarce equal to the tenth, and morals unworthy of the lowest. He never gained either man or woman but as he paid for them. Giddy with power, base to those who assisted him in his distress, ungrateful to those who were the instruments of his advancement, and treacherous to those who preserved him from disgrace, he endeavours to divert the general hatred of the people from himself by putting his master upon measures which naturally tend to alienate their affections."

The taste of that period did not condemn the style, or think it misbecoming the character of a Prime Minister to emulate it. In the 'Remarks on the Craftsman's Vindication of his two honourable Patrons,' which if not from Walpole's own pen was inspired by him, Pulteney was denounced as "a turn-coat and tool of veteran Jacobites." He was represented as "a sophist, who would prove that his Sovereign, by his natural affection for Hanover, had violated the Act of Settlement, and thereby broken the solitary link by which his house held their crown." He was reproached in the same document with blind inconsistency, in assailing as traitors the negotiators of those treaties, to which he had himself, when in office, been a consenting party, and in railing at a systematic corruption by which he had once not disdained to profit. Pulteney, with his views of the latitude of controversy and particular talent for abuse, was, as we have seen, nothing loth to accept the report of the authorship of the paper. Taking it for certain, he at once assumes, in his 'Answer to One Part of an Infamous Libel,' that he has convicted the Minister of a breach of confidence, in having divulged certain unpalatable facts to which he imagined no one privy but themselves. Thence, with that dangerous incapacity to pass by an occasion for an attack, which in some measure justified Horace Walpole's sneers at "Lord Bath's treachery," and the more modern censure of Lord Stanhope, that "he sometimes attempted to prove that he could keep new secrets by revealing old ones," he inferred a right to unclose audaciously the floodgates of political confidences.

"Now that they were upon the heads of secret history, which Walpole had opened," was the time for putting the public right as to the reconciliation between the late and the present monarch, which had led to the present quarrel between the two statesmen. As in that transaction, he attempted to show, Walpole had only learned to honour the present King when he could be advanced by him, so he still confounded servility to the Minister with loyalty to the Sovereign, and the lavishing of the public treasure on himself and his family, down to his menials, with public munificence. Pulteney, the pamphlet continued, had been upbraided with inconsistency in reviling the man now, whom he had formerly loved. But had he ever loved or respected Walpole? "Do you think, most noble sir, that all those that played at nine-pins with you in the Tower, had for that reason regard for you on account of your personal integrity?" As it was in defence of sacred principles that he then sympathised with him, so now he would accept the help, in aid of his country, of men, whether Whigs or Tories, not in aid of factiousness or intrigue, as the other did, "when a country gentleman, nay, as he does now." "You, sir, have been an intemperate zealot against France, a most obsequious dupe to France, and seem to be now relapsing into your old aversion to the same." Pulteney had neither countenanced nor shared the "dirty job," by which the Premier, having had himself, for form's sake, constituted, in addition to his regular office, a Secretary of State, on the absence abroad of the two actual Secretaries, claimed the salary, even the plate of a Secretary of State, nay, even the secret-service money, though with no possible secret missions to defray. It had been asked why, if Pulteney could, through Guy the Secretary of the Treasury, whose heir he was, derive £9,000 a year, should the actual head of the Treasury be grudged his hard earnings? "Impudent and silly falsehoods these!" £50,000 in all was the sum of Guy's bequest. By the economy necessary to keep a man independent of the smiles and favours of a Court, he had made it, with the addition of his paternal and his wife's inheritances, into a fortune which raised him above the suspicion that his wrath arose from vexation at the loss of an office however lucrative. Could Walpole, a man unable at one time to have obtained £100 upon his personal security, account for his estate and expenditure in the same way, for that profuseness, miscalled generosity, to spies, and "the scribblers of the atheistical stuff, and vile political magazines, propagated by him at the public expense," for which he was accountable in a much stricter sense than was Pulteney for the Craftsman? Lord, sir, if an inquiry was to be made into your estate, what a scene of iniquity would be disclosed." How much would be traced to the Treasury, how much to 'Change Alley! What jobs we should discover it took to build the new house, how many manors were bought by the sale of so many peerages and garters, places, pensions, pardons! In the list would be secret-service money, exchequer bills, debentures, and public securities, "from the infamous Bank contract down to the last bargain you made with the East India Company!" "Only one other establishment had ever been scraped together by such means, his whom you last saved from the gallows, from sympathy." Well, "that pedler in politics" might go on misapplying the public treasure, and prostituting his royal master's name in his own dirty service; sooner or later the time of vengeance would come. He had already, doubtless, often seen Pulteney in his dreams, armed with axes and halters; he had, doubtless, often felt "the same terror which, on the revelations of a penny-post letter, made him hurry, pale and trembling, to secure that gentleman's protection, as his neighbour, from incendiaries." From disclosures affecting the private reputation of his family he was safe through his antagonist's honour. From menaces of illegal personal violence he was also secure. "But let him know that the first condition in any treaty with His Majesty's Opposition, must be to deliver up the guilty Minister to the justice of his country."

Amidst all this controversial frenzy, personal intimacy was not altogether dropped. The thin veil of anonymous authorship, or the pseudonyms eked out by a "noble sir," and "honourable gentleman," enabled the adversaries to interchange calls and civilities, chats on the Treasury bench, and good-humoured bets, with epithets and imputations not equalled by the yells for vengeance upon a Strafford or a Danby in the previous century. The details of such a state of society, picturesque as they may be, are rather painful. Between the hot wrath of a nation, which was, or certainly believed itself misgoverned, and the mutual complaisance of the statesmen, who, while they echoed or ridiculed that indignation, could tranquilly negotiate about leases and feesimples, or bandy compliments, there is too abrupt a gap. The generosity of a rival, who could beg a deanery for a friend, and urge upon the new dean the obligation on him to employ all his electioneering influence for the Government, was sincere, and even romantic; at the same time, it jars with a political vocabulary in which the Minister thus to be supported by votes, is always a "traitor," and a perjured "wretch." It produces a suspicion that the popular champions felt themselves a distinct caste from the people they affected to represent. An undercurrent of social familiarity and recognition of common responsibility to the bar of the inner circle to which they with their antagonists belonged, went on flowing beneath the surface of outraged patriotism. The student of the period derives from it an impression that the patriotism, though not hypocrisy, as it seemed to Walpole, must have been hollow and artificial.

So in the essence it continued to the end, as the circumstances of the close of the contest showed, to the disgust and disenchantment of the country, which throughout had been in real earnest. Nevertheless, gradually, as the disputants warmed, they began to appear to be almost in earnest themselves. Walpole at any rate was combating for the only existence he valued. His place was being struck at, and he retaliated in kind. His notion of a final rejoinder to the 'Answer to One Part of an Infamous Libel' was to turn his critic into a martyr. The King himself had been equally exasperated. All that Pulteney had revealed of Walpole's language on the reconciliation of the Prince with the late King, was true; but it was a most unsavoury truth. George II. had quietly swallowed the feeling, that his Minister had once despised him, perhaps despised him still. He could not do without him, or he would have had Compton; and now here was the whole world informed of the opinion conceived of the monarch by so sagacious an observer as Sir Robert. He was pushed into the disagreeable predicament of having to choose between sanctioning that opinion, by retaining about him the person who had formed it, and the impossible alternative of dismissing the friend of Hanover and master of finance. He was, at all events, resolved to avenge himself on the author of his perplexity, and readily fell in with his Minister's view. Pulteney was forthwith struck off the Privy Council, and ceased to be Custos rotulorum of the County of York. Popular adoration converted his disgrace into glory; but he does not seem to have appreciated it, and thirsted for an opportunity to strike back.

In 1733, an occasion offered for bringing to bear upon the Commons, impregnable by unaided Parliamentary eloquence, the pressure of external opinion. Walpole, a profound and economical financier, had planned the conversion of the customs into duties of excise. He hoped to augment the revenue, prevent frauds and smuggling, save disbursements on the preventive service, and simplify the collection. The imposts were never meant to be extended to necessaries or raw materials, and he intended to apply the scheme, in the first place, tentatively to one or two commodities. As a bribe to the House, he offered to abolish the land-tax, the bugbear of the country gentlemen. The project was divulged. Though recommended later by Adam Smith, it was denounced with all that fury which the threat of an importation of the Dutch excise system had once before in our history raised, in the reign of Charles I. The necessarily inquisitorial powers of the officials have always rendered excise odious, notwithstanding its economy. Before the plan was mooted in

Parliament, it had been compared out of doors to "a monster feeding on its own vitals," or "the Trojan horse, which contained an army in its belly."

The Craftsman led the chorus of execrations, and its attacks were republished weekly, in the form of 'Arguments against the Excise.' The Opposition sought to force the Cabinet into bringing forward the bill while the whole kingdom was in a ferment, and every town was menacing or encouraging its members. Pulteney dragged it into a debate on alienating part of the sinking fund. "There is another thing," he suddenly broke out, "a very terrible thing, impending! A monstrous project! yea, more monstrous than has yet been represented! It is such a project as has struck terror into the minds of most gentlemen within this House, and into the minds of all men without doors, who have any regard to the happiness or the Constitution of their country. I mean that monster the Excise! that plan of arbitrary power which is expected to be laid before this House in the present Session of Parliament." Wyndham seconded this assault, discussing, as an abstract question, "whether we should sacrifice the Constitution to the prevention of frauds in the revenue." Sir John Barnard, the Opposition Chancellor of the Exchequer, without whose aid Pulteney confessed he could not have competed in finance with his rival, bore witness to the detestation of the bill by the trading classes. Walpole reserved his defence for his motion for leave to bring in the bill. "Such a scheme as a general excise, he denied had ever entered his head, or, for what he knew, the head of any man with whom he was acquainted. His thoughts had been confined solely to the revenue arising from the duties on wine and tobacco." His argument from the frauds inseparable from custom dues, was met by the bold assertion, that losses from this cause were rated by the Commissioners of Customs themselves merely at from £30,000 to £60,000 a year. To his details of the generous intention of Government, should the bill become law, to give up the land-tax, as well as the income accruing from forfeitures and fines, Pulteney rejoined: "The honourable gentleman was pleased to dwell on the generosity of the Crown, in giving up the fines and seizures to the public; but, in my opinion, it will be but a poor equivalent for the many oppressions and exactions which the people will be exposed to by this scheme. I must say, that he has been of late mighty bountiful and liberal in his offers to the public. He has been so gracious as to ask us, Will you have a land-tax of 2s. in the pound, a land-tax of 1s. in the pound, or will you have no land-tax at all? Will you have your debts paid? Will you have them soon paid? Tell me but what you want. Let me but know how you can be made easy, and it shall be done for you. These are generous offers; but there is something so very extraordinary, so very farcical, in them, that really I can hardly mention them without laughing." Again Wyndham seconded the attack led by Pulteney, and threatened the Premier with the fate of Empson and Dudley. In his reply, Walpole, though he had not at first caught the historical allusion, aptly inquired how the punishment of the revivers of obsolete laws could be adapted to the mover of what was represented as a dangerous innovation. To his Whig antagonist he returned sneer for sneer: "I know that my political and Ministerial life has been by some gentlemen long wished at an end; they may ask their own disappointed hearts how vain these wishes have been."

But neither his proof of its virtues, nor his proffered repeal of the land-tax could save the project. Members were intimidated by their constituents, and by a vast mob which thronged all the avenues to the House. Inch by inch the ground was contested, and the Administration saw its majority dwindle from 61 on the first to 17 on the third division. The country was in a state of agitation, to which the Minister could not blind himself. His protest against the crowd at the doors as "sturdy beggars," by which he explained he meant merely that they were petitioners, became a gathering cry against him. He was too cold a politician, too sincere a lover of power, to sacrifice what he thought sober realities to visions of reform. He summoned his colleagues, and told them, that, "if their resolution was, as it seemed, to proceed with the bill, he would instantly ask his Majesty's permission to resign; for he would not enforce a tax at the expense of the blood which must, in the present state of popular inflammation, be shed." Immense was the exultation of the large towns, where the scheme gave a blow to Walpole's old popularity with the trading interest. The Monument in London was illuminated. Oxford ran riot. "The night that the news came here that the Excise Bill was dropped," writes the Rev. Mr. Meadowcourt to Horace Walpole, "bonfires were made, moppets with stars and blue garters were burnt, and the old cries of Ormond, Bolingbroke, King James for ever, revived."

Walpole could not help dissolving. He had to go to the country, with the cry of "No excise" against him, in the midst of the popular madness. The result showed how incomplete was the representation, and how potent the influence of Government and borough-mongers. The new elections gave Ministers an assured majority, and all the hunters after place were in despair. Bolingbroke withdrew for a season to a noble mansion in Touraine, and the delights of the chase in the Royal Forest of Fontainebleau. Walpole's famous peroration on Wyndham and Bromley's motion, discountenanced by their Whig allies, for repealing the Septennial Act, with its menacing portrait of the mock patriot, may not have been without its share in his retirement. His own account attributed it to general dejection, while Pulteney ascribed it to a love of display, and a prodigality which had exhausted his moderate means. His main motive undoubtedly was, as he hinted, a want of sympathy between him and the chiefs of Opposition. But the despondency was universal in the ranks of the party, and in proportion to the confidence with which they had marched to the assault. It is very visible in the irregular, but most interesting, correspondence between Swift and Pulteney. Pulteney himself had peculiar matter for discouragement.

s 2

The captain of a mighty league, he had after the deaths of his cousin, Daniel Pulteney, a deadly foe of Walpole on account of that Minister's estrangement from Sunderland, his patron, and of Mr. Watts, his right hand and his left, as he called them, positively no staff in which he could confide. The temper of society and the nature of political confederacies had changed since the time when the Kit-Cat and the Brothers were recognised by their respective parties as representative committees, available both for supplying lieutenants, and for feeling the pulse of the public. His followers were but loosely knit together, and still less bound to their leader. Not a few hated him as a Whig; many affected to despise his popularity as the sign of a radical and demagogue, though they were not therefore the less jealous of it. He was not sure of Bolingbroke, whom the contrariety of their moral sentiments, and the similarity of some of their intellectual endowments, had always led him to mistrust, but with whom the influence of Daniel Pulteney had persuaded him to unite. He could no longer calculate with certainty upon the services of that redoubtable pen. Ill-health, besides, was operating upon him. A fit of sickness, which resulted in attracting to him, he writes, "the attacks of five eminent physicians for five months together," at the end of the year 1736, had, in the summer of the same year, reduced him so low as to induce him to receive attentions from the Court with civility. He displayed to the elder Horace Walpole, at the Hague, a lowness of spirits, which, to the envoy's hopeful eyes, seemed rather to arise from his being dead-hearted than sick in body.

He and his party had no real right to complain. Though their assault in the last Parliament had been withstood, the victory of the Government was one of those which are virtual defeats. The rottenness of its defences had been discovered. Lords Chesterfield, Burlington, Clinton, and Marchmont, with many Commoners, for agitating against the Excise Bill, were turned out of their posts at Court and elsewhere, with circumstances of rudeness which drove them thirsting for revenge into the opposite camp. In the Commons, Pitt, and Lord

Polwarth, the friend and correspondent of Bolingbroke, helped to hamper the plans of the Administration. This accession of force may not have been altogether agreeable to Pulteney personally. It introduced too many chieftains of independent pretensions into the confederacy. They were not ready to yield proper obedience, and some brought the disrepute and bad habits of veteran placemen under a corrupt Government. Very soon after the sudden influx into the ranks of Opposition, we discover hints in the correspondence of Lyttelton and Chesterfield of a factious repugnance to Pulteney's supremacy. Measures were on foot for the construction of a Parliamentary cabal, in direct contravention of the views of their leader, who believed that the straightforward maintenance of "public and national" interests would secure them the sympathies of the people much more fully than such conspiracies. But if the secession from the Ministerialists increased Pulteney's difficulties of management, the mutiny was fatally ominous for Walpole; it indicated a decay of faith in his stability.

The attacks upon him were resumed in the new Parliament with unabated spirit, and in both Houses. The House of Lords now begins to share with the Commons in the interest of the conflict. After a set of the usual charges against Ministers of a plot to introduce an extended excise, and of general corruption, a Parliamentary provision was asked for the Prince of Wales, lately married, of £100,000 a year. The motion was sufficiently reasonable. At the same time, it was admirably adapted to stir the King's jealousy of his son's independence, to compromise Walpole with the Heir Apparent, and to give Opposition a hold on the gratitude of the future sovereign, which, had he lived, he would doubtless have quickly evaded. The address on Frederick's marriage with Princess Augusta of Saxe-Gotha had been the occasion for Pitt's maiden speech, which, we are told, electrified the House. Lyttelton, another of the Prince's especial courtiers, had then spoken excellently. They now again, with Pulteney, produced a great effect. Pulteney laid especial weight on the precedent of the present King's allowance as heir. Only by the help of Shippen and forty-five Jacobites, from dislike, they said, of Parliamentary interference with the King, though, it was suspected, more really from displeasure at seeing the Prince assume the authority among the Opposition which they thought the right of the Pretender, was the Government able to defeat the motion by 234 to 204.

In 1738 Pulteney moved for the production of papers on the exercise by Spain of its alleged right of search. A defeat did not hinder him from declaiming against the infamous pusillanimity of the Administration in not having taken vengeance for the manifold wrongs done by Spanish officials. The conduct of Ministers on the capture of our merchant vessels, he would, he said, illustrate by the story of a gentleman, who, upon receiving a box on the ear, asked him that gave it if he were in jest or in earnest; upon the other answering he was in great earnest, the honest gentleman replied only, "I am glad you are, sir, for I do not like such jests." He called for vengeance, not restitution or reparation now. "The captain or the governor must be hung in chains upon the island where the outrage was committed." Bloodier measures still, he cried, were needed to compensate England for what Burke has called the "fable of Jenkins' ears." Apparently, that mariner's grievance of the cropping of his ears, except perhaps in the pillory, was as fictitious as the counter anecdote in vogue in Spain, of the two noble Spaniards who had been forced by some of our half-privateering men-of-war's crews to devour their own noses. However, the captain's narrative evoked a gust of rage throughout the kingdom. Amid the indignation against Government and the Bourbons, Pulteney proposed a series of resolutions, comprising assertions of our right freely to navigate the Southern Seas, and to cut logwood in Campeachy Bay. Walpole by his argument on the insolence of setting before Spain a carte blanche to sign, when a conference was to commence, obtained a postponement of all but the first. Yet an address to the King was carried to demand redress of Spain. In the House of Lords, even the Ministerialists consented to put on record a solemn denial of the Spanish right of search.

In January, 1739, the Anglo-Spanish Convention was signed. Pitt first, in a masterly speech, and, a little later, Pulteney and Wyndham, made fierce attacks on it, repulsed by majorities only of 260 to 232, and 244 to 214. But the thirty were stanch; and it was resolved to appeal to the country from the present Parliament by a secession. The responsibility for the step has been disputed. Bolingbroke, still in France, admitted he had recommended the policy, but not the occasion selected. Pulteney doubted, but suffered himself to be overruled. It did their party no good, as a desertion of the trust committed by their constituents to members never will. Wyndham in vain defied the House as he bade it farewell. He hoped to rouse the sympathies of the country by being sent to the Tower for the statement of his regret that not even for once would his opponents be won over " by unanswerable arguments to distinguish themselves from a faction against the liberties and the properties of their fellow-subjects." The experienced Premier restrained Pelham's eagerness, and expressed his joy that his adversaries had declared themselves: " We can be," he exclaimed, " upon our guard against open rebellion, but it is difficult to guard against secret traitors." He frustrated the calculation that a call of the House fixed for the next Monday would give his adversaries the excuse of compulsion, and enable them to return to their seats without shame; for he moved that the Commons should adjourn over that day.

The secession had been abortive. Circumstances favoured the seceders. The Whig Duke of Argyle had, as all readers of Scott know, been patriotically indignant at the Porteous Bill of 1737 against Edinburgh. To the surprise both of Pulteney and of the ever caballing Duchess of Marlborough, who equally disliked him, he now came over to the Opposition, and converted their hatred into ardent affection.

Pulteney had previously, when the negotiation was going on, taken advantage of the presence of the Duke in the Commons, to break out into a panegyric on his splendid qualities, concluding, " He wants nothing to make him still greater, but to be stripped of all the posts, of all the places he now enjoys; but that they dare not." This was one fortunate event; another was the refusal of Spain to ratify the Convention, and its consequence, a declaration of war in October. The nation exulted; hostilities were a triumph over the Government. The Prince of Wales accompanied the heralds to Temple Bar, and, at the Rose Tavern, drank success to the war. The contest was, men thought, to be one succession of victories; the galleons should pay the fleet; the kingdom would have the mines of Mexico and Peru. " They may ring the bells now," said Walpole, in the strain of a Greek chorus, " before long they will be wringing their hands."

In November, 1739, Parliament met: and all the seceders were there. Pulteney, after various wild remarks, that he would go no more to the House, though he should be sorry were others to follow his example, was among them. Ministers, he declared, had confessed themselves in the wrong; for, if the war were now necessary, so was it then. He and his friends consequently had returned. He hoped that the meanness, tameness, and submission, which had resulted in the shameful Convention, would not operate to make us resign our conquests on the restoration of peace. Walpole sneeringly retorted, that Parliament was glad to see gentlemen return to their duty, but had not felt their absence. The common accusations of corruption had been launched. " The stale argument of corruption never shall have any weight with me," said Walpole; " it has been the common refuge of the disappointed and disaffected ever since government had a being; it is an accusation that, like all other charges, though unsupported by proof, if advanced against the best and most disinterested Administration, and pushed with a becoming violence, will never fail to meet applause among the populace." His demeanour was higher than ever;

but he felt power slipping from him, as he perceived the growing disaffection of his partisans. He had to turn aside the edge of Wyndham's philippic, by allowing an Address to be sent up to the throne against any peace by which the Right of Search should be allowed. The death of that orator in June, 1740, though it broke the chief link between the two sections of Opposition, did not save the Ministry.

Yet 1741 came, and Sir Robert had, at least, the pleasure of seeing his foes once more baffled. Supposing, from their new strength in the Lords, and their compactness in the Commons, that the time was ripe, they let loose Sandys, the motion-maker, as he was called, upon him on February 13, 1741. Sandys ascribed our want of allies to the friendship with France and the treaty of Hanover. Corruption, the waste of public money on "Spithead expeditions and Hyde Park reviews," while Haddock's and Vernon's fleets were destitute, the criminal lenity to the South Sea Directors, and the dismissal of officials for their votes, were, he asserted, all due to one " who had usurped regal power, who had arrogated to himself a place of French extraction, that of Sole Minister." Were he not guilty, " in a free government too long a possession of power is highly dangerous." The charges could not be examined while he kept his office. Besides, " he is bewildered in treaties, and has forfeited his word with every Court in Europe." Pitt declared, with a prevision of his own career, that " when the greatest scene is opening to Europe that has ever before occurred, he who had lost the confidence of mankind should not continue at the head of the King's Government. Pulteney, flushed with an easy triumph over Walpole's bad Latin, " nulli pallescere culpâ," and his winnings of a guinea, " the only money he had received from the Treasury for many years, and, he hoped, the last," followed with thunder against the treaty of Hanover, " the source of all subsequent degradations." The bombardment was ineffectual after all. The vagueness of the indictment, and the ominous sound of cumulative and constructive guilt, and credibility of common report, brought to the Minister's aid not only

Stephen Fox and Pelham, but the Tory Lord Cornbury. Edward Harley heaped coals of fire on the head of the persecutor of his brother, Lord Treasurer Oxford, by challenging for him a different treatment to that he had meted to the Earl. Other allies rallied round him. Shippen and thirty-four Jacobites withdrew; their ringleader, who had been bribed perhaps with an indemnity, remarking, "that the motion was but a scheme for turning out one Minister and bringing in another." Walpole rose to the level of the occasion, and made good Pulteney's opinion, that he could be a great orator when he pleased. He classed Opposition members as "Boys," "ripe Patriots," and "Tories." Demerit with Tories ought to be a merit with the nation. Nevertheless the Tories he respected. His greatest crime against them had been the duration of his power; but would they endure to be partners of such mean creatures as rebel Whigs, after having divided the public opinion of the whole nation! Could they share with "the men of yesterday, the boys in politics, who would be contemptible, did not their audacity render them detestable?" The patriots he simply despised. "A patriot, sir! Why, patriots spring up like mushrooms. I could raise fifty of them within the four and twenty hours. I have raised many of them in one night. I have never been afraid of making patriots. They clamour for change of measures; they only mean change of Ministers." The dismissals for contrary votes he excused as the acts of the King, who might wish "Crown favours to circulate." He appealed to his financial services,—"Is not credit at an incredible height, and to whom must that be attributed?" Where, lastly, were the proofs of the crimes he had perpetrated while invested with that "mock dignity of Prime Minister?" "A strange phenomenon! a corrupter, himself incorrupt!"

A clear majority of 184 pronounced him free of all the charges. This great majority proved Walpole's ruin. It threw him, wrote a contemporary, into a lethargy of power. Loss of memory, and other maladies of years, began to impair his energies and destroy the trust of his followers in their chief. From over confidence in his strength, or carelessness, he gave, on the meeting of a new Parliament in December, 1741, an excuse for a rebuff to Government by proposing for chairman of Election Committees the unpopular Giles Earle. The consequence, the election of Dr. Lee, a member of the Opposition, cost the Government a most important advantage. The unseating of the members for Westminster, two Ministerialists, by a majority of four, and the Berwick election decision, warned him of his mistake when it was too late. He once more shook off his fits of silence, alternating with fretful captiousness, to deliver a masterly answer to Pulteney's motion of January 21, 1742, for referring the papers on the war to a secret committee. The self-compassionating old Whig houses congratulated themselves on their preservation by this speech, and by the timely conversion of two Tories, from four and twenty tyrants. The division was close. Ministers had been deceived as to the purport of the motion; the ranks of the Opposition were full, though only the chiefs had been told the cause. "Sir William Gordon was brought in like a corpse; some thought it had been an old woman in disguise; others, who found him out, expected him to expire every moment. Mr. Hopton was carried in with crutches." This victory was the last. The substance of the same motion was agreed to without a division in a few days; and the decision on the Chippenham election against Government by a majority of one on January 28, was followed on February 11 by the resignation of the invincible "Prime Minister." He would have fought on but for the cowardice of his colleagues. More loyal believers had predicted that he would never give up. They reckoned that he could, if matters came to the worst, bribe the whole Opposition into submission by the offer of a few sinecures. The timorous officials were right.

It had been a hard thing to gain the victory. To divide the spoil satisfactorily was an insuperable task. The conquerors acted like the brigands who prepared poison for their comrades, and then drank deep of the deadly flasks. Each esteemed his own merits engrossing, exclusive; the veterans of Opposition, because they never had taken a place; the ex-Ministerialists, because they had sacrificed so much, and so recently. At all events, they could with one consent fly at Pulteney. Many of them thought him not sufficiently decided in the struggle; some malignant minds imputed to him, and his friend Carteret, systematic treachery. "They desire to get in," had written Chesterfield in the September of 1741, "by negotiation, and not by victory with numbers, who, they fear, might presume upon their strength, and grow troublesome to their generals. . . . The only effect of our strong minority will be to raise the pride of Pulteney. He has a personal influence over many, and an interested influence over more. The silly, half-witted, jealous Whigs, consider him as the only support of Whiggism; the interested Whigs, being persuaded that he has opened the door of the Court a little, will hold fast by him to squeeze in with him." All believed him to have a paramount influence; so that anything not done to please them was left undone through him. Both Tories and calculating Whigs deemed his professions of purity a screen for motives no better than their own. Walpole did all he could to encourage the schism in the camp of his enemies. He hoped in the discord to escape an impeachment.

Pulteney had an apparent supremacy enough to explain though not justify his hardly loyal language, "If the King wished to open any treaty." But his positive power was gone with the accomplishment of the object for which it had been placed in his hands by the nation. He had no large principles of policy to expound; he had not even experience in the commonplace system which his predecessor had administered. He had been, for all his mature political life, feeling his way along the path engineered by the man he was pursuing to the death. The flight of his enemy left him alone in the dark forest; and the road, as an American poet has said, suddenly turned into a squirrel track and ran up a tree. He had no right to complain that he did not remain the popular idol; neither, for that, had the people, that he had deceived them. He had done their work in casting down Walpole; they had helped him to attain his revenge. It was his own fault and his own merit too, that he missed the opportunity of striking a blow for his sovereignty. He had appeared to be "once in the greatest point of view in which a subject has been ever seen." To him was confided the choice of a plan of reformation, or a revival of old systems. To please all was impossible. As a contemporary, Lord Egmont, remarks in his 'Faction Detected,' a Place Bill was, in some men's eyes, good government; others were for annual Parliaments; others desired a reduction of the civil list. Some cried for justice on the Minister, and others for pensions for themselves. The plans for his guidance were as various as the sections of the Opposition he had led. Many of them might be good; very few were feasible in the struggle of party feeling. He could have pleased most by hounding them on to the destruction of his late rival. Nothing was easier; but he was not a man of blood, and "had meant by the Minister's destruction the annihilation of his power, not of his person." Perhaps it would have been his most popular course to constitute himself absolute Minister in Walpole's stead. He would have been overturned, and more speedily than his predecessor, but the fall would not have been ignominious. The rage of the people was not unjustly excited that he had won a signal triumph by their help, and then led them round by another route, not only to the old system, which they might have pardoned, but to the old officials as well.

The not unreasonable public disgust had plenty of mouthpieces among his unsatisfied followers. When there were forty or fifty claimants of seats in a Cabinet, it could not have been otherwise. He rashly alienated Chesterfield, whom he left out of his arrangements, from a notion that he had betrayed the party once to Queen Caroline; also Bubb Dodington, that magnificent lover of himself in deep brocade and embroidery, tie periwig, and laced ruffles, who used to amuse himself with politics and sigh for a peerage; lastly,

Lyttelton and Pitt, immediate retainers of the Prince. Three hundred, Peers and Commoners, met at the Fountain Tavern, to arraign their leader. Argyle observed, in allusion to Pulteney's wealth, that a grain of honesty was worth a cartload of gold. He asked where was the extinction of party, if the Tories were to be excluded from the Ministry. Pulteney, although ever shrinking from general party meetings, and steadily refusing to call them at Chesterfield's and Dodington's suggestions in former times, took up a bold attitude. He declared, in what seems an official manner by the side of his old style, that "Government neither can, nor will, nor ought to be, taken by storm;" that all the old Ministers could not be turned out; that "it must depend upon the prudent conduct of the Tories themselves to abolish the odious distinctions of party;" finally, that "it was not just, dutiful, or decent, to dictate to the King how to dispose of every preferment." His remonstrances did not carry conviction; and a second meeting, confined to the chiefs, was held in the presence of the Prince of Wales, when the Tories were promised that one of them, Sir John Hynde Cotton, should be a Lord of the Admiralty.

For himself, Pulteney had demanded an earldom and a seat in the Cabinet without office, conceiving himself bound by a foolish vaunt in the past that he would never again be a placeman. He was tired of the responsibilities both of a leader and of a member of the House of Commons. He had some time back complained, "that he was weary of being at the head of a party; he would rather row in the galleys, and was absolutely resolved not to charge himself with taking the lead." The events of the last few months had proved to him the truth of his own comparison—used to Hardwicke and Newcastle when they came from the King to drink negus and talk of a Cabinet—of the head of a party to "the head of a snake which is carried on by its tail." As well dislike of the duties of a chief in the Commons, as his desire to add hereditary rank to fortune, decided him to go up to the Lords. He was glad to quit the Commons while his fame was fresh and living. The Court and King, originally reluctant, had been taught by Walpole to consider this elevation the best means of disarming a dangerous demagogue. The late Minister exulted in having turned the key of the Closet upon his rival, at last brought to a conference with the Sovereign. He had a true perception that the public would not discriminate between one seeming confidant of the Court and another. It was not the mere peerage which irritated the popular mind against its former hero. On the contrary, his delay in taking the earldom, though it arose from the futile hope of passing a bill against bribery at elections, of forcing Lord Hervey from Court, and especially of procuring a show of royal favour for the Tories, was imputed to greedy haggling after a higher price for his mercy to Walpole. An old calumny as to the terms on which he had exchanged his long lease of part of Piccadilly for the fee-simple, was vamped up. Against such charges it might have been thought he was proof. He would not have taken them to heart, except for the evidence he knew their facile acceptance bore to the intensity of his present discredit. In his agony on discovering the change which had come over the spirit of his adherents, he appealed to the King to take back his earl's patent; he is said, when it was delivered to him, to have stamped and trampled upon the parchment, in a paroxysm of angry mortification.

Walpole had despised the motives of his opponents too much to arm against their reasoning. He was himself by no means guiltless as a statesman, or a mere scapegoat of popular prejudices. His partisanship treated Toryism as necessarily treasonable. He disgusted the nation at large with sound Whig principles by a bigoted and exclusive adherence to a few maxims embodied in the Revolution of 1689. A radical defect of his organisation was that he looked on a temporary state of things as the preordained and permanent rule. He could never emancipate himself from the ideas of the tempestuous period when he had himself entered public life. He could not help believing that the nation still abdicated the privilege, in abeyance during a crisis, but assured to it by the Bill of Rights and Act of Settlement, of thinking for itself on politics, and choosing its own legislators and Ministers. Attending only to the moods of the Sovereign and of Parliament, taking them as his infallible gauge and test of public opinion, he at length fell into the fatal delusion, that to persuade them, no matter how, was the one duty of a statesman. Not endeavouring to guide Parliament by external public opinion, but making its consent or opposition his single measure of popularity, he glided naturally into disbelief in the superiority of one member of that assembly, or of one argument, to another, into an arithmetical computation of men's powers by the votes they could command. He miscalculated most of all the determination and perception of the people. He allowed too little force to the length of time during which the passions of the previous century had been cooling down, and to the weariness of his own protracted predominance, unvaried by any danger to remind the Whigs themselves of the advantages of his judgment and foresight.

But if Walpole had, in his arduous position, failed from a misconception of the times and circumstances, and his own relation to them, the failure of his opponents, with their lofty pretensions, was infinitely more egregious. Walpole was their mark. As long as he was in office, their principles and their tactics were always the same. Corruption in Parliament, and without; care for Hanover; peace; financial parsimony; and a confederacy with France, had been the key-stones of Walpole's policy in the reign of George I. They remained the same in the reign of George II. They furnished the sole themes of the declamation of his rivals. We search vainly for evidence in their oratory and acts that they had conceived any idea of an administrative plan or doctrine by which they expected better than by his to secure the welfare of the kingdom. The repudiation of worn out party badges is a noble cry. Though we know that they adopted it from self-interest, we should still have had reason for gratitude to them if they had realised its meaning, and testified to their personal faith in it by their conduct. Not a fragment of proof to that effect can be discovered in their measures whether rejected or carried. Their attacks on the Administration indicate freedom from party spirit as little as the defence by the Ministry of its emoluments. Whig-seceders were as frightened as any placeman of the reproach of desertion of their ancient Whig standard, while the battle was proceeding. When the enemy's camp was in their hands their course evinced no genuine understanding of the motto on the flag they had waved. Dislike of party is a profession easy to make, and hard to disprove, when there exists a multitude of common topics of hostility to those in power. The points on which any two bodies of disappointed politicians disagree with a third body in office are so many as to make their junction the easiest thing in the world. When the battle is over the time comes for proving the truth of their professions of unanimity. If the two sets of leaders unite then, on an equal footing, in forming a Government, and if, as a Government, they think out and pursue a common policy, their coalition from the first is entitled to praise for good faith and unselfish public spirit. Judged by this test, Pulteney's and Bolingbroke's Whig and Tory Opposition cannot claim from posterity a reversal of the condemnation passed upon it by its own age. The most positive end it accomplished was to elevate to official supremacy the paltriest statesman who ever trafficked in a nation's fortunes. Pulteney and Bolingbroke tore the control of patronage from Walpole that the field might be free for the Duke of Newcastle to hawk it about.

The personal collapse of Pulteney's influence was yet more remarkable than that of his party. He would have liked always to overshadow the Minister for the time being without substituting himself. He did not comprehend the impracticability of such a character, until he had lost his chance of changing it. In 1743, Lord Wilmington, the First Lord, died; and Pulteney's old associates, jealous of the suspected secret preponderance of Walpole with the King, persuaded him to retract his resolution of never accepting place, and ask for the Treasury. The King coldly declined his services, and nominated Mr. Henry Pelham. The loss of his importance was subsequently again indicated to him. The Privy Seal which he demanded for Lord Carlisle was given to Lord Cholmondeley, Walpole's son-in-law, and his remonstrances against the return to office of Henry Fox, one of the most corrupt of the old Administration, were quietly neglected. The glimpse of power, called "the Revolution of three days," which visited him in 1746, only lighted up the barrenness of his political prospects. George had found the yoke of the narrow-minded, selfish bureaucracy, represented by Newcastle, intolerable. He entreated Lord Bath to overthrow it. The commission was accepted; the financier Gideon and the moneyed interest agreed to countenance the plot, and Granville was suddenly nominated Secretary of State. It was just such a conspiracy as might have been expected from Carteret, who, always drunk with claret or imagination, loved a combination in the inverse proportion to its practicability, and from the eagerness and reminiscences of Pulteney, who had once been able to gather a host about him by a nod, and forgot he had abdicated. An official mutiny ensued; all the Ministers had at once resigned; Lords and Commons refused to have anything to do with the plot; the nation looked on with the most irritating apathy; and Granville and Pulteney had to retire disgracefully. "Your victory is complete," wrote Chesterfield from Ireland, where he was viceroy, to Newcastle. "Good policy, still more than resentment, requires that Granville and Bath should be marked out, and all their people cut off. A general run ought to be made upon Bath by all your followers and runners."

Persecution was not necessary. Pulteney was not, in the Lords, a politician to be feared even by Newcastle. He could not comprehend the flight of his popularity. To himself he appeared the purest of patriots, because he had constantly refused office. But, though he could not explain his downfall, he was fully conscious of it. The satirical odes of Sir Charles Hanbury Williams inflicted, says Horace Walpole, deeper wounds on Lord Bath than a series of Craftsmen by him and Bolingbroke for several years could inflict on Sir Robert Walpole. Akenside, once a hot radical admirer, hurled an angry ode at his retirement from the post of tribune, which would touch him less sharply. Pulteney was a member of a different world to Akenside's. He was much more provoked by the epigrammatic irony of the fashionable writer of *vers de société* than by the wrath of the poet of Imagination.

In that world of which he was an ornament he found many consolations for his disappointments. He was the guide and friend of the great original of modern literary ladies, the celebrated " blue-stocking," Mrs. Montagu. Through her he was admitted to intimacy with Mrs. Elizabeth Carter, the translator of Epictetus. With them he could develop to the uttermost his genius for Greek and punning, suffer himself at Tunbridge Wells to be dragged up the rocks of Mount Ephraim, and be inveigled into spending his money on nosegays. He was playful, affectionate, and in private life universally courteous. Friends who half lived in his house, Bishop Newton, originally his chaplain, and Bishop Zachary Pearce, bear testimony to his unvarying kindness, goodness of heart, and even munificence. He loved his wife, and was loved in return. " She," says Newton, " was a wonderfully agreeable woman when she pleased, but was often clouded and overcast." By her love of speculation and hoarding, which made her brother call her dressing-room, with its levee of moneybrokers, " the Jews' synagogue," she encouraged her husband's natural love of money, till it became a deformity in his character. He had not accumulated without an object; all his thoughts and hopes were concentrated on his only child, Viscount Pulteney, a young man of moderate abilities. His son died abroad. The intelligence had reached the guests at his table before himself. He learnt it from their faces while he was drinking the dead man's health and happy return, as may be read in a pathetic narrative by Newton. Thenceforward he became indolent and indifferent about the disposal of his riches. From want of interest, not, as his enemies insinuated, from reluctance to repeat those self-denying words, "I give and bequeath," he left the whole, to the amount of £1,200,000, in a few words to a cousin.

Letters to his adopted nephew, the brilliant, but indolent George Colman the elder, picture the statesman in old age. We see him careful before his son's death of any device by which he might save five pounds, informing his young correspondent that he must get his living "by toil and drudgery;" that he will be "closely watched at Lincoln's Inn." At another time, he reminds him of a debt to himself—"the first thing that an honest man has to do is to pay his debts"—and warns him against wasting his time and money on going to the theatre. With all this, there is much affectionate thoughtfulness manifested; and he regrets Colman's absence from any scene he had enjoyed. He writes from Spa, that it is a pity he had not been there, "to play writs with a vast number of princes and princesses at twopence a corner." We can perceive, also, indications of the old tendency to love whatever was popular, in his sudden acquiescence in his nephew's dramatic pursuits, and willingness to have 'The Jealous Wife' dedicated to him, with his eagerness to cultivate Garrick's acquaintance. Whether at Spa, Bath, or Tunbridge Wells, he betrays the same concentration of interest and curiosity on the world of London. He requests Colman to be sure to send him, with Churchill's new poem, which he admired, "all the chit-chat he can pick up, whether in Lincoln's Inn, in Grub Street, or St. James's, let it be private scandal or political falsehoods."

In 1760, his dormant passion for pamphleteering revived. His anonymous 'Letter to Two Great Men,' Pitt and Newcastle, on behalf of the retention of Canada, triumphed in the coffee-houses, though by statesmen in office not more heeded, asserts Horace Walpole, than would have been their own effusions, had "they survived patriotism and power twenty years." In the same year the influence at Court, which he flattered himself he had never lost, became more actual on the accession of George III., who remembered Lord Bath as an amiable and lively visitor at Kew in the days of his father. It roused the jealousy of the Ministry; but an old man of seventy-eight was not a very dangerous competitor for power. A proof was the ill success of his efforts to gain permission for the exhausted Bishop Pearce to resign, and to procure the translation of Dr. Newton to a richer see. During the year and a half by which he survived his son, he ceased to cherish political schemes, either occupying himself with pious meditations, or innocent gaieties. His enemies saw in him only a politician who had been the tool of his allies, and a miser. Horace Walpole sums up his character, "he died very rich;" and Lord Chesterfield, on the news of his death in 1764, spitefully writes to his son, "the public, which was long the dupe of his simulation and dissimulation, begins to explain upon him." But there had been much happiness in the life of Pulteney, and some advantage to the nation. Of neither could impersonations of polite society, such as Chesterfield and Horace Walpole, form any idea.

To us the period in which Pulteney flourished is the stock and source of our present stage of political and social history. The fashion of our modern literature, our everyday language, much in our manners, and almost our modes of thinking, can scarcely be traced to a higher fountain-head. The same social interests as now, the same political questions, the reciprocal calumnies of the opposed coteries of fashion, the whispers of Mayfair, and the gossip of St. James's, the balance of power, the policy of subsidising foreign states, or the limits and expediency of direct taxation, were the topics of discussion. Except one broken range of hills marking the epoch of the French Revolution, there is little to intercept the view over the vast plain which embraces our times and his. This space comprises many modifications of feeling, and of the relations of classes; but there has been, since the strife of Bolingbroke, Walpole, and Pulteney, one continuous progress of reform. There have been various constitutional transitions, but no mental revolution. Readers find few violent contrasts with our own day to fix their attention, and are not tempted to dwell on discussions and contests apparently on the same questions with those now agitated. History engaged with the topics and in the form of a file of old newspapers is unattractive. Far from a deficiency of materials being the explanation of the neglect of the period, their abundance has tended to that result. Letters, biographies, and anecdotes are among the genuine sources of history; they are by no means history itself. Politicians and gossip-mongers have always found occupation in the last century. The period has been used, like the palaces and temples of old Rome, as a quarry whence to house the thoughts and fancies of the present; the surrounding country has become a desolate campagna, where the student is unwilling to linger. No novelty or certainty of conclusions is anticipated from a Parliamentary history crowded with discussions about yet unsettled and open questions, and little amusement from lives which have already furnished collections with their tritest stories, and supplied the moral of many an obvious proverb.

Yet in that wilderness lie concealed many pleasant spots; and grand torsos may still be dug up from among its forsaken monuments. To include the whole in one immediate and comprehensive survey is all but impossible. There are too many seemingly distinct centres of action to allow of such a treatment. No one great idea pervading and tempering all the rest at first can be discovered. The most that can be done is to trace in some section of the group of events an index and type of the rest; to fix our attention on the life of some representative man, some disposer of circumstances, over the formation of whose character we have a right to consider the diverse circumstances of his age must, by the law of action and reaction, have had in turn a control. The nature of the time invites to the use of such a method. With all its air of flatness it is the most individualising period of our history. Unlike the half-heroic, half-feudal age of the Tudors, it was not an age in which great minds monopolised history; it was not, as the reigns of the Stuarts, remarkable for distinctions of doctrine and sentiment; it was not diversified by the socio-political turmoil, the clubbist tendencies of the three post-Commonwealth reigns, when high-born and low-born, statesmen and writers of squibs, courtiers and poets, had each his engrossing political programme to elaborate, when every private circle had its public objects, and social distinctions were in the pervading excitement ignored, though not effaced or forgotten. It displayed very little national sentiment. The biographical age of history, it yet adds scarcely any but the post-dated portraits of Bolingbroke and Wyndham to the world's gallery of types. Above all others, the age of Walpole was the era of social badges, when society loved a coronet chiefly for the personal precedence it gave, honoured a dukedom less than a blue riband, and wealth combined with fashion more than either. The boundaries of the social line were strictly defined; those of long descent were lightly overleaped. Society became all in all, and avenged itself for having been absorbed in a former reign by politics, by drawing politics within the relaxing fascination of its own sphere.

This close union between society and politics, and their inverted relation invest the period with its most picturesque hues. Norman blood was disregarded, but eminence in the recent epoch of the Revolution was admitted as a source of distinction, a circle within a circle. Many pocket boroughs, or the commanding, even crushing, endowments of a Pitt, were required to mate the arrogance of families which boasted a representative among the founders of the Kit-Cat, or some champion on one side or the other in the mortal conflict between Harley and St. John. Within this line every one of riches sufficient for moving in the same social sphere knew every one. St. James's Square and Piccadilly had a vested right in the distribution of offices, or to be consulted on the strategy of the Opposition. Each new Ministry was a family, or a drawing-room, compact; and the choicest artillery of public warfare was drawn from the storehouse of private life and old familiarity. Individuals, to be fit representatives of the period, must have been leaders of society, as well as of Parliament. They must not have been too much above slander themselves, or of characters too elevated, to avail themselves of similar weapons. The first half of the eighteenth century is not a time of heroes in politics, or of architects of a national policy. It was a time which had its heroes, though incomplete. Its records can show politicians of undaunted courage, inflexible against threats, caresses, and bribes. Eloquence had not died with St. John's expatriation; while losing something of its fire and strength, it had gained in variety. Jest and earnest, comedy and tragedy are observed mingling in the Parliamentary drama. Even that retribution which always, sooner or later, waits upon the diversion of public spirit to private ends, and the awakening of national passions for the gratification of private animosity, is not wanting. All their wealth and reputation, their powers of mind, and the patriotism which some possessed, did not save the chiefs of the mightiest Opposition ever known from an utter and irreparable fall. We are not left for a moment in doubt of the moral of the series of events. The morrow of their triumph witnessed their humiliation.

V.

AN AMERICAN REVOLUTIONIST
AND
AN ENGLISH RADICAL.

BENJAMIN FRANKLIN,
1706–1790.

WILLIAM COBBETT,
1762–1835.

BENJAMIN FRANKLIN.

STAGES of history, as I have already intimated, will not keep symmetrically to centuries. In many respects the eighteenth century terminated, and the nineteenth opened, long before the end of the former as reckoned by years and calendars. The period in which the career of Franklin became inseparably blended with English history shows little of the spirit of the eighteenth century as manœuvred in politics by Bolingbroke, and dictated to in literature by Pope. The lines of the era to which he is assigned must be drawn so as not to shut out Cobbett, and the dawn of modern Radicalism. Theirs was a season no longer of pamphleteering skirmishes, and spectacular Parliamentary tournaments. It occupied itself with the tearing asunder of nations' flesh and blood. Its combats were between causes wrestling in grim earnest for nothing less than death and life. The battle raged first on the other side of the Atlantic for State independence. It did not close there. When American liberties had asserted themselves, the scene of the strife shifted to England. France caught some of the impulse, and England some. The Thirty Years' War for the rights of English citizenship which lasted till 1832 was a sequel to the American War of Independence. Different as were their forms, the two revolutions, in America, and in England, were animated by principles of kindred origin. The victory of English Parliamentary reform was won in part across the ocean. Franklin's demonstrations of the rottenness of the administrative work of a corrupt representative system prepared the way for the battering-ram swung with beneficial results, if not from the most scrupulous motives, against the crumbling edifice by the editor of the Political Register.

If the several causes of the foundation of the Republic of the United States were ranged according to their respective importance, first of all would come the perverse policy of Mr. George Grenville, and the want of moral courage in Lord North to resist the unenlightened obstinacy of George the Third. If not demerits but only merits were classified, an equal rank, and that the highest, must be assigned to George Washington and Benjamin Franklin. So far as any historical events can be appropriated to individuals, those two men were the joint authors of the great Republic. The common English impression of Franklin recognises only two stages in his career. From the struggling printer he is transformed at a bound into the powerful diplomatist who rent in twain Great Britain and her American colonies. The actual Franklin rose gradually to this enormous influence. He had already become independent in fortune before he engaged in public affairs. When he had once taken to public life, he made it his profession, though he sighed after science. Step by step he grew to be the most prominent citizen of Philadelphia. He was appointed Clerk of the General Assembly of Pennsylvania; he became a justice of the peace, an alderman, a burgess of the Assembly. He established the first public library in America. He founded an academy and an hospital. He set on foot a militia force for the defence of the province against the French in Canada. "There was," he writes in his Memoirs, "no such thing as carrying a public-spirited project through without my being concerned in it." If it were so small a matter as clearing away the dust from the roadways or lighting the city, he had to set the example. One question was always asked when subscriptions for an improvement were requested: "Have you consulted Franklin, and what does he think of it?" From Pennsylvania his influence spread throughout the American colonies. He was appointed Postmaster-General for America. That office he kept for over twenty years. His enemies in

England often hoped to taunt him into surrendering it. But he lacked, he was in the habit of saying, "the Christian virtue of resignation." It was his rule "never to ask for offices," but also "never to resign them." Franklin had passed his seventieth year before he arrived at the Court of France as the champion of American independence. A long and active life had preceded his greatest exploit, the conclusion of the Peace of 1783.

In view of an impending war with France in 1754, he drew up a plan for "the union of all the colonies under one government, so far as might be necessary for defence, and other important general purposes." The scheme roused jealousy in England, and Franklin attributes to that feeling the despatch of General Braddock from England with two regiments of regulars for the expedition against Fort Duquesne. Though the project of the campaign was not Franklin's, only by his help was the army able to move a step. Horses and carriages could not be procured until Franklin had personally guaranteed payment to the lenders. He accompanied the force, and in vain endeavoured to dissuade the General from marching in a slender line nearly four miles long through a country infested by hostile Indians. The General's answer was: "The savages may indeed be a formidable enemy to your raw American militia; but upon the King's regular and disciplined troops, sir, it is impossible they should make any impression." In the panic which followed Braddock's defeat, Franklin carried a Bill in the Pennsylvania Assembly for the embodiment of a militia force. To concentrate more attention on the movement, he persuaded the Governor to proclaim a fast, that "the blessing of Heaven might be implored on our undertaking." He even obtained subscriptions from Quakers for gunpowder under the euphemism of "bread, flour, wheat, and other grain." He raised and commanded a regiment. Governor Dunbar offered to commission him as general of a force which he was to raise and lead against Fort Duquesne. Franklin had the modesty to decline the service which had proved fatal to Braddock.

But he might reasonably have esteemed himself not much inferior in soldierly competence to incapables such as the British Government thought good enough for colonial commands. Of Braddock's successor, Lord Loudoun, he writes: "I wondered much how such a man came to be entrusted with so important a business as the conduct of a great army; but having since seen more of the great world, and the means of obtaining and motives for giving places, my wonder is diminished."

In the years between 1743, when he began to have leisure for public affairs, and 1757 when he came to England as Agent for his province, he was preparing the lesson he applied eighteen years later. He was learning to despise the Home Government's method of managing colonial affairs, and to value aright the internal strength of the colonies for their own defence. He arrived in London on July, 27, 1757, no obscure stranger, but the most prominent citizen of the most important foreign possession of the Empire. The object of his journey had nothing in it of hostility to the Crown. The real sovereigns of Pennsylvania were not the House of Hanover, but the family of William Penn. The heirs of Penn appointed the Governor of the province, and their governor's one care was to see that none of the public burdens touched the vast estates of the Proprietary. Their nominee, the Governor, refused his assent to any tax from which his principals were not expressly exempted. At every step for the protection of the province by the maintenance of an efficient militia, the Assembly found itself checked in its measures for raising the necessary revenue by a veto from the Governor. Franklin was the most energetic enemy of the Proprietary. His future implacability against the American "Loyalists" originated probably in his early resentment against the Penns, who were among the foremost of them. So far the province felt itself drawn to the Crown through their common interest in defensive measures against hostile Indians and Frenchmen. Indeed, at the Privy Council, Lord Mansfield used his authority to break down the Proprietary's obstinacy. Yet even so early as this, Franklin's indignation was stirred by the exorbitant claims of the Crown to authority over the colonies. Within a few mornings after his arrival in London the accomplished and eccentric Lord Granville, better known as Carteret, who was President of the Council, granted him an interview. Lord Granville then surprised him by the statement that "the King's instructions to his governors, being first drawn up by judges, then considered in council, after which they are signed by the King, are, so far as they relate to you Americans, the law of the land, for the King is the legislator of the colonies." "His lordship's conversation," wrote Franklin, "a little alarmed me as to what might be the sentiments of the Court concerning us." For the moment Franklin's aim was to extort liberty from the ungenerous domination of a private family. He registered, however, the pretensions of the royal prerogative as matter of warning.

On his second visit to England he bore originally a commission only from the Pennsylvanian Assembly. To the Agency for Pennsylvania were gradually added the Agencies for Georgia, Massachusetts, and New Jersey, as the colonies found that what had been only a theory of the royal prerogative was in process of conversion into practice. He had come once more in 1763 to intercede against the King Log of the Proprietary Constitution. He found himself confronted with much more formidable claims of the British nation and Parliament. He still is seen, as in old days, appealing to the Sovereign; only formerly it was against the Penns he besought his aid, now it is against the King's own Ministers. The Stamp Act was passed by Parliament on the pretext of reimbursing this country for the cost it had defrayed in expelling the French from Canada and Nova Scotia. Franklin, by conversation, by private letters, and in the public press, was always forward to deny that the colonies owed any debt to the mother-country. The mother-country had engaged in war with France for its own ambitious purposes. The war was not a colonial, but an imperial war. The colonies had, he would have admitted, benefited by the results of the war. He was always forward to express his delight at the subjugation of the French territories. But he rejoiced "not merely as a colonist, but as a Briton." A moral duty lay on the colonists, their Agent confessed, to pay their share of the expenses because they were Britons. The fact, however, he asserted, was that they had already paid their share, and more than their share. "Every year during the war requisitions were made by the Crown on the colonies for raising money and men. They made more extraordinary efforts in proportion to their abilities than Britain did." What was that proportion, he urged, was: matter for grave consideration. He complained that it was a favourite device, "in order to render the taxing of America a popular measure, to insist continually on the topics of our wealth and flourishing circumstances, while this country is loaded with debt, great part of it incurred on our account." The truth was, according to him, that, magnificent as he accounted American prospects, the present was discouraging. Colonies, he forcibly argued, are not, like their countrymen at home, heirs to many generations of laborious ancestors. They have to do all for themselves; their expenses press so closely on the heels of their resources that a great part of the charges for the rout of Braddock and the triumphs of Wolfe and Amherst " lies still, in 1766, a load of debt upon them."

Even had Great Britain made them its debtors by relieving them from the perpetual terror of French attack at its own sole cost, the discharge of the moral debt should have been matter of mutual arrangement. But the colonies were being taxed by a Legislature in which they were not represented. When their aid in money had formerly been required, the custom had been to ask it of their Assemblies, as the Crown asked it of Parliament. On all proper occasions they were ready to grant aid as Parliament granted it. "We of the colonies have never insisted that we ought to be exempt from contributing to the common expenses necessary to support the prosperity of the Empire." They did insist that the money of the King's subjects in America could no more be taken from them without their own consent, obtained through their representatives, than from the King's subjects in England. "If the Parliament has a right thus to take from us a penny in the pound, where is the line drawn that bounds that right, and what shall hinder their calling, whenever they please, for the other nineteen shillings and eleven pence?" Franklin's theory of the relation of the colonies to Great Britain was that they were "only connected, as England and Scotland were before the Union, by having one common sovereign, the King." The founders of the colonies expressly went to the New World to escape from the tyranny of English statutes. "They took with them, however, by compact, their allegiance to the King, and a legislative power for the making a new body of laws with his assent, by which they were to be governed. Hence they became distinct States, under the same prince, united as Ireland is to the Crown, but not to the realm, of England, and governed each by its own laws, though with the same sovereign, and having each the right of granting its own money to that sovereign."

The weak point in Franklin's theory of colonial rule is that it implies the King could come to the consideration of colonial questions as if for the time he were transported bodily, and unattended by any of his Parliamentary advisers, across the Atlantic. Franklin would have been as unwilling that Lord Hillsborough should dictate to the colonies under cover of the King's name as that Parliament should dictate. Probably he would not have been disposed to deny the difficulty of emancipating the King whenever he had to exercise his colonial prerogative from an English sovereign's deference to the Ministers delegated by Parliament. But when Englishmen dwelt upon the "inconvenience" of a theory which supposed the division of "an empire into many separate states," he answered that "an inconvenience proves nothing but itself." It was, however, his consciousness of the difficulty of fastening upon the King double functions which doubtless suggested to him, as to his friend Lord

Kames, a consolidating union of Great Britain and the American colonies as the way out of the dilemma. If the colonies sent members to Parliament, Parliament in taxing them would not have been disjoining taxation from representation. The King, in exercising his colonial prerogative at the instance of his Parliamentary advisers, would have been exercising it with the implied assent of his colonial subjects. Franklin's logical objection to the actual mode in which the King and the British Parliament claimed to rule the colonies was that colonists were treated as possessed of inferior liberties to their fellow-subjects here. They were governed without having a voice in their government. The grant of proportionate representation in the Imperial Parliament to Pennsylvania and the rest would have brought their subjection to the supremacy of Parliament at all events into logical conformity with the theory of the British Constitution.

That any such Parliamentary union with the North American colonies would have been permanent it is impossible to believe. Franklin affected to think " it would probably subsist so long as Britain shall continue a nation." On the contrary, the first occasion on which the colonial representatives had been overborne by the English and Scotch members would have dissolved it. Franklin himself would have been the first to denounce a connection in which British representative heads were counted as against colonial. Great Britain and the American colonies were doomed to part by the very incompatibility of their rival greatness. The projects Franklin and some of his English and Scotch allies devised with a view to averting the catastrophe carried on their face proof of their want of reality. It was, however, a gratuitous addition to the shock of predestined separation that British politics should at the time have been passing through a stage of moral degradation which intensified the violence of the wrench. Almost more grievous still was the coincidence that it was the fate of England to have Franklin, of all men, for witness to the decay.

In the earlier years of the reign of George III. the whole

body of British politics was sick, it seemed, to death. Franklin's letters home reveal it in all its ghastly infirmities. The few statesmen who were incorrupt were technical fanatics, like Mr. George Grenville, or "inaccessibles," like Lord Chatham. Public men were commonly of a much weaker moral or mental fibre. There was the careless King's Minister, like Lord North, who for the sake of peace with his colleagues, "some of whom could not be brought to agree to the repeal of the whole Stamp Act," suffered his better sense to be overriden, and consented to maintain "the duty on tea, with the obnoxious preamble, to continue the dispute." There was the man of pleasure, like Lord Clare, who, "after we had drunk a bottle and a half of claret each, hugged and kissed me, protesting he never in his life met with a man he was so much in love with." There was the official, incapable of understanding that a colony could have rights, like Lord Hillsborough, "whose character is conceit, wrong-headedness, obstinacy, and passion." There was the Minister with an instinct of equity, but without the moral courage to adhere to it, like Lord Dartmouth, "with dispositions for the best measures, and easily prevailed with to join in the worst." There was the mob of peers, not vouchsafing even to consider, still less to understand, Lord Chatham's plan for pacification: "Hereditary Legislators! There would be more propriety, because less hazard of mischief, in having, as in some University of Germany, hereditary professors of mathematics." There was a House of Commons, costing "no less than four thousand pounds for a member." There was the abandonment of London for days to "a drunken mad mob," which had made a hero of "an outlaw and an exile of bad personal character." "I went last week to Winchester, and observed that for fifteen miles out of town there was scarce a door or window-shutter next the road unmarked with 'Wilkes and Liberty,' and 'No. 45.'" There was, at least in the American's eyes, "in short, a whole venal nation, now at market, to be sold for about two millions, and able to be bought out of the hands of the present bidders, if he would offer half a million more, by the devil himself."

This was a population which talked of "our colonies," as if Pennsylvania and Massachusetts and Virginia were private possessions of every ignorant Englishman. To Englishmen an American's apology for existence was that he made a market for English goods. These people, who thought themselves competent to legislate for America, could scarcely point out its place on the globe. They would not of themselves have seen any incongruity in Franklin's jest that the King of Spain had contracted for the casting of a thousand guns at Quebec, or detected the absurdity of his assurance that " the grand leap of the whale in the chase up the Falls of Niagara is esteemed, by all who have seen it, as one of the finest spectacles in nature." For a time the King was the refuge of Americans enraged and outraged by the pretensions of men they despised to lord it over their superiors in character and public spirit. Franklin records with delight so late as 1772 how "the King has been heard to speak of me with great regard." He loved to contrast the goodness of the King with the stupid selfishness of the nation. But gradually he begins to "suspect, between you and me, that the late measures have been very much the King's own, and that he has in some cases a great share of what his friends call firmness." He hopes still that, "by some painstaking and proper management, the wrong impressions the King has received may be removed." At length the suspicion becomes certainty, the hope fades, and he is forced to the conclusion, which was unhappily only too true, that "the King hates us most cordially" in the aggregate, and "that insidious man," Franklin, in particular.

King George thought all who disagreed with him madmen or rogues. We know from the Shelburne Correspondence how he consoled himself at the end of the American war with the reflection that "knavery seems to be so much the striking feature of the inhabitants, that it may not in the end be an evil that they will become aliens to this Kingdom." At all events, his instinct of aversion from Franklin did not deceive him. Whatever was vicious and out of joint in the relations between England and its colonies showed uglier and more misshapen as reflected through Franklin's eyes. It was not by any design or desire of Franklin that his mission in England irritated every disposition in the two peoples to quarrel. His correspondence shows that, though he could not avoid perceiving the blunders of English dealing with America, he would have been far from disinclined to aid in correcting them. He had shown himself so temperate a mediator between the two countries, that when the Stamp Act was promulgated in America in 1766, his house and family in Philadelphia were threatened by a mob. His complaint in 1768 had probably not been insincere that, as he had rendered himself suspected in England of being "too much an American," in America, on the contrary, he was suspected of being "too much an Englishman." He argued that "between the governed and governing every mistake in Government, every encroachment on right, is not worth a rebellion." To the very eve of the civil war he was ready to discuss ways by which it might have been avoided. Yet an agent of the colonies much less acute, much less of an impassioned enthusiast for peace, with a far inferior title to gain an audience of Ministers and orators, would have had more chance of success in appeasing the feud. As we read the correspondence which Mr. John Bigelow has compiled and condensed in his 'Life of Franklin,' published in 1879, we feel the issue of the controversy to be a foregone conclusion. Franklin taught his countrymen to despise the mother-country. He seemed always to be presenting an ultimatum. In 1766 he writes of the Stamp Act: "As to executing the Act by force, it is madness, and will be ruin to the whole." In 1771 he writes to the Massachusetts Committee of Correspondence about the exaction of customs in America by Parliament, that civil war is the certain result. "The bloody struggle will end in absolute slavery to America, or ruin to Britain by the loss of her colonies; the latter most probable from America's growing strength and magnitude." Another representative of the colonies would probably have begun by assuming the indissolubility of the bond which united Great Britain and its American settlements. Franklin showed himself to his countrymen perpetually in the act of testing the chain, to judge where were the weak links at which it might be expected to break. Instead of a mediator come to negotiate a removal of colonial grievances, he appeared in the character of a judge pronouncing a divorce of the Colonies from Great Britain for British infidelity, cruelty, and general desertion of duties.

Jobbing English politicians felt and resented the tone of scornful superiority in Franklin's remonstrances on behalf of his constituents. They exulted in the opportunity afforded them for a retort by his appearance before the Privy Council to give evidence on the petition of Massachusetts for the removal of Governor Hutchinson and Lieutenant-Governor Andrew Oliver. The ground of the petition was that correspondence which had fallen into Franklin's hands between them and a Mr. Whately, who had been private secretary to Mr. George Grenville, convicted them of having incited the British Government to the measures whence had issued the strife between it and the colonies. The scene in the Council Chamber on the historical 29th of January, 1774, was an explosion of wrath long pent up. The whole, as Franklin wrote to Mr. Cushing, was "in all probability preconcerted." The thirty-five Privy Councillors, forgetting that they were sitting as judges, "frequently laughed outright," as Dr. Priestley narrates, "at the sallies of "Mr. Wedderburn's sarcastic wit." They were charmed to retaliate thus on the Transatlantic moralist who, they well knew, had been for seventeen years cataloguing their follies and corruptions. They were not altogether wrong in condemning the conduct of Franklin in that transaction. It is not necessary to accept Wedderburn's insinuation that Franklin had employed his opportunities as American Postmaster-General to intercept Governor Hutchinson's letters home. Mr. Charles Francis Adams's account is probably true, that the papers were delivered to Franklin by Sir John Temple. Not the less had both Franklin and the Assembly of Massachusetts violated, in the use they made of them, the confidence of private correspondence. Franklin's defence has been commonly accepted by Americans. It was that private letters written by a highly placed official on public questions to a member of the British Parliament could not be described as private letters. That was the conclusion also of the Massachusetts House of Representatives. The fallacy of such a position is apparent. It is at least as extraordinary that Franklin should have thought the misuse of Governor Hutchinson's correspondence balanced by the publication and despatch to the English Government of the letters sent by Franklin as the Agent of the Massachusetts Assembly to the Assembly. Obviously publicity, though within a limited circle, was contemplated by the writer himself as a property of the letters to the Assembly, and privacy as a property of those of Governor Hutchinson to Mr. Whately. Most extraordinary of all was Franklin's profession of amazement in the account he published of the whole transaction that the British Government should not have profited by the occasion and left Governor Hutchinson and his brother officials "like the scapegoats of old to carry away into the wilderness all the offences which have arisen between the two countries." He did not understand, any more than after the war, when Great Britain interceded for the restoration of the Loyalists who had suffered in its cause, that a Government cannot with any self-respect cast the consequences of its blunders on subordinates who have served it. He actually appears to have anticipated gratitude from British Ministers for the part he had played in the miserable business. " A Court clamour," he exclaims in his narrative, " was raised against me as an incendiary! The very action upon which I valued myself as, it appeared to me, a means of lessening our differences, I was unlucky enough to find charged upon me as a wicked attempt to increase them. Strange perversion!"

The 29th of January, 1774, shattered what Franklin was fond of calling that "China vase," that "beautiful porcelain vase," the British Empire, as then constituted. From that day, though Franklin himself was possibly as yet unconscious of the catastrophe, no hope remained of reconciling the claims of Great Britain to sovereignty, and of the colonies to equality. On the day following the baiting at the Council Office, he was informed that " his Majesty's Postmaster-General had found it necessary to dismiss him from the office of Deputy Postmaster-General in North America." He lingered in England for another year and four months, observing "a cool, sullen silence" to Ministers. He kept, he writes, "a separate account of private injuries, which," he adds, " I may forgive." He certainly never forgave them. But, though henceforth he did not court, neither did he reject, overtures for an arrangement of the difficulty between the two kindred peoples. Interminable negotiations passed between Franklin on one side, and Lord Howe, Lord Hyde, Dr. Fothergill, Mr. David Hartley, and Mr. Barclay, on the other, for a basis of settlement. Franklin visited Lord Chatham at Hayes, to consult on possible means of accommodation. The great man's equipage was seen at Franklin's door in Craven Street, "on the very day twelve months," as Franklin proudly notes, "that the Ministry had taken so much pains to disgrace me before the Privy Council." Franklin by no means repulsed the assistance thus proffered for the reunion of the two countries. He remarked, with pleasure, the sympathy of Dissenters and Irishmen, and other victims of English legislative exclusiveness, with the resistance of the colonies, and their belief that "the salvation of English liberty depended now on the perseverance and virtue of America." The negotiations went on as merrily as if none of the parties to them entertained any suspicion that the subject-matter of their conferences had ceased to exist, that the British Plantations in North America had expanded into a nation. Even at this distance of time, an English student is sensible of a sort of despair, from the consciousness how only the surface was stirred by these elaborate discussions. The deliberations commonly accompanied or followed a game of chess between Franklin and Lord Howe's sister. They had neither less nor more of seriousness about them than the tournament of the chessboard. On points of detail Franklin was ready enough to give way. He offered to pledge his personal security for the repayment to the merchants of their losses on the tea thrown into Boston harbour. When it came to the question of conceding legislative independence to the colonies, neither could he abate, nor the English volunteer pacificators yield, a jot. The utmost to which Franklin's English friends felt they could even offer to pledge the British nation was, that the bare right of Parliament to supremacy should be so guarded in its exercise as to be practically dormant. Chatham himself could not presume to ask of the nation at large anything higher. When, moderate as was Chatham's plan for a settlement, and enormous as was his personal authority, the Peers would not so much consider it as to allow it to lie on their table, it may easily be conceived how utterly insoluble had the crisis become.

Yet of the two sides there was on the English more, it may almost be said, of good faith than on the American. We are far from imputing conscious insincerity to Franklin. He foresaw war as the necessary consequence of a failure to repair the breach; and his common declaration may be believed, that he was almost inclined to think "there was never a good war, nor a bad peace." He was no fanatical admirer of particular forms of Government. But circumstances, he obviously felt, had cut off from England its American Colonies, and there was no possibility of healing the wound. His Quaker, Dissenter, and Chathamite friends could scarcely believe in such a schism in the imperial unity. At the moment of recognising the independence of the United States, seven years later, statesmen looked forward to a possible return of the colonies to their allegiance. No Englishman could comprehend, as could Franklin, the capacity of the colonies for standing alone. In exhorting, when the British Ministers had shown themselves unbending in 1775, the Americans to resist, for that " nothing could secure the privileges of America but a firm, sober adherence to the terms of the association made at the Congress," men like Barclay and Fothergill hardly suspected that the firmness meant final separation. In asserting that "the salvation of English liberty depended on the perseverance and virtue of America," they were thinking of Americans as fellow-subjects, whose voices in favour of liberty would be added to their English voices in right of their common country. We can see more clearly in these days, and so could Franklin in his. An United American Congress was sitting at Philadelphia, and Benjamin Franklin had been scolded and sneered at by the Solicitor-General of England and the King's Councillors as a thief. It would have been wonderful surgery to reincorporate the bleeding limb in the old body. It would have needed nothing less than a miracle when the fragment torn from the mutilated British trunk was itself grown into a breathing being.

Franklin shook the dust of England from his feet as a subject of King George when he set sail for America in 1775. When he returned to Europe it was to watch and to baffle from Passy the clumsy efforts of British Ministers to make a solitude where they had failed to maintain peace. He was so far a diplomatist that he had studied human character for seventy years. Yet in England his diplomacy had only exasperated. In France he accomplished as much against England as Washington with all his victories. His knowledge of French was so indifferent, that on one occasion during the sitting of the Academy he was observed to "applaud the loudest at his own praises." He did the work, he never learned the dialect, of diplomacy. He was that strange creature, a Republican at the Court of a pure monarchy. In Paris his defects were virtues. His scientific fame spoke for itself in purest Parisian French. As a politician, he was to the Court the dire enemy of England; to the jaded society of Paris he was the representative of a new world of feeling and thought. His New England astuteness seemed to Parisian courtiers patriarchal innocence. His naïve stories and illustrations, which a thousand admirers were ready to translate and repeat in every circle of the town, were as bracing as quinine. His very costume, "his hair hanging, his spectacles on his nose, his white hose, and white hat under his arm," in the midst of absurd perukes and brocaded suits, came like a revelation of free nature to the slaves of fashion. He became, to his own amusement, the idol of Paris. "Mr. Franklin," writes a contemporary Parisian, "is besieged, followed, admired, adored, wherever he shows himself, with a fury, a fanaticism, capable no doubt of flattering him and doing him honour, but which at the same time proves that we shall never be reasonable." He tells his daughter that incredible numbers had been sold of clay medallions of him, "some to be set in the lids of snuff-boxes, and some so small as to be worn in rings." "Pictures, busts, and prints have made your father's face as well known as that of the moon." A great Parisian lady wrote fifty years later to the respectable Ticknor in language which implied that she thought Bostonians and Patagonians kindred peoples. After the same fashion, Versailles was never perhaps quite certain that the New England philosopher was not of Red Indian descent. But love does not reason. Paris had fallen in love with Franklin, and in homage to him grew enamoured of simplicity.

No Englishman was ever so caressed in Paris, for the very reason that Franklin was, and was not, an Englishman. As the American sage and philosopher, he performed as much for his country as he accomplished by his diplomatic skill. But he was a diplomatist too, and of high rank in the art. Colleagues and rivals, like his detractor Arthur Lee, or even Jay and Adams, who, as Mr. Fitzherbert wrote, in a letter quoted by Lord Edmond Fitzmaurice in his Life of Lord Shelburne, " rather fear than are attached to him," might be pardoned for inability to understand the source of his influence. They did not venture to deny the fact. In the only serious instance in which, with reference to the disputed fishery and boundary rights, he was accused of neglecting the interests of his countrymen, his colleagues certified that he had defended those interests with his counsels and his authority.

On another and more important point, he not merely cooperated but took the initiative. Englishmen and Canadians, who mutually cherish the connection of the Dominion with Great Britain, may well shudder at the contemplation of the extreme risk that connection ran from British statesmen's weariness of the war, and from Franklin's superior diplomatic keenness. A man who had gone through the campaign with Braddock, who had shared in the alarms and labours of the period which followed the British defeat, and exulted in the triumph of Wolfe, was not likely to depreciate the value of Canada. The moral right of the colonies to the old French possessions in North America had been a special question in the futile negotiations between himself and Lord Howe in England. When the war commenced, he sought to induce France to help the colonies to wrest Canada and Nova Scotia from England. As soon as the negotiations for peace with England opened, his great efforts were directed to persuade the English Commissioner, Richard Oswald, to see the utility of ceding those territories as proofs of a desire for that "sweet" thing, a "reconciliation," and as a safeguard against future causes of strife. Oswald, a prosperous Scotch merchant, was, as Franklin says of him, an old man who had "nothing at heart but the good of mankind, and putting a stop to mischief." He does not seem to have been fit to cope with a philanthropist like Franklin. He had happened to let fall an opinion, that "the giving up of Canada to the English at the last peace had been a politic act in France, for that it had weakened the ties between England and her colonies, and that he himself had predicted from it the late revolution." Franklin, who had been preparing the ground by asserting the title of the United States to reparation over and above the mere grant of peace for the injuries England had inflicted, proposed that Canada should be given and accepted as such reparation. He applied Oswald's own argument to the future: " I spoke of the occasions of quarrel that might be produced by England continuing to hold Canada, hinting at the same time, but not expressing too plainly, that such a situation, to us so dangerous, would necessarily oblige us to cultivate and strengthen our union with France." Oswald "appeared much struck with my discourse." Franklin had already developed a scheme on paper which he lent to Oswald to read and meditate upon. The plan was, that "Britain should voluntarily offer to give up the province, though on these conditions, that she shall in all times coming have and enjoy the right of free trade thither, unencumbered with any duties whatsoever; that so much of the vacant lands shall be sold as will raise a sum sufficient to pay for the houses burnt by the British troops and their Indians, and also to indemnify the Royalists for the confiscation of their estates." Oswald, he says, "told me that nothing in his judgment could be clearer, more satisfactory, and convincing, than the reasonings in that paper; that he would do his utmost to impress Lord Shelburne with them." Franklin, in reporting by letter this conversation to his brother Peace Commissioner, Adams, describes Oswald's remarks rather more fully than in the semi-official journal he kept. He tells Adams, on April 20, 1782, his proposal about Canada: "Mr. Oswald liked much the idea, but said they were too much straitened for money to make any pecuniary reparation; but he should endeavour to persuade their doing in this way." Oswald went to England to confer with Lord Shelburne, taking Franklin's paper with him. On his return to Paris, he informed Franklin that "it seemed to have made an impression, and he had reason to believe that it might be settled to our satisfaction towards the end of the treaty; but in his own mind he wished it might not be mentioned at the beginning; that his lordship indeed said he had not imagined reparation would be expected, and he wondered I should not know whether it was intended to demand it." A day or two after, Franklin conversed again on the subject with Oswald. "Oswald repeated to me his opinion, that the affair of Canada would be settled to our satisfaction, and his wish that it might not be mentioned till towards the end of the treaty." Franklin relied on the assistance of French statesmanship in pressing his advantage against British dejection.

But the extracts from French despatches printed in M. de Circourt's translation of Mr. Bancroft's history demonstrate that no one was more bitterly opposed than the French Ministers to the annexation of Canada to the United States. Eager as they had been to promote the separation of the British provinces in America from the mother-country, M. de Vergennes was entirely opposed to any extension of the emancipated territory. Perhaps he still cherished a hope that the French provinces in America, which had been conquered by England only twenty years before, might one day be brought back to their allegiance to the Court of Versailles.

Franklin, as a diplomatist, was not peremptory in insisting on abstract rights of his country, still less on his own dignity. But he studied the French men and the French women who ruled France, and he probed to the bottom the instincts of the French governing class, without losing his own. About alliances in general he was not solicitous. Before he started on his own mission to Europe he had in Congress, though in vain, deprecated the sending a "virgin" republic "suitoring" for the friendship of European Powers. "It seems to me," he writes, "that we have in most instances hurt our credit and importance by sending all over Europe begging alliances, and soliciting declarations of our independence. The nations, perhaps, from thence seemed to think that our independence is something they have to sell, and that we do not offer enough for it." Writing to Jay, at Madrid, in April 1782, he exclaims: Spain has taken four years to consider whether she should treat with us or not. Give her forty, and let us in the meantime mind our own business." Five years before, in 1777, he and his fellow-representatives of the United States in Europe had received instructions that, "in case France and Spain will enter into the war, the United States will assist the former in the conquest of the British sugar islands, and the latter in the conquest of Portugal, America desiring only for her share what Britain holds on the continent." Americans must blush to think that their new-born commonwealth should have condescended to purchase aid towards its emancipation by offers to help in enslaving another free state which had never done it any injury. We are glad, for the credit of Franklin, that he simply recites these instructions in a letter to Arthur Lee, who was at Burgos. He adds not a word implying approval of the dishonourable bribe to Spain.

He cared indeed little for European alliances except the French. To consolidate that he was all complaisance. His tact alone prevented a rupture with the French Ministers through the signature, in December 1782, behind their backs, of the preliminary treaty between Great Britain and the United States. His brother Commissioners, Jay and Adams, suspected that the French Government wished to protract the negotiations for its own objects, however the United States might suffer by the prolongation of the war. Their suspicion was not without foundation; and Franklin, when he understood the facts, concurred with their decision to proceed independently. But he had the wisdom, which his colleagues lacked, to be content with starting peace on its route without breaking down the bridge by which it had crossed before he knew whether it might not be useful for a retreat. To the French Minister's reproaches on the departure from good fellowship, he replied by the soft answer which turns away wrath. He defends himself, and Jay and Adams, against the charge of anything worse than "indiscretion," and "neglect of a point of *bienséance*." To those two offences he pleads guilty. But he warns M. de Vergennes not to forget the effect of a quarrel upon "the English, who, I just now learn, flatter themselves they have already divided us." The friendly relations of France and the United States had seemed in danger of being completely overclouded when Franklin's amiable apologies restored peace. Two days after the French Ministerial remonstrance, the United States actually received from the French Treasury a loan of six million francs, which infused new life into their military operations. Jay and Adams, "who," observes M. de Vergennes, "do not pretend to recognise the rules of courtesy in regard to us," could never have obtained that aid. Franklin's brother Commissioners underrated the gain to the United States from French succour. Without the diversion France created in Europe, and the subsidies she granted, it is almost impossible that the Congress should not have been compelled to conclude a humiliating peace with King George. Franklin understood that the French alliance was vital to his people, and he spared no pains that he might confirm it. As Jefferson said of him, in extolling his diplomatic dexterity, he, by his reasonableness, moderation, and temper, so won the confidence of the French Ministers that "it may truly be said they were more under his influence than he under theirs."

Englishmen were not so criminal, nor was England so near to the close of its greatness, as Franklin supposed. On the other hand, neither was the power of France so deeply rooted as it appeared to his friendly eyes, nor French assistance to the struggling Republic so generous as he habituated himself to represent it. While he was quick to detect the perversion of free institutions to the purposes of selfish corruption in England, he chose to be for the most part utterly blind to the more radical vices of French government and society. He remarks, almost as if it were matter of praise, that "the noblesse always govern here," and that "trade is not their admiration." On his journey, in 1785, through France to Havre, where he was to embark for America, he was entertained at the magnificent chateau of the Archbishop of Rouen, Cardinal Rochefoucauld. He seems not to have felt the Revolution in the air, and goes out of his way to testify that "the Cardinal is much respected and beloved by the people of this country." In England the foundations were sound. Much practical liberty, and even good administration, were compatible with electoral dishonesty and political perversity. But Franklin could perceive no hope of a remedy for the inconsistencies between theory and practice which disgusted him. Not altogether in jest does he advise Englishmen to "dissolve your present old crazy Constitution, and send members to Congress." The entire order of things in France was rotten at the core, yet Franklin was more than half inclined to live and die there. When the tempest had actually begun to rage, he still regarded it as a passing gust. He writes in October, 1788, to his friend M. le Veillard: " When this fermentation is over, and the troubling parts subsided, the wine will be fine and good, and cheer the hearts of those who drink of it." Had his life lasted a little longer, he would have had to lament the deaths on the scaffold of the correspondent to whom he wrote thus confidently, and a multitude of other friends.

Franklin simply did not see the instability of that charming Parisian society to which he discoursed in his shrewdly witty parables. We suspect that he only affected not to perceive the selfish motives at the bottom of the invaluable assistance the French nation and Government afforded his country. Chivalrous Frenchmen like Lafayette, in advocating the American cause, were protesting more against Court absolutism at home than against the imperial tyranny of Great Britain. Frenchmen generally and their rulers, when they succoured the United States, were merely fighting, as they had fought a generation earlier, England in America. They longed to recover Canada. When they had convinced themselves that their American allies would not consent to their return as sovereigns to any part of the North American continent, they liked better to leave their old dominions in the hands of England than struggle for their transfer to the emancipated British colonies. Whilst Great Britain remained still a neighbour they believed the Republic would not be able to dispense with the shelter of French protection. Franklin, who weighed human motives, especially when not altogether noble, with unerring sagacity, was possibly more desirous to convince Robert Livingston than himself convinced, when he wrote : " The ideas of aggrandisement by conquest are out of fashion. The wise here think France great enough; and its ambition at present seems to be only that of justice and magnanimity towards other nations, fidelity and utility to its allies." With this amiable construction which Franklin puts on the motives of French kindness to the American colonies of England in 1783, it is interesting to contrast his view of

French official civilities sixteen years before. In 1767, after his examination by the House of Commons on the subject of the Stamp Act, the French Minister Plenipotentiary in London, M. Durand, called upon him. "M. Durand," writes Franklin to his son, "is extremely curious to inform himself on the affairs of America; pretends to have a great esteem for me; invited me to dine with him, was very inquisitive, makes me visits. I fancy that intriguing nation would like very much to meddle on occasion, and blow up the coals between Britain and her colonies; but I hope we shall give them no opportunity."

The certainty that, had the American connection with Great Britain survived the Stamp and Tea Duty Acts, it must have collapsed in wider ruin a little later, produces a feeling of indifference to the personal incidents which contributed to the actual catastrophe. Otherwise, English readers of these volumes might be disposed to repine that Franklin should not have bestowed on the task of reconciling England and the colonies some of the unfailing *bonhomie* which kept the peace between the United States and France. As, when the war was once begun, every feature in the French national and political character was interpreted by him too kindly, so all in the English were interpreted too harshly. He made no account of the difficulties inherent in the relations of the colonies and the mother-country. To him there could be no fault on the former side, because there was nothing not faulty on the latter. He hears with delight of the vengeance of which the "No Popery" mob was the unconscious instrument upon Lord Mansfield and Governor Hutchinson. "Lord Mansfield's house is burnt. Thus he who approved the burning of American houses has had fire brought home to him. He himself was horribly scared, and Governor Hutchinson, it is said, died outright of the fright." He speculates with pleasure on the possible wreck of the whole British Empire: "If the English lose their Indian commerce and one battle at sea, their credit is gone, and their power follows." He foretells that the war "must end in the ruin of Britain, if she does not speedily put an end to it." He believes every tale of the "cruel captivity" to which "our brave countrymen," "martyrs to the cause of liberty," are subjected, "fed scantily on bad provisions; without warm lodging, clothes, or fire." He denounces the war "on the part of England as, of all the wars in my time, the wickedest, having no cause but malice against liberty, and the jealousy of commerce." He despairs of seeing its end because, he writes to an Englishman, "your thirsty nation has not drunk enough of our blood." Every Englishman is held by him guilty of complicity. But he attached especial guilt to politicians. He had written while fresh from England, in 1775, to his old friend, William Strahan, the King's printer : "Mr. Strahan, you are a Member of Parliament, and one of that majority which has doomed my country to destruction. You have begun to burn our homes and murder our people. Look at your hands; they are stained with the blood of your relations. You and I were long friends; you are now my enemy, and I am yours." Guilty above other Members of Parliament were, in his eyes, the King's Ministers. "I never think," he writes to Mr. James Hutton, in 1778, "of your present Ministers and their abettors but with the image strongly painted in my view of their hands, red, wet, and dripping with the blood of my countrymen, friends, and relations." Upon King George himself, once his admired mediator between a despotic Parliament and oppressed colonies, he pours out all the vials of his wrath. He charges upon the King the destruction, "in a continued course of bloody wars, of near one hundred thousand human creatures." To Franklin the King must account for two thousand scalps torn from defenceless farmers, their wives, and children, by the savages he hired. To Franklin the royal wickednesses are the best evidence of immortality. "The more I see the impossibility, from the number and extent of his crimes, of giving equivalent punishment in this life, the more I am convinced of a future state in which all that here appears to be wrong shall be set right."

The disposition in Franklin to misjudge England impresses readers of his correspondence the more that he was by theory and practice generally indulgent to principles and conduct differing from his own. So ostentatiously violent are his outbursts of anger at the English King, Ministers, and nation, and, with this exception, so universally philanthropic and moderate are Franklin's general sentiments and language, that it is sometimes hard to smother a suspicion that the harshness against his former fellow-subjects and Sovereign was a species of affectation. A more probable hypothesis would be that it was nature's revenge for the regular and continued repression to which from early manhood he had subjected his natural disposition. From the training his Autobiography shows him to have undergone, we can infer something of his original temper. In that unique work, now for the first time, through Mr. Bigelow's care, printed as Franklin wrote it, and with the addition of the last few pages which had never before been published, Franklin alludes to his native impetuosity, and to the means he took to correct it. When young, he was, he says, of a "disputatious turn," a very bad habit, he remarks, into which "persons of good sense seldom fall, except lawyers, university men, and men of all sorts that have been bred at Edinburgh." Noticing that "disputing, contradicting, and confuting people are generally unfortunate in their affairs," he exchanged the habit, after reading Xenophon's 'Memorabilia,' for the Socratic method. "I dropt my abrupt contradiction and argumentation, and put on the humble inquirer and doubter." He became so expert a master of dialectics, that a controversial printer with whom he worked at Philadelphia would at last "hardly answer me the most common question, without asking first, 'What do you intend to infer from that?'" As that very irritating substitute for dogmatism proved not more likely to make friends than his former practice, he set himself to curtail it. He retained of the Socratic method "only the habit of expressing himself in terms of modest diffidence." "I never use," he writes, "when I advance anything that may possibly be disputed, the words 'certainly,' 'undoubtedly,' or any others that give the air of positiveness to an opinion, but rather say, 'I conceive or apprehend a thing to be so and so,' or 'It is so if I am not mistaken.'" When he set up his "club of mutual improvement," the Junto, the rules drawn up by him were framed on the same principle. "Everything was studied which might prevent our disgusting each other." "To prevent warmth, all expressions of positiveness in opinions, or direct contradiction, were after some time made contraband, and prohibited under small pecuniary penalties." Restraint at the meetings of the Junto may be responsible in part for the freedom with which, when patriotism seemed to license him, the unlucky Lord Hillsborough is characterised as a compound of "conceit, wrongheadedness, obstinacy, passion, and insincerity." If King George once "the very best king in the world, and the most amiable," is condemned to Tophet for not letting the American colonies go free on their own demand, the warmth of the denunciation may only have been compensation for the careful veneer of calmness upon a nature apparently by no means devoid of passion and excitability.

Franklin had brought himself to regard varieties of doctrine and opinion as not worth the friction of loss of temper, with the one exception of the question of national liberty and independence. That appeared to him on a different level altogether. On that he esteemed anger lawful and virtuous, and he seems to have found an occasional fit of temper by no means disagreeable. He could bear vituperation with the stoicism of a tortured Indian, and then turn and wither up an assailant with lightning flash and fire. But the extraordinary feature both in his tolerance and in his intolerance is that no one can ever suppose his indignation was not as much under his command as his patience. His Autobiography and Correspondence are of high value as contributing to the history of a great political and historical epoch. They possess as much value of a different sort, as offering together the most marvellous representation of a formed and built-up character to be found in the whole of the records of pyschology. There was the raw, original Franklin, who might have developed in this or that direction; and there was a very different creature, the actual Franklin, as Philadelphia, London, and Paris knew him. The rough material had been hewn and carved and polished into the finished moralist, statesman, diplomatist, fabulist, and general worker in human wit, by a third self, a moral censor who was continually surveying and criticising the new fabric as it grew.

Franklin was at an early period dogmatic. As we have seen, he discovered that was an inconvenient character in which to make the pilgrimage of life. He corrected it at first by enquiring into the foundations of the dogmas of others, instead of propounding dogmas himself. People liked no better to be obliged to render an account of their own beliefs than to have another person's forced upon them; so, his inner monitor accommodated matters by engrafting a habit of suggesting an opinion. Whoever chose were left at liberty to suppose they had elaborated it out of their own heads. There was restlessly free blood in the veins of the Franklins. His father, Josiah, had quitted Ecton, in Northamptonshire, for Boston in 1682, for the sake of liberty of worship. He had a library of "books of dispute about religion," and Franklin when a mere boy read them out of a mere natural "bookishness." Later, when he was about fifteen, "some books against Deism fell into my hands; they were said to be the substance of sermons preached at Boyle's Lectures. It happened that they wrought an effect upon me quite contrary to what was intended by them; for the arguments of the Deists, which were quoted to be refuted, appeared to me much stronger than the refutations; in short, I became a thorough Deist." There worked the natural Franklin. But he argued from his new point of view to such effect as to convert his friends, and several of them ended by defrauding him. Consequently his monitor "began to suspect that the doctrine, though it might be true, was not very useful." Deism was put out at the door, and "trust, sincerity, and integrity," together with an apparently very sincere faith in Providence, were introduced instead. He accepted even Revelation, to such an extent at any rate, as to assume that, though certain actions might not be bad because they were forbidden by it, or good because it commanded them, yet probably those actions might be forbidden because they were bad for us, or commanded because they were beneficial to us." A man's belief is commonly part of himself, the growth of his own nature. Franklin ceased to be a rationalist because his inner monitor had examined the reasons for and against, and arrived at the conclusion that it was for his general advantage, comfort, respectability, and internal satisfaction to be unenthusiastically religious.

His own devotions he performed at home, but he had so good an opinion of the utility of public services that he persuaded the Federal Convention to open its sittings with prayer. Of the advantages of a regular liturgy he was equally convinced. To popularise the Prayer Book he helped the reformed Lord le Despencer, once the friend of Wilkes and "Abbot" of Medmenham, in abridging it. For his share he took the Catechism and the Psalms. This edifying work was published by a bookseller in St. Paul's Churchyard in 1773. Franklin's heart, however, was at all times more susceptible of charitable than of theological emotions. Writing in 1758 to his sister of an acrostic on her name, in which faith was described as occupying the Christian's ground floor, hope the first floor, and charity the garret, he bids her "Get as fast as you can into the garret, for in truth the best room in the house is charity. For my part, I wish the house was turned upside down; it is so difficult, when one is fat, to go upstairs." Religion moved him, not dogmatic theology. Every one knows his remark: "Orthodoxy is my doxy, and heterodoxy is your doxy." He could not understand why some American gentlemen desiring to officiate according to the rites of the Church of England in the United States, whom the Archbishop of Canterbury refused to ordain unless they took the oath of allegiance, should not ordain one another. As they objected, he asked the Papal Nuncio in Paris to direct a Roman Catholic bishop in America to ordain them. He was surprised that the Nuncio insisted they should turn Catholics first. Mr. Whitefield, he mentions in the Autobiography, "used sometimes to pray for my conversion, but never had the satisfaction of believing that his prayers were answered."

Followers of Whitefield could specify the day and even the minute of their conversion. Franklin had his conversion and its date too. But, as with his religious views and practices, so his morality was done to order. The natural Franklin was ordered by his ruling self "to acquire the habitude of all the virtues." In the year 1728, being then twenty-two, "I convinced the bold and arduous project of arriving at moral perfection. I wished to live without committing any fault at any time. As I knew, or thought I knew, what was right and wrong, I did not see why I might not always do the one and avoid the other." He accordingly divided all the virtues into thirteen, temperance, silence, order, resolution, frugality, industry, sincerity, justice, moderation, cleanliness, tranquillity, chastity, and humility. Humility was not in his first draft. He introduced it, "a Quaker friend having kindly informed me that I was generally thought proud, being in conversation overbearing and rather insolent, of which he convinced me by mentioning several instances." He kept a kind of diary, with a page allotted to each of the thirteen, and "determined to give a week's strict attention to each of the virtues successively." Order he found the hardest of all the virtues to acquire. "In truth, I found myself incorrigible with respect to order; and, now I am grown old, and my memory bad, I feel very sensibly the want of it." Humility was another difficult virtue. But, writes Franklin, "though I cannot boast of much success in acquiring the reality of this virtue, I had a good deal with regard to the appearance of it." "On the whole," he adds, "though I never arrived at the perfection I had been so ambitious of obtaining, but fell far short of it, yet I was, by the endeavour, a better and a happier man than I otherwise should have been if I had not attempted it." Mr. Bigelow found a marginal note appended to the original MS., from which his edition of the Autobiography is printed : "Nothing so likely to make a man's fortune as virtue." The natural

Franklin was guilty, as his own censorious self often remarked, of various "errata" in youth. In his Autobiography and in his letters to friends he avows a wish to have his life come over again, that he might enjoy "the advantages authors have in a second edition to correct some faults of the first." But that probably was only a show of tribute to the virtue of humility. His conscience seems to have cleared itself of all uncomfortable twinges for his youthful misdeeds. Of misdeeds in after life, except in the matter of an occasional second bottle and a preference of riding over walking, he shows no consciousness. Even the glass too much and the bodily indolence brought their own sufficient penalty in visitations of gout, which balanced the account.

Franklin's description of himself, both in the Autobiography and in his correspondence, resembles a little too much the portrait of a self-sufficient, self-made, pompous tradesman. Vice is represented as want of practical wisdom, not as something to arouse shame or moral indignation. Such a disposition would have broken up an empire and plunged the world in war in revenge for London not agreeing with a Philadelphian alderman's estimate of his own merits. He has misrepresented himself. The universal testimony of America, and France, and of a large body of the most upright and honest Englishmen, pronounced Franklin the brightest and least egotistical of companions, the warmest of friends, the most devoted and disinterested of patriots. George the Third's condemnation of his "insidiousness" was testimony to the frankness and simplicity which the King believed to conceal continual intrigues. The King was similarly prejudiced against the French envoy, Rayneval, for having "the appearance of an inoffensive man of business," since "cunning will be more dangerous under so specious a garb." Franklin was simply one of that class of men to whom the capacity has been given of surveying themselves from the outside as well as from the inside. He desired to judge himself as a stranger would have judged him. Some men do that towards the close of their lives, when their careers are become to them mere matter of history. He did it not in his Autobiography alone, but in every incident of his busy life. The quality in one sense is not very rare. But commonly they who are their own critics lose in courage and decision what they gain by appraising themselves at their proper value. They escape the danger of exaggerating their real merits, and they succumb to the evil of frightening themselves with their own shadows. Self-consciousness and timidity dwarf in them all vigour of growth. The happy peculiarity of Franklin's character was that it remained buoyant and independent in spite of the sense that at the end of each day it was sure to be called up to render an account of itself. His original self took advice from his educated self, yet never ceased to be natural. He studied humanity as mirrored in his own disposition. There he traced the varying strength of motives, and the mode in which they operate. What he saw he was ready enough to expose to the view of other men. The world at large was fascinated and charmed by being admitted to the contemplation of the most masculine and capacious of minds, through which its owner himself was always ready to act as guide.

The strength and variety of his friendships are among the most conspicuous features of his career. We know the fact by his correspondence; and also why it should have been so. As a lad he won predominating influence over more brilliant acquaintances, like Osborn, the "eminent lawyer" with whom Franklin "made a serious agreement, which Osborn never fulfilled," that "the one who happened first to die should, if possible, pay a friendly visit to the other, and acquaint him how he found things in that separate state." Keith the Governor of Pennsylvania, Burnet the Governor of New York, conversed with him, while a journeyman printer, as almost an equal. Whitefield would not resign the hope of converting so illustrious a moralist. Lord Kames, a forgotten Scotch celebrity, whose fame once ranked with that of Hume and Gibbon, was his intimate, with whom at various times he "passed weeks of densest happiness." Though politics, and perhaps the contrast between his measured equability of manner and Johnson's strongly accented temperament, kept them apart, Boswell was proud to be his acquaintance and his host. Cowper treasured the praises of his poems by "one of the first philosophers, one of the most eminent literary characters that the present age can boast of." Chatham sought his friendship. Fox eagerly claimed him still for a countryman. Lafayette haunted him, much to the disgust of the English Peace Commissioners, who thought they could understand Franklin, but not the French knight-errant. Mirabeau was the bearer of letters of introduction from him to America, and encircled his memory when dead with the halo of his meteoric eloquence. His successor at Paris, Jefferson, agreed that "no one could replace Dr. Franklin," for the reason that no one could excite so much interest as a man. Washington was proud to be counted among his friends. He was honoured by all the kings he ever had an opportunity of meeting, except his own. He was loved by the old lodging-house keeper in Craven Street where he lived. None could have been better company. He could play chess, and the next moment be weaving a new web of politics. He could fathom the secrets of nature, and explain them as if he were telling a fairy tale. He could make a real fairy tale the vehicle for a moral lesson, and hide a political sarcasm in a mock proclamation by the great Frederick. If the company loved its wine, he could drink as stoutly as Dr. Johnson. He had no fear of the gout before his eyes when fair ladies filled the glass, and wits were hanging upon his lips.

He enjoyed a large share of happiness in life, and was grateful for it. He himself has written: "The felicity of my life, when I reflected on it, has induced me sometimes to say that, were it offered to my choice, I should have no objection to a repetition of the same life from its beginning." At the age of twenty-one, he nearly died of pleurisy. "I was," he says, "rather disappointed when I found myself recovering, regretting in some degree that I must now, some time or other, have all that disagreeable work to do over again." As life proceeded he found enough of what was agreeable in it to make up for the vexation of its finiteness. At the age of sixty-three, he could say : "Take one thing with another, and the world is a pretty good sort of world." He would have been content to go on enduring its vicissitudes: "Though living on in one's children is a good thing, I cannot but fancy it might be better to continue living ourselves at the same time." In one way old age itself, which otherwise he would not object to have cured in himself along with other diseases, had its advantages. "As I grow old I grow less concerned about censure." As he grew old, he did not grow less willing to continue that exertion of the energies which to him meant happiness. At the age of seventy he accepted the dangerous and delicate mission to France. "I am," he told the Congress, "but a fag-end; you may have me for what you please." At seventy-nine he still found enjoyment in the management of affairs. Two years later, at the age of eighty-one, his legislative inventiveness was of the greatest benefit to the Convention which met in 1787 to frame the definitive Constitution. Though opposed personally to the system of two legislative Houses, he made the project practicable by his device that all the States should be represented equally in the Upper House, and according to population in the Lower House. If he sighed over his toils at seventy-nine, it was a sigh of satisfaction at the prospect of being "harnessed in the country's service for another year" as President of Pennsylvania. My countrymen, he wrote with manifest pleasure to a friend, "engrossed the prime of my life. They have eaten my flesh, and seem resolved now to pick my bones." At the age of eighty-three he still composed poetry, not very good, but not worse perhaps than that he was in the habit of writing sixty years before. Attacked simultaneously by gout, the stone, and old age, he comforted himself that "only three incurable diseases had fallen to his share, and that these had not deprived him at the age of eighty-one of his natural cheerfulness, his delight in books, and enjoyment of social conversation." If obliged by his three assailants to anticipate death, he solaced himself, by thoughts of a term of higher activity, and therefore enjoyment, in another stage of existence. He began to doubt whether the building, his body, did not need so many repairs that in a little time the owner would "find it cheaper to pull it down and build a new one." He avowed "a growing curiosity to be acquainted with some other world," and longed, "free from bodily embarrassments, to roam through some of the systems Herschel has explored, conducted by old companions already acquainted with them." His only hesitation at the age of eighty-two about dying is whether it were not a pity to quit this particular universe at a time of extraordinary "improvements in philosophy, morals, politics, and even the conveniences of common living, and the invention and acquisition of new and useful utensils and instruments." He whispers a wish that the final advance had been made in the particular art of physic, that, " we might be able to avoid diseases and live as long as the patriarchs in Genesis ; to which I suppose we should have little objection." "It was almost as well that, though in 1788 he had heard rumours of John Fitch's "boat moved by a steam engine rowing itself against tide in our river," and though he appeared to think the construction might be so simplified and improved as to become generally useful," he could not foresee the full application of the principle. It would have been too tantalizing to know he was leaving life on the eve of such a revolution.

The secret of his happiness was his power of doing whatever was his work for the moment with all his might. He could enjoy the pleasures of life as heartily as he performed its toils. Both were pleasures, if only one kind bore the name. Every faculty of his nature was permitted, and even commanded, to seek in its turn occasions for exercise. His bodily senses were encouraged to gratify themselves as well as the mental. For a sage Franklin seems to have liked good eating and drinking, perhaps even a very little too much. As a boy he was trained to be "quite indifferent what kind of food was set before me, and so unobservant of it that to this day if I am asked, I can scarce tell a few hours after dinner what I dined upon." He took a little later on to a vegetable diet, and used the money he saved to buy books. All the world knows how at Watts's printing-house, in Queen Street, Franklin drank water-gruel to his companions' beer, and outworked them all on the diet. As he became prosperous he acquired a decorous taste for less hermit-like fare. He was fond of madeira. He confesses "for one that if I could find in any Italian travels a receipt for making Parmesan cheese, it would give me more satisfaction than a transcript of any inscription from any old stone structure." Parmesan had still some savour of Arcadia. But in another letter from Craven Street he remarks: "Just come home from a venison feast, where I have drunk more than a philosopher ought." Already at the age, for him very juvenile, of sixty-two, he was becoming stout. He observes: "Men of my bulk often fail suddenly." Paris was not likely to teach him plain living; parties accompanied by innumerable glasses of champagne in his honour must have been so many challenges to gout. At seventy-eight he writes to Strahan, whom he had taken back into friendship, a letter of "chit-chat between ourselves over the second bottle." The next letter in these volumes, addressed to Henry Laurens, begins significantly: "I write this in great pain from the gout in both feet."

His talk of the bottle perhaps savours a little of humorous exaggeration. Certainly, in most points he would have contented Plato himself by his "temperance" and "justice" in respecting the independence both of his neighbours and of the various constituents of his own nature. It was this admirable orderliness of his organisation which leaves on those who only read what he wrote an impression of coldness and absence of generous fervour which his contemporaries did not feel. Franklin, as English politicians knew only too well, could be impassioned and fiery. There are signs in abundance that his heart could be touched as readily and more genially by private griefs and joys. If his acquaintances included a cross-grained aunt and her youthful niece, he could appreciate the tediousness of the companionship for the girl, yet compassionate even more the infirmities of body and temper of the poor old woman. "Invent," he writes to his younger friend, "amusements for her; be pleased when she accepts of them, and patient when she perhaps peevishly rejects them." He lifts up his powerful voice in an appeal for mercy to the "numbers of little innocents who suffer and perish" from its being unfashionable in London, and yet more in Paris, for mothers to nurse their children. In the midst of the turmoil over the Stamp Act, he is anxious in London for news of his young grandson in Pennsylvania: "You have so used me," he writes to his wife, "to have something pretty about the boy, that I am a little disappointed in finding nothing more of him. Pray give in your next, as usual, a little more of his history." We are afraid his admirers must admit that he too easily resigned himself to accept his wife's dread of the sea as a sufficient excuse for their separation during many years. But he thought she was happy with her walnut-trees and grandson; and he soothes the pangs of remoteness compelled by "duty to my country," by choosing London novelties for her, "a crimson satin cloak, the newest fashion," and a gown of flowered tissue, sixteen yards, cost nine guineas; I think it a great beauty." While the Stamp Act was still in force he would not violate the colonial self-denying ordinance by sending Mrs. Franklin presents of British goods. The moment it was repealed, in 1766, he despatches "a fine piece of Pompadour satin, fourteen yards, cost eleven shillings a yard." For his wife's comfort, so long as she remained at Philadelphia, he is ready even to sacrifice the completeness of his electrical apparatus. "If the ringing of the bells connected with the iron rod frightens you, tie a piece of wire from one bell to the other." I am, however, bound to say that he adds: "Though I think it best the bells should be at liberty to ring, that you may know when they are electrified; and when you are afraid, you may keep at a distance."

His purse was always open to a tale of distress. He had an ingenious method of circulating alms, by charging it on the honour of the recipient to pass on the gift to another deserving object, if he should have the means of making payment. He sends five louis d'or to an English clergyman, who had been taken by a French privateer, or perhaps by Paul Jones, and was in prison in Paris. "Some time or other," Franklin tells him, "you may have an opportunity of assisting with an equal sum a stranger who has equal need of it. If so, by that means you will discharge any obligation you may suppose yourself under to me. Enjoin him to do the same. Let kind offices go round." To an American in distress he gives ten louis, bidding him follow the same course: "I hope it may thus go through many hands before it meets with a knave that will stop its progress. This is a trick of mine for doing a deal of good with a little money." He adopted the same system with the salary he received, on quitting his French mission, as President of Pennsylvania. He held that "in a democratical State there ought to be no offices of profit." An envoy might receive a salary, he appeared to think; and an American Postmaster-General might for seventeen years receive the salary in London, and perform its duties by deputy in America. But he drew the line short of Presidents of Assemblies and States. Accordingly, he bequeathed his Presidential salary and its accumulations on trust, among other things, for loans to young artisans. These loans, unlike Franklin's louis d'or, were to be repaid with interest; but the principle was the same. A limited sum was to circulate illimitably in charity from hand to hand. The scheme was unsuccessful, partly from the want of proper objects, and partly from the failure of the legacy to realise the amount it should, by Franklin's estimate of the profits of compound interest, have produced. By the end of two hundred years, two thousand pounds, he computed, should yield eight millions one hundred and twenty-two thousand pounds sterling. As in the eighty-two years from 1790 to 1872 the two thousand produced only a little over ten thousand, that magnificent arithmetical vision would seem to have had some flaw in it. However, the intention was equally benevolent, though the trust in compound interest proved as much a broken reed in Franklin's benevolent hands as in the exceedingly selfish ones of Mr. Thellusson.

His pen was as ready as his purse in the service of all human kindliness. And what a pen it was! It could discourse on metaphysics so lucidly as to make the finest subtleties seem plain moralising. It could tear a sophism to pieces by a query. It could make a simple tale read like a philosophical argument. He could be grave and he could be gay in a breath. On a 'Craven Street Gazette,' composed to amuse an old lodging-house keeper away from home, and probably fearful that the world, or the Strand, would be out of joint before her return from Rochester, he could spend as much wit and humour as on a State paper designed to fire America and sting England. In another tone he translates into human language, for the amusement of a Court lady, the reflections, in the garden of her house, of a grey-headed ephemera, full seven hours old, on the vanity of all things. His 'Petition of the Left Hand' might have been composed by Addison. In it the left hand bewails the partiality which educates the right hand exclusively. Some of Franklin's fables and tales have been so absorbed into the thought of the world that their source is absolutely forgotten. In this manner we may account for a plagiarism not long since by an eminent sanitary authority of Franklin's 'Economical Project for Diminishing the Cost of Light.' The economy consists in rising at six o'clock instead of nine or ten. A wakeful Parisian is represented as having discovered to his great astonishment that the sun actually began to shine at that hour. He calculated the saving to Paris in candle-light, should the city take advantage of the fact, at ninety-six million francs. But the philosophers of the town denied the fact. They proved by common notoriety that there could have been no light abroad at six o'clock, and therefore none could have entered from without. Their explanation was that the "windows, being accidentally left open, instead of letting in the light, had only served to let out the darkness." No one who listened to the recent reproduction of this bright little satire appears to have doubted the re-discoverer's originality. That is a tribute to its modern air. But, in truth, ideas such as Franklin's never become superannuated. Few who use the expression, "to pay dear for one's whistle," know that the dear whistle was a purchase made by Franklin, when seven years old, with a pocketful of pence. Franklin's store was too abundant for him to mind, though some of his fame went astray. "You know," he tells his daughter, "everything makes me recollect some story." It was not recollection so much as fancy. His fancy clothed every idea in circumstances. When the illustration had served its turn, he was indifferent what became of it. If he cared at all, it was that, when borrowed by a newspaper or magazine, it should have its proper allowance of long-tailed s's and italics, and capitals to the substantives. With his old printer's prejudices, he could not understand the modern "fondness for an even and uniform appearance of characters in the line." He was less delighted at the complimentary censure by Lord Mansfield of his witty and bitter 'Edict of the King of Prussia' when reprinted in the Chronicle, than indignant that the Chronicle should have "stripped it of all the capitals and italics that intimate the allusions and mark the emphasis of written discourses, to bring them as near as possible to those spoken." He thought such appeals to the eye help to raise a writer to the level of a speaker, who has at his command both accent and gesture to point his periods. Franklin did injustice to himself when he fancied he wanted such poor mechanical aids. His English had been learnt from The Pilgrim's Progress and the Spectator. It had the force of Bunyan without his ruggedness. It had much of the serene light of Addison, with more raciness and tenfold the vigour. It sparkled with sarcasms as cutting as Voltaire's, but all sweetened with humanity.

If David Hume might condemn here and there a sprinkling of such words as "pejorate," it was not from poverty but from exuberance of diction that Franklin exposed his vocabulary to criticism. Many of his inventions, or adaptations,

such as "colonise," have long been stamped as current
English. But he did not covet the fame of an inventor,
whether in language, in morals, or in politics. In language
he was even a declared foe to change. Writing to Noah
Webster, the lexicographer, in 1789, he protests against the new
verbs, "notice," "advocate," and "progress." He had as little
ambition to be a classic as to be an innovator in English. He
wrote because he had something at the moment to say, with a
view to procuring that something should at the moment be
done. In religion he confessed to a certain liking for heretics,
all of whom, so far as he had acquaintance with the class, he
declared were virtuous men. What, however, he liked was
not their heresy so much as the spirit of self-sacrifice which
led them to brave persecution. As a moralist he did not
aspire to alter the materials with which he had to deal. He
was satisfied that men should make something more of their
life, as their life was, without expecting to transform them
into angels. When he proposed to himself moral perfection,
he was aiming at nothing superhuman. He pared his defini-
tions of the virtues he had resolved to practise down to the
moderate level to which he felt himself not unequal. If a
defect did not appear to be of a nature necessarily to injure
a man or his neighbours, he was not prepared to banish
it as a vice. Humility had forced its way in among his
ostensible virtues. But humility in his sense is not incom-
patible with a certain intermixture of vanity. "Most people,"
he writes, "dislike vanity in others, whatever share they have
of it themselves; but I give it fair quarter wherever I meet
with it, being persuaded that it is often productive of good
to the possessor and to others that are within his sphere of
action; and therefore in many cases it would not be
altogether absurd if a man were to thank God for his
vanity among the other comforts of life." His model of
life was adapted rigidly to the ordinary circumstances of
humanity. If men seemed to be substantially the better
off for the ownership of a quality, Franklin inserted that
quality among his virtues. He was always more ready to
admit a new candidate to his Olympus than to risk rejecting

an addition to the sum of human happiness. He himself believed in a Providence, and apparently in "a particular Providence;" he was not disposed to deny to others the right to disbelieve. When, however, Thomas Paine, whose work on Common Sense he had warmly patronised, submitted to him a manuscript treatise against "a particular Providence," he earnestly dissuaded its publication. He urged not only the odium it would bring upon the author, but the danger of withdrawing from the weak, the ignorant, the inexperienced, and the inconsiderate, the support which religion affords to virtue. His ideas on the origin of evil were probably not very completely developed. But he thought a Devil very useful for the punishment of criminal wretches who cheated starving orphans of the alms entrusted for their relief. Whatever quality could prove by results that it had contributed to render life more harmonious he was glad to enshrine in his Pantheon, as Romans borrowed foreign gods. His ideal, in morals, in religion, and even in politics, was entirely inductive. He examined life and history to see in what circumstances of belief, education, and government men had enjoyed happiness. The same circumstances might not have suited his character; but he was content not to disturb what appeared to suit others.

One province of his nature there was in which, so far as we are permitted to penetrate it, he was not always weighing the dangers of zeal to the evenness of the balance he was constantly engaged in adjusting. In natural science he was an enthusiast; but that was a matter for himself and not for the outside world. He just mentions in his Autobiography the fact of his electrical experiments, and "the rise and progress of my philosophical reputation," between 1746 and 1753, when the Royal Society bestowed its medal. His Autobiography contains nothing more on the subject, and his correspondence very little. When his views were resisted, he was content to leave them to the judgment of posterity. He writes to an admirer in 1777: "I have never entered into any controversy in defence of my philosophical opinions. If they are right, truth and experience will support them; if wrong, they ought to be refuted and rejected." He had been told King George had exchanged the rebel Franklin's favourite pointed' conductors for blunt ones. "If I had a wish about it," remarks Franklin, "it would be that he had rejected conductors altogether as ineffectual." Physical science was too grand a thing for him to care to soil it with controversy. He would gaily dispute upon metaphysics, morals, and politics; upon the philosophy of nature never. Though he loved riches reasonably, he would not mix up so sublunary an application of science even as a stove with money. This typical American was so un-American in one respect as to set his face against monopolies in inventions. His love of his science itself he limited by the sense of other duties. He vigorously deprecates a friend's design to try a balloon journey across the Channel in 1785 as a risk unfair to his family.

Except in science, so far as direct personal influence over posterity is concerned, Franklin did not go the way to secure it. "Poor Richard" was a great power in his own time, just because the object of Richard's mission was not very sublime. For the making of a hero and a leader in the ages to come an admixture of divinity is needed. In Franklin's teaching there was nothing but what had been found in human life as it was. The matter of the teaching was after all ignoble. The world tired of it when it had come to perceive that the ideal propounded was nothing but ordinary prosaic humanity with something pruned off it. While the teacher survived there were a strength and freshness about his doctrines which came from himself, and kept them wholesome and pure. Whatever they might be the man was not ignoble. Somewhat earthy he may have been; he was great in himself; he was greater in his power over himself. His fame was common to two continents, and vital to his own. If George Washington more than any one man saved America from being overrun by German mercenaries, and American liberties from being dragged in the mire by the owners of pocket British boroughs, it was Franklin more than any one man who had made Americans too self-respecting to consent to be slaves; it was Franklin who took the new-born Republic by the hand and seated it among the nations.

WILLIAM COBBETT.

WILLIAM COBBETT and Benjamin Franklin agreed in the enjoyment of absolute independence of judgment and self-reliance. But Franklin canonised humility as a virtue, though in an appendix to his calendar, and sanctified rather out of due time. In Cobbett's creed, humility, modesty, or by what other name it might choose to be known, was nothing but a contemptible meanness. In the dusty volumes of the Political Register their extraordinary editor can be most accurately studied; and their foremost and most obtrusive characteristic is his amazing egotism. Not a measure was debated in Parliament, not a treaty was negotiated by the Foreign Office, but Cobbett claimed to assist as the self-appointed representative of English popular rights. He seated himself like a Roman tribune by the senate doors, and protested if he could not veto. This egotism is so candid that it never seduces him to colour facts in his own defence or glorification. It is so restless, intrusive, and universal that a student of his career is led by him into the inmost recesses of national policy and individual character. His criticisms of acts and motives are often as far as possible from being equitable or right. Any one who obediently followed the Register's estimates of public transactions and public men would soon find his political principles in a whirl. Cobbett does not solve political problems; far from it; but his blunders are more instructive than the wisest answers. If he does not bring down his birds, he is, at any rate, an incomparable pointer. Over all the long strife which issued in the Act of 1832 he interposes his own passionate personality. His faith in his exclusive genius for putting the world right is like quicksilver for its power of interfering with everything, and separating into the several elements whatever it touches. A first introduction to the hundred volumes of Peter Porcupine and the Weekly Political Register may even inoculate the student with the writer's own belief that in an age of bloodthirsty Jacobins, overreaching Americans, and jobbing or stolid Englishmen, William Cobbett was the one incorruptibly wise and fearlessly benevolent politician. That sentiment will be evanescent. When, however, the hero has ceased to be one to his reader, the time spent in studying him will yet not seem to have been lost. The curiosity aroused by the idiosyncrasies of an individual character will be not unwillingly transferred to the social and political enigmas which a perfect self-confidence convinced Cobbett that he alone had the wit and the integrity to guess.

Cobbett had, like Franklin, the self-made man's fondness for describing the steps of his rise, and, like Franklin, a born writer's art of narration. In every pamphlet he penned there are touches of the most vivid autobiography. His origin and early life he related to prove to American controversialists that, if he attacked democracy, it was from no prejudices of aristocratic blood or associations. It is delightful to think of Cobbett finding it necessary to demonstrate that he was not reared a gentleman. His grandfather had worked for one employer from the day of his marriage to that of his death, upwards of forty years. His father was a Farnham farmer, who had raised himself from the grade of a day labourer. He had learned some mathematics and land-surveying. What he knew he taught his children. Still more of their schooling was in the fields. Cobbett declared he never remembered the time when he did not earn his living. His father used to boast that his four boys, from fifteen years of age downwards, did as much work as any three men in Farnham parish.

When the supply of farm employment failed, William Cobbett worked in the Bishop of Winchester's gardens at

Farnham Castle. That led to an experience which gave his tastes a strong anticipatory bent towards controversial literature. A gardener fresh from Kew Gardens, by his account of their horticultural splendours, fired the imagination of the lad of eleven. Next morning, without a word, he started for Kew with sixpence halfpenny for his fortune. Twopence spent on bread and cheese, a penny on small beer, and a halfpenny lost, brought him to Richmond with threepence in his pocket for supper and lodging. His eyes suddenly fell on a little volume in a bookseller's window, 'Tale of a Tub,' price threepence. He spent his board and lodging on the book with the odd title. So impatient was he that he sat down by the side of a haystack and began to read. A boy could not understand it all: but perhaps the mystery was not the less suggestive. He said himself in after years: "It produced what I have always considered a birth of intellect." He read on till it was dark, and then slept in the hay. In the morning he resumed his walk to Kew, where the gardener, a Scotchman, gave him work for some weeks or months. The 'Tale of a Tub,' became a sort of Bible to him. His little copy perished with a box which fell overboard in the Bay of Fundy. "The loss," he wrote, " gave me greater pain than I have ever felt at losing thousands of pounds." This was Cobbett's introduction to something beyond a village schoolboy's idea of literature. His first political views came from his father. His father was a vehement opponent of Lord North's mischievous policy. Cobbett remembered how, when a hop factor offered to read an account in the Gazette of a British victory, his father and a dozen other farmers went and supped in a different room, where they toasted Washington.

All this, with much more which is equally interesting, is to be found in the autobiographical sketch, 'The Life and Adventures of Peter Porcupine,' printed by Cobbett in America. The public should be grateful to Mr. Edward Smith for popularising by its insertion in his 'William Cobbett: a Biography,' which was published in 1878, a narrative as picturesque as was ever written. A debt is due to Mr. Smith generally for much information carefully and zealously collected. The obligation would have been greater had the biographer been less conjectural in his inferences, had he quoted more, and moralised less. Thus tempestuously does he pass to the incident which drove Cobbett from the quiet hop gardens of Farnham into his restless noisy career: "A head and shoulders above the average of his mates, his mind is likewise, on a higher level. Not so high, but as yet to be infinitely dark as to any purpose: a healthy spirit in a healthy body, there stood, working as hard and as cheerily as ever; but ready for the first impulse—which impulse came, in no uncommon way; in no more romantic style than that which sets a ball rolling, upon the impact of the foot." A casual reader might suppose that Cobbett had become involved in some village brawl, and been "in unromantic style" kicked by a rival. What happened was, that the young farmer, now twenty, while visiting a relative at Portsmouth, saw the British fleet at anchor, and was forthwith inflamed with an English lad's passion for maritime adventures. He was fortunate in applying to a captain who, taken by something in his manner, refused, out of sheer pity, to let him sacrifice himself to such a lot as a common sailor's then was. He returned to the plough perforce; as he himself wrote afterwards, he was "spoilt for a farmer." The next year, on a sudden impulse, he mounted a passing stage-coach, and was set down at Ludgate Hill with half-a-crown in his pocket. But he had that in him which always made friends as well as foes. A fellow-passenger, a hop merchant who knew his father, interested himself in his fortunes, and procured him a place as a lawyer's copying clerk in Gray's Inn. This was not quite the career he had aspired to when he sighed after a voyage in a three-decker. His regular working hours were from five in the morning till eight or nine at night at earliest. An old laundress was his substitute for society; and his single recreation a Sunday walk in St. James's Park. The life was intolerable for one bred up in the pure air of the

South downs. He gasped after any opening for escape, and to enlist was the outlet which offered itself. He thought he had taken the King's shilling for the Marines; in fact, he found himself a recruit of the 54th Regiment of the Line then serving in Nova Scotia.

The life of a private soldier might not at first sight appear favourable to intellectual development. Cobbett it suited admirably. There was almost starvation, but there was abundant leisure. He had a devouring curiosity, which the plough first, and then a copying clerkship, had quenched in sheer fatigue. Now he became a student, and employed his year at the Chatham depôt in reading through, "more than once," the miscellaneous collection of a neighbouring lending library. His training at Gray's Inn recommended him as copyist to Colonel Debbieg, the commandant of Chatham garrison. His grammatical knowledge, however, was still imperfect; and, in his desire to escape the colonel's criticisms, he bought Bishop Lowth's grammar. He learnt it by heart, and would repeat the whole whenever he was on guard. There he was, at all events, in quiet. His reading and writing had to be done amidst the talking, laughing, singing, whistling, and brawling of some ten idle soldiers. Downright hunger was an additional hardship. Fourpence was as much as could be saved for food out of the sixpence a day, after washing, clothes, hair-powder, and pipeclay. "The whole week's food was not a bit too much for one day." For pocket-money there remained twopence a week. One Friday, Cobbett had managed to economise a halfpenny. He determined to buy a red herring on the Saturday morning: but as he undressed, he found he had lost his halfpenny. "I buried my head," he wrote nearly fifty years after, "under the miserable sheet and rug, and cried like a child."

His ability to read and write soon raised him to the rank of corporal, which brought him an additional twopence a day. On his arrival with this rank in Nova Scotia, the post of clerk of the regiment was also conferred on him. According to his own subsequent account, the whole of the regimental business, military as well as financial, fell within a year into his hands. "Neither adjutant, paymaster, nor quartermaster could move an inch without my assistance." At this period the drill was revolutionised by 'Dundas's system.' It was ordered from headquarters that the change should be introduced before the next annual review. This wonderful corporal effected it, explaining the whole matter in lectures to the officers, including the colonel himself. He made out for them on large cards little plans of the position of the regiment, with lists of the words of command they had to give in the field. Probably a good many corporals would similarly explain how they virtually commanded their regiments; but Cobbett had the literary gift, and could put the boasts of the barracks in a form which gave them credibility. It is sufficient to believe that Cobbett made a smart soldier, without charging his officers with gross incapacity. They saw, at any rate, his merits. After speedy promotion to the rank of sergeant, he was, at the end of little more than a year from his disembarcation at Halifax, appointed sergeant-major. That brought him into yet closer relations with his officers. They were jealous; and he would, he declares, have been more than once flogged for his freedom in speaking of his superiors had they not depended upon him for "easing them all of the trouble of even thinking about their duty." In the autumn of 1791 the Regiment was sent home. Its sergeant-major might have hoped for a commission; he had seen enough of soldiering, and had fallen in love. He had conceived also a scheme which required that he should be out of the army. He applied for his discharge, and it was granted with a laudatory testimonial from his major, the unfortunate Lord Edward Fitzgerald, to the services he had rendered to the regiment. His future bride, Ann Reid, the young daughter of an artilleryman, had already returned to England, entrusted with her lover's savings of a hundred and forty or fifty guineas.

The grand project Cobbett had conceived as his new introduction to civil life was nothing less then the prosecution of several officers of his old regiment for defrauding the men of their bread, clothes, and fuel, and cheating the revenue by false musters. His position had enabled him to collect testimony; and the War Office agreed to submit the case to a court-martial. When, however, the trial was at hand, disputes arose between Cobbett and the Judge Advocate General on the manner of conducting the enquiry. Cobbett refused to proceed with it. On the day the court met no prosecutor appeared. The charges were read out, and an acquittal recorded. The Attorney and Solicitor General were consulted whether Cobbett could be criminally prosecuted. As there was no evidence of conspiracy with others, their opinion was that he could not be, but that the officers he had slandered might bring actions for damages. But by this time Cobbett was in France, where he passed a few months before his final departure to the United States of America. The affair of the court-martial is a perplexed one. On such evidence as has been produced, though the War Office archives might clear up an obscure question, it seems likely that the sergeant-major had discovered a mare's nest. Cobbett, at a later period, ridicules his own bookkeeping. His publishing accounts he defies "the devil to unravel." The Judge Advocate probably came to the conclusion that the main offence of Cobbett's former officers consisted in keeping accounts of much the same character as those subsequently kept by their accuser. If Cobbett discovered that the battery he had laboriously charged against his regimental superiors would not go off, the shame, and some apprehension of private retaliation, may have driven him from England. That the War Office had resolved to procure an acquittal of dishonest officials requires more proof than the assertion of a man who launched an accusation and ran away before it was brought home. This is not Mr. Edward Smith's way of judging Cobbett's acts. The London Chronicle of March 28, 1792, had explained what certainly looked like a flight by the suggestion that "some misconduct" was the motive. Mr. Smith thereupon apostrophises the circulators of such rumours in a tone recalling equally Mr. Carlyle and the prophet Jeremiah: 'No such thing at all, paragraph-monger! And no such thing at all, ye rapid writers! You don't know this man. You don't know how he retires from the unequal conflict with money, prescription, aristocratic influence. Let him flee from anticipated vengeance; and see him return one day, himself always incorruptible, with such a budget, such a quiverful!'

Cobbett had gone to France to learn French. But the Revolution was entering into its savage stage; and the feeling between the Revolutionary Government and England was growing so exasperated that he prudently took ship for America. The money he had saved as a sergeant had nearly evaporated during his attendance in London on the affair of the court-martial. He had to look about for a means of subsistence at Philadelphia. Translating French authors for the bookseller's was one resource. He could translate a dollar's worth while his wife was preparing breakfast, and another dollar's worth when she and their child were asleep. Another, and at first his principal occupation, was giving English lessons to Frenchmen. His own English education was only half finished; and there could be no better training for his future literary career than having to elucidate the peculiarities of his native language for foreigners. Talleyrand was among the later arrived French refugees; and the Prince, Cobbett used to declare, asked to be received as his pupil. Cobbett, who was known to have stigmatised him as an apostate and a hypocrite, saw in the request proof that he was a spy in the service of the French Republican Government. Talleyrand, says Cobbett, knew English as well as himself. The obvious inference, in his judgment, was that the ex-Bishop of Autun wanted to take a survey of his desk. Certainly Talleyrand's habitual shrewdness deserted him when he experimented so grossly on Cobbett's literary vanity as to enquire whether it were "at Oxford or at Cambridge he had received his education."

But this was after he had become famous enough to make it worth while for Talleyrand to flatter him. He had been gradually educating himself in politics as well as in composition. His court-martial experiences had turned him into a Republican in London; a very short residence in Philadelphia changed him into a violent Tory. Mr. Smith says: "When he soon comes to see all sides of Republicanism, he reverts to his intrinsic love for the Constitution under which he was born." Cobbett's peculiar advantage in contentious politics was that he never saw "all sides" of any question. He might see one side at one time and another at another time; he could never believe that there was any side but that at which he was pleased for the moment to look. Whoever asserted there was another aspect to a topic must be a blind bigot or a Mr. Facing-both-ways. Dr. Priestley, tired of controversy and Tory mob law, came to New York in 1794. He was received with enthusiasm, which was directed as much by jealousy of England as by admiration for the Birmingham philosopher. Cobbett's spirit burned within him at all this stir about a "philosophi-theologi-politi-cal empiric." Forthwith he launched forth 'Observations on Priestley's Emigration.' The kind of logic Cobbett wielded at this time may be inferred from his indignation that a man who claimed "the right of thinking for others" would not "permit the people of England to think for themselves," and to decline his offers to enlighten their stolidity.

Cobbett's first pamphleteering adventure in Philadelphia was pecuniarily not very lucrative. Published on the half-profits system, the 'Observations' brought him in "the enormous sum of one shilling and sevenpence halfpenny, currency of the State of Philadelphia, or about elevenpence three-farthings sterling, quite entirely clear of all deductions whatsoever." But he had learned that he could use his pen, and, profits or no profits, his vocation was manifest. The Federal against the Democratic policy of the States, Washington and Adams against Jefferson, and British influence against French, were the chief subjects of his pamphlets. 'A Bone to gnaw for the Democrats' and 'A Kick for a Bite' followed the attack on Priestley. Then Cobbett became "Peter Porcupine." He had been for some time suspicious of the fair dealing of his publisher, Bradford, in the matter of profits. The Farnham ex-ploughboy was yet more indignant that a bookseller had presumed to promise his customers that Peter Porcupine should continue one of his works, and make it "very interesting." "What! a bookseller undertake to promise that I should write, and that I should write to please his customers too!" He denounced booksellers as a race of slave-drivers who "have adopted the birdcatcher's maxim: 'A bird that can sing, and won't sing, ought to be made to sing.'" So on July 11, 1796, he turned bookseller himself.

The most important part of his stock in trade was the goodwill and copyright of Peter Porcupine's brains. He opened a shop to sell his own tracts. But he meant to carry on besides the miscellaneous trade of a bookseller. He determined to make his entrance into business an event in Philadelphia. Philadelphia contained a large colony of Irishmen and Frenchmen. All the Irishmen and very many of the Frenchmen hated Great Britain, and they threw in their lot with the Democrats who opposed the policy of Washington as having monarchical and British tendencies. When Cobbett's shutters were taken down for the first time, his windows were seen to be filled with portraits of kings, queens, nobles, bishops, and judges. There was George III., whose portrait had not been exhibited in the States for twenty years; there was William Pitt; above all there were two tableaux four feet long, labelled "Lord Howe's decisive Victory over the French Fleet." A paper war broke out, and kept the excitement at fever point for months. He writes home to his father, wondering what the old man will think to hear that his boy's picture is "stuck in the windows." The portraits were not flattering; the glory was in being sufficiently notorious to be caricatured. Gilray's pictures of Cobbett, which were, though much more clever, probably not less coarse than the Philadelphian, were prized in after years at Botley. Quarter was neither given nor asked. He was declared to be a garret-scribbler, who did a little occasional "night business," we suppose, as a burglar, "to supply unavoidable contingencies." He had quitted England to save his neck, according to one critic. According to another he had been publicly flogged while in the army. The Aurora, a journal of Democratic views, inserted a counterfeit invitation from Cobbett to Philadelphians to come and receive ocular demonstration that his back showed no marks of flagellation. Then followed a controversy in the same newspaper between imaginary correspondents, one asserting that he had seen the scars, another explaining that they were the scars of a private whipping. Cobbett had studied Swift to some purpose, and he struck back with equal scurrility and more point. His opponents could never meet him in fair pamphleteering combat. They threw mud, and he threw it back; but he argued while he reviled.

The 'Scarecrow,' the 'Bone to Gnaw,' and other publications of the sort have no interest now except for persons curious in the literature of abuse. The 'Life and Adventures of Peter Porcupine,' belonging to the same time, has a permanent autobiographical interest. But Cobbett began to go deeper into the political controversies of the United States. When he first took up his abode in the country, hostility to Great Britain and friendship for France were axioms of popular American policy. France presumed upon the benefits her alliance had conferred on the Republic at its birth, and her dictation was resented. Cobbett was ever prompt to further, according to his lights, British interests, by embittering the American sense of the arrogance of French diplomacy. His monthly Political Censor preached intermittently on his text, and it was the daily burden of his later Porcupine's Gazette. Its editor and proprietor always boasted that its three years' life, 1797–99, was a main instrument in preventing an offensive alliance between France and the United States against Great Britain. Cobbett was able to produce evidence in after years that the British Government recognised the advantages it received from his pen. Through the British Legation it made several offers, which he declined, to advance his interests.

Americans deserve credit for the fact that, fiercely as Cobbett assaulted their prejudices, they confined their retorts to the same weapons of pen and ink. He had professed apprehensions of the kind of mob violence which drove Dr. Priestley from Birmingham, which, in Dr. Priestley's case, Cobbett was inclined to justify. Neither he nor his shop suffered. Not even a stone broke those windows full of royal and noble portraits. Cobbett never admitted a good trait in an opponent. Far from having the candour to remark on this self-restraint and good police of Philadelphia, Cobbett probably despised it as a sign of Democratic or French and Irish cowardice. There was, however, something formidable in having not the rabble merely, but the local authorities of Pennsylvania arrayed against him. This prospect threatened him in 1797. Chief Justice M'Kean, a zealous Democrat and an enemy of everything English, had been elected Governor. A recent attempt to indict Cobbett for libelling the Spanish Envoy had failed, notwithstanding the partisan bias alleged to have been shown by the Chief Justice, whose daughter the Envoy had married. But Cobbett thought it prudent to withdraw from M'Kean's jurisdiction, and he moved his bookselling business to New York. Porcupine's Gazette was at the same time discontinued. There is no evidence that Cobbett contemplated departure from America when he migrated from Philadelphia. One most obvious cause of that step was the result of an action for libel brought against him by a well-known physician of Philadelphia, named Benjamin Rush. Cobbett had ridiculed him as a Dr. Sangrado, a quack who had murdered his thousands by his specific of bleeding during a destructive epidemic of yellow fever. Rush, at the end of the year 1799, obtained a verdict for damages of five thousand dollars, and Cobbett, in June, 1800, sailed for England.

Cobbett had scoffed at Republican institutions and sentiments, and finally been mulcted in damages for a scurrilous libel. Later on, when afflicted by the yet more flagrant ingratitude of Englishmen in authority, he persuaded himself to forgive and forget, "with some few exceptions," all the injuries with which the worst of the people of the United States had, in their "folly and madness," endeavoured to load him. For the present so sublime a temper of charity was beyond him. Full in view, eager to welcome its champion, was the country, his own country, of ancient loyalty and incorrupt good faith, where there were no Sangrados in medicine or politics, and consequently no actions for libel. Government officials and the Government press, in effect, received with joy so redoubtable an advocate as Peter Porcupine. John Gifford, sub-editor, under Canning, of the Anti-Jacobin, who had prefixed laudatory prefaces to the English editions of some of Cobbett's Philadelphia pamphlets, the Rev. William Beloe, joint editor with Archdeacon Nares of the British Critic, a paper friendly to Government, which had praised them, Dr. Ireland, afterwards Dean of Westminster, and many other gentlemen called upon him at his lodgings in St. James's Street. Mr. Windham, the Secretary at War, became a warm friend of the ex-sergeant who was supposed to have quitted England to avoid the consequences of having slandered his former officers. He actually dined, as Windham's guest, at a Ministerial dinner in August, 1800, in company with Canning and Pitt himself. Cobbett then and there resolved to set up a daily paper. He used to relate how Mr. George Hammond, who was Under-Secretary for Foreign Affairs, as was his son more than fifty years later, acting on behalf of the Government, offered him as a gift the proprietorship of a Ministerial paper, the evening Sun, or a half share in another, the morning True Briton. He refused the bribe; he had resolved to support the Government, but he would be his own master.

On his arrival in England he possessed no more than £500; but in September, 1800, he very courageously started a sixpenny morning newspaper, Porcupine's Gazette. Porcupine's Gazette began by being a panegyrist of Pitt; but it avowed its dislike of the concessions he had desired to make to the Catholics. Its proprietor, with that perversity which he commonly displayed, abhorred the Peace of Amiens. He had his windows broken on October 7, 1801, by the mob, for refusing to illuminate in honour of the Preliminaries. For two days the publication had to stop, "until," as Cobbett informed his subscribers, "the delirium of joy shall have subsided." In the following month the Porcupine shot its last quill, being sold to Mr. John Gifford and merged in the True Briton. Cobbett had carried on the publication, while it lasted, with energy. Newspapers fought in those days against each other like famished wolves: and in this department Cobbett had served an incomparable apprenticeship. He had the more honourable advantage of contributions by such correspondents as Lord Grenville and Jeremy Bentham. In general, he professed not to know his correspondents, requesting that communications should not be accompanied by the real names of the authors. The fault of the English Porcupine doubtless was that its editor regarded a newspaper as an enlarged pamphlet, and newspaper readers wanted news. Cobbett himself affected to be relieved at his journal's untimely fate. "He who has been," he exclaimed, "the proprietor of a daily paper for only one month wants no Romish priest to describe to him the torments of purgatory." His time, with or without the charge of the Porcupine, was fully occupied. In March, 1801, he had opened a bookseller's shop at the Crown and Mitre, Pall Mall, under the especial patronage of the royal dukes and princes. At the commencement of the next year he embarked on a new literary venture. He belonged to the so-called New Opposition. To Windham, Lawrence, and Lord Grenville, who were its chiefs, Cobbett recommended the establishment of a weekly organ, which should be "something between a newspaper and a magazine." Six hundred pounds would be required to launch it, and he had no money to risk. He would edit it, on the terms of disclaiming "all desire to derive pecuniary advantage from the proposed undertaking, and all idea of personal obligation towards any one who may think proper to contribute towards it." The requisite £600 was at once raised, and January, 1802, witnessed the issue of the first number of Cobbett's Political Register, under the title originally of Cobbett's Annual Register. January, 1802, is an epoch in the history of journalism.

Cobbett, when he returned to England in the year 1800, was liquid metal which a Bolingbroke might possibly have cast into a rough copy of Cobbett's literary model, the great Irish Dean. But Pitt had scarcely any more real capacity for appreciating the value of literary auxiliaries than Walpole. The Whig party itself was only gradually taught it by the success of the Edinburgh Review. Statesmen assumed that a place or a pension for a layman, a benefice for a clergyman, satisfied any claims mere literary eminence could assert. It was well for the country which required the rude audit to which Cobbett subjected the policy of its authorised leaders that Pitt and his brother statesmen did not understand the worth of such a pen as Cobbett's, and the price at which alone it could be retained. Cobbett had a habit of proclaiming his contempt for money. He liked money as much as most people, and had a noble capacity for spending it. He spoke the simple truth when he boasted of the impossibility of purchasing him by pecuniary offers. An invitation to help to pull the strings which directed the policy of the kingdom might not have been rejected if skilfully addressed. He would have found it very hard to resist the flattery of continual appeals to his patriotism and his intelligence for co-operation, or to break the delicate chains of repeated Ministerial dinners. Criticisms by a writer who had been a warm ally, and who might be one again, should have been received with indulgence. On the contrary, the colleagues of Pitt who formed the Addington Ministry let loose their press on "a certain American scribbler," for whom "the pillory or the gibbet" was declared to be "an appropriate reward." The Government itself soon intervened openly. Mr. Justice Johnson's letters in the Register, under the signature of "Juverna," against the Irish Administration of Lord Hardwicke were made the subject of proceedings against the proprietor. The Irish judge, among other sarcasms, compared the appointment of Lord Hardwicke to setting the surgeon's apprentice to bleed the pauper patients. Perceval, as Attorney General, conducted the prosecution, and taunted Cobbett with not being a man of family. Lord Ellenborough, who presided, had not in those days lost the art of compelling a verdict of guilty. Cobbett was sentenced to pay a fine of £500. The man who returned to England in 1800 glowing with Tory admiration of Pitt, the House of Lords, and the bench of bishops, convicted in 1804 of libel, became a Radical. The conviction opened Cobbett's eyes to the fact that "the race that plunder the people, the Court sycophants, parasites, pensioners, bribed senators, directors, contractors, jobbers, hireling lords, and Ministers of State were not the people of England."

Addington was the first object of Cobbett's attacks, but his hostility was not so much to a particular Minister as to authority. In August, 1805, the Register commenced the practice of publishing pension lists, that the impoverished country might see where a million a year of its hard earnings went. Sometimes a Tory Minister was pilloried. The Register emphasised the moral of the startling statistics of jobbery and corruption disclosed through Lord Melville's impeachment. Another week the butt was some leader of the Whigs, whom Cobbett hated with a hate far exceeding that he felt for their adversaries. Sheridan had once hinted a charge against the Register of having incited sailors to mutiny. Four years later, the slander, having been laid up in Cobbett's memory, which was extraordinarily retentive of such things, bore fruit. In a series of letters Cobbett expatiated on the descent of the Sheridans from a playactor, that is, from a "vagabond." He promised to furnish details some day of twenty-five public pledges which Sheridan had given and broken. When the scandal of Mrs. Clarke's abuse of the Duke of York's patronage burst, he was careful not to let the public forget it. The Register was eager to discover any pretext for assailing authority, so only the attack left no visible loophole for authority to shoot back into.

Considering the burning ploughshares of legal censorship amid which Cobbett had to tread, he picked his way with marvellous dexterity. But at last the Register was caught tripping, and the Attorney General did not miss his opportunity. Some militiamen at Ely had mutinied in June, 1809, on account of a stoppage of pay to provide knapsacks. The rising was suppressed by a body of Hanoverian cavalry quartered at Bury, and five of the ringleaders received the barbarous punishment of 500 lashes apiece. Cobbett, who never forgot that he had served in the ranks, was sincerely enraged that Germans should have been imported to flog Englishmen. But with the oil of his pity for the soldiers he rubbed in plenty of pepper for his official countrymen. Out he burst in the Weekly Political Register of June 1, 1809: "Five hundred lashes each! Ay, that is right! Flog them! flog them! flog them! They deserve it, and a great deal more. They deserve a flogging at every meal time. Lash them daily! lash them daily! What! shall the rascals dare to mutiny, and that too when the German Legion is so near at hand? Lash them! lash them! lash them! They deserve it. Oh yes! they merit a doubled-tailed cat! Base dogs! Mutiny for the price of a goat's skin; and then upon the appearance of the German soldiers they take a flogging as quietly as so many trunks of trees. This occurrence at home will, one would hope, teach the loyal a little caution in speaking of the means which Napoleon employs, or rather, which they say he employs, in order to get together and to discipline his conscripts."

As soon as the article was published, Cobbett felt that his chance of escape was remote. He even anticipated the sentence: "They may probably confine me for two years, but that does not kill a man." As months passed by, and the Attorney General still stayed his hand, Cobbett resumed a tone which unsympathetic critics might call blustering. He declared himself "no more afraid of the rascals than he could be of so many mice." If there should be "an honest jury, it would be a famous thing altogether." Probably he honestly believed that Ministers were afraid of meddling with so formidable a free lance. But it was only Sir Vicary Gibbs's way of playing with his victims. More than a year after the offence had been committed the trial was brought on. Cobbett, who would never employ counsel, delivered a speech in his own defence, in which he apologised for the article as "written in haste." He was immediately found guilty. Sentence, however, was not yet passed, and Cobbett was free in the interval to return to his pleasant Hampshire house.

It was the kind of home to make a prospect of Newgate especially gloomy. If Cobbett was obliged to live in Bolt Court, his imagination made him hear the caged birds "sing better and sing louder and more and stronger than they do when at large." Naturally, he liked better, when he had the choice, to declaim among hop-gardens and young woods against the corruption of Downing Street and St. Stephen's, than to imagine hedgerows and orchards in Fleet Street. When the Register had seemed securely established, he had left its management to Mr. John Wright, formerly a bookseller in Piccadilly, and his English correspondent when he was trading at Philadelphia and New York. Quitting Duke Street, St. James's, he bought "a most delightful house and more delightful garden" at Botley, near Southampton. Frequent allusions to the place are to be found in the Register. They occur everywhere in the two hundred manuscript letters, now in the British Museum, which contain much of Cobbett's weekly correspondence with Wright, and from which Mr. Smith has extracted some of the most interesting portions of his memoir. But the most vivid sketch of the sort of life Cobbett now led is in Miss Mitford's 'Recollections of a Literary Life.' A common love of coursing drew together Cobbett and her father, a man of no worth whatever. Miss Mitford, in her father's company, visited Cobbett's house, "large, high, massive, red, and square," which stood opposite to the village, on the further side of the river Hamble. The river was full of jack, and trout, and salmon, and Cobbett could catch in a week enough fish to defray the cost of a trammel net, for which he paid several pounds. He never sold the fish, but the calculation was a good excuse for buying the net. What with the savings he was to make by dispensing with a town house, by having milk three times as cheap, bread one-ninth, fuel a half, and meat an eighth cheaper than in London, he reckoned he should economise to the extent of at least £300 a year. The money he spent on the purchase of the Botley house and in stocking the garden he never estimated at all. Yet he did not produce for nothing his " green Indian corn, his Carolina beans, which could hardly have been exceeded at New York, his wall fruit, equally splendid," and his flowers, than which Miss Mitford " never saw more glowing or more fragrant."

His expenditure must have been enormous on " the large fluctuating series of guests for the hour, or guests for the day," whom Miss Mitford met there, " of almost all ranks and descriptions, from the earl and his countess to the farmer and his dame." The maintenance of a house " always open," according to Cobbett himself, to give his labourers " victuals and drink whenever they happened to come to it," with invalid comforts and full wages in illness, was probably still more costly. " They called it," says Miss Mitford, " a farmhouse, and everything was in accordance with the largest idea of a great English yeoman of the old time." Two or three small farms were, in a year or two after Cobbett's establishment at Botley, bought and thrown together, and there was " a vast nursery raised chiefly from seed of almost all the different sorts of forest trees known on the Atlantic side of the middle States of North America." All this Cobbett treated as money invested at compound interest payable in the future. In May, 1808, he purchased sixty-seven acres of wood. " The new purchase has upon it above 6,000 trees that would cost me from a shilling to two-and-sixpence apiece, and that, in twenty years' time, will be worth £3 apiece at the very least. This, I think, is the best way of insuring a fortune for children." He cannot even attend a dinner in honour of Sir Francis Burdett's election for Westminster, for "the health and growth, as well as the future beauty, of a hundred acres of the finest woods in England depend upon my personal attendance between Saturday and Wednesday." Fishing, and coursing, and planting seemed to make up his Botley life. Of course it was only seeming. The Register was really a weekly essay by Cobbett; and the weekly essay never failed. But Cobbett at Botley was accustomed to reserve the business of life for his study. "Of politics," writes Miss Mitford, "we heard little, and should, I think, have heard nothing, but for an occasional red-hot patriot, who would introduce the subject, which our host would fain put aside, and got rid of as speedily as possible."

Back to this prosperous home and these joyous labours, in which politics seemed to his children only an interlude, came Cobbett from Westminster Hall, a convicted, not yet a sentenced, libeller. All the associations of Botley pleaded for a compromise. Cobbett was induced to negotiate one. Seven years later he asserted that "something very near to the chopping of my right hand should be done before I would cease to write." But he admits that he authorised his attorney to offer in his name to discontinue the publication of the Register. Though he asserts that he countermanded the offer before it had been made to the Government, cause exists for doubt whether the proposition were effectually withdrawn. The Government, however, would seem to have had the folly to expect, like Queen Mary in her dealings with Cranmer, the penalty as well as submission. Cobbett, if he were to be immured in Newgate in any case, preferred to spend his time there as proprietor of the Register. Ten years to the very day from the time he had landed in England, "having lost a fortune in America solely for the sake of that same England," he stood up in Westminster Hall to hear himself sentenced to pay a fine of a thousand pounds and undergo two years' imprisonment, and at the end of that term to give security in a total amount of £5,000 for his future good behaviour during seven years. The punishment was not the worst disaster of this period of Cobbett's career. Newgate was made tolerable to him by the admiring kindness of Mr. Sheriff Wood, afterwards the famous Sir Matthew. He was not cast down. Not even his sturdy constitution suffered. One or another of his family was always with him. He had a levee of visitors. Major Cartwright often came. So did Francis Maseres, Cursitor Baron of the Exchequer, who appeared "always in his wig and gown, in order, as he said, to show his abhorrence of the sentence." The discipline of a soldier's life made the mechanical routine of prison regulations endurable. Want of liberty of locomotion was the worst hardship. He was allowed to purchase, at an expense in all of £1,200, the privilege of a separate room. He was never without abundance of "violets, and primroses, and cowslips, and harebells," from his own Botley meadows.

A calamity, which the scent of Botley violets had no power to cure, was the sudden discovery that all his fancied affluence was founded on a quicksand. He must have learned the truth soon in any case; the comparative leisure of Newgate precipitated the revelation. The Register was started in January, 1802, with three hundred subscribers, as a fortnightly journal, tenpence in price. Its immediate success warranted its issue weekly after the first two numbers. By 1803 the circulation had risen to four thousand, which implied, Cobbett reckoned, forty thousand readers. In 1809 it was nearly six thousand, and the price was raised to 1s. As late as 1816 the circulation of the Times was only eight thousand, of the Courier five thousand, and of the Morning Chronicle less still. Cobbett, reasonably enough, believed himself possessed of a mine of wealth. He added field to field at Botley, paying with money borrowed from his paper-maker, Swann, of Wolvercot, to whom he gave bills. The profits of the journal, which some years later he estimated at

£10,000 a year, were, though not equal to that sum, very great. But the love of publishing, which is as ruinous as a love of building, had bitten him. He commenced the Parliamentary Reports, now designated after Cobbett's printer, Hansard, who bought the property of Cobbett. To Cobbett belongs the praise of having instituted the first regular reports of debates. He derived no pecuniary profit from his patriotic enterprise. Another ambitious and bulky work in which he engaged was his Parliamentary History. A third was the great collection of State Trials. Of the last he had appointed a very learned barrister, Mr. Howell, editor. His expressions of indignation at Howell's views, as at the views of "all your authors," of the proper remuneration for brain-work, show that he had forgotten very completely his own anger at the Philadelphia bookseller Bradford's mode of reckoning duties and profits as between writer and publisher. "Authors," he says, "think that every book that is printed is so much money coined." Cobbett could not have described more exactly his own mode of keeping publishing accounts. He reckoned income and not outgoings. In fact, the sale neither of the State Trials, nor of the Parliamentary History, nor of the Debates, nor of a work soon dropped, called The Spirit of the Public Journals, covered the expenses. The Register staggered under a dead weight of paper and printer's ink; but Swann made advances, and Cobbett gaily bought farm after farm, as if he were fast growing into a millionaire.

Cobbett's story was repeated later in a more ruinously sumptuous edition by Walter Scott and the Ballantynes and Constable, with the close parallel of the intolerable load of unsaleable historical quartos, and the fields added to fields, which the Waverley Novels strove so gallantly to sustain. Cobbett, unlike Scott, had, however, always half suspected his own prudence. He warns Wright by letter in 1805 against "speaking or hinting, in the presence of Mrs. Cobbett, anything relative to my pecuniary concerns, or concerns in trade, of any sort or kind. She has her own ideas about such matters, which cannot be altered. She knows that I have lost so much by printing that she is fearful of everything of the kind." The good orderly honest-minded wife, who, when a young girl, had kept so faithfully Cobbett's savings from his sergeant's salary, Cobbett's conscience told him could not be made a confidante of a business about which Cobbett writes on another occasion to Wright: "Only think of having another person invested with a right to make us account—us whose accounts the devil himself would never unravel. No, no; you and I were never made to have our accounts examined by anybody but ourselves." Subsequently it appeared that he had not looked at his balance for six years. Yet nothing could be more beautifully prudent than his advice to others. "You should economise," he tells Wright, "as much as possible. A horse, a cow, a house, is soon gone in even trifling things, which we give in to from mere want of strength, and not from our love of the things themselves." Wright was not likely to take advice his counsellor never tried. The collapse came as soon as Cobbett was in Newgate. On the accounts, such as they were, being made up, it appeared that Wright owed £6,500 to Cobbett. Not a penny of that debt was forthcoming to pay the thousands which Cobbett owed on accommodation bills to Swann. The debt to Swann was settled by an advance Burdett made of £3,000, which was never repaid. Other friends defrayed Cobbett's fine of £1,000, and Hansard took over the Parliamentary History, the Debates, and the State Trials.

The man's nature must have been magnificently buoyant. There is no sign that he suffered any real affliction at the collapse of what had seemed to him boundless wealth. The Register fell into a temporary eclipse, but its proprietor's virtual insolvency had nothing to do with that. The cause we believe to have been that Cobbett composing Registers in Newgate lost temporarily his intuitive sympathy with the emotions and passions of the market-place. For the time Cobbett had ceased to write with the force and edge which had made him a dangerous adversary. His denunciations were comparatively neglected by friends and foes. He speaks in his letter of January 1, 1817, to "old George Rose," as if there were a conspiracy to suppress him by an absence of criticism. "The press of corruption," he complains, "as if it acted under one common command, abstained from even alluding to me or my writings for more than six years." It was all very well to write his series of articles on Paper against Gold, and to declare that he had crushed the Government. This, he writes, "at the end of thirteen years I hold up to the noses of the insolent foes who then exulted over me, and tell them 'This is what you got by my having been sentenced to Newgate; this was the produce of that deed by which it was hoped and believed that I was pressed down never to be able to stir again.'" The Castlereaghs and the Sidmouths were aggravatingly indifferent to that which Cobbett describes as "this new epoch in the progress of my mind." Articles on the flogging of militiamen terrified them; they bore placidly a reproach, in which their enemy coupled them with Malthus and Ricardo, of being bad political economists.

The currency was a momentous question, it must be acknowledged, in the years which preceded and followed Waterloo. Very properly its fascinations never released their hold upon Cobbett's fancy. But he resumed, with his restoration to liberty, less recondite enquiries. Personally he may, as he boasted, have preserved his equanimity during his two years of gaol; at their close his pen ran riot. The name of Cobbett became a word of terror and loathing to whole orders of men. He had already attacked tithes. He now never mentioned a clergyman without an insulting epithet. He taunted the profession continually with not supplying more spiritual arguments than the Attorney General's specific of the pillory against Paine's 'Age of Reason.' Landholders feared the man whom Lord Sidmouth and Mr. Perceval feared. Farmers instinctively recoiled from the avowed champion of the emancipation of their labourers. Farm labourers could not, except here and there, read the Register, and, if they had read, would not have understood it. But a new class began to study it. The weavers and mill hands and small tradesmen looked to the Register as their educator. In November, 1816, Cobbett published a number at twopence. Lord Cochrane, his constant political confederate, had suggested the experiment. "General Lud" and "Captain Swing" were both in the field. Mills, frames, and ricks were alike being burned. Cobbett might, Cochrane thought, turn a warning to work-people against futile crime to the purpose of goading the country to a sense of the necessity of representative reform. No. 18 of the Register, addressed to "The Journeymen and Labourers of England, Wales, Scotland, and Ireland," is a model of political and argumentative invective. The sarcasm hisses, but the surface remains smooth and cool. The subsequent letter addressed to the Luddites is an admirably plain demonstration of what was not self-evident in those days as in these. Its object was to demonstrate the benefit of machinery to the whole community. The argument grows as regularly tier by tier as the story of the house that Jack built. In Cobbett's reasonings links are never left to be understood. He prided himself on an invincible love of making things intelligible, and he gives his readers all the premisses, from which they may see for themselves that the conclusion follows. Political economy and logic are barbed with mockery and gibes at the remedies sinecurists and borough-mongers propose for the relief of the prevalent destitution. Charity subscriptions have been set on foot, and eleemosynary soup is being given. "What!" he exclaims, "are you to come crawling, like sneaking curs, to lick up alms to the amount of forty or fifty thousand pounds round the brim of a soup kettle, while you are taxed, with the rest of us, to the amount of £175,000 in order to give relief to French and Dutch emigrants, and to the poor clergy of the Church of England? I trust that my countrymen have yet English blood enough left in their veins to make them reject such alms with scorn and indignation."

But he prays them not to let their scorn and indignation

exceed the bounds of law. He inculcates the warning in the name of the vengeance he wishes them to enjoy upon the "hirelings" who oppress them. These are not "the landlord, the farmer, the tradesman, the merchant," classes equally burdened with themselves. They are the men who "live upon the taxes," for whose benefit the State takes £10 out of every £18 of wages. He entreats the workmen to bide their time, though they be mocked at as "lower orders," "swinish multitude," "mob," "rabble," "population." He tells them that, if they let themselves be goaded into physical violence, they will be favouring "the cause of corruption, which is never so much delighted as at the sight of troops acting against the people."

The circulation of the cheap edition of the Register, 'Twopenny Trash,' as Cobbett was content it should be styled, leaped to 44,000. In his 'Last Hundred Days of English Freedom' he declares that of the number published after the issue of Lord Sidmouth's circular of March, 1817, against seditious pamphlets, 20,000 copies were sold in London on one day. He gave a general license to any one who wished to republish No. 18, and "within two months," he states, "more than 200,000 copies of this number were printed and sold." Had the Newspaper Stamp Act applied to such a reissue, the circulation broadcast of this Twopenny Trash would have been impossible. But it did not come within the class of periodicals. Cobbett became a power in the State. He had engaged in a single-handed combat with the Government, and he beat it. At first the word went forth from the Home Office to "write him down." Anti-Cobbett tracts were all of no avail. It was Cobbett's boast that Lord Sidmouth's suspension of the Habeas Corpus Act was, "though he did not actually name it," aimed directly at the Political Register. Though Cobbett had a habit of appropriating attacks, here probably he was justified. Yet, if the Government feared the Register as a propagator of open sedition, it was wrong. There is truth in the interesting extract Mr. Smith cites from Samuel

Bamford's 'Passages in the Life of a Radical,' in which Bamford declares that, with the growth of the authority of Cobbett's writings, " riots soon became scarce." " Instead of riots and destruction of property, Hampden clubs were now established in many of our large towns and the villages and districts around them. Cobbett's books were printed in a cheap form; the labourers read them, and thenceforward became deliberate and systematic in their proceedings." Cobbett gave long-smothered wrath a vent. Men assembled to read the new gospel instead of breaking frames. A Government, however, like that led by Sidmouth and Castlereagh and Eldon, might easily be more panic-struck at the ground-swell of such an agitation as the twopenny Register was exciting than even at the burning of ricks and mills. Agrarian and anti-machinery riots might be dealt with by yeomanry and Hanoverians; a demand by weavers for Parliamentary reform had all the terrors of the unknown. Whether the weavers themselves generally understood Cobbett's arguments may be questioned; it was enough that they were starving, and Cobbett told them their poverty came from pensions and paper-money. The wrath and consternation of their rulers were proof to them that there was reason in what he said. His prayers to his new disciples to curse their oppressors, but not throw stones, indicated, in the judgment of Southey and of Downing Street, some deep plot to which more material weapons would not be wanting.

Cobbett was to be suppressed, and some have suspected that, had he been imprisoned under the powers given by the Habeas Corpus Suspension Act, the advice of Southey would have been followed. Southey's recommendation, in a memorandum he addressed at this time to Lord Liverpool, was that Cobbett, Hone, and the editors of the Examiner should be subjected to such good discipline, or even transportation, as would "prevent them from carrying on their journals." While the Suspension Act was still in incubation, Cobbett did his worst. The country was in a miserable condition, and he probed every sore. If alleviations were proposed, he jeered

at them; they were not the one thing needed; they were
not reform of Parliament. George Rose established savings-
banks, the greatest boon the working classes have ever had
conferred upon them. Cobbett poured the burning lava of
his ridicule upon the scheme of philanthropy. Rose had
patronised friendly societies once; but the members met to
hear the Register read. By his new plan the pennies of the
few poor who were not paupers might be put together to lend
to the Government "while their persons were kept asunder."
If the salaries of Rose himself and one of his sons, not counting
the payments to another son, an ambassador, were capitalised,
the amount would make a round £300,000 of principal. This
at compound interest, "if it had remained among the people,
might have formed a very nice savings-bank." To recom-
mend savings-banks to a nation in which "it is notorious that
hundreds of thousands of families do not know, when they
rise, where they are to find a meal during the day," is, next
only to the old company for making deal boards out of
sawdust, "the most ridiculous project that ever entered into
the mind of man."

The moral of all Cobbett wrote at this time, the zenith of
his career, was that the country was being stifled by placemen
in Parliament, and that radical representative reform alone
could save it. "Petition, peaceable petition," was his constant
cry. He desired to hear that a million of names at least had
been signed to such petitions. "That would be two-thirds of
the able male population of Great Britain, excluding those
who live on taxes." Petitioning could hardly be called rioting, and the continual injunction he laid upon his friends was
to be "peaceable." If his reasoning were false, the remedy
was obvious. There were "20,000 parsons, 4,000 or 5,000
lawyers, the two Universities, the two Houses of Parliament,
many thousands of magistrates, many hundreds of writers
for pay." Surely it must be easy for these myriads, "with all
their learning and all their weight, to counteract the effect of
one poor twopenny pamphlet." Ministers had on their side
"the greater part of the London press," mercenaries who "threw

their poison from behind a curtain." With all their power the whole legion of friends of authority could not stand up in fair fight against the man who was not ashamed to sign what he wrote. "It was a combat of argument, and they have taken shelter under the shield of physical force." Lord Sidmouth, Cobbett knew, would have preferred to lock him up once more in Newgate as a libeller; "but the pamphlets," by which he meant the Register, "had," Lord Sidmouth avowed in Parliament, "been submitted to the law officers; they were found to be written with so much dexterity that he was sorry to say hitherto the law officers could find in them nothing to prosecute." Consequently, according to Cobbett writing in the Political Register, in March, 1817, a new statute must be passed: "Whereas one William Cobbett, an old offender in the same way, has been, by the means of a certain weekly trash publication, endeavouring to throw down the Corinthian pillar of corruption, and at the same time to preserve the peace and restore the happiness of the United Kingdom; and whereas these efforts tend directly to do great and lasting injury to all those who directly or indirectly live and fatten upon the profits of bribery, corruption, perjury, and public robbery; . . . and whereas no one has been found to answer the writings of the said William, notwithstanding corruption pervades nineteen-twentieths of all the reviews, magazines, and newspapers in the kingdom; and whereas it is expedient to prevent the said William Cobbett from proceeding in the said dangerous courses: Be it therefore enacted that the said William shall write and publish no more, and that he shall neither talk, nor think, nor dream, without the express permission of the proprietors of the Courier and Times, or of their supporters and abettors." In other words, according to Cobbett's egotistical but not wholly unfair inference, Lord Liverpool's Government suspended the Habeas Corpus Act to catch a criminal who was so perverse as to refuse to commit a crime.

But Cobbett would not be caught. His farewell of April 5, 1817, to his countrymen is a masterly apology for what even some of his admirers, like Wooler, "the Black Dwarf," denounced as a desertion. He urged that, if he stayed in England, he would have, as Brougham said, to write with "a halter about his neck." He could not write except as his love for England and English rights inspired him. Yet write he must. "Any sort of trial" he would have stayed to face. "Against the absolute power of imprisonment, without even a hearing, for time unlimited, without the use of pen, ink, and paper, against such a power it would have been worse than madness to attempt to strive." So he departed to a land where he might write for Englishmen, and write freely. He pledged himself that he "would never become a subject or a citizen in any other State, and would always be a foreigner in every country but England." Very superfluously he added: "Any foible that may belong to the English character I shall always willingly allow to belong to my own." His brother Reformers or Reformists, to adopt their own hideous name for themselves, were not all of them as convinced as he seemed himself that the flight to America was not a flight, but a flank movement. The sceptics had reason for their doubts. It is a cruel ordeal for any crusader of politics to know that the Attorney General is leaning over him as he writes, and meditating whether to give him more rope, or to despatch him incontinently to the nearest gaol. Cobbett, brave enough before an open enemy, was not particularly well fitted to bear this supreme test of moral courage or insensibility. He had not endured with equanimity the suspense of the interval between the conviction and the sentence of 1810. He had a right, moreover, to believe that the Hones, and the Woolers, and the Hunts might risk being silenced with less harm to the cause. Perhaps their danger was, as he remarked to them, inconsiderable. A certain Mr. White, of the Independent Whig, had reproached Cobbett for abandoning his post in the army of Reform. Cobbett retorted: "Brave man Mr. White to remain at his post! It is the mastiff and not the mouse that Secretaries of State wish to muzzle." Nevertheless, Cobbett's own apologies for his emigration leave the impression that, after all, it was to be excused as prudent rather than to be panegyrised as magnanimous.

Reasonable doubt may be entertained whether the Government would have gone to the extremity of imprisoning Cobbett without trial. It did not use the power against his fellow-agitators, though that, he would have argued, only confirmed his vaunt that the Suspension Act had him and only him for its object. In any case, his menaces despatched by every mail from Long Island, where he had settled himself, no longer disturbed very greatly either friend or foe in England. Somehow the darts which sped so lustily from New York seemed to fall short of the hearts of his old disciples in cottages and workshops. Within a few months of his departure England was once more enjoying a fair measure of material prosperity. To Cobbett's foreboding eyes the prospect remained black and gloomy; but farm labourers and mechanics were content to feel that they were no longer starving, and petty farmers that they were not becoming bankrupt. The interval of Cobbett's expatriation was not propitious for agitation which had its chief seat at present in the stomach. The mere mechanical fact of absence was more influential still in relaxing Cobbett's hold upon the English people. He was emphatically a journalist, who wrote on the events of a day to be read in the day. English hearts could thrill but feebly to the two-months-old echoes of indignation at incidents they had half forgotten. Cobbett felt this, though he did not confess it. He waited only for a fitting juncture to return. At length he believed that another crisis of commercial depression and discontent at the material conditions of existence was at hand. Like a stormy petrel, he reappeared.

Parliament was contemplating the resumption of cash payments by the Bank of England. Cobbett hated paper-money. But men had for years been keeping their accounts in depreciated paper. He supposed that a sudden return to cash payments would jar the whole of the commercial relations of the country. The shock he looked forward to as his opportunity for urging on Parliamentary Reform, just as at different times he would express pleasure at the prospect that the price of a quartern loaf was soon to be half a crown. His gloomy anticipations or hopes of such an auxiliary as a series of commercial crises in his Reform crusade were disappointed; but he found what might seem a more direct occasion already made for him. The Peterloo massacre was in August, 1819. The meeting of which it was the catastrophe itself marked the resurrection of the Reform agitation. A movement of the small Radical party was converted by the savagery of the yeomanry into an awakening of all the elements of Liberalism in the land. A natural presumption would be that, in this high tide of popular feeling, Cobbett, if he had been powerful before his flight to New York, was likely to become supreme. On the contrary, Reform, in growing into a national movement, had glided beyond Radical control.

He had been converted since his previous residence in America from a specially scornful opponent into an enthusiastic worshipper of the political and economical doctrines of the author of the 'Rights of Man.' Thinking Paine's bones insufficiently honoured by burial "in a little hole under the grass and weeds of an obscure farm" in Long Island, he had them dug up and managed with some difficulty to pass them through the Liverpool Custom House. They made a very cumbersome part of Cobbett's political luggage. At once the cry of Atheist was raised against him by the clergy. But the incident, though it confirmed Cobbett's foes in their aversion, scarcely affected his influence with his faithful Radicals. His return was the signal for an outburst of enthusiasm which terrified authority. The Lancashire magistrates imprisoned for ten weeks a bellman, John Hayes, for proclaiming at Bolton that Cobbett was come back. The borough-reeves of Manchester brought cannon into the town when his approaching arrival was announced. He was clearly still the accepted mouthpiece of English Radicalism. As the battle of Reform proceeded, it speedily was apparent that relatively his power was no longer what it once had been, because the comparative power of Radicalism had waned too. Reform had other champions now than Cobbett, and Hone, and Wooler, and the Hunts. Radicalism and he lost their sharpest weapon when Representative Reform was adopted as the corner-stone of the creed of the historical Whig party. His supplanting by the Whigs was a crime which Cobbett never forgave. From the opening of this the last chapter but one of his political career, and thence to the end, his attacks upon the fortresses of corruption and misgovernment were liable to be blunted by sudden turns about to charge into the ranks of his unacceptable fellow-combatants. The cause of Reform grew and prospered; Cobbett's dominion did not grow with its growth. When it triumphed he was carried on into the captured citadel by the impetus of the assault; it was not his flag which waved above the ramparts.

The year or two which followed Cobbett's return from Long Island were clouded by more material troubles than party jealousies. He had never repaid Burdett the £3,000 lent to settle Swann's claim. That trivial circumstance did not prevent him from accusing Sir Francis of lukewarmness in the cause of Reform. Praiseworthy as it may be not to let private ties stand in the way of a public duty, Burdett's many friends and Cobbett's more enemies raised not unnaturally an outcry of ingratitude. Then his old manager, Wright, had made bad blood between Orator Hunt and Cobbett, who were now close allies. Cobbett had warned him ten years before against relations with Hunt, as "a sad fellow, who goes riding about the country with the wife of another man, having deserted his own." This confidence Wright divulged. Cobbett, who already attributed to Wright's dishonest indolence the wreck of his fortunes, retaliated on what he thought an act of treachery by styling him "a rogue unparalleled in the annals of infamy." For this outburst Cobbett, that is to say, a friend for him, had to pay £1,000 damages. He could not himself have raised the money. The

Register can scarcely have been as remunerative as in the days before 1810. In a controversy he held with Perry, of the Morning Chronicle, who had alleged that at one period, before Cobbett left England, the sale of the Register had fallen to 750, he seems himself not to put the number of weekly copies higher than 1,600, and the yearly profits than £1,500. He declares, indeed, in a previous letter from Long Island, that he enjoyed, at the time he sailed for the States, "a current income from his writings of more than £10,000," beside "copyrights which apparently were worth an immense sum." In the same paragraph he appears to reckon his Botley property as worth more than double the mortgages of £17,000 upon it. If the £10,000 a year from the Register were not more substantial than the value of the copyrights and the farm, we must make great deductions from his estimate of the net profits of his newspaper. In any case, he succumbed to his embarrassments soon after his return from America. He gave up Botley, and passed through the Bankruptcy Court. When that ordeal had been surmounted, the family, in its Brompton lodgings, found itself, according to Cobbett, with "only three shillings in the whole world." That mattered little to him with his unfailing spirits and courage. Looking back over seventy years of life, he once said: "I have led the happiest life of any man that I have ever known." He adds: "Never did I know a single moment when I was cast down, never one moment when I dreaded the future."

A garden at rural Kensington for the moment replaced Botley. If he could not plant acacia woods, he could raise seedlings for friends like Lord Folkestone to plant. He could at Kensington, as at Botley, inculcate the virtues of maize and the vices of potatoes. In course of time he took to seed-farming at Barn-Elms, in the neighbourhood of Jacob Tonson's old house, and later at Normandy Farm, on the borders of Surrey and Hampshire. This was the period in which the 'Rural Rides' were ridden and written. That narrow circumstances could not subdue him is perceptible in every line of that delightful volume. It is a reprint of articles from the Register, describing expeditions, chiefly in the south of England, between the years 1821 and 1832, undertaken for the purpose of inquiring into the condition of the peasantry and the farming interest. Cobbett, as he rides through England, is genuinely happy. For him, as a politician, the earlier of these years were years of fruitless, however noisy, agitation. He boiled over with indignation; his indignation provoked only an unreal popular echo. He worried the topic of paper and cash payments. If anybody, from a "loanmongering" Baring to an Attwood, "a Brummagem banker," discoursed on the subject against the Government, he accused the speaker or writer of stealing his ideas. If Peel's Bill for resumption of cash payments should be carried "without a reduction of the interest of the debt," he offered to give himself up to be "broiled alive." The repeated allusions subsequently in the Register to the "Feast of the Gridiron" reminded men of the falsification of his prediction, and his determination to put a good face upon it. He wrote, in the cause of Catholic emancipation, his 'History of the Reformation.' The successive numbers, as they appeared, gained a circulation of 40,000. But the book injured his clients as much as all Eldon's bigotry and Wetherell's vituperations benefited them. No advocate of toleration, with any self-respect, can read the work without shame for the assumption by scurrility of the disguise of liberality.

Others of his failures were his canvassings of Coventry and Preston. Among his successes he would himself have reckoned his manifestos on behalf of Queen Caroline. Were the mere number of readers a test of a writer's authority, the circulation of Cobbett's publications in the Queen's equivocal cause might be accepted as evidence of triumphant popularity. No doubt, scores of thousands admired the sad fustian of the Queen's letter to the King which was Cobbett's composition. But that unsavoury discussion endangered the monarchical system, of which Cobbett professed himself the most strenuous of champions against the republicanism he instinctively hated; it added no momentum to the downfall of jobbery and corruption at which he aimed his manliest blows. The best tribute to the real durability of his might as an agitator was a renewal by authority of the old homage of fear in the shape of a fresh prosecution of the Register. Portions of the Register were in 1830 republished monthly for twopence, under the title, which Cobbett had already made familiar, of Twopenny Trash. It was a time of agricultural desperation, and Cobbett adopted his ancient tactics. His Twopenny Trash, and he himself orally in his habitual peregrinations, warned the farm labourers against violence. In the same breath he threatened Ministers that the labourer must not be expected to "lie down and die." The Whig Government, new to power, was timorous of the suspicion of abetting Cobbett's attacks on the prosperous classes. Denman, as Attorney General, indicted him for " a libel, with the intent to raise discontent in the minds of the labourers in husbandry, and to incite them to acts of violence, and to destroy corn-stacks, machinery, and other property." Cobbett, as usual, defended himself, and had subpœnaed half the Ministry to give evidence of the former sympathy of its members with his teaching. He was able, as Mr. Greville mentions in his Memoirs, to produce a letter from the Chancellor himself, requesting leave to use some former publications of Cobbett's, which Lord Brougham thought " would be of great use in quieting the labourers." The request was actually made while this prosecution was pending. The jury, which had for its foreman a strong Cobbettite, could not agree upon a verdict, and was discharged amid a scene of tumultuous enthusiasm.

Cobbett, in his defence before the King's Bench, had accused the Whig Cabinet of resolving to ruin him by fair means or foul. The Ministerial motive was the knowledge, he explained, that "if he were to get into the House under a reformed Parliament, he would speedily obtain a cheap Government for the country, and, by doing away with places and pensions, prevent the people's pockets from being picked." Had Ministers been moved by the reasons Cobbett imputed to them, his presence in the House must have quickly undeceived them. He was elected for Oldham in December, 1832, and signalised his introduction to the House by taking possession of a seat on the Treasury bench. Mr. Greville, while noting that "some very bad characters have been returned," and instancing, among others, Cobbett, adds, "though I am glad that Cobbett is in Parliament." Greville had the sense to understand that power such as Cobbett possessed, or had possessed, if a danger, as probably he honestly believed, to the country, would be less of a danger for the yoking of its owner to a seat in the Commons. The demagogue yielded himself as a hostage to Parliament for the acts of his following outside. Cobbett in the House was tiresome rather than formidable. The Register itself was necessarily a bar to sympathy between him and the House. Members could not quite forget that their colleague, as likely as not, was meditating a statement of his views next week on "the hideous bellowings at the back of Althorp, and the half female ya, ya, ya, ya, ya, of the sucking cubs at the back of Peel." Peel himself betrayed the feeling when he promised to attend to Cobbett's observations exactly as to those of "a respectable Member." Even the weekly amenities of the Register might have been forgiven; Cobbett's offences outside the House might have been condoned, as are after-dinner gibes of Long Vacation orators, had he added weight to the deliberations within. He appeared to the House only to twaddle; and he thought the House of Commons indulged, as he told it in his first speech, in "a great deal of vain and unprofitable conversation." When each judged in this way of the other, it is not strange that his brief Parliamentary career was disappointing. But his programme was altogether too impracticably ambitious. He had taken with him into the House of Commons a special mandate which he charged himself to fulfil. Its articles he had recounted to the electors of Manchester when he was canvassing them before the Reform Bill was passed. His work in the House was to obtain the abolition of tithes, of sinecures, and of the majority of pensions, the reduction of the standing army, an equitable readjustment of the currency, and a remission of taxation. The last result was to be compassed by the sale of ecclesiastical and Crown estates, and misapplied corporate property. With the proceeds the national debt was to be wiped out. He accomplished no single point in this comprehensive scheme. The solitary impress his warmest admirer can prove to have been left by his election for Oldham on Parliamentary history is the dismissal of one William Popay from the police force for acting the part of an amateur spy. William Popay was the scapegoat for a bureaucracy still unexpurgated by William Cobbett, a Church still endowed with un-apostolic wealth, armaments still bloated, a currency still left to be adjusted by a financial bungler like Peel, a national debt still a cancer eating into the prosperity and happiness of "this industrious nation."

If it were necessary to characterise Cobbett by a single quality, he might best be described as a good hater. The abundance and variety of his enmities and the copiousness of his vocabulary of contempt surpass the gift in that direction of his illustrious model and exemplar, the Dean of St. Patrick's, "the first author after Moses I ever read." Sometimes even *facit indignatio versum*, though we prefer the angry prose. His satire lost no antithetical point by not being in heroic metre. He had a perilous faculty of embodying his wrath in epithets which stuck. While only revelling in the intoxication of political strife, and as yet unsoured by Newgate and "gagging bills," he had compunctions, which might sometimes seem almost excessive. He tells Wright: "In the copy last sent you there is the phrase '*old* G. Rose.' Upon second thoughts it may as well be left out. It is perhaps right to cease to use that and the like phrases. One puts them down under the influence of indignant feelings but they probably do more harm than good." Even at this period the second thoughts seldom obtruded themselves.

Later on the mocking devil in Cobbett had absolutely free course. He was never at a loss for an object. A public man for the forty years of Cobbett's active literary career must have been harmless to the verge of nonentity to escape without an opprobrious epithet from that inexhaustible treasury.

Many vivid flowers of plain speaking might be culled from the American pamphlets. But Cobbett does not find out how infinitely villainous is public life till he is back in England, and conducting the Political Register. Pitt, once the heaven-born, descends in time, through various gradations of cold and doubting respect, into "great, empty, staring, botheration Pitt." "Mr. Pitt's young friends," including, of course, Canning, "would have put the Tartuffe to the blush, lads that would literally sing you a smutty song to a psalm tune." Perceval, "the little, malignant Perceval," "the favourite of the Church," is a minister who would destroy a Plymouth tinman for offering to buy a petty place, and connive at "the swapping of office for seats." Lord Chancellor Eldon is exquisitely burlesqued as "that plain, frank, and sincere old nobleman," who, on giving his assent to what Cobbett terms the Dungeon Bill, "nearly shed tears." The courtesies of the Register are sometimes retrospective. Edmund Burke is "the sycophant" who trafficked his principles away for a large pension for several lives. A remoter personage yet, "that famous Judge Holt," is "a barrister who had the baseness, after he had received his fee, to desert his client, Mr. Prynne." Holt's still more famous contemporary Locke is "the placeman Locke, who, compared with Paine, was, as to subjects of finance, a mere babbler." Sir Francis Burdett is figured as "an old, tall, bare-ribbed, and broken-down chaise-horse" who will not drag the Reform cart a yard, unless he feel the wheels at his heels. His oratory is held up to ridicule; he "labours till he is out of breath in the utterance of sentences two minutes long, each containing in its belly two or three parentheses, and each of these two or three little ones one within another, as Swift calls it, 'like a nest of pill-boxes.'" Malthus is "the nasty and greedy parson," with "a parson's bawl" and "a muddled parson's head." "I have," writes Cobbett to him, "during my life detested many men, but never any one so much as you." Mr. Jenkinson is accused in 1819 of stealing and spoiling Cobbett's attacks on the fictitiousness of paper-money. His conduct reminds Cobbett of the "scoundrels who, when they have stolen a horse, cut off his tail and ears, and knock out an eye." "Shallow and impudent, hole-digging Castlereagh," "dull and arrogant daddy Grenville," "profligate Sheridan," "stupid Lawyer Horner," are all assailed either for not perceiving or not acknowledging the perspicacity of Cobbett's arguments against that "usurping muckworm," paper currency, or for intercepting the credit which belongs by right to him alone. But of all the mean detractors from his merit, "the meanness of my Lord Folkestone," Cobbett's constant patron, "surpasses that of all the rest." The crime was that Cobbett had sent to Lord Folkestone, afterwards Lord Radnor, a voluminous petition for presentation to the House of Commons against paper-money. Its length precluded its presentation, and Cobbett charges his friend with appropriating its wisdom in a speech of his own without acknowledgment. "You were ashamed to own your obligations to one of the 'lower orders,' but not at all ashamed to pillage him; like your broods of uncles, cousins, and dependents, who, while they are too proud to speak to the common labourer, are not too proud to eat part of his dinner, under the name of offices, sinecures, and pensions."

The only two deserving political economists, though Cobbett would have scorned the name, are himself and Tom Paine. Ricardo's volume is "a heap of senseless Change-Alley jargon, put upon paper and bound up into a book." Tooke's 'Theory of Prices' is "a conundrum," "absurdity upon absurdity." Adam Smith, "if Paine had been a canter and a crawler instead of a man of sincerity and spirit, would have been laughed off the stage years ago." He hates Adam Smith both as a political economist and as a Scotchman. "I will be bound," he writes at another time, "to find a couple of Scotch economists who shall by their own individual exertions outlie the father of lies himself." Mackintosh, the reformer of the criminal law, is sneered at as "Lawyer Mackintosh," who has, like every lawyer, his bill. The whole London press is "corrupt" and malignant, especially the Courier and the "bloody old Times." The writers are politely designated "wicked old hacks." Perry of the Chronicle, whom he had been forward in congratulating in 1810 upon his acquittal in a Government prosecution, and declared to have "done more good than any man of his time," is in 1817 "the basest of all the base tools of corruption." To Cobbett William Wilberforce appears a mere writer of "canting pamphlets." Wilberforce had appealed to "the inhabitants of the British Empire" to help to transmute the wretched Africans into "the condition of free British labourers." Cobbett's comment is: "Empire in your teeth, you retailer of bombast!" Cobbett wants to know if the appeal for the blacks is addressed to the free British labourers to be seen at the Kensington gravel-pits "with bits of sack round their shoulders and with haybands round their legs," or to "the emaciated, half-dead things who crack stones to make roads as level as a die for the tax-eaters to ride on." Frederick Robinson, afterwards Lord Goderich, whose sound common sense while he was Chancellor of the Exchequer retrieved British finance, is scoffed at as "Mr. Frederick Prosperity." He is more particularly denounced for claiming the credit for the sitting Parliament of a reduction of taxation. Sir James Graham is "a proud, insolent, unprincipled writer," on account of his pamphlet on Corn and Currency. The pamphlet Cobbett declares to contain a proposition for robbing the whole nation, if the landowners, "who have all the legal power in their hands, have but the *pluck* to make use of it." But Cobbett "has taken the Baronet of Netherby down a peg." Miss Martineau, for her advocacy of the new Poor Law, is "Mother Martineau." The most proverbially honest of statesmen is actually "sly Althorp," "cunning Althorp!" With this supreme effort of extravagantly perverted indignation the forty years' flood of invective ceases to flow. Cobbett sat up in bed to dictate the Register which contains the attack on the Whig leader on June 10, 1835. On June 18 he was dead.

No chivalrous sensibility ever checked his aggressiveness. If person or cause could be struck at through a woman, he would strike as ferociously at the woman as at a man. Death gave no shelter from his satire. A long and wrathful article is devoted to the misdeeds both of the second Mrs. Coutts, afterwards Duchess of St. Albans, for succeeding to the wealth of "late Banker Coutts," and of her dead husband for having endowed her with it. He is indignant at the national sorrow for the murdered Perceval. If a man was fallen, that, in Cobbett's eyes, was no reason for sparing him if he had not spared Cobbett. A story he tells in the 'Farewell to England,' published on the eve of his departure for the United States in 1817, illustrates his view of what for him was fair fighting. A butcher and a west-country grazier quarrelled at Barnet fair, and the butcher drew his knife. The grazier ran off, but returned with a long ash stick. With this he gave the butcher a blow on the wrist which brought the knife to the ground. "The grazier then fell to work with his stick; the butcher fell down and rolled and kicked; but he seemed only to change his position in order to insure to every part of his carcase a due share of the penalty of his baseness. After the grazier had apparently tired himself, he was coming away, when, happening to cast his eye upon the knife, he ran back and renewed the basting, exclaiming every now and then as he caught his breath, 'Dra thy knife, wo't?' He came away a second time, and a second time returned, and set upon the caitiff again; and this he repeated several times, exclaiming always when he recommenced the drubbing, 'Dra thy knife, wo't?'" Cobbett was perpetually casting his eye upon the knife he considered his adversaries had drawn against him. Prostrate though they might be, he was perpetually tempted to "recommence their drubbing." "We are told," he says at another time, "to love our enemies; but there is a condition attached to this; they are to repent and make atonement first; for otherwise this would be the most immoral maxim. God says, 'An eye for an eye'; and this is the rule, the plain unmystical rule, that I pursue."

Former favours were no bar to present enmity. No one had stood by him so faithfully as Lord Folkestone. Burdett's example made him a reformer. Burdett had saved Cobbett from a load of pecuniary embarrassment. Yet he assailed both Folkestone and Burdett with the utmost virulence. His old patron Windham, to whom, it must be admitted, he was generally faithful, is stamped, on occasion, as "the misguided." The single character which seems to have escaped even a side buffet, was that of Cochrane. Cochrane's expulsion from the House of Commons for fraud was his protection. Ingratitude, or what bore the semblance of ingratitude, to old friends was taken by Cobbett's friends as evidence of his incorruptibility; and incorruptible by money or place he was. He might have agreed to be silent in order to buy exemption from Newgate; he would never have sold his pen to authority. That in the course of his political career he had veered round to opposite sides of the compass did not take the edge off his consciousness of rectitude. His opponents wasted their time in endeavouring to confute him by dwelling on his printed and published inconsistencies. He might hallow Paine dead whom living he would have gibbeted. He might, in 1795, have eloquently execrated the "murderous" French Revolution, and the "cannibal" atrocities of the emissaries of the Convention at Lyons. That was no reason why he should not, in 1816, justify the vengeance, no greater, he alleged, after all than that of Moses, taken by a "cruelly treated and starving people" for "a tyranny under which it had groaned for ages," and compared with which "the bondage of the Israelites was light as a feather." No doubt ever crept over him whether possibly he might not be in error now, since he must otherwise have certainly been in error before. He was himself apparently insensible for the most part to the changes which had been operating in him. He would appeal bravely to his part in early controversies as evidence for his new theses. His disciples never cared to confront the Cobbett of the present with the Cobbett of the past. For them each Weekly Register as it appeared was a new genesis; it had fulfilled its destiny if it slew a reputation.

Cobbett cared neither for consistency in his opinions old and new, nor for the consistency of his position at any one period of his career with itself. No Englishman could be a more genuine lover of honest industry. He was cut to the heart by the horrible state of degradation into which the British labourer had sunk during, and for twenty years after, the great war. Yet he asserted that "the English system of poor law," the system under which Coventry with 20,000 inhabitants had 8,000 paupers, was "the best in the world." He mocked at Whitbread's and Romilly's schemes for "enlightening the people." Modern "facilities of moving human bodies from place to place," which were beginning to lift the British labourer from the debasement of a thrall, he, as he rides his way on a good horse, holds to be "amongst the curses of the country, the destroyers of industry, of morals, and, of course, of happiness." He would not have his son taught "outlandish Greek or Latin;" but he detested utilitarianism. He invited the nation at large to yearly exhibitions of rough old English sports at Botley, and defended bull-baiting as an innocent mode of procuring cheap beef for the poor. Week by week, and year by year, he went on thundering against the governing classes; but he always inserted saving clauses in his indictment for old descent and the trappings of royalty. "Loanmonger Baring," "baronets," like Peel's father, "of the spinning jenny," and the "paper aristocracy" generally, he could not tolerate. He was careful to qualify the existing house of Percy as "Smithsons (called Percys)." The Duke of Buckingham is "the new" duke. He taunted Ministers with having "sneakingly withdrawn the title of 'King of France' from the King and from his coins." He scoffed at "the lowness, the dirtiness of the villainy, the vulgarity, the disregard of all sense of morality and of honour" among republicans. No man was ever prouder of having lords among his acquaintances. For estates "which had descended from ancestor to heir from the Norman Conquest" he professed an admiring respect. He denounced "the Administration of Mr. Pitt," the more bitterly that it had promoted the transfer of immemorial patrimonies to "brokers and jobbers."

How much of all this was real and how much was acting it is hard to say. Cobbett himself did not know. He had acquired a habit of attitudinising before the public; if a sentiment of the proper sharpness of emphasis did not spring up naturally, it had to be forced. He made himself the central subject of interest or curiosity for his readers. He always uses the first person in his newspaper attacks upon Pitt and Addington. He is to be met everywhere riding about the country. He is a guest from time to time at every farmers' ordinary. Speaking of the farmers of Herefordshire, a district which was strange to him, he says in his 'Rural Rides': "If I were to live in the county two months, I should be acquainted with every man of them." On the county hustings the petty farmer's son, the farm labourer's grandson, the ex-sergeant, dared to oppose a more penetrating power than Pitt's, that of "old Rose" himself. When an attorney of the Rose party attempted to excite a clamour, "I fixed my eye upon him," writes Cobbett, "and, pointing my hand downright, and making a sort of chastising motion, said: 'Peace, babbling slave!' which produced such terror amongst others, that I met with no more interruption." On the Westminster hustings he beards as an equal the great Whig orator, Sheridan. He might be planting an acacia copse at Botley. He might cudgel a rival journalist for maligning him, or be threatened with the whip by a political barrister for his most laudable refusal of a challenge. In every case the whole English public was taken into his confidence. He mixed up himself and his personality with every social problem, with every affair of State. No author has left in his works so complete an autobiography. We are told by him in the Register and his earlier publications so much about himself that it might be supposed no character could have been drawn more distinctly. No character, on the contrary, is more bewildering. The bluff plain English yeoman is continually being transformed under our very eyes into a shrewd, wily Yankee. Beneath the Radical peep forth infinite possibilities of Tory prejudice.

Whatever may have been the real Cobbett, the actual Cobbett impressed himself in all his various phases very deeply on the shifting scenes of the first five-and-thirty years of the nineteenth century. His influence had its evil side. A popular leader of whose character rancour, inconsistency, forgetfulness of kindnesses, prejudice, and incapacity for recognising that there may be good motives for mischievous acts, are essential constituents, is not one to bridge over social chasms and pacify class feuds. The faintest spark of envy and jealousy which Cobbett detected in the relations of Englishmen he fanned into a flame. Yet any one who has studied the administration of England during the great French war and the period which was its sequel, will pause before condemning the influence of Cobbett, or perhaps the man himself, too absolutely. It was a period of pretences, subterfuges, and hypocrisies. The rulers ruling under one title exercised powers that title was never meant to cover. The Political Register had its birth in a period when they who were supposed to represent the British people represented either Downing Street, or a score of boroughmongering peers, or a heavy balance at their bank. Wages were a species of poor rate, and the poor rate a form of wages. The criminal law was a lottery in which the least guilty might draw the penalty of the most atrocious outrage. Finance was reduced to mere juggling; and Lord Castlereagh appeared to be plotting to acclimatise the principles of foreign despotism on English soil.

Cobbett, though he had blinding prejudices of his own,

could see through the prejudices and sophisms of others. He chose both his weapons and their mark often wrongly ; but even his perversity compelled politicians to render account of their constitutional faith. When Chancellors of the Exchequer were still in darkness, he saw the grotesque absurdity of borrowing to maintain the Sinking Fund. He saw the fallacy of bounties on corn. He saw the superiority of leases to yearly tenancies. He saw that a large currency does not make a nation richer than a small currency ; that the one virtue of a national currency is that it should continue to represent equivalent values when a debt is contracted and when it has to be paid. In his highest flights of extravagance—when he railed at Protestantism, as though he were not a rampant political Protestant himself, when he extolled the old poor law, when he raged against potatoes, "hog potatoes," "the suitable companions of misery and filth," a thing which can be "raked half ripe out of the ground with the paws," "and without the help of any utensils, except, perhaps, a stick to rake it from the fire, can be conveyed into the stomach in the space of an hour," when he reviled all Liberals who scrupled to unroof the house of politics before they had got the inmates out—his impulse was often right. The abuses he assailed were generally flagrant, though the personal antipathies he founded on them usually were grotesque, and though the remedies he proposed might be as bad as the disease. A more temperate politician might not have stirred farmers and mechanics to educate themselves in politics. Without the proportion of earthiness in his intellectual composition there would have been slender sympathy between himself and the ill-used and uneducated classes which he taught to feel their wrongs, if not their rights, as Englishmen.

The power he had won he believed was only a beginning. The echoes his burning appeals had woke in deadened souls he heard reverberating through the ages. "All the celebrity," he boasted, "which my writings have obtained, they will preserve long and long after Lords Liverpool, and Sidmouth, and Castlereagh are rotten and forgotten." Liverpool, and Sidmouth, and Castlereagh may be forgotten; but neither are the writings of Cobbett remembered. The many volumes of the Political Register, Sermons on the rights of the poor and the extortion of the clergy, parodies of the Protestant Reformation, and Legacies to labourers, to Peel, and to parsons, did their work, and are at rest. The student of politics must be a student of Cobbett if he would understand the rudiments out of which existing tendencies have been developed. The statesman who [does not know the Register forfeits a master key to the passions of his countrymen. Yet thousands of Englishmen go through what they suppose to be a complete course of English literature, without a suspicion that Cobbett should be read as well as Burke. We cannot wish for Cobbett a place among English classics. Insolence and spite are the spirit he breathes. He speaks in the accents of an age as much one of civil war as if the weapons had not been bitter thoughts, but more innocent swords and muskets. Of such literature the life is necessarily brief; and it is useless to deprecate a fate for his writings which was inevitable. Not the less lamentable is it that a style so piquant, such power of marrying argument to declamation, such spontaneous transitions from wrath against the oppressor to pity for the oppressed, with such sudden gleams of illustration by biting apologue of pots and pans, or tender reminiscence of "my dear old grandmother" and her rushlights, should be mixed up inextricably with withering sarcasms upon the sins, which no longer arouse indignation, of statesmen whose names no longer evoke memories.

Recollections of nature-printed bits of English scenery, taken with the dew and the sunlight glistening upon them, plead for a reprieve from oblivion of one book of Cobbett's, if no other. English literature may be searched in vain for such another miniature of southern England as the 'Rural Rides.' It is an ambulatory history of Selborne, with the parish of Selborne expanded into a dozen counties. But the smoke from the monster "Wen" poisons the air even on the breezy Surrey downs. In great leafy western woods the diarist scents, as it were, the carcase of a "fundlord" beneath the violets. The eye is lingering fondly on some sweep of fruitful valleys and green hills, when the foot stumbles on the brink of a forsaken mine of rustic happiness, exhausted and desolated by commercial or official greediness. Guidebook makers have always quarried in the 'Rural Rides.' Those transcripts of scenery never grow obsolete. But the volume itself gathers dust; few and far between are its new editions. Cobbett chose his lot, and it is too late to dream of mending it. His Register stung vindictively a hundred political reputations, and his own fame is dead of his revenge.

VI.

PURITAN AND CAVALIER ENGLAND TRANSPLANTED.

NEW ENGLAND,
1620–1784.

VIRGINIA,
1607–1799.

NEW ENGLAND.

FRANKLIN and Cobbett, in varying modes and degrees, both serve as points of contact between English and American politics. But the America to which they call attention is America moulded and transformed by Republican institutions. There is another aspect in which American history may be viewed; and it also has its English counterparts. American provincial history, the period of American antiquity, to Franklin himself was grown obsolete before his career ended; it was always invisible to Cobbett as a sojourner; yet it deserves study not less for the light it sheds outside its immediate circle than for its own merits. It tells much about the direction of the American national character, and not a little concerning English character as well. For experimental purposes nothing is more instructive than to transport outside its habitual circumstances an element of which the force needs to be measured. A retention of vigour by it in its new quarters attests inherent vitality. Its choice of the same line to move along is evidence of a genuine tendency, and cannot be attributed to accident. Explorers of particular veins and strata of English history enjoy that kind of opportunity for gauging some of their distinctive characteristics in pictures of the social life of Virginia and New England as it existed before their emancipation from British rule. Cavalier England, the England of country squires, not feudal and baronial, not unconscious of the advantages of commerce, but despising the economy and assiduity which trade demands, is plainly reflected in the former. Puritan England stereotyped itself in the latter and preserved the impression long after it had faded off the original type. Both offer an interesting spectacle. In the younger of the two the traits were so deeply graven that they have never been effaced. The Puritan bias, though no longer more distinctly religious at Boston than at Geneva, continues in its own modern fashion to stamp the character of New England. By its influence over a national constituent so important as Massachusetts it remains an active leavening force in general American progress.

Populations, when all their life and energies have been absorbed and dominated by a particular type of feeling, seem sometimes to have a capacity of throwing off into space an exact facsimile of it. The image does not revolve in the same orbit, or undergo the same developments as the state of society of which it is the product. It obeys simply the special laws which it illustrated at and by its birth. Its tendencies, which may be various, continue ever after unchangeable. Thus, the result of a most radical revolution may manifest subsequently equally extreme conservatism. Never has the principle been more plainly exemplified than in the course of the annals and thought of New England.

The story of the plantation of the New England colonies belongs to a heroic chapter in English history. It reproduces the spirit which animated its leaders at home, unadulterated by the suspicion of cunning and scheming with which, whether true or false, the art of the English Thucydides has overspread their policy. Every now and then, one of the actors in the great coming drama of the Commonwealth is seen directly associated with the Colonial knight errantry. Of the more permanent settlers the Bellinghams, Dudleys, and Winthrops were English all over, with the prejudices generous, or narrow, as they might be, of English gentlemen and yeomen. The land they chose was not one of nature's treasure houses. Such as it was it suited their mood. Captain Goswold found Martha's Vineyard "replenished with the blossoms of strawberries and raspberries, with cranes and hernes, and courteous salvages." But it was, " by reason of some occult and secret accident, known by experience to partake a little too much of the two extremes of heat and cold;" the latter, however, cleansing the air's lower chambers, "and the earth as to its fruitfulness being beholding to the summer's heat, and the influence of celestial planets." Englishmen are inclined to think this somewhat stormy land of Puritan refuge sterner than it seemed then. Few English tourists examine the country at all. So late as 1796, an American travelling through it for curiosity was a marvel. Judging from the meagreness of more recent tours and American handbooks, we may conceive he would be so still. New England scenery, in general, though not romantic, is of a domestic picturesqueness. Everywhere rise up lichen-covered rocks, partially covered with the native forest, or boulders of bare gneiss bordering the level and fertile plain. Now you come upon swamps fringed with red cedars; now on one of the multitudinous, glittering New England lochs, each, writes President Dwight, like "a delightful morning in spring." Then again appear stretches of aboriginal forest, great groves of whispering white pines, birch, and oak, and sumach, and glorious maples, contrasting with what the same author terms the "cavern-like darkness of the massy green hemlock." All are gilded and vermilioned by the first breath of the summer of All-Saints. Interspersed now are bright white villages, shadowed with luxuriant avenues. Down the broken forest-lands the waters, always pure and sweet, flow with unceasing rapidity; and, to their pleased surprise, emigrants, natives of our eastern counties, found grassy hollows and thickets ever dry and healthy. There were not smooth lawns, or heaths, or ancient oaks; but the yellow tulip-tree and blush pink dogwood, and fragrant shad-blossom illuminated the landscape. Every common had its glossy candleberry and sweet fern, golden rods and asters, and everlastings. Generally the hills were low downs rather than mountains; but the clear northern atmosphere made the crests of the White Mountains, pearl-like, or projected, as before a storm, a continual presence within a circle of eighty or a hundred miles.

The Virginian tobacco-planter might taunt the colonists with the sugar, indigo, ginger, and cotton, which the industry of their twenty thousand would have produced had they come thither, instead of selecting a region "so barren, that, except a herring be put into the hole that you set the corn or maize in, it will not come up." But rocky Massachusetts was blown upon by the rough animating winds of England, and its sand dunes, pools, and levels, reminded of old homesteads amid the fens of Lincolnshire and Essex. Even English weeds loved the soil which was friendly to English grain. The colonists were fugitives in the cause of religious liberty, and had no reason to meditate with gratitude on their native rulers. They might have, in this remote region, practically renounced Privy Councils and Stuarts. The thought never entered their imaginations. They would be Englishmen in all points still. At the moment of departure, the leaders of the main body of emigrants put forth to the world a manifesto of ardent love and gratitude to the land and Constitution which had indifferently cherished them.

A forlorn hope for making the experiment of a settlement, was furnished by the congregation of Mr. Robinson, that audacious controversialist who, a chronicler tells us, " at length arrived to that confidence, that he began to play with Dr. Ames his name, styling him in one of his pamphlets 'Dr. William Amiss.'" After a brief trial of Holland they tired of its fogs, and were the more disposed to be tempted by Captain Goswold's report of the dry bracing air in the region he had just visited. They had been encouraged also by a prediction of "Mr. Brigges, that famous mathematician," as people then politely termed their Murphys and Moores, that "the disappearing of the blazing star in the west, in the year 1619, betokened the death of the natives in these parts through some notable event." In a dreary December, after a tedious passage over "the vast and wide ocean," the little company reached the shore, "to be entertained with no other sight than that of the withered grass on the surface of the cold earth, and the grim looks of savage enemies." They were comforted a little by "stumbling, through an accident, upon some baskets of Indian corn, which did, in some sort, resemble the grapes of Eshcol, more to the apprehension of faith than of sense."

Miles Standish was elected captain of Plymouth, "the Old Colony." He had been "bred a soldier in the Low Countries, and was very expert in things of that nature, though not at that time of their chnrch." Mr. Robinson, indeed, seems to have been somewhat alarmed at the tales of the prowess of this mail-clad, fiery, little warrior, as shown in the slaying, with his own hand, of the naked Indian brave, Pecksuct. The Pastor wrote in 1623 to his people, " to consider the diposition of their captain, who was of a severe temper. He doubted whether there was not wanting that tenderness of the life of man, made after God's image, which was meet." His congregation was less scrupulous, and did not look censoriously into little incidents of murder and marauding which might diversify the marches and countermarches through the forest of him and his

"Twelve men all equipped, having each his rest and his matchlock,
Eighteen shillings a month, together with diet and pillage."

In memory, some assert, of his ancestral hall in Lancashire, of which, they say, he had been unjustly deprived, he called his own village Duxbury According to another tradition, it gained its name from his office of Dux. Perhaps it was an equivoque. There he hung up his sword and snaphance, the terror of the Indian tribes from Massachusetts Bay to Martha's Vineyard, from Cape Cod to Narraganset, and married. Faithless John Alden and fair Priscilla were his near neighbours. Whatever his failures in wooing, or carelessness of Indian rights, he was a successful public servant for the young settlement, and he tolerated no lawlessness among his people. Order was strictly maintained under his command and the magistracy of Mr. John Carver. In September 1630, one Billington was executed for murder in the forest; and so the colony took root among lawful nations. Soon beneath the brow of the pine-clad plain, overlooking the ocean, avenues of drooping elms were planted. Beside them arose houses with panelled walls and huge protruding wooden beams. The exteriors were constructed in Leyden style of brick imported with the settlers from Holland, and fitted with house-martin boxes to remind them of the stork-nests on friendly Dutch roofs. There dwelt many a Jerusha, Eunice, Dorcas, and Experience, making comfortable, if very serious, homes for their Adonirams, Seths, and Considers, during the residue of the eighty or ninety years which it was granted to many of them to see out in the Old Colony; all which the primitive churchyard shows.

In the meantime Salem had been planted by some dissidents from the principle of religious separatism upheld by Plymouth. Soon, with the help of a rich and powerful company, which had obtained a charter to hold the land in common socage of the manor of East Greenwich, it grew and prospered, until it became the most characteristic of New England settlements. There was gathered, in 1629, the first "Church," that of Boston being but seventh in order of date. In wealth, literature, contributions to works of charity, and population, though year by year with a wider interval, it still stands next, among the cities of its State, to Boston. On it Nathaniel Hawthorne, the most national of American writers, concentrates his chief wealth of description and historic fancy. In itself, nothing can be more prosaic. That does not make it less of a type. The novelist describes its flat, unvaried surface, covered chiefly with wooden houses, few of which pretend to architectural beauty, with an irregularity which is neither picturesque nor quaint. He expatiates on its long and lazy street, lounging wearisomely through the whole extent of the peninsula, with its Gallows-hill at one end, and a view of the almshouse at the other. "Such," he continues, "being the features of my native town, it would be quite as reasonable to form a sentimental attachment to a disarranged checker-board. And yet, though invariably happiest elsewhere, there is within me a feeling for old Salem, which, in lack of a better phrase, I must be content to call affection." Round about the sandy plain on which it stands, washed by the salt water on each side at every tide, with stormy Cape Anne stretching mistily far out to the north, rise rude hills. Great swamps are interspersed, Pine Swamp, Blueberry Swamp, Cotton Swamp, Round Swamp, and hosts of other swamps, with rocks, downs, and pasture lands, and wild, melancholy pine groves. The name of Wenham Lake, a few miles away, is better known than all the rest in England now. It suggests cheerful summer and strawberry ices, and is worthy of the pleasant associations. According to the testimony of a traveller a couple of centuries ago, it is "a delicious paradise, abounding with all rural pleasures; the lofty trees on each side being a sufficient shelter from the winds, and the warm sun so kindly ripening both the fruits and flowers, as if the spring, the summer, and the autumn had agreed together to thrust winter out of doors."

Formerly the name of Salem required no accidental aids to remembrance. The whole early history of New England may be read in the names of its runs, and coves, points, and "dungeons." Many wealthy families still reside in it, or the neighbourhood, in mansions disguised under the democratic name of farm-houses. Such are Fitch's Farm, possessed, by a descendant of King Derby, as one merchant prince was styled, Castlehill Farm, with a vast decaying hall, and Pickman's Farm. The munificent family which sprang direct from Sir Richard Saltonstall, a founder and patron of the new colony, lived splendidly at Saltonstall Place. In the town itself, with its dull monotony of wooden houses and unpaved streets, occasional edifices of wood, rich in fanciful decorations, show the "House of the Seven Gables" to be only one of a class. Its quaint figures stamped on the glittering plaster; its gables presenting the aspect of a whole sisterhood of edifices breathing through the spiracles of one great chimney, with spaces in between for fair flowers to colour, and humming-birds to flit over; its carved globes of wood, and spiral rods of iron; its many lattices with diamond panes, and deep waves of shadow thrown over hall and chamber by the full projecting eaves, are native facts of Salem topography. The seat of these Pyncheons stands, or stood not long since, in spacious Summer Street. In the same street is the almshouse, though neither to that, nor to the new one on the common, had Uncle Venner to retire. Essex or Main Street contains all the principal houses, and the two old-fashioned wooden churches. At the corner of it and North Street, Curwen-house, gabled and peaked, and dating back to 1642, is another witness to the love the adventurers had of recalling their quaint Essex or Lincolnshire homesteads amid the lanes and high streets of an American village. The dress and portrait of Captain Curwen, still or till lately there preserved, with flowing neckcloth, lace sash, and coat with short cuffs showing the plaited shirt, octagon ring, and cane, is, or was, a sort of material guarantee of the deeds and characters of the whole stern resolute race.

The founders of Salem were no vagrants, leaving home for the sake of subsistence. They were well-to-do landowners. Many, if not most, had enjoyed the advantages of a complete university training, and some, as Wilson and Governor Dudley, had attained academical distinction. They came of the same stock with the men who faced Rupert's horsemen at Marston Moor and Naseby, and they anticipated them in disdaining the idea of subservience. Such were the Curwens, and Hawthornes, or Hathornes, and Pyncheons. The first of the New England branch of the Curwens left, at his death, £5,964 in money; 621 oz. of plate; much merchandise; three farms near Salem; ships, houses, warehouses, and wharfs, both there and at Boston. The Hawthornes came from England at the same period. Major Hawthorne very early founded Dorchester, and planted its rich orchards and gardens, though retaining his Salem domicile. We hear of them on special commissions, in the Council of the province, and in the town magistracy. In 1652 the town voted for the building of a fort on the south-east point of Winter Island, to be under the care of Governor Endicott and William Hawthorne. The same W. Hawthorne, "the bold and worthy captain, a man of an undaunted courage, with his lieutenant Lothrope, led the band of Salem." Perhaps he had, like his major, "the stout and active Robert Sedgwick," been nursed up in "London's Artillery Garden," whence, we must remember, came Sir Arthur Hasilrigge's valiant cuirassiers. The Pyncheons were a still more important house. Beside being the squires of Springfield and Northfield, they generally held the office of Assistant; and their head, even under the despotic sway of Sir Edmund Andros, kept his seat in the Council of the province. William Pyncheon was Provincial Treasurer in 1636, the same year in which Sir Henry Vane, soon to figure on a larger field, was Governor. The Honourable Major and Colonel John Pyncheon was a man of war, often charged by the Council with the drilling and mustering of the trainbands against Marquas and Sineques. He was a friend of the unpopular Mr. Secretary Edward Randolph, and one for whom, writes the latter, "his Excellency the Governor has a great kindness." The race continued to flourish in Salem, and the Pyncheon Papers constitute some of the most important documents of Massachusetts history.

The names of a few families meet us at every step, in tracing the history of the old New England settlements. The migration included capitalists and merchants, such as Browne and Humphries, younger sons seeking a fortune, and individuals of all ranks fleeing from persecution. The groundwork of any one of its several sections was a body of Lincolnshire, Dorset, or Essex villagers, dissatisfied with the whole home system of government. But all, leaders and followers, were men of prompt energy, ready to improve every opportunity. In 1629 Salem consisted of six houses; in 1636, Endicott was exploring as far as Narraganset Bay, and marching, with his score of warriors, deep into the heart of the hostile Pequod territory. The sickly flocked over to a land where rheumatic and phlegmatic diseases were said to be unknown; for, writes one of the first ministers, "a sup of New England's aire is better than a whole draught of Old England's ale." Peasants hoped for rich returns from a virgin soil. Hardy seamen found wealth in the fisheries of bass, cod, and mackerel, which yielded draughts often enough to break strong nets. No long time, and the Desire sailed forth from a Salem dockyard, a printing-press was set up, and the first American Almanac issued. Opulent merchants began to build themselves houses in the Puritan villages, where 80 per cent. was no uncommon rate of profit. The general tone of comfort was increased; and "green pease growing in the magistrates' gardens, as good as ever he eat in England," seem to have startled and tickled worthy Mr. Higginson's palate. As plentiful a crop of English weeds, which, imported with seed-corn, made holiday in New Essex, completely beating out the native tribes, was a less pleasant proof of the indiscriminate congeniality of air and soil.

While the Endicotts, Pyncheons, and Curwens were guarding the land from the Indian foe with the great ordnance which was a matter of high pride to the settlement, Hugh Peters, afterwards the regicide, stimulated commercial activity. His influence is always spoken of under the term "sovereignty." A refugee City of London preacher, he had come over from Holland in the capacity as much of a merchant as of a minister. At one time he was excommunicating Roger Williams's adherents; at another, reforming the police of the town. He was an autocrat. Rich men, the Brownes and William Hawthorne, flocked into Salem, and bowed to his authority. He founded salt-works, water-mills, and glass-works. By him the marsh was drained; and a great ship, for those times, of 300 tons burden, was equipped, and bore the name of Salem to every mercantile port of Europe. Governor Endicott he wrested from the dominion of Roger Williams. Williams was too kind and gentle for him, though a religionist so zealous as to have compelled the impetuous Puritan captain, to the indignation of the Conservative Browne, to cut out from the royal standard the red cross as a Popish emblem. He rebuked Harry Vane himself for abetting the heresies of Anne Hutchinson. He was a powerful preacher; his coarse, familiar images and strange analogies "making whatever he said sure to be remembered." At the same time, he would not suffer the Church to interfere with secular business, and went so far as to suppress the crowd of weekly and occasional lectures to which Cotton Mather at Boston confidently ascribes the remarkable prosperity of that town. He nobly rebuked the people for pretending a private revelation from Heaven, to eke out insufficient evidence against a woman accused of child-murder. He woke up the energies of the Puritan farmers; and Endicott, aided by his counsels, triumphed over the Indian borderers. To missions for propagating the Gospel among the tribes he never showed favour in Old or in New England. To his solid, prosaic understanding, there appeared something ridiculously visionary in all the arguments and theories on this topic of Roger Williams, and even the "Apostle of the Indians," Eliot. He seems to have held, as completely as Cromwell in regard to the wild Irish, that the savages were vermin made to be exterminated. Magnificent educational schemes were not favoured by him. A project, for instance, for the institution of a college at Salem he denounced as the mere result of jealousy of the metropolitan claims of Boston. But all sober plans of the sort he furthered; and to him was due the introduction to the settlement of Mr. John Fisk, a Cambridge graduate of great wealth, and equal liberality, the father of education in New England. Sir George Downing, subsequently celebrated as Cromwell's and Charles II.'s ambassador in Holland, was a pupil of Fisk's, and the first New Cambridge graduate. Against the earnest remonstrances of Endicott, and the agricultural members of his congregation, who valued his ministrations above his commercial genius, but at his own request, and backed by the wishes of the mercantile party, Hugh Peters was elected delegate to England, to represent the sense of the colony on the laws of excise and trade. Local tradition continues to associate Wenham Lake with the memory of his bold oratory and strong, rough sense, ringing out amid the queerest of grammar, and sometimes the most inconclusive of arguments, from Peters' Hill over the waters. At home, only his last words, on the scaffold, are remembered: " In a revolution, burn the whole and begin anew."

Peters had indoctrinated with his own passion for orthodoxy, as he understood it, that "sociable warrior, of a cheerful, loving, and austere spirit," Captain Endicott; and the Captain, with all his gaiety, did not bear the sword in vain. Mrs. Oliver and the Hutchinsonians were hardly dealt with; and in 1658 Quakers were threatened with the penalty of death, though not with the consent of the minister, Mr. Norris. There seem to have been two parties in Salem, and New England generally, the democratic and enthusiastic, and the conservative. Men like Vane and Roger Williams, and, at one time, Cotton, were on the side of the former. So originally had been Endicott; but we find him in 1652 joining Dudley, Bellingham, Bradstreet, and Hibbins, husband of a future victim of the witchcraft delusion, "bitter-tempered Mistress Hibbins," in excusing themselves to Vane, by this time exalted in power at home, from showing forbearance to William Pyncheon, who had, though a magistrate, written a book in favour of the radical tenets. Winthrop and Peters, and most of the ministers, were consistent in discountenancing innovations. An extreme section of the same party, comprising Hawthorne, Humphries, and Sir Richard Saltonstall, actually proposed a high property qualification for office, and would have converted the Council into a permanent oligarchy.

Boston was founded after Salem. On the 7th of April, 1630, had Winthrop, Fiennes, and the rest of the Council, put forth from on board the Arbella their solemn declaration of love for England, and entreaty for the prayers of the Church. On June 12, the Admiral galley, followed soon by the Mayflower and the rest, reached Massachusetts. They met a hearty welcome. Venison pasty and strong beer refreshed the great men. The rest, in addition, it may be presumed, to more solid food, feasted on strawberries, with which, says the old historian in a regretful tone, "the woods were at that time everywhere well furnished." The whole land was gay and bright, as in old Hubbard's description. "Now, in May you shall see the woods and fields curiously decked with roses, and an innumerable multitude of other delightful flowers, not only pleasing to the eye but smell; so that you may behold nature contending with art, and striving to equal, if not excel, many gardens in England." But second impressions were gloomier than the first. Young Henry Winthrop, the Governor's second son, "a sprightly and hopeful young gentleman," was drowned on the second day; and, within a month, was buried at Salem, only a few weeks before her husband, Isaac Johnson, the Lady Arbella. The poor lady died heart-broken at the "change from a paradise of plenty and pleasure, in the family of a noble earldom, into a wilderness of wants;" all which sorrows, says the pious chronicler, "proved too strong a temptation." Winter, too, came like a surprise upon the new-comers, before they had become habituated to their new abode. Happily, writes one of themselves in a rapture, "we have plenty of fire to warm us. Nay, all Europe is not able to afford to make so great fires as New England." If the blaze they kept up had a habit of setting the huts on fire, the structures were easily rebuilt.

In the following spring Governor Winthrop, John Wilson, late Fellow of King's College, Cambridge, the learned Williams, and Cotton, established themselves on the peninsula. The settlement was called, from the native town of Cotton and other chief men, Boston; soon to become "the metropolis of the wilderness, environed as it was with the brinish flouds, furnished with a beacon and lowd babbling guns, . . . the wonder of this modern age, whose continuall inlargement presages some sumptuous city." The fertile black earth about the town grew grass for the cattle, all manner of wheat, pumpkins, grapes, and strawberries, and "divers physicall herbs" for both men and turkeys; with other free gifts of nature, rocks and rivulets, "damaske roses verie sweete," lobelias, fire-flies and humming-birds, green coast-islands and gleaming lakelets, with sweet-scented water-lilies. Governor Winthrop's house stood a little north of the Old South Church, where, on the 6th of March, 1770, the townsmen were to meet, animated by Winthrop's spirit, to remonstrate with a Governor very unlike him for introducing troops into the city. His descendants of the fifth or sixth generation still flourish in Cambridge.

Before Boston Charlestown was founded, between "the pleasant river of Mistick" and the Charles; and speedily grew up "a fair market-place, near the water-side, built round with houses comely and fair, forth of which there issues two streetes orderly built, with some very fair houses, beautified with pleasant gardens and orchards." The suddenness of the creation seems to the old narrator wellnigh miraculous. High up the Charles, Sir Richard Saltonstall and the Rev. Mr. Philips dwelt, with store of cattle and servants, in Watertown amid a labyrinth of waters. Gradually farmers betook themselves to the richer lands in the interior of the county of Middlesex. By the side of the slumberous Concord sprang up, nineteen miles from Boston, a town of the same name as the river, embosomed in apple-trees, corn lands, meadows, and onion fields, on a site purchased from a female chieftain, at the liberal price of a hat and greatcoat for her husband. There, at the North Bridge, Gage's troops were beaten by the county militia, on the memorable 19th of April, 1775, and the first blood in the war was shed. The opening up of the river Connecticut, with its succession of rich valleys, rude bluffs, and shaggy mountains, and the example of the Rev. Thomas Hooker, attracted various controversialists, who "could not bear two suns in one firmament." They were encouraged by the countenance, though not much more, of the Marquis Hamilton, who owned a territory, sixty miles in length, between this stream and the Narraganset country, and of the Lords Say and Brooke, republicans at home, who desired to establish in America an hereditary magistracy and aristocracy. The Fort of Saybrook was built; and William Pyncheon, become by his book unpopular in Salem, commenced a town beneath the shadow of

Mount Tom. It took its name from Pyncheon's estate near Chelmsford, Springfield, Thomas Hooker's native place. To a modern New Englander, the mention of Springfield suggests not the Puritan divine, but bright green jalousies, neat precise porches to white wooden houses, and many flower-pots. Negligent of claims to the land put forth by the Prince of Orange, or, as the local historian prefers to render the title, "Ourania," the new settlement flourished. It was strong in the assistance of energetic men like Mr. Peter Prudden, pastor of Milford, though not the wearer of Hawthorne's "Black Veil," who could "provide comfortably for a numerous family, without indecent distractions from his study," and laymen like Mr. Theophilus Eaton, once well known in the Baltic Company, and a thriving merchant. Eaton, finding husbandry more suitable for his new locality than trading, "applied himself, though he had more than once, with good advantage, stood before kings, dexterously to the mean and low things of New England." He was perpetual Governor of Connecticut, till "too excellent a supper carried off his excellent princely face and port." Then Massachusetts, where the rulers had not left behind in their Lincolnshire and Essex homesteads and halls the capacity for jealousy of a neighbouring squire or county, managed to prove, perhaps by the aid of the Pyncheons, still citizens of Salem, that Springfield, the chief ornament of the new province, lay within its territory.

A master motive, the craving for a community representing each man's especial views, carried these stouthearted farmers far into New Hampshire. Very early, Portsmouth was settled within distant view of the mysterious floating peaks of the White Mountains, and the echo of strange stories of the wonderful gem set on one of their cliffs. The settlers ploughed almost in the shadow of the hills; but none but a few Irishmen cared to hunt after the treasure there hidden. The chronicler's summary of the result of their expedition is, simply, that they found "several rivers strong enough to turn a mill."

In each and every division of the province the dispersed

homesteads betrayed a propensity to expand into affluent villages, with paddocks and wall-fruit. The numerous lists, still on record, of " charges for magistrates and attendants at dinner at Quarter Court," recall the joviality of Elizabethan quarter-sessions. Though grave Winthrop somewhat damped the festivity, by discountenancing the English practice of drinking one to another, the essence of the good cheer was preserved. "This poor wilderness," writes a contemporary, "hath not only equalised England in food, but gone beyond it in some places for the great plenty of wine and sugar, apples, pippins, and russets, and jennetings, and quince tarts instead of pumpkin pies. Of poultry they have plenty, and great rarity; and, in their feasts, have not forgotten the English fashion of stirring up their appetites with variety of cooking their food."

Learning was not neglected. New England could even boast a Latin poet, Morell, who had come out with young Gorges as general Episcopal Commissioner, but, having nothing to do in this office, suppressed his patent, made verses, and translated them. He was more fortunate in his themes than the learned Stephen Parmenius of Buda, who accompanied Sir Humphrey Gilbert's expedition to Newfoundland, and found, as he writes, bemoaning himself, to Hakluyt, nothing to sing but cod, "piscium inexhausta copia!" Morell was at no loss for topics. He glorifies the land for the abundance of

> "The turtle, eagle, partridge, and the quaile,
> Knot, plover, pigeons, which doe never faile.
> With these sweete dainties man is sweetly fed;
> With these rich feathers ladies plume their head."

Soon the province could boast of a learned grammarian, Ezekiel Cheever, afterwards master of Cambridge Grammar School, of whom the erudite Cotton Mather has written the epitaph in his 'Magnalia,'—

> "He lived and wrought; his labours were immense,
> But ne'er declined to preterperfect sense."

By the advice of such men, and with the help of a legacy of

£700, bequeathed by John Harvard, of Southwark, increased by grants from the Legislature, as of a right of ferry and a couple of thousand acres of land, an university was established in Massachusetts. Newtown, a plantation of Deputy-Governor Dudley, in a plain a little above the bay, half a mile broad, formed by the Charles, with a common stretching to the north-west, was chosen for the locality. To it from English Cambridge, the university at which Dudley and others of the magistrates had been educated, "the Muses were invited to emigrate." It began under difficulties; for "that hidden Jesuit, Mr. Nathaniel Eaton, proved a mere Orbilius, thrashing his ushers," and welcoming his fair guests themselves from Parnassus, according to the assertion of his local censor, with a plentiful stock of cudgels. When, however, he had been ejected, its fame, under Dunster and Mitchell, soon rose high. A fine edifice, one hundred feet long, was erected in a few years, and the germ of a library collected, augmented by the munificence of Baxter, Sir Kenelm Digby, and Sir John Maynard. By the College statute, "none are to be admitted before they can make and speak true Latin in verse and prose, suo, ut aiunt, marte," though it was enough to be able to decline in Greek "the paradigms." The ordinary academical curriculum included Hebrew, Logic, Metaphysics, Natural Philosophy, and Astronomy. So the state of education must have been advanced indeed. English poetry does not seem to have been equally cultivated. In 1639, the first printing-press was set up in the university town, according to the precedent of Old England. The ambition of Mather of Dorchester, and Eliot, the preacher of Roxbury, at once set it to work on what was to have been an improved edition of Sternhold and Hopkins. But their "regard for conscience rather than rhythm" landed them in so dreary a rendering, that the following reproof might have been to their ears a model of melody:—

> "Ye Roxbury poets, keep clear of the crime
> Of missing to give us very good rhyme;
> And you of Dorchester, your verses lengthen,
> But with the text's own words you will them strengthen."

The pretty villas, bordering broad winding roads, with flower-gardens and old mossy fruit-trees, indicating by their size a former richness of soil which is said to have now evaporated, shelter perhaps hardly as weighty scholars, but far more tuneful ears. In a roomy house, overshadowed by a huge elm a couple of centuries old, and ornamented with gay terrace parterres and Georgian pilasters and verandahs, once sojourned Washington. It became the happy and hospitable home of Professor Longfellow.

The prosperity of Massachusetts was advancing surely and steadily, unchecked by tyrannical Boards of Trade or intriguing Governors, when a fearful calamity assaulted it from within. The extraordinary epidemic, the witchcraft scare, burst upon it. By the year 1692 almost all the worthies of the first generation, men endowed with the authority of patriarchs and of founders, had died. Such was Thomas Hooker of Hartford, "of whom," says modestly an old New England writer, "some may think too much said by his friend," who declared, in reviewing the glories of the rest of the earth, that America

> "Yet thinks she may into this catalogue come
> With Europe, Africk, Asia, for one tomb."

Such, too, were "that ancient gentleman, Governor Dudley,"

> "Helluo librorum, lectorum bibliotheca,"

solicitor, soldier, statesman, and scholar, who yet was content to indite for his epitaph, "I died no libertine;" Nathaniel Rogers, "son of the famous preacher of Dedham, the only Boanerges of his age;" and Governor Bradford of Plymouth, if a zealot, "for one of that persuasion very gentle;" Captain Standish, "allied to the noble house of Standish, and inheriting some of the virtues of that honourable family as well as the name;" and Cotton of Boston, "a glory to both Englands." Shortly after these the grave had received "the very ancient gentleman, Governor Bellingham, bred a lawyer, though his will did not show his skill, a great justiciary and noted hater of bribes, firm and fixed in any resolution, who, had he not been a little too much overpowered with the humour of melancholy, the infirmities of which tincture did now and then appear in his dispensing of justice, had been very well qualified for a governor."

A majority of these men, but not without resistance, had carried severe enactments against the Quakers. The pertinacity of that sect, as disorderly then as now order-loving, in the parade of their extravagances, had provoked to the utmost men who had left behind them prosperous homes and schemes of honourable ambition, to seek in a savage wilderness, as to them it seemed, not merely a refuge from active persecution, but the right to worship in a community fashioned and regulated entirely after their own hearts. Endicott especially had sympathised with this feeling. By his efforts, mainly, harsh edicts had been promulgated against the sect. He had countenanced the sale of the seniors of a Quaker family in 1659, and the whipping of others through all the towns of a district. But many eminent ministers had protested against Endicott's cruelties to the Quakers. It is at least to be hoped that they would have been still less tolerant of the vulgar panic against witchcraft, and that they would have had on their side on this occasion in combating the delusion the stern common sense of "strong valiant John," as his epitaph entitles him. The Endicotts, Winthrops, and Wilsons could scarcely have had sympathy with the metaphysics of the wise Salem justices, who on the Cartesian doctrine of "effluvia," condemned men and women on account of the cure, by their touch, it was alleged, of their supposed victims. Their argument was that "by the touch the venomous and malignant particles ejected from the eye, do, by this means, return to the body from whence they came." The madness was not confined to a town or class. The whole land was implicated. Members of the Court which sat in Salem for the trials were from Boston. In Boston were cherished traditions of "the strange form like a man, over against Castle Island, that would sometimes cast out flames and sparkles of fire, with a dreadful voice, heard between it and Dorchester, crying over the waters, 'Come away, come away!' Immediately afterwards "Captain Chaddock and his crew of necromancers were blown up by the kindling of some gunpowder." There too, so long before as 1656, against the voice of Governor Bradstreet, Dunforth, Increase Mather, Saltonstall, and others, but by a sentence of the General Court, had Dame Hibbins, widow of a man who had served on commissions with the Dudleys, and Bellinghams, and Pierpoints, been put to death on a similar charge. "Vox populi, some people thought, was the chief part of the evidence against her." Margaret Jones, of the neighbouring Charlestown, was executed on a like accusation, the possession of a malignant touch which brought on deafness and vomiting. This murder had been followed by the arrest of her husband for causing the rolling of a Barbadoes ship lying in the harbour, in which he had been refused a passage. The conclusive proof was, that on the production by the officer of his warrant the agitation of the vessel had subsided.

Salem, however, had a miserable preeminence in this shameful episode of New England history. Yet, in 1685, though there might be a sort of ground-swell of indignation and fear, arising from the arbitrary policy of James II. and his Governor Andros, Salem seemed to John Dunton, he tells us in his amusing 'Life and Errors,' one of the most agreeable and well-to-do towns in New England. Fine houses abounded. They were tenanted by magistrates, such as Sewel, "than whom neither Abraham nor Lot were ever more kind to strangers;" by generous merchants, rich enough to woo and wed English beauties, who, reversing the later fashion, had, as Mrs. Hickes, "come over with the valuable venture of a beautiful person;" by eminent scholars, "with much of the gentleman," but the eccentricities of German professors; and by eloquent preachers, as Higginson, "for whose sake all men," Dunton says prettily, "looked on old age as a reverend thing," and Noyes, famous for his Election sermons, a man "of delightful conversation," soon to have the weight of nineteen death-warrants on his heart. Suddenly, in 1692, from a predisposition it is true of the whole community, but, directly, from the murderous mischievousness, as in Scotland at an earlier period, of a few children, who subsequently confessed the conspiracy, the storm burst. The whole country seemed, we are told, "to behold the sudden descent of wicked spirits from their high places." The weak-spirited who pleaded guilty were reprieved. The brave ones, "who could not, who durst not belie their own souls," were sent to the stake and the scaffold. "For a time," writes another contemporary, "no life was safe; the scene was like a torrent, sudden, irresistible, and momentary." Few of the victims belonged to the town. They were generally from Salem village, now called Danvers, or dwellers in cottages among the pine groves, or on the melancholy seashore, and by the solitary pools of the outskirts. It was the neighbourhood in which good Mr. Norris had encouraged spinning, to employ the evening leisure, and divert the fancy from gloomy tales and alarms. The whole people became a mob, in which individual sagacity counted for nothing. The assessors of the Salem judge did not resist. Saltonstall left the Board, but did not veto the proceedings; and Ex-Governor Simon Bradstreet, the son-in-law of Ex-Governor Dudley, acted the same cautious part. Increase Mather and Willard of Boston disbelieved the charges and succoured the fugitives; they had not the hardihood, or perhaps the entire conviction of the falsity of the accusations, to stand up boldly in Salem against the majority of justices, or, out of it, against men of the authority of Increase Mather's son, Cotton Mather. Of him it had prophetically been said a few years before, " He has read much, but there are many that won't allow him the prudence to make a seasonable use of it."

Thus the second generation of New England opened in sadness and gloom. But the land had already shown signs of revival, before even 1697, when died the last Old Charter Governor, and the last Governor who had made Salem his residence. This was old Simon Bradstreet, "vir judicio lynceario præditus," who yet did not see his way openly to resist a delusion originating with a couple of wretched children, and supported by the fright of weak women. The recovery was complete by the time of the death, in 1709, of John Massey, the first "town-born child;" or, as he styles himself, in 1694, in a petition for the grant of a ferry, "the ancientest planter, and the oldest man now living in Salem that was born here." Trade increased every day. It had sufficient influence, even in 1670, to have lands made liable to debts by leave of the Court. In lazy, luxurious, agricultural Virginia, down to the Revolution, real property was exempt, and entails were stricter than in England. "Stately ships," too, "with great ornament of carving and painting, and much strength of ordnance," were built by native shipwrights, and freighted for Old Spain and the Isle of Sables. They might be cast away, and with them scores of sailors, "who went to provide for old age, but now wanted nothing but a grave, being buried in the rude waters." Others undaunted forthwith sailed out from the docks of Cambridge and Boston. Many wealthy freebooters spent their wealth there. A good example is that magnanimous Captain Cromwell, whom his fellow-townsmen likened to Cæsar for his refusal to desert "the thatched cottage of the poor man who had entertained him in his mean estate" for the mansions of the rich to which he was invited in his prosperous days. Everywhere in New England a spirit of mercantile adventure sprang up, especially at Boston. Boston ships, first of any belonging to American merchants, sailed round the world. At Boston the proposal for the establishment anywhere of a depot, or a colony, found readiest acceptance. Salem was not far behind, if at all, in commerce, hospitality, and public spirit. The merchants of Salem were known in every port of Europe. "Some of them," writes Sir Charles Lyell, "sailed to India by the Cape without a single chart or map, except that small one of the world on Mercator's projection, contained in Guthrie's Geography. They used no sextants, but working their dead reckoning with chalk on a plank, guessed at the sun's position with their hand at noon. They had usually no capital, but started with a few beads and trinkets, and, in exchange for these trifles, often obtained the skins of sea otters in the Oregon territory, each worth no less than one hundred dollars. They also collected sandal wood in the Sandwich Islands, and bartered these and other articles in China for tea. On such slender means many merchants of Salem laid the foundations of the princely fortunes they now enjoy." Such was Peter Hooper of rocky Marblehead, who bought all the fish caught on the coast, after its hardy race had left off working the mines and betaken themselves to the cod-fisheries, and sent it to Bilbao and other ports of Spain. Thence he brought back store of golden ingots, with which he purchased for the American market English cloth and hardware. "He rode," says a Salem author, "in a chariot like a prince," and was known as King Hooper. Of the same character was his contemporary, King Derby, whose wharf was 600 feet long. He, in 1799, built the most sumptuous house in the whole county of Essex.

In wealth and mercantile enterprise Salem was nearly Boston's equal; in the tone of society and politics it was much more Conservative. With all its riches, it did not possess, to the end of the eighteenth century, a single four-wheeled private carriage. Royalist principles, all but obsolete elsewhere, were sheltered in the bosom of many of its old families. They were professed by Colonel Saltonstall, one of the historical grandees of the place, who kept up old English hospitality in his seat at Haverhill; rich John Vassall, an exile with him at the time of the Revolution, who would not after that event, continue to bear his family arms, "sæpe pro rege, semper pro republicâ;" Judge Curwen or Curwin; and William Pyncheon, the last of whom left, for years un-mended, as a reproach to mobocracy, the windows in his old house in Summer Street, after they had been broken for his refusal to recant the unpopular address to Governor Hutchinson. The extreme measure taken by the General Court of the Province, held, at Salem, by General Gage in 1774, of electing delegates to the Continental Congress, fixed their Royalism. Before this, they had been by no means the most docile of subjects. When compromised, and pensioners of the British Government, they used, as freely as Sam Slick, to express their disgust at having the Province spoken of in England as, "our colonies, or our plantations, with such an air as though," writes Judge Curwin from London, "our property and persons were absolutely theirs, like the villains." Most of them had left the country soon after the successful stand of Colonel Pickering, himself of an honoured Salem name, on the bridge which provided Hawthorne with the scene of a pretty prose idyl. But the town could not bear to part with them for ever. Curwin relates how, on his return from exile in England, "not a man, woman, or child, but expressed a satisfaction at seeing me, and welcomed me back." In fact, Royalism and Republicanism were, in Salem, always tending to overlap. They were but the two sides of the shield, and Essex federalists and monarchists would have been, in the mouth of a Virginian democrat, interchangeable terms. The stately Curwins and Pyncheons clung to their allegiance to George III., on the same principle as that to which Clarendon imputes the attachment of Lord Newcastle to Charles I.; they felt their own social precedence to be connected with a shadow of royal suzerainty.

In these long tedious streets, with their neat, dull, two-storied wooden houses, agreeable variety is created for the eye by green and golden lichens. Within, there was and is abundance of hospitality: The great merchants, even after they had their wharfs at Boston, went on living at Salem. There they kept, and probably keep old-fashioned good cheer without the splendour of the society of the capital. They are commended for exhibiting universal sympathy with their fellow-townsmen, "the few who are poor being too strongly allied to the rich by kindred to be separated from them." Before the war of North and South it could boast that, almost alone of anti-slavery cities, it taught in the same schools black and white children. There is no better town type of New England than it, with its succession of villages, each with its church, and a school library, containing often even formerly Plutarch's Lives, with the addition now of volumes by Prescott, Irving, and Herschel. Each is "not a mere cluster of brick, or rude stone cottages," writes President Dwight enthusiastically, "but is composed of neat houses in their several house-lot meadows, adorned with gardens, meadows, and orchards, and exhibiting the universally easy circumstances of the inhabitants." The whole makes "one of the most delightful prospects which the world can afford."

But though Salem has most closely adhered to the ideal of its founders, and has maintained a sort of religious metropolitanism in New England, political preeminence quickly passed away, both from it and the "Old Colony," to Boston. Boston was the acknowledged representative of the whole land, on all occasions when its independence was menaced by English statesmen and prelates, or insolent admirals. Its resistance was generally successful. The attempt of Commodore Knowles to press some ship carpenters in the port excited a terrible riot. Archbishop Secker's scheme, suggested by the philosophical and liberal Bishop Butler, for giving a legal establishment to Episcopacy, was triumphantly opposed. The motives of the leaders of an opposition were, it is true, not always as pure as their apparent objects. The richer Bostonians "had the reputation," we are told by Dunton, "of being lavish in promises, but not in payment," whilst "the most uncommon practice with them was the custom of telling the truth." Such is alleged to have been the character of Governor Hutchinson, who was a native. Such, too, was in part that of John Hancock. The latter was the son and grandson of reputable but by no means rich country clergymen. His uncle, a Royalist, had gained great wealth by smuggling tea from St. Eustatia in molasses casks, the popular rumour being that he had bought for a trifle an immense diamond. He left his radical nephew £50,000 in hand, with the interest of £20,000 more, beside houses and ships, with troops of workmen attached to them, "from whose aid his heir acquired great influence." John

Hancock was suave, and supplied the want of genius by a popular demeanour. He loved place and applause so inordinately as to lavish his wealth upon those objects, till, we learn from President Quincy, who had suffered through him, he ended by becoming, as Treasurer of Harvard College, a great defaulter. The seizure, the first made by the new Commissioners of Customs, of a vessel laden with wine belonging to him, covered a multitude of faults. It saved from ridicule the prodigious vanity itself, which made him grasp, not contented with the Presidency of Congress and Governorship of Massachussets, at the command of the federal armies against England.

With Hancock's name we find often joined that of Samuel Adams, a considerable lawyer, and a skilful political intriguer. Boston had men of a far higher order, men like William Pepperell, merchant and landowner, who, an amateur soldier, in the scarlet cloth and gold lace of a courtier, captured Louisburg to the astonishment of Europe. But generally the more prominent pioneers of the Revolution in Boston were unscrupulous partisans. They could plead they had to do with officials yet more unscrupulous, men whom all honest men at home reprobated, as ex-Governor Bernard. General Oglethorpe, famed alike for benevolence, for Dr. Johnson's friendship, and for having shot snipes in what is now Regent Street, ejected him ignominiously from the Smyrna coffee-house, declaring, say the contemporary journals, that "he smelt strongly of the hangman." Though it is not a satisfactory apology for dishonesty that the offender's adversaries are worse, it is a very common excuse, and, in some measure, a reason. The system of corruption, fraud, and violence employed by British Secretaries of State, by the Hillsboroughs, Sandwiches, and Sackvilles, and by Boards of Trade, and their delegates, the Bernards, Hutchinsons, Olivers, and Randolphs, with the whole plentiful crop of Surveyors, Collectors, and Attorneys General, had corrupted Colonial morality almost as completely as the policy of Clifford and Danby marred the delicacy of that of Sidney in Charles II.'s reign. The new England patriots kept agents in the mother-country, to bribe, promise, or threaten on occasion, and themselves were not averse from any sharp practice on the side of freedom.

The Revolution blew aside the vapours, and brought into sight a nobler set of men, whose ambition, if as engrossing as that of their political predecessors, was of a kind to identify them with their country, not to narrow their country to themselves. They remained to the full as Conservative; for so, in the essence, was New England. The elder race of statesmen had not conceived themselves bound to follow republican ways while giving republican pledges, any more than Charles James Fox felt an obligation to pay his tradesmen, because he was canvassing the shopkeepers of Westminster. John Hancock and the others had the gout, and arrayed themselves in lace and embroidery, like their prototypes at home. Their successors were contented with simpler fashions. Ex-President Adams dined at one, went to church twice on Sunday, and prided himself on being, like Cincinnatus, a practical farmer. But the difference, after all, was not very material. Gold lace was by that time gone out of fashion, and his practical farming was on an old ancestral estate in the midst of a population which venerated him. "In Massachusetts," writes Jefferson to him, "there exists a traditionary reverence for certain families, rendering public offices nearly hereditary. This is from the merit of those families, and from the strict alliance of Church and State." Younger representatives of the governing houses required as implicit obedience from their followers as the elder, and were not slow to "gnash their teeth and curse the people," as we are told was a habit of the statesman of Quincy, when the least resistance was offered to their policy. Honorary titles they claimed with punctiliousness, and the country readily rendered them. The Governor of New England has always been most rigidly His Excellency, and every representative "the Honourable." There was a time when many repented of having lost King George, and would have readily made a King George of their own out of the most unselfish of soldiers. Perhaps Hancock fancied a King John might more suitably have opened a new dynasty. Boston society, as reflected in local literature, continues to believe in definite class distinctions. The town has its recognised division into first, second, and third families, with reference to wealth; and, above all, "the old families." Sir Charles Lyell tells us in his Transatlantic journal, half a century ago, that he considered himself a Liberal in England, but he found himself regarded as a Radical in Boston, and our Reform Bill of 1832 denounced as a perilous innovation.

The Conservatism of New England was, and is, of a peculiar kind. It was powerful, even tyrannical, when local prejudices or national institutions were attacked. It was powerless as an active principle, when the relations between its country and another were called in question. Two things impress the mind after an investigation of provincial New England history. One is that the Cabinets of George III. were abundantly short-sighted, that they either could not understand the Colonial character, or were insolently defiant of the warnings of knowledge. The other is that our own generation could not, however anxiously conciliatory, have long maintained the Imperial unity. We see the men of Boston, and Salem, and Plymouth, from first to last, chafing and fretting at the notion that a land they had bought and won for themselves, could be in any degree directed by strangers. A Navigation Act was as much an abomination to them as a Stamp Act; but they were not powerful enough to secede in the seventeenth century. Englishmen of the age of George III. knew little of New England and its people, and paid as the price of their ignorance the costs of a tremendous war. In another way modern Englishmen are as ignorant. We will not remember that, until the war of the American Revolution, New England's history is a page of our own. We insist on regarding New England as a manufactured article of the reign of Charles I. Allusions by native authors to the presence of old families, old houses, and old prejudices in settlements planted two centuries and a half ago, are treated as efforts of fancy. We do not consider that the oldest tree, if transplanted with its roots and soil about it, will bear to its new home its pride of branches, and much of the dignity, as well as some of the defects, of age.

VIRGINIA.

NEW ENGLAND and Virginia both show characteristics of age. But age in New England is displayed in the tone of thought, and has to be searched for. It is spread over the whole surface of Virginian history, and, until the War of Secession, was deeply imprinted on every institution. Countries differ like wines, some become ripe and mellow, or vapid, as it may be, with years, while others, their contemporaries, are still effervescing with youth. In the midst of the prevailing newness of the United States little ever was new about Virginia, the original Virginia. In its three centuries of existence the Old Dominion has lived through as varied a series of national fortunes, and as many social and political experiences, as any ancient realm in our hemisphere. Long and doubtful was its struggle into life. Storms seemed to blow which have never raged since, and new forms of disease were discovered, as though to balance, in proper tragic antithesis, the Eden-like beauties which revealed themselves to the admiring eyes of North Devon mariners. The contrast is a strange one between the luxuriant beauty of these southern regions of the New World, as they presented themselves to the eyes of the first discoverers, and the aspect they showed to the same men become regular residents, and no longer amiable and casual guests. The sunny air was then a parching Arabian atmosphere; the zephyrs, sharp withering breezes; cool, shadowy woods, gloomy jungles; and bright flowers, the poor apologies for west country grain and orchards.

Only after several calamitous expeditions, connected with the name of the knight-errant who hovers strangely between the Sir Lancelots and the Marlboroughs, between romance and prose, the gallant who spoiled a cloak, and the somewhat jesuitical plotter with atheists and seminary priests, at length a little village slowly emerged on the banks of the broad James. Fresh bands of eager adventurers flocked in. In vain they met their predecessors in full retreat, despairing and disgusted, their harvests grubbed up, and their huts in ruins. As they floated up the glorious Virginian estuaries, they forgot all evil omens. "Their senses were ravished," writes one of themselves, "with the beauty of the prospect, the fragrancy of fields and gardens, the brightness of the sky, and serenity of the air," till they exclaimed that no two European kingdoms could approach the rich abundance and luxuriance of this. The flaunting crown imperial, the cardinal flower, the mocassin flower, and the tulip tree, were on every side; not in gardens, but in the woods, running wild. Malochotons, cherries, and peaches were there, too many for any but the hogs to eat; and, in short, "scarce a flower or a fruit exists which does not flourish better in Virginia than even its own native soil." Gradually, even wealth poured in. The scent of tobacco began to captivate European senses. The Grand Turk and the Tartars of Samarcand appreciated the discovery. The Virginian Company condescended, though reluctantly, to "this degradation of the Virginian glebe," relinquishing grand visions of rivalry with Potosi, Italian silkworms, and French vineyards. James I. gave up devoting his leisure to "Blasts, and Counterblasts," abandoned his paternal fears lest "one hundred thousand English rustics should smoke at the plough," and betook himself to the more serious task of devising how to turn the new taste into the most profitable vehicle of taxation.

Before the Revolution, the social condition of the tidewater region of Virginia was well known to the merchants of Liverpool and Bristol, who were often the guests of the planters

on the shores of those great highways, the James and the
Potomac. They knew it better than the present generation. Modern highways and railways pass far on one side
of this once famous territory. Guide-books neglect it; and
Americans themselves seem scarcely to understand the nature
of this division of Virginia, or its inhabitants. While the whole
land has lost its primacy in the Union, this district has in
its own State lost its relative rank. Formerly it was everything; and its history was the history of Virginia. It included the shores of the great rivers, with a depth of many
miles into the interior. It was fringed with spacious
mansions, up to the very doors of which frigates could sail, and
laden merchantmen, with the fashions of London to exchange
for the renowned sweet Virginian tobacco. The sea-breezes
showed favouritism to it; they were then never felt above
Williamsburg; now they are welcomed, at close of midday,
in the hot woods on the slopes of the mountains. Out
of the whole number of members returned to the first
Congress by the State, a large majority came thence; now it
sends an inconsiderable minority. Thence sprang all the
leading men, foremost in the Union as in Virginia, of the
epoch of the Revolution, and there they lived. Patrick
Henry, the Radical and democrat, dwelt just on its verge.
Now all that is changed. The life and vigour of the land,
as seen in politics, have oozed away from the tidal territory.
Tobacco, the staple of Virginian trade and wealth, requires
across the Atlantic a virgin soil, though the peasant proprietor
of the Bergstrasse cannot apparently afford to hold any such
doctrine. So the Virginian capitalist was ever removing
farther and farther into the interior. His exhausted plantation he left to become a wilderness of cedars, oaks, wild vines,
tulip and judas trees, strawberries, azaleas, and roses, pastur-
age for hosts of butterflies and humming-birds. The West
received the owner, or the region beyond the barrier of the
Blue Mountains. New counties were, even in settled times,
ever in process of formation in the West. Thus, Albemarle
had originally been a portion of Gooch County, and Gooch

County, the native district of Jefferson, was itself a fragment of another.

Though the land is generally poor, the course of the great rivers and their tributaries is marked by a fertile strip of country, sown usually with maize, cotton, and palma Christi. This is bounded, at a mile's distance, by the interminable forests of black pitch-pine. Such is more peculiarly the character of the James. Forty-three miles from its source it is fourteen miles broad, a sort of inland sea. The edging of dark fir and cedar of various sombre tints on its shores appears to grow straight out of the water; so low is the surrounding level. After a time the banks begin to display soil of a good quality, covered thickly with the mulberry, walnut, and sycamore. Every now and then a great house comes into view, heralded, as in France, or in Italy, by solemn columns of Lombardy poplars. The Potomac flows through more picturesque scenery. Its magnificent falls are bordered by huge black cliffs, a combination of Alpine grandeur with tropical vegetation. The great bluffs and long wooded ridges throw massive shadows over the broad silent river on towards the rich shores of Maryland. It does not, however, water a larger breadth of fertile land on the whole. All through those flat alluvial regions stretches the broad belt of Pine Barrens, running parallel to the coast through the Atlantic Plain, overspread with gigantic long-tufted firs. They give way to swamps clothed with evergreen oak and cypress, with wild vines clinging round the trunks, and their branches hung with the white berries of the mistletoe. The largest, which has the name of the Great Dismal, is forty miles long and fifteen broad. It is described as looking like an inundated river plain, the water vibrating with a sort of mysterious current, and the whole fen being higher than the dry land round. Trunks of fallen trees lie beneath a dense deposit of peat in the interior, and a carpet of moss spreads over the surface. Washington set on foot the construction of a series of canals through the midst. Now and then a boat emerges from under the overarching aisles into the central lake, called Drummond's Pool. The occasional snarl of a wolf, and the crash of boughs dragged down by a bear in quest of acorns interrupt the sighing of the cedars.

The barrenness of the chief part of the district, and the narrow limits within which all industry was confined, cherished, as in a hothouse, the prosperity of the tide-water plantations. They were kept to the bounds within which trade could most readily find them. So early as the days of Governor Berkeley, and partly in consequence of the sympathy between the settlers and that fiery old cavalier, this region had become important. In 1649 we learn from a description of the settlement given by a gentleman in a letter to a friend in England, that it had so increased as then to contain 15,000 English, including the King's occasional presents to the Company of a hundred or two of "dissolute persons," and 300 negroes. There were 2,000 head of cattle, and innumerable swine ranged the woods. Thirty ships, with a complement in all of a thousand sailors, sailed up the estuaries in autumn, returning with their freight of tobacco in March. The land was full of valuable timber, often sixty feet high and three square, with no underwood, so that the cumbrous coaches-and-six of the period could make their way through the forest. Already the orchards, in parts, had begun to bear as richly as in Herefordshire, and cider was added to the excellent metheglin, the final result of the wild flowers which the bees, we are assured, found, notwithstanding their flaunting pretentiousness, "most excellent food." So late as the close of the seventeenth century, when the population had now grown to 70,000, pork "the best in the world," and capons might be had almost for the asking, and deer sold at eight shillings the head. It was reckoned that the tobacco trade was at this period carried on in fifty ships in the year from Liverpool alone, and in the same, or a yet larger number from Bristol, which paid on their cargoes £60,000 to the revenue annually. At least a hundred sailed from the Thames.

In such a land capital soon made its weight felt. The richest portions of the country on the banks of each of the four great rivers were parcelled out among a score or two of planters dwelling in ample homesteads, not much farther apart than in a rural district of the mother-country. There they kept open house, "every one's contempt falling upon the sordid wretch who should offend against that laudable custom of the country," says Oldmixon, in his 'New State of Virginia.' "In England," he continues, "a hospitable man is reckoned a sot or a bubble, and hearty feasts are thought disreputable. Not so among the prudent, careful, generous, hospitable people of Virginia." Of this class, so early as 1649, was "that worthy Captain Matthews, one of the Council, and a most deserving Commonwealth's man, who hath a fine house, and keeps weavers and a tan-house, with eight shoemakers and forty negro servants, whom he brings up to trade. His wheat he selleth at four shillings the bushel, kills store of beeves, and sells them to victual the ships, hath abundance of kine, and a brave dairy." "With his wife, the daughter of Sir Thomas Hamilton, he keeps a good house, lives bravely, is a true lover of Virginia, and is worthy of much honour." Such were the hearty merchant-farmers of Virginia of the first generation, in whom some of the refinement of courtiers was conjoined with the adventurous temper of West of England mariners. In his own ships and from his own wharves the rich landowner loaded for Bristol the tobacco crop grown on his own lands. In the meantime he entertained nobly at his house the merchant or supercargo the whole winter through, gathering up tales of popular resistance to prerogative at home.

He was as keen a champion of popular rights as any feudal baron struggling for Magna Charta, or a Puritan Eastern counties squire fretting under the sway of a cavalier peer. It is impossible to take in at a glance both sides of his character. The planters, more particularly those of the second generation, spent on pleasure and luxury the profits, and often something more, of a hundred commercial voyages.

To one set of men they held the relation of liberal democratic traders, to another that of despots and task-masters. The spectacle of a Leicestershire fox-hunter, driving a troop not only of negroes, but of whites, now convicts from the hulks, now cavaliers, Commonwealth men, or Jacobites, whichever cause was undermost in England, would not be pleasing. Its Virginian counterpart was inharmonious. But these careless Transatlantic squires, who loved no sport in which the dangers of a fox-chase were not exaggerated, hunting wild horses in the interval of a drinking-bout, and dashing about over roads at least as bad as English highways in the reigns of the Stuarts, managed to keep the two characters apart. With the very easiest of consciences, they transferred all of the slave-owner's attributes, except his profits, to their bailiffs, clerks, and stewards. Themselves, far from brandishing the whip, were busy in their parlours with thriced-voyaged madeira, or strong Cheshire ale, or in the Parliament-house and many coffee-houses of Williamsburg they were declaiming on the equality of man, and the limits of prerogative.

Centralisation was their great bugbear, both before the Revolution and after. The establishment of fixed depots of trade was a pet object of jealousy. In vain did Charles II. command Governor Berkeley to have a law passed in the Colonial Legislature to oblige all ships to unlade at Jamestown, and for the erection of forts, as well for that purpose as to guard against breaches of the Act of Navigation. Both merchants and planters were obstinately opposed to any policy of the sort. The former held that it was not for their interest that great marts should arise. At them the growers might learn the urgency of the demand for the tobacco crop. They would no longer be, as under the actual system, entirely dependent on the offer of a single ship-owner, who had obtained a monopoly, in many cases by lending large sums on the security of the harvest for years to come. They were reluctant also to resign their agreeable sojourn of three or four months amid the luxuries of a planter's mansion. The planters, for their part, were, on their land, as absolutely independent as an old Norman lord of a manor. Each estate had its appropriate name, not being called, as in the north, such and such a lot in such a township. They went up to the seat of government to spend the season together, to dine merrily at taverns, and to feast or be feasted by a popular nobleman and his wife. But they were as unwilling to resign their rank of squires for that of regular residents in a small country town, as would be Highland lairds or English county families. They hated the appearance of centralisation: and nothing in appearance less like centralisation could have existed than the Virginian system. The Governor or his deputy lived in a palace, had his guards, titles, and a salary liberal enough to tempt English peers. He could veto acts of the Assembly, and appoint colonels of militia, and lords-lieutenant of counties. He was lord-general, and high admiral, chancellor, chief justice, and his own prime minister. Yet no government could be less of an absolutism in its practical working. The whole body of planters felt a national pride in the name of Virginians, and their grief was moderate whenever the tobacco trade of rival Maryland, or the commerce of New York or New England was supposed to be in peril. So far, however, as they cared practically for aught beyond the verge of their estates, their cares were bounded by their several counties.

County government was modelled in a way to gratify their dislike of the appearance of dependence. The county courts of Virginia retained down to the War of Secession a constitution which appears exceedingly anomalous, till we have gained a clear insight into the character of Virginian democracy. "The number of magistrates composing them," we learn from Professor Tucker, a Virginian writer on political economy and government, " is kept up from persons nominated by the courts themselves. It is true that the executive of the State has the power of rejecting the nominations of the county courts; but, as the public necessity for the magistrates may be very pressing, and as the motives to reject can seldom be so strong as to induce the executive power to put itself into collision with the court, the recommendation is virtually an appointment. There has not been a rejection perhaps in one case in a thousand. The consequence is, that the power is substantially possessed by the courts, and is concentrated in a few families, who naturally endeavour to strengthen and perpetuate their influence and authority. They have criminal jurisdiction in all cases of misdemeanour, the power of acquittal in all cases of felony, the power of nominating, which is equivalent to that of appointing, all militia officers below the rank of brigadiers, and of making all the lucrative county appointments, as well as of filling up the vacancies in their own body; the high sheriff is taken from the body every two years, and then returns to it; they have the power of levying poll taxes for county purposes; they establish or put down all the roads and bridges. There is no individual in the county who may not be made to feel their power or ill will." Nevertheless, "the great mass of State politicians regard these oligarchical courts as the anchor of safety to the State, which has hitherto kept her to her moorings, in spite of the shifting currents of opinion, and would keep her against the driving tempest of popular fury."

Not by standing forward boldly as the people's representatives did the great Virginian houses attain their influence. It was their own by right of property. In many cases they were most unpopular with the yeomanry, "philippizing," says Jefferson, somewhat in a partisan spirit, "in every collision between king and people, with a view to a seat in the Council," so that after the Revolution made the old social precedence a reproach, "a Randolph, a Carter, or a Burwell must have great personal superiority over a common competitor to be elected even at this day." Few Virginian planters had made their own fortunes. Fortune-making was not a quality which flourished on Virginian soil. It was enough if they kept that which family interest at home had procured for them by lavish royal grants. Oldmixon, a notorious perverter of facts, writes that there was "no need of a Heralds' Office at Jamestown, the honest merchant and industrious planter being the men of honour in Virginia." He confesses, that when the condition of the settlement began to improve, "many men of small fortunes but good families came out." There was country gentlemen's blood in their veins, and the instinct in their hearts that the serious business of life for their class was sport. They defied royal governors and orders of Boards of Trade with the zeal of Radicals when their pockets were attacked; they were steady Conservatives when social relations were the subject of controversy. Both Oldmixon and De Foe confound Maryland and Virginia. The latter even declares, in 'Colonel Jack,' that "Maryland is Virginia, speaking of them from a distance." In Maryland classes mingled; in Virginia, those who began life as yeomen left to their descendants a similar status; and the same was the rule with the great planters.

In right of their apparent possessions and landed interest, on the faith of the legend of their ancestral wealth, they maintained their predominance. The great families of the country received but few accessions to compete with and outshine them. Their estates groaned under all the excrescences of an old landed system, which they had imported with them from England to a new world. They were burdened with many mortgages, liens, settlements on younger children, and elegits. Usually the soil was so fast tied up that its transfer to other hands did not emancipate it. The possessors might be treated with the greatest insolence by the merchants, their guests and creditors. As between themselves and their countrymen, they maintained their superiority as fully as an insolvent Irish landowner besieged in his dilapidated castle, before the establishment of the Encumbered Estates Court, with its compulsory liquidations. They bore their dignity by no means meekly. In later days, northerners were, according to Sir Charles Lyell, forced to confess that, though the majority, "they were held in political thraldom by the southern planters." The causes were the greater leisure planters could devote to questions of politics than the small farmers and merchants of New York and New England, their superior power of "banding together as one man in defence of what they called their property and institutions, their general eloquence and political tact, and the high bearing, which often imposed on northern men, much superior to them in real talent, knowledge, and strength of character."

They could not be expected to be less domineering towards the lower orders of their fellow Virginians. At home they saw none but courteous or complaisant neighbours of their own rank, obsequious overseers, or silent bondsmen of whom a planter occasionally held a levee, seated on high, as De Foe describes it, in a large hall, "like a lord judge on the bench, or a petty king on his throne." The interests of the first were the same with their own, and they met only to indulge in an outcry against the Government, or to dance away the long summer evenings. The last they suffered to be ruled with a rod of iron; for these jovial olive-hued squires would, without scruple, commit the extreme power of torture into the hands of men proverbially cruel. They did not concern themselves with the fate of the last purchase from the convict-ship. It might sometimes be an abandoned fellow, sent to contaminate the tobacco-fields; sometimes a chivalrous gentleman from Preston, transported for defence of the cause which planters loved to toast on their knees. Sometimes it might be a kidnapped child, or honest peasant. They recked not. To neighbours not of the same degree with their own they behaved with extreme haughtiness. The "half-breeds," as, we are assured by Mr. Wirt, the biographer of Patrick Henry, the younger scions of great families were nicknamed, were just admitted within the circle, not as members, but appendages. The integral constituents of the order formed a true oligarchy, defined, that is, by wealth as well as birth. The few who had raised themselves from a dependent condition, could not hope to be admitted till, by the third generation, they had purged away the stain of mechanical industry. The substantial independent yeomanry, "looking askance at, but not jostling their betters," were treated by their chiefs as only made to pay taxes.

Public expenditure in general was defrayed by a capitation tax. The heavy expense of making the roads was borne equally by all males over sixteen. The landowners absorbed a considerable portion of the income when collected. By limiting the suffrage to freeholders, they insured, for the most part, the return of their nominees. There was as fine a show of the recognition of popular privileges at an election of a burgess as in an old English rotten borough. Much band-playing and drinking went on at the expense of the candidates; but the poorer freeholders were commonly as deeply in debt to the richer, who were in the habit of supplying them with imported goods, as were these to the merchants. Hence the free choice was a farce. The leading landowners selected representatives. They paid them out of the contributions of the masses an exorbitant remuneration for defending their own monopoly against the prerogative of the Crown as represented by the Governor. During the reign of Charles I., when the aristocracy was entirely absolute, the salary was, for each day of attendance, 150 lbs. of tobacco, the common currency of the tide-water region, and 100 lbs. more for the maintenance of a horse and servant. Altogether it averaged about twenty-five dollars daily. One of the chief complaints of young Colonel Bacon, in an insurrectionary manifesto he published, concerned these extravagantly high salaries. His opponents retorted, no doubt with much truth, he being one of themselves by birth and fortune, that his sole object was to obtain a monopoly of the Indian trade. Governor Berkeley, who, we are told, ruled as "a Governor with a landed interest," made common cause with the aristocrats; but the Royal Commissioners sent out to examine into the origin of the rebellion reported so strongly against the amount of the payment to members that it was reduced. It still, however, continued so high as to be a perpetual source of murmurs among the farmers, and a good electioneering cry for the Crown. Thus, James II., on the rejection of a recommendation from the Privy Council by the Assembly, took care to insinuate that the contumacy of that body arose partly from a wish to prolong the session for the sake of the pay. He commanded that his popular charge should be read in all the churches. In the same way they monopolised the honours of the Council. They accepted them, not as a pledge of submission to Government, but as an acknowledgment of their rank and power. Very few of them were, their adversaries allow, Tories, that is, supporters of prerogative. But the Council was the avenue to various lucrative posts, such as the Auditorship, endowed with an income of $7\frac{1}{2}$ per cent. of public money; the Treasurership, with 6 per cent. of all passing through that office; the Presidency of the Council, and place of Attorney-General. We find, accordingly, Dudley Digges, Randolph, Byrd, and other aristocratic names perpetually on the Council roll.

Not content to pay for their thousands of acres no larger a share of the charges for the support of administration than fell on the farm of fifty, while they had themselves the lion's share in the expenditure, they were not ashamed to pillage the public secretly. The Speaker of the Assembly, who was also, by virtue of his office, Colonial Treasurer for the twenty-five years preceding 1765, was Robinson, the acknowledged head of the landed aristocracy, with a keen love of pomp and titles, but popular and courteous to his equals. It was he who addressed the celebrated compliment to Washington, when utterly confounded, and incapable of uttering a single word in reply to the vote of thanks by the House of Burgesses for his military services, after Braddock's defeat. Party management was his pride, and to catch a vote he did not scruple to lend, on personal security, large sums of public money to embarrassed trading squires. In the year 1765 he felt a crisis was approaching. All his own private means were exhausted, and, backed by the tide-water oligarchs, he proposed the establishment of a State Loan Office, with the intention of entering the old transactions as new ones. By the eloquence of Patrick Henry, who, without impeaching the honesty of the powerful Speaker, excited the jealousy of the members from the upper counties, and laid up for himself a future tempest of hatred on the part of the aristocracy, the iniquitous scheme was defeated. The next year Robinson died, irretrievably insolvent, and, it was discovered, 100,000 dollars in debt to the Treasury. These men lived in splendour, while they consoled their neighbours, who in every creek starved on shell-fish, with the fact that they were not slaves of the Crown. Amidst professions of rigid orthodoxy they plundered the revenue of the Church. Till late in the seventeenth century, only one Nonconformist chapel existed in Virginia. But their ecclesiastical orthodoxy was of a negative character; they had early prevailed to have the right to induct transferred from the Crown to the vestries, which were formed by cooptation of the twelve leading men of the parish. They used their power to keep the rectory legally vacant. Church and parsonage they let fall into decay, while they allowed the officiating clergyman so humble a stipend out of the very liberal provision made at the establishment of the Colony, that he was forced, in most cases, to eke it out by keeping a school. The Assembly itself sympathised with this policy. It had the effect of curbing any disagreeable disposition on the part of a minister to reprove the morals of his wealthy parishioners.

Altogether no favourable impression is produced by the social and political aspects of the tide-water districts. The planters were selfish, indolent, and rapacious. They did not even possess the ideas of taste and comfort. Their domestic architecture so offended Jefferson's ultra-classical proclivities, though he did not scorn Philadelphian neatness, that he exclaims, "The genius of architecture seems to have shed its malediction over this land." Its eccentricities would not have roused English instincts against it. But they betrayed only ostentation. In vain we look in old Virginia for traces of rural ease and amenity. There we find no orchards or bright flower-gardens, no dairies or lawns; no well kept farm-houses, as in New England. Every acre they had sufficient slave-labour to cultivate was used for the growth of tobacco, to supply the demands of rapacious English creditors. Solely by the law of entail, and the assistance they managed to obtain from the State Treasury, were they maintained in their hereditary position. Strict settlements had been, very soon after the planting of the colony, imported from England, along with many other legal traditions, by the cadets of county families. There were many Colonel Esmonds in those old times. At first, entails could, as at home, be barred, and the property alienated; but by the end of the seventeenth century, the old cavalier spirit was become so triumphant as to have completely driven beyond the Chesapeake, into Maryland, and the North, the habits of thrift proper to a new country. Mortgages were in headlong process of eating up the vast domains with which noble families had been endowed by the Crown. In a short time the whole land seemed doomed to pass into the hands of a small guild of merchants. These were accustomed, writes Jefferson to Lister Asquith, to accommodate their reckless host with loan upon loan, and then, "having got him immersed in debt, they reduced the price given for his tobacco. Let his shipments be ever so great, and his demand of necessaries ever so economical, they never permitted him to clear it off. The debt became hereditary from father to son for many generations, so that the planters were a species of property annexed to certain mercantile houses." After the Revolution the same state of things existed, and Virginians by no means themselves guiltless in this respect have lamented it freely. Jefferson, for instance, whilst indulging, to the ruin of his private means and family position, in a love of the fine arts and of hospitality, writes regretfully from Paris, where he was Minister, that "he looked back to the war as a time of happiness, when we could not run in debt because nobody would trust us; when we practised, of necessity, the maxim of buying nothing but what we had money in our pockets to pay for; a maxim which, of all others, lays the broadest foundation for happiness." For a generation before the war statutory law had stereotyped landownership. In the year 1705, the docking of entails, to restore to the limited owners control over the estate, was expressly prohibited. Thus the land was bound up indissolubly with the family, unless the Legislature chose as a favour to an individual possessor to set it free.

The contest begun by Jefferson and Patrick Henry for the abolition of the doctrine of entail with all its incidents, and of the rights of primogeniture, opened the eyes of the Virginian aristocracy to the nature of the struggle then opening. In New England, the main object of the Revolution was to break the bond of dependence on the mother-country. In Virginia this was only one motive; it was inseparably connected with another, which was, as its own supporters phrased it, "the substitution of an aristocracy of virtue and talent for the aristocracy of birth and wealth." Few of the old aristocracy could be called Tories. Adversaries who hated the system, speak of "only half-a-dozen aristocratic gentlemen, angry at the loss of their preeminence, venting their indignation at the change from a monarchy to a republic, and more worthy of pity than punishment." The main perplexity of the old families arose from the fact that they found the natural stay of their own dignity to be the throne they had ever opposed, and could not now bring themselves to aid in re-establishing. This inconsistency was the weak point in their fortress. Men like the Randolphs had always been Whigs, or more advanced still. They had resisted the Court, the Governor's party, with a self-approbation the most sincere. They had travelled to London, and intrigued in the purlieus of Whitehall for a century. All this had been in the interests of their own order. They were bitterly indignant at agitators who now demanded for themselves a share in the glory of patriotism, and still more fiercely suspicious when they found them impertinently interfering in matters which concerned private property. A monopoly of popularity had long been arrogated by the Randolphs, Flemings, Says, Eldridges, and Murrays, all of renown in the State, if not actually, in right of their descent from Princess Pocahontas, princes of the blood royal of Virginia, as James I. had intimated they should be accounted. They could point to portions of their estates as having once formed part of the demesne of that Indian emperor and puissant English baron, Powhatan. Another member of the coterie was the family of Digges. Its representative made it a point of pride always to receive George Washington, himself not averse, with all his modesty, from gay apparel and splendid equipages, on the broad bosom of the Potomac, in a barge of English make, rowed by six negroes in fine attire.

A redeeming trait in the history of the order, is that, when its members found they must either abandon their old principles of political, and as they thought it, patriotic opposition, and go over to the side of the English Government, or else acquiesce in the destruction of many of their cherished privileges, they did not choose the course of apparent expediency for a single moment. Further, though the whole system which they had instituted in Virginia had been cumbrous and effete, under it the land reached, and for some time maintained, a priority, relatively to the rest of the New World, which it was unable for long to understand it had lost. It contributed a revenue to the mother-country; it consumed a large quantity of elaborate and expensive English products; it furnished the world at large with luxuries, which general use has almost converted into necessaries. On the spot there was a vast display of expenditure, if not of elegance. The shores of broad tide-ways penetrating far inland between majestic forests, were studded with a succession of sumptuous villas, and wharves crowded with shipping. The aspect of the country was that of a Liverpool broken up, and spread up and down a hundred miles or so of estuary. To see that the country was crippled with debt, and the prey of gross extravagance, it was necessary to wander into the interior, and examine more closely. We are told by

Professor Tucker, writing before the War of Secession, that Jefferson's laws promoted the distribution of wealth, that "a much larger number of those who are wealthy have acquired their wealth by their own talents or enterprise; and most of these last are commonly content with reaching the average of that more moderate standard of expense which public opinion requires, rather than the higher scale which it tolerates." He adds: "There were formerly many in Virginia who drove a coach-and-six; now such an equipage is never seen; there were probably twice or three times as many four-horse carriages before the Revolution as there are at present; but the number of two-horse carriages may be now ten or even twenty times as great as at the former period;" "a few families could boast of more plate than can now be met with; but the whole quantity in the country has increased twenty if not fifty fold." That may well be true, and the condition of the middle and working classes in Virginia may have sensibly improved after the War of Independence, yet the fact be that Virginia, in the period between that war and the War of Secession, was relatively one of the least flourishing members of the Union, though it had inherited the most extraordinary natural advantages for trade. For the first two-thirds, or more, of last century it was clearly foremost both in the show of material prosperity, and, still more, in political distinction.

The State furnished the Union with four out of the first five Presidents. From it came a large proportion of the most eminent diplomatists and Ministers, men who have stamped their character and theories of government on the policy and constitution of America. According to contemporary testimony, the Virginian State-Assembly, before the Revolution, was a fitting nursery of orators and statesmen. Its panegyrists, though their diction may sometimes be inflated and confused, produce an impression of its possession of real ability and Parliamentary dexterity. Among its leaders, when Patrick Henry first appeared in it, an uncouth country lawyer, with a stolid abstracted air, and in his coarse hunting dress, startling the propriety of the glittering lobbies and committee-rooms, were Speaker Robinson, a very Sir John Trevor in powers of management and want of integrity, and Peyton Randolph, a noted intriguer, though Attorney-General, solid rather than eloquent. They were two of those business men, heirs to an historic name, who can direct discreetly all men's affairs but their own. Another non-rhetorical debater was Richard Bland, the Virginian Antiquary, as he was called, learned and logical, but apt to retreat startled from the conclusions to which his own arguments had led his hearers. Edward Pendleton, the Conservative lawyer, with silvery voice, and almost equal in management to his friend Robinson, and George Wythe, afterwards Chief Justice, the law tutor of Jefferson, a ripe scholar, charged with an excessive love, from which at all events modern members of Congress are free, of the Elizabethan writers, and an amount of eccentricity which could scarcely be believed to be the possible possession of one man, sat together, originally on the Liberal-Conservative side. With them was Richard Henry Lee, one of the few members who, though no lawyers, were perfect masters of practice and forms; a Cicero in debate, "and," we are informed by an admirer of his, "with a Cæsarean nose," a man, in short, who, though "no Niagara, Homer, or Patrick Henry, flowed through banks covered with the bloom of spring." These American Old Whigs of the generation anterior to the Revolution manifested a peculiarly English faculty for Parliamentary tactics. They did not talk for talk's sake. They were sure of their position. They had no particular reverence for public opinion, and there was nothing they hoped to gain from promiscuous popularity. Their object was to maintain a reputation for business powers among their fellow-magistrates. Political perturbations threw up tyrants of debate like Patrick Henry, men who, when entrusted by acclamation with the task of drawing up a simple resolution, faltered, and at length produced a paper at once, with as universal a consent, consigned to oblivion. They were the Addisons of oratory, superseded by an under-clerk. The old

Virginian statesmen seldom spoke on matters of grave public interest for longer than ten minutes at a time. They did not argue for victory, but to expound the motion which they knew the rest would accept.

Virginian politicians of the period of the Revolution divide themselves under three heads. There were the Conservatives, that is to say, Conservative Republicans; monarchical Conservatives were few at a period when the words British Tory, we are told, "threw any company into a rage, and suggested tar and feathers." Next came the theoretical Democrats, men not from the people, and as sensitive about their personal rank as the aristocracy, but desiring to lead the people. Lastly, there were the real popular champions, such as Patrick Henry. These were actually of and from the masses, though from masses which themselves, in relation to a yet inferior body, constituted a highly privileged class. In the tide-water region, especially on the banks of the James, thorough aristocrats might be found, of families which had never broken off their connection with the English stock. They might have been educated at Oxford or Cambridge, or have served for a campaign in Flanders. They never, from first to last, pretended to popularity. In many cases the heir had been sent to Europe on the first signs of the rising, and had there remained till the conclusion of peace. But the more influential of the Conservative party had always been Liberals as to the relations between the colony and mother-country. Their Conservatism was restricted to social questions and home politics. Of these, Washington, living towards the verge of the Conservative district, and with the more energetic and innovating Maryland stretching out in the distance, is a favourable, perhaps too favourable an example. He is their ideal, their apology, and in some measure the reflection of what this class imagined itself to be. He is acknowledged by political adversaries to have possessed a judgment unsurpassed in soundness, though better adapted to decide on the plans of others than to originate; to have been of an exact integrity and justice, and though naturally of an irritable temper, and a slave-owner, self-restrained and forbearing. He was liberal but exact in his expenditure. He was far from fluent in speech. With little learning but reading, writing, arithmetic, and surveying, he advocated all schemes for the promotion of education; he confessed to a great respect for Latin, and something of a mysterious reverence for Greek. He could dance, while Republican commander-in-chief, three hours at a time, and, when President, envy those whose rank did not scare partners. He enjoyed the more serious reputation of being the best horseman of his time. His good family and estate did not hinder him from being the most practical as well as most honest of farmers. His brand, "George Washington, of Mt. Vernon," passed a flour-barrel through the most suspicious West Indian custom-house.

Mount Vernon is in the district of the Potomac, before the river becomes the rocky romantic stream it appears at its picturesque junction with the Shenandoah, at Harper's Ferry. This region, not yet crowned by the City of Washington, was in Washington's youth, with its bold cliffs and wooded ridges, the waters beneath sparkling with shoals of countless herrings, carp, sturgeon, and bass, in their seasons, and covered with canvas-back ducks, the favourite Virginian resort. Now and then, a frigate would sail up from the broad Chesapeake, and, anchoring opposite the verandah of a wealthy planter's mansion, pour forth a troop of officers and letters of introduction, to greet the squire who might, as George Washington's elder half-brother, Lawrence, have himself served in the English navy. The river acted as a highway for gay barges to carry the planters and their wives to each other's houses, or to the court of the Governor of Maryland, at Annapolis, with its balls, and dinners, and private theatricals. The shore line was marked by primitive but well-to-do farmhouses, such as the General's birthplace, on Bridge's Creek, with its steep roof sloping into low projecting eaves, its single story, with the attic over, and great chimney at either end. Many stately edifices adorned the slopes above the water.

Arlington, the house of Mr. Custis, Washington's step-grandson, with marble columns and porticoes, long recalled the old days along with the new. Of a style of architecture not so classical, were Mount Vernon and hospitable Belvoir, built on the same ridge. Belvoir was the residence of William Fairfax, Lawrence Washington's father-in-law, and was just enough miles distant to make a pleasant ride on a bright autumn morning.

Many, especially after the arrival of Lord Fairfax, were the meets on the lawn of one or the other house, to beat the wild woods, indented with rocks and rivulets, and natural deep dells, loved by fox and deer. The sportsmen would return to a jovial hunt dinner, at which Washington seems to have had a capacity for being as merry as the most pleasure-loving of Diggeses or Randolphs. How proud he was of his stud his diary shows. There we read, set forth with some gentle boastfulness, the genealogies of Ajax, and Magnolia, and of keen fox-hounds, Music and Sweet-lips and Ringwood, and a host of others. Mrs. Washington, the blooming widow of John Parke Custis, whom readers of Mr. Thackeray will remember, was a lady of birth and connections not to be despised even by a Madam Esmond. She had brought her second husband 100,000 dollars, and she had, for her part, her carriage-and-four, with black postilions in scarlet and white liveries, as gorgeous as a high sheriff's equipage. In it he and she were wont to proceed in solemn state to one or other of the two parish churches of which the General was a vestryman. Both were conspicuous figures at festivities of all kinds, some splendid, others resembling the simple Alexandria subscription balls, which he, in his bachelor days, describes as "bread-and-butter balls," where "the tea and coffee had a deep resemblance to hot water, and pocket-handkerchiefs were made, without apology, to serve the purpose of table-cloths." He himself was not ashamed on occasion to deck himself in fine clothes. When he rode forth, to the admiration of the simple north-eastern cities, on a splendid horse, with mounted negroes behind him, to meet Governor Shirley, his more personal accoutrements we may be sure, were in conformity. We know something of the resources of his wardrobe, the "fashionable gold-laced hat," the "drab-coloured riding frock with plain double-gilt buttons," the "superfine scarlet cloth waistcoat," "livery suits to be chosen by his London tailor by the Washington arms and housings, with the Washington crest," and "the very neat and fashionable Newmarket saddle-cloth." Of all these his account-books make particular mention.

His kitchen was thronged with servants, and his cellar well stocked with old wine. Beautiful gardens surrounded the house. That was an improvement peculiarly his own on the comfortless carelessness of tide-water proprietors about anything in the way of plants but tobacco, or ornamental copses but poplar-trees. He was ever trying to naturalise foreign trees; and profound were his meditations on the superiority of one in shade to another. In his diary we find noted, under January 16th, that the whitethorn was in berry; on the 20th, he is busy clearing the pine-groves of the underwood, and, in February and March, transplanting ivy to adorn his garden-walls, and evergreens to make a cheerful winter prospect; or he is opening vistas through his woods, and twining scarlet honeysuckle round the columns of his verandah. We discover even sentiment in his embellishments. He is careful to plant horse-chestnuts from his native county of Westmoreland, Virginia, sent him by his favourite, Harry Lee, the son of the "Lowland beauty," a "chaste and troublesome passion" for whom he had been, he tell us, forced, before the mature age of sixteen, "to bury in the grave of oblivion."

He had more industry as well as taste than the majority of tide-water proprietors. He was a busy country gentleman, pruning his own plantations, beside being, like the rest of his landholder class, his own game-keeper and water-bailiff, ready to chastise corporally, without fear of bludgeons and guns, trespassers on his rights over water-fowl and oyster-beds. He kept his own books. Week by week, with the cares, never neglected, of a struggling nation upon him, he conveyed to his agent, by maps, his views on the culture of each special field. With precepts of economy he mixed benevolent orders, after the Sir Roger de Coverley school of country squires, to his steward to maintain hospitality in his place, and to "let no one go hungry away." He says of himself that he was not a very skilful farmer; at any rate, he was an enthusiast, not only procuring balsam-trees from New York, and vines from Languedoc, but ploughs from no less an agriculturist than Arthur Young. He showed his zeal by inventing one himself, and nearly ruining two of his best carriage-horses by forcing them to drag it over the heavy sward. He rose before dawn, lighted his own fire, though a slave-owner, and one whose every look was studied, out of love, not fear, by his troops of servants, and took a morning ride of four or five hours over his estate. The whole had been most systematically divided by him into four different farms, each having its own allotment of labourers, and particular crops. With its woodland, pastures, cornland, eleven miles of fisheries, and villages stocked with tailors, shoe-makers, smiths, and warehousemen, it constituted a fertile self-contained principality of three to four thousand acres. The result was, that he made agriculture pay, unlike most of his neighbours. Their estates were first gnawed by encumbrances, and, at length, after the new Constitution set them free from entails, sold to the overseers at the rate of about four dollars an acre, the master emigrating, with a portion of his slaves, beyond the Blue Mountains. Washington's estate, when he was gone, exhibited the same tendency. Tourists many years before the War of Secession described it as falling into the normal Virginian condition, the shrubberies overgrown, the lawn obliterated, and the whole in process of relapse into a haunt for bears and wolves.

The Blue Ridge was then, as later, the land of hope, or, it might be, the forlorn hope, of the broken-down landowners of the James or Potomac. A hundred miles away, amid the noxious exhalations of the marshy tide-water region, and over its black foliage, those azure peaks can be seen floating in air. In early Virginian history we hear of powerful Indian chieftains, whom the English colonist loved to awe himself by styling kings, Powhatans and Oppecancanoughs, whose sway was supreme throughout the hill-country. Round the base was a belt of land more fertile than the lowlands; but the strength of the natives long intimidated poorer settlers. The richer would in any case have preferred for their residence an inlet of the sea, by which they could communicate directly with the mother-country. Water too, in the general absence of good roads, was a necessity for the carriage of crops to their markets. By Charles II. a great grant of land in this direction was made to the Earl of St. Albans, Lord Berkeley, Sir William Martin and others, as Proprietaries. Under grants from them, or in defiance of them, the district gradually began to be settled, though the boundary of Virginia, till 1744, was still considered to be virtually the mountain range. By a new grant subsequently made, overriding the old, the royal rights over the land between the Potomac and Rappahanock, called the Northern Neck, were ceded to Lord Culpepper, who had, says Oldmixon, "trumped up a title to it." Very indefinite powers were conferred. In vain the adventurers who had already occupied portions appealed. Culpepper had shrewdly managed to have appeals in such cases transferred to the Crown from the Assembly, which had formerly cognizance. The answer was that, if they had encroached without a licence, they had acted at their own risk. They were forced eventually to compound with Culpepper for the payment of a quit-rent. Colonel Richard Lee, and Colonel Robert Carter, two leading Virginians, members of the Council, and large freeholders on the Neck, consented to officiate as his agents.

Thus the lands at the foot of the Blue Ridge became by degrees peopled; but, down to 1748, no white men except a few Irish had made their way into the valley between it and North Mountain. The objection of Virginian planters to companionship with Irishmen interposed a fresh barrier, we are told, over and above the bugbear of Indian forays, to emigration thither from the alluvial country. Early in the reign of George II., however, Lord Fairfax was cast off for a duke by the reigning London belle. Culpepper, whose favourite employment during his governorship seems to have been buying up light pieces of eight at five shillings, and then, by proclamation, raising their value to six, left no son to inherit his ill-gotten wealth. Fairfax, his daughter's son, was his heir. In his rage at the coquette, this cornet in the Blues, who had studied at Oxford, and written a paper in the Spectator, made his succession to a Virginian domain a pretext for quitting England. His cousin, William Fairfax, a brave soldier, formerly Governor of New Providence, which he had helped to reduce, and Chief Justice of the Bahamas, was already residing on the Northern Neck as his agent. The peer was delighted with the taste for country sports he found existing on the Chesapeake. He went to England only to procure an explanation of the grant to his ancestor, which extended it to a great tract beyond the Alleghanies. Then he returned for good to plant, and to teach his neighbours scientific fox-hunting.

This immense area of rich waste land had never been surveyed. Lord Fairfax found that squatters were making their way up the stream, and securing an occupancy in the best plots. They neither sought licences from him, nor thought of paying quit-rents, such things having been ever most abhorrent to American instincts. Washington, who was perpetually about Belvoir, was become an especial favourite. He showed a remarkable capacity for comprehending lessons on sporting matters, though he himself disclaims the fame of an accomplished fox-hunter. Fairfax commissioned him to survey the region, at a rate of salary which enabled him to earn a doubloon, or as much as six pistoles, a day. The district, between the Blue Ridge and the Alleghanies, is the third of the four zones into which geographers and politicians agree in dividing Virginia. It enjoys the most temperate climate, and the most fertile soil. The hills, rarely rising to more than 2,000 feet, and presenting "one continuous waving line, with intervening glens like gigantic wrinkles and furrows," are covered so thickly with beech, cedars, and oak, red, white, and black, hung with roses and wild vines green in the midst of March, that surveyors long afterwards were obliged to climb to the top of a tree to examine the country. The turf beneath is a garden. Rhododendrons, azaleas, the shumac, and kalmia fringe the cliffs of many colours which crop up beside the pathway. Over all, are the blue summits melting away in the distance. The defect of the ridge as a landscape is that it is not sufficiently broken; and there is a want of individuality about the several mountains. But it compensates for this deficiency in picturesqueness by its universal fertility. Even the higher slopes are now tilled.

Beyond the wooded hill country Washington entered, in company with young George Fairfax, surveying as he went along, a grand valley twenty-five miles broad. He found it bounded by the Blue Mountains, with "their soft liquid tints of mingled blue and green," on the one side, and North Mountain, a division of the Alleghanies, on the other. Throughout it is irrigated by the Shenandoah, "daughter of the stars," as the Indian tribes named it for its beauty. This great central valley of Virginia became later the chief pride of the State. Often it was denominated "Virginia" simply. It is a country of wheat and Indian corn; and the slopes of every hill glow with peach and apple orchards. Its social aspects before the War of Secession were described as intermediate between those of the birthplace of sweet-scented tobacco, and the maize and cotton plantations of the lower tide-water country, on the one hand, and those of the Northern States on the other. The number of slaves was smaller than in the tide-water country. Labour, which is also much more agreeable there to the physical constitution of the white man, did not involve a loss of caste. The estates were generally for the same reason more moderate in extent. The tone of comfort was greater. Farmers did not, as further south, live from year to year on pork, salt fish or corn bread; they made the soil yield fruit and garden vegetables. It was the home of the class described by Jefferson: "I know no condition happier than that of a Virginian farmer might be. His estate supplies a good table, clothes himself and his family with their ordinary apparel, furnishes a small surplus to buy salt, sugar, coffee, and a little finery for his wife and daughters, enables him to receive and visit his friends, and furnishes him with a pleasing and healthy occupation." Along with these moderate holdings were also many estates on a far ampler scale, large enough to afford their owners leisure for studying politics and for refinement, and to provide a surplus for the exercise of the profuse hospitality which delighted a southern planter anywhere. Some domains were princely in their dimensions.

The country a hundred years later became fashionable for its medicinal springs of sulphur, red and white, first made known by Washington himself, who purchased the site of one of the principal. Its modern aspect would have amazed Solomon Hedge, Esquire, his Majesty's Justice of the Peace, to whose supper party the young explorer, and the rest of the company, brought their own knives, doing without forks. Washington was in ecstasies with the valley, its beauty and its richness, its oaks, and sugar-maples. Lord Fairfax was so fired by his report, that within a short time he moved from his cousin's house at Belvoir across the Blue Ridge, with horses and dogs, books, retainers, and coat of arms. He laid out a manor of ten thousand acres, with pastures, woodland, and cornland, to be entitled, with the manor-house he was designing, Greenway Court. For the present, he took up his residence in his steward's "quarter," a long stone house on a green knoll overlooking the Shenandoah, one story high, with dormer windows, and two wooden belfries, a roof with low eaves, and a long verandah the whole length of the house for summer evening sauntering. At the foot of the knoll were outhouses for servants, stables, and kennels, and a hut twelve feet square, in which it pleased the master, from some eccentricity, to sleep, away from the main building. In the library, Washington, a constant guest, loved to read English history, and the Spectator. He was not likely to neglect the old lord's particular contribution.

The gaunt old man, with his near sight, light grey eyes, and sharp features, and generally strange appearance and manifold oddities, won the hearts of his neighbours. He acted with ardour the part of road-surveyor. In the character of lord-lieutenant of the county he was in the habit of feasting, during the assizes at Cumberland, all the notables of the vicinity. At one time he would be drilling a militia cavalry troop on his lawn; at another, when game happened to be scarce at Greenway Court and Belvoir, he migrated with his whole household to some rustic inn in the heart of the wild forest, and there entertained all who could join his hunting party for weeks at a time. When the Indian tribes were in arms all about him, at the date of Braddock's fatal expedition, he disdained to remove to the lower country, and, with his negroes and half-breed huntsmen and friends, beat the woods as before. The Revolution was a heavy grief to him. No one ever dreamt of molesting the old man, though he did not disguise his royalism; but the surrender of Cornwallis at Yorktown to his friend and surveyor is said to have killed him, if it be necessary to look for any special reason for death at ninety-two. Thus pathetically does a local poet, Weem, in a 'History of Mount Vernon,' sing that catastrophe, after a prose prelude to the valet, " Come, Joe, carry me to bed; for it is high time for me to die."

"Then up rose Joe, all at the word,
And took his master's arm.
And thus to bed he slowly led
The lord of Greenway Farm.

Then oft he called on Britain's name,
And oft he wept full sore,
Then sighed, 'Thy will, O Lord, be done,'
And word spake never more."

To this new country, opened up by Washington, and

purged by so magnificent a resident as an English baron from equivocal associations, thronged adventurers. Thither came, in 1772, Horatio Gates. Once he was well known in fashionable London circles, and he had served in Braddock's luckless expedition. He was now, at the age of forty-six, a disappointed half-pay officer, somewhat corpulent, and " with a disagreeable proneness to wheedle," caught by haunting ante-chambers and Pall Mall. He bought an estate beyond the Blue Ridge, in Berkeley County, called the " Traveller's Rest," a name suggesting preexistence in the shape of a roadside inn. Thence he looked out to see how he could best turn the circumstances of his troubled period to account. About the same time, his friend Lee, major-general in the service of the King of Poland, and aide-de-camp to his Majesty of Portugal, was, among other birds of prey, who seem to have scented the war from afar, wandering about America. His journey ostensibly was undertaken to establish some claim upon Government to a grant in the South; but he had already been strongly suspected of tampering with the New England patriots. Gates wrote eagerly to him, expatiating on the advantages of a neighbouring farm, then for sale, with a flour-mill, and 2,400 acres, sure in ten years, he affirmed, to have doubled their value. In the meantime, he offers him "a good bed, and two or three slaves, at the 'Traveller's Rest,' to wait on his whimsies." One of these whimsies, which was peculiarly disagreeable to neat Mrs. Washington, was a habit of taking troops of dogs to the houses of friends, and insisting on having them accommodated with seats at the dinner-table. Rough quarters were fitted for rough ways; and General Lee's farmhouse on the Shenandoah was a mere shell. The different apartments were indicated by lines chalked on the ground. At least, he would argue, it was economical; he could, from any part, without the least inconvenience, overlook the entire establishment, and regulate library, bedroom, harness-room, and kitchen, without stirring a foot. To this primitive abode the tattered soldier of fortune, suspected, neglected, and virulent, retired about the middle of the war, to abuse his "Small Friends," and, with a sneer at Washington, declare his belief that "hoeing tobacco must be the best school to form a consummate general."

Washington, although he had done much, in youth and age, to render the region known, and had sagaciously bought some very fertile portions of it, cannot be considered a representative of its planters. He was the old tide-water planter, with the fine equipages, manners, and prerogatives of a feudal lord of a manor joined to the spirit and industry of a merchant of Amsterdam. Other proprietors in the "great valley," of the grand seigneur type as Lord Fairfax, and sojourners as Lee and Gates, were never American in thought and feeling. President Jefferson, though not locally belonging actually to the Shenandoah, is a fair representative of the intermediate state of society which flourished on its banks. He owned large possessions, both at Poplar Forest, in Bedford County, and at Monticello, close to the town of Charlottesville. Some of the wonders of the district were close to his own lands; the Natural Bridge was his property. He always considered himself a born enemy of the tide-water aristocracy. Washington, in common with the latter class, doubted the future of a republic; Jefferson believed in it most implicitly, and was in doctrine a liberal as to social, as well as a republican as to national relations. By fortune he belonged to the higher ranks. He had in the rich hollows of the Blue Ridge Highlands an estate of from five to six thousand acres, and at Poplar Forest a tobacco plantation which ought to have been lucrative, with flour-mills, canals, and locks, leading from the Rivanna, constructed at a cost of thirty thousand dollars. He was also a considerable slave-owner, possessing about a couple of hundred slaves. In his 'Notes on Virginia' he denounces the system, and solemnly exclaims, "The only firm basis of national liberty is the conviction that liberty is the gift of God."

In his theories Jefferson was consistent enough. In practice his assertion of the right of all human beings to equal privileges, and outcry against presidential titles and levees, and tables of precedence, were combined with the prejudices and habits of a Virginian gentleman. He was especially jealous of any assumption of a right to intrude upon his privacy, upon the ground of his public character, or to criticise his personal conduct. The visitor who introduced himself with the remark that "he had availed himself of a common privilege of calling upon him," was met with a far more chilling rebuff than Scott's American persecutors at Abbotsford. In the same tone he complains to his brother-ex-president Adams of the multitude of letters with which his leisure was fretted and worried. "Is this life? It is the life of a mill-stone. To such a life that of a cabbage would be paradise." Neither was his general mode of life in the least democratic, in the European sense of the term. The care of his Poplar Forest estate he left wholly to an overseer, a course fatal, he acknowledges, to the profits of a southern plantation. He declares that "from breakfast to dinner, he was always in the shops, his garden, or on horseback among his farms;" and that "he talked with his neighbours of ploughs and harrows, seeding and harvesting." He affected a lively interest, while abroad, in the probable returns from his "little essay in red clover." But his agricultural experiments seldom were remunerative; and a seminary of young politicians he kept in the neighbouring village of Charlottesville, directing their studies, and conversing frequently with them on statesmanship, was the object of many of his farm rides. Or perhaps he was composing Greek epitaphs, or criticising Plato, whom, it is shocking to find, he had the want of taste to decry as "full of puerilities and unintelligible jargon." He had a fondness, too, for fine horses, spending, for instance, at one time, a couple of thousand dollars on the purchase of four. With this extravagance he united a polite taste for French cookery, to the indignation of Patrick Henry, who called it "treason against one's native victuals." Every stranger who brought to Monticello letters of introduction, was invited to stay. He was never without occasional guests. His neighbours would come over from Marrowbone, Horse Pasture, and Poison Field, and other localities which his letters have made classical. All, of whatever phase of politics, might reckon on being received with courtesy. The federal Tories of Bedford County, who, he knew, detested his principles, as he did theirs, were of the company. So were musical prisoners of war from Burgoyne's staff, for whose stay in Albemarle he pleaded successfully with the Legislature, on the ground that they had planted gardens, and collected for themselves poultry. They were no less heartily welcomed than their predecessor at Collé, the Italian Mazzei, whose vineyards they treated as ruthlessly as did Czar Peter Evelyn's holly hedge at Saye's Court. An incessant flood of visitors poured in from the neighbouring University of Virginia, built among the woods on the same skirts of the Blue Ridge as Monticello, under his immediate superintendence, after a quasi classical model. It is satisfactory to learn that he had not excluded from its programme of studies those Latin and Greek classics, which, in his first burst of zeal for experimental philosophy, he abuses, in the description of William and Mary's College in his 'Notes,' as " disgusting and degrading " to " young gentlemen already prepared for entering on the sciences."

He not merely planned educational reforms ; he believed he had a vocation also for improving the architecture of his native State. The four parallel ranges of his university, with the glittering dome of its rotunda, are monuments of his views on the subject. His own residence was a favourable specimen of gentlemen's houses on the outskirts of the Blue Ridge. It commanded a wide view to the east, over an undulating forest plain. The mountains were visible, stretching away to the distance of a hundred miles. Aboriginal forest-trees surrounded it on three sides, the fourth being occupied by a spacious hanging garden. Necessarily, the mansion had a Grecian portico, and cupola, and raised terraces. Saloons, and hall, and drawing-rooms were crowded with curiosities, moose and elk horns, Indian weapons and Italian statuary. The library was well stored with books, and mathematical and philosophical instruments; indeed, on journeys, he was in the habit of taking with him, somewhat after the fashion of Dr. Johnson, a set of logarithm tables. Walls and floors were adorned with paintings, and with mosaic work executed by his slaves.

Unhappily, his various elegant tastes aggravated a southern planter's habitual and ruinous instinct of living beyond his income. His presidential salary of 25,000 dollars a year did not prevent him from quitting office, at the end of eight years, ten thousand dollars out of pocket. His estate gradually dwindled away. Bad crops were looked upon as mere accidents which would not recur, and plots of land were sold to defray the loss; a good harvest was treated as a windfall, and not as compensation for any defect of the previous autumn. His labourers, who should have been at the plough, were engaged on works of art. A consequence of all this was, that the statesman who had, in and out of office, vehemently discouraged lotteries, was, like Lamartine, persuaded finally, in his necessity, to ask as a charity from the State Assembly the right to institute one, for the more profitable sale of his plantation. This being the ex-President's own financial condition, he laboured to induce Short, Monroe, and Madison to fix their residence near, for the sake not more of the opportunity of social intercourse than of the example of economy he and they together might show the whole country side. Albemarle County was not to have the happiness of watching these economists in direct collocation. Only Monroe went so far as to build a house in the mountains. He was soon called away to pursuits in which he earned, from first to last, 400,000 dollars, yet died insolvent. Jefferson and he forgot, in their own cases, though they were always reminding others and each other of the truth, that a Virginian planter must, to remain solvent, ever think of himself as a merchant and farmer.

Virginia, beside its great proprietors, whether tide-water oligarchs, Shenandoah farmers, or theorists and statesmen in the villas of the Blue Ridge, had its class of yeomen, composed indiscriminately of the old colonists, more recent emigrants, and emancipated bondsmen. By the constitution of the settlement, it was intended that the chief part of the land should belong to this order of men The original scheme, as that of New England, contemplated that only a few of distinguished rank or wealth, fitted to give a tone to the province, or if necessary to defend its rights at home, were to be allured into residing by grants of domains. This plan had been perverted, partly by fraud, and partly by avarice. Governors and surveyors-general gave to any single individual, who had sufficient wealth or influence, many lots of fifty acres. With official connivance, ship captains obtained in different counties independent allotments, in virtue of the same voyage. Such yeomen as there were, if often of inferior energy, on account of the relaxing climate, do not seem at first to have been in kind unlike the farmers of the north-east. They had set up no pretence to grandeur. They did not ride the magnificent horses found by Cornwallis in Virginian stables, which La Fayette styles " racers." Their steeds were ill-groomed, and they dwelt in log huts. The oppression of capitalists, who lent them goods and money at enormous interest, gradually spoilt their attractive qualities. As they appear in late præ-Revolutionary descriptions, they do not form a very prepossessing feature of Virginian society, with their arrogance, their slovenly lazy ways, and their addiction to hunting, racing, and mortgaging.

However, to this class belonged Patrick Henry, and he was not ashamed of it. With its members he eat, drank, and talked, dressing in their rough costume, and even, at the height of his fame, using much of their accent. At one time he managed a store. When this failed, with more of the spirit supposed to mark a Yankee than a Virginian, he betook himself to practising in the county courts, in one of which his father presided. Occasionally he would officiate in place of his father-in-law, Skelton, at a bar of a different kind, kept at Hanover Court-house. Hunting and dancing still occupied much of his attention; and his first meeting with Jefferson, was at a ball given by Colonel Dandridge. Often he would rush in to conduct a case, fresh from the chase, in a slouched hat and tattered clothes. A New Englander of the middle class is consistent in his ways; he dresses for his common business in good broadcloth, he does not change it for extraordinary occasions. Patrick Henry was a Virginian; for appearances at the bar of the general court he arrayed himself in a full suit of black velvet, and an elaborately powdered tie wig. On his election into the House of Burgesses, he had advanced to a peach-coloured coat, which Goldsmith would have admired. When he took his place as Governor of his native State, and migrated with his household into a palace, as Government-house had been styled, he blazed forth in a trailing scarlet robe, and other Roman-senator-like magnificences. All this furnished copious matter for sarcasms to the young gentlemen fresh from European Courts, who used to profess that they did not think it of importance, "whether a country were ruled by a despot with a tiara on his head, or by a demagogue with a red cloak and caulbare wig."

His merit and that of his class was exuberant life and energy. The Randolphs and Robinsons, when they laid down an office, withdrew to the superior dignity and influence of country gentlemen, surrounded by troops of admiring friends and dependents. Henry and his class had, on retirement, to resume their practice or other business. He, for instance, betook himself to the drudgery of the petty district courts of Prince Edward County and New London. But Henry and his fellows succeeded in effecting what was beyond the reach of the old families. They realised fortunes. Not till after a double career of labour did he retire to live out the evenings of many summers under the shade of a huge walnut-tree in which he most delighted. He ever acknowledged himself, and was acknowledged by his old equals, as from and of them, and their representative throughout. It can hardly be but that the stock retains a capacity for the qualities which he developed so fully. Now, the Virginian Capes are no longer a name of power in Bristol and Liverpool, and on the London Exchange. Trade, wealth, and political power have drifted round the Alleghanies, eastwards and westwards. The Old Dominion, which once esteemed the Presidency its all but vested right, has gradually sunk below many juniors in the amount of representation in Congress. Its progress, where any is discernible, is due to strangers, not to its own people. Farmers from Maine locate themselves on the rich shores of the Potomac, and gather in abundant harvests from land which overseers had reported to be thoroughly exhausted. Companies from England, Old and New, have worked mines, the very existence of which was unknown to the native Virginians. They hire local labour to do what it would never have consented to undertake on its own account. Virginians have deserved to fall behind. Few populations have enjoyed greater advantages, and had a fairer start towards prosperity, or have more misused the whole. Friends of Virginia who have looked forward to its resurrection since the blight of slavery was removed, build their hopes, not on the old lineage still vegetating on the river estuaries, or on the memory of a party of dexterous statesmen, who happened to choose for their retreat the Shenandoah, or the belt at the foot of the Blue Ridge, but on the race of yeomen who survive, in whatever part of the State, and of whatever origin, whether descended from courtiers of King Charles, or from convicts sold for a few pounds of tobacco.

www.ingramcontent.com/pod-product-compliance
Lightning Source LLC
Chambersburg PA
CBHW030549300426
44111CB00009B/908